BRANDS AND BRANDING

OTHER ECONOMIST BOOKS

Guide to Analysing Companies
Guide to Business Modelling
Guide to Business Planning
Guide to Economic Indicators
Guide to the European Union
Guide to Financial Management
Guide to Financial Markets
Guide to Investment Strategy
Guide to Management Ideas and Gurus
Guide to Organisation Design
Guide to Project Management
Numbers Guide
Style Guide

Book of Obituaries
Business Consulting
Business Strategy
China's Stockmarket
The City
Dealing with Financial Risk
Economics
Emerging Markets
The Future of Technology
Headhunters and How to Use Them
Mapping the Markets
Successful Strategy Execution

Essential Economics
Essential Investment
Essential Negotiation
Essentials for Board Directors

For more information on these books:
www.bloomberg.com/economistbooks

The
Economist

BRANDS AND BRANDING

Rita Clifton

with
Sameena Ahmad
Tony Allen
Simon Anholt
Patrick Barwise
Tom Blackett
Deborah Bowker
Jonathan Chajet
Deborah Doane
Iain Ellwood
Paul Feldwick
Jez Frampton
Giles Gibbons
Andy Hobsbawm
Jan Lindemann
Allan Poulter
Max Raison
John Simmons
Shaun Smith

Bloomberg Press
New York

THE ECONOMIST IN ASSOCIATION WITH PROFILE BOOKS LTD

This edition published in the United States and Canada by Bloomberg Press
Published in the U.K. by Profile Books Ltd, 2009

Printed in Canada

1 3 5 7 9 10 8 6 4 2

Library of Congress Cataloging-in-Publication Data on file

ISBN 978-1-57660-350-5

Contents

The authors

Rita Clifton is a leading practitioner, author and commentator on brands and branding, and has worked with many of the world's most successful companies. After graduating from Cambridge, she spent her early career in advertising, becoming vice-chairman and strategic director at Saatchi & Saatchi. A frequent speaker at conferences around the world, she is also a regular contributor on CNN and the BBC and to all the major broadsheets and business magazines. She edited *The Future of Brands*, and since 1997 has been CEO and then chairman in London of Interbrand, a global brand consultancy. She was made Visiting Professor at Henley Management College in 2006, and holds a number of non-executive directorships as well as being a trustee of the Worldwide Fund for Nature (WWF).

Sameena Ahmad has been *The Economist*'s consumer industries correspondent based in London and New York, and the Asia business and finance writer based in Hong Kong.

Tony Allen is CEO of brand consultancy Fortune Street. He has been a hands-on practitioner leading international branding projects for over 20 years. Before founding Fortune Street he was a director of corporate identity firm Newell and Sorrell, running its offices in Amsterdam and New York and working for clients including Rabobank, Barclays, Pharmacia & Upjohn and IBM. He then worked at Interbrand as CEO of its London office. His main area of expertise is branding in financial and professional services. He has extensive experience of brand development in emerging economies including Russia, Turkey and Azerbaijan.

Simon Anholt is an independent policy adviser, author and researcher who originated the concept of nation branding in 1996 and is today regarded as the leading authority on the identity and reputation of places. He is a member of the UK Foreign Office Public Diplomacy Board and has advised the governments of countries in Europe, Africa, Australasia, the Caribbean, East Asia and Latin America. He publishes the Anholt Nation Brands Index and Anholt City Brands Index, which use a panel of over

5m people in 20 countries to monitor global perceptions of 50 countries and cities. He is editor of a quarterly journal, *Place Branding and Public Diplomacy*, and his books include *Brand New Justice*, *Brand America* and *Competitive Identity: the New Brand Management for Nations, Cities and Regions*.

Patrick Barwise is emeritus professor of management and marketing at London Business School. He joined LBS in 1976, having spent his early career with IBM. He has published and consulted widely on management, marketing and media. His latest book, *Simply Better*, co-authored with Seán Meehan, won the American Marketing Association's 2005 Berry-AMA Prize for the best recent book in marketing. In 2004, he led an independent review for the UK government of the BBC's digital television services. He is a Fellow of both the Marketing Society and the Sunningdale Institute, a virtual academy on public service management. He is also a Council member (and previous deputy chairman) of *Which?*, the UK's leading consumer organisation, and an experienced expert witness, having worked on commercial, tax and competition cases in London, Brussels, Paris, Cologne, and Washington.

Tom Blackett is a leading expert on brands and branding. He is the author of *Trademarks* and co-editor of *Co-branding: the science of alliance* and *Brand Medicine*, and has contributed to many other key texts about brands. He was with the Interbrand Group for 25 years, retiring as deputy chairman in March 2008, and during his career worked for many of the world's leading brand owners. He continues to write about brands and to speak at conferences; he also acts as an expert witness in disputes concerning brands and has appeared in several prominent cases.

Deborah Bowker has 30 years' experience in strategic planning, organisational communication, media and government relations. She has helped public- and private-sector organisations achieve improved reputation and performance through stakeholder analysis, issues management and brand-based public relations. Before forming Deborah Bowker Communications & Consulting she was a managing director at Burson-Marsteller where she led the US Corporate Practice. She was also director of PricewaterhouseCoopers' Centre of Excellence for Strategic Communications and a technical adviser in communications and marketing planning to numerous PWC clients. She has served as an assistant postmaster general and vice-president at the US Postal Service and has directed major projects for USPS, a worldwide Olympic sponsorship and a national literacy programme. Her promotion of the Elvis postage stamp earned her a place in the Ad Age 100. She is a Sloan Fellow of the Massachusetts Institute of Technology.

Jonathan Chajet manages Interbrand's business in China and oversees strategy for the Asia-Pacific region. He is an expert in brand strategy, business planning, market research, naming, visual identity, multimedia communications, packaging and employee training. He has helped create, enhance and manage some of the world's most recognised brands including Adobe, Nestlé, Dow, Dell, Intel, Microsoft, Sony Playstation, Motorola, Nokia, Samsung and Wrigley. He was previously strategy director at Siegel & Gale and a management consultant at Oliver Wyman Management Consulting. He began his career in advertising at J. Walter Thompson, Rapp Collins Worldwide and the Arnell Group.

Deborah Doane is head of sustainable consumption at WWF-UK, leading innovative strategies to work towards an 80% reduction of our footprint by 2050, working with sectors such as food, housing and finance and with both local and national governments. For the past 15 years she has worked with NGOs, think-tanks and the private sector on ethical trading, human rights and sustainable development issues. She was director of the CORE (Corporate Responsibility) Coalition, campaigning for mandatory social and environmental reporting of all large companies. Previously, she was a programme director of Transforming Markets at the New Economics Foundation in London, and head of the Humanitarian Ombudsman Project, based in London and Geneva. She lectures at the London School of Economics and London Business School, and writes internationally on a range of CSR issues. She is on the Advisory Board on CSR for the Institute of Chartered Accountants of England and Wales and is chair of the Board of Anti-Apathy, which supports people who take creative approaches to social and environmental issues.

Iain Ellwood is head of consulting at the London office of Interbrand and leads the strategy, brand valuation and analytics, and brand engagement teams. Previously he worked at Prophet Management Consultancy, where he led a number of global strategic marketing engagements and helped grow the London office from start-up. He is a seasoned management consultant with over 15 years' international experience, leading commercially effective engagements for clients such as British Airways, Barclays,

Godrej, InterContinental Hotels, Mitsubishi, Orange, The Orient Express and Thomson Reuters. He is the author of *Wonder Woman: Marketing Secrets for the Trillion Dollar Customer* and *The Essential Brand Book* and a regular press commentator on marketing and branding issues. He is a Fellow of the Royal Society of Arts (FRSA), a member of the Chartered Institute of Marketing (MCIM) and a member of the Marketing Society.

Paul Feldwick worked for over 30 years at BMP, now DDB London, one of the agencies that invented Account Planning. He has been convenor of judges for the IPA Advertising Effectiveness Awards, chair of the APG and of the AQR, and is a fellow of the MRS and of the IPA. He is well known as a writer and speaker on advertising and brands; author of the book *What is Brand Equity, Anyway;* and three times winner of Best Paper at the MRS Conference – most recently in 2007 for the paper "Fifty Years Using the Wrong Model of TV Advertising" with Robert Heath. He is a visiting research fellow at the Centre for Research into Advertising and Consumption (CRiAC) at the University of Bath School of Management. He now works as a consultant, advising agencies and advertisers on issues of communication, creativity and change. He also runs Fine Frenzy, a series of workshops which apply the experience of writing and reading poetry to organisational creativity and change.

Jez Frampton is the global CEO of Interbrand, responsible for managing the firm's worldwide interests and enhancing the strategic and creative offering. Previously CEO of the firm in the UK, he has worked with many different clients including Budweiser, the BBC, IBM, Orange, Diageo, Carlsberg-Tetley, Nestlé, Marks and Spencer and McLaren Cars. He began his career in advertising while working in the United States. On returning to the UK, he moved into account planning at DMB&B and was executive planning director at Saatchi & Saatchi before joining Interbrand to manage the European interactive branding offer.

Giles Gibbons is the founder and CEO of Good Business, one of Europe's leading corporate responsibility (CR) consultancies. He began his career at Cadbury Schweppes, serving in the marketing department on the development and launch of some of the UK's most successful consumer products. He moved to advertising agency Saatchi & Saatchi, where he managed a wide range of domestic and international marketing campaigns. He then helped set up M&C Saatchi in 1995 before starting Good Business in 1997 with Steve Hilton. His first book, co-authored with Steve Hilton, is *Good*

Business – Your World Needs You. Giles writes a monthly column for *The Times* on business and consumer trends in the social and environmental arena and is a regular speaker at corporate responsibility conferences. He plays an active role in the voluntary sector advising a number of charities and is currently vice-chair of We Are What We Do, a social enterprise focused on creating consumer-led social change.

Andy Hobsbawm established the first international web agency in 1994 and was a founding director of leading British new media company Online Magic that merged with Agency.com in 1997. Since 2005 he has been European chairman of Agency.com. He has been a weekly columnist about the new economy for the *Financial Times*, and published a widely acclaimed report, "10 Years On: The State of the Internet a decade after Mosaic". He is currently writing *Small is the Next Big Thing* to be published by Atlantic Books. Andy was recognised by UK internet industry professionals as one of most influential 100 individuals over the past decade and also received a Special Lifetime Achievement Award in 2005. In *Campaign* magazine he has been voted New Media Innovator of the Year and named by industry peers as one of the most admired digital pioneers. Most recently, Andy co-founded an award-winning public service, Green Thing (Dothegreenthing.com), which inspires people to lead a greener life.

Jan Lindemann is a leading authority on value-based brand management and the impact of brands and other intangibles on shareholder value. He has advised many companies such as Samsung Electronics, ING and Prada Group on building leading global brands with sustainable economic value. He was global managing director of brand valuation at Interbrand, where he built the firm's global brand valuation and analytics business. He established and managed the ranking of the Best Global Brands published annually in *BusinessWeek*. In his earlier career he was a mergers and acquisitions adviser for Chase Manhattan Bank. He has an MA in international economics and politics from the School of Advanced International Studies (SAIS) at Johns Hopkins University in Washington, DC.

Allan Poulter is a partner at Field Fisher Waterhouse LLP, a London-based law firm, practising within its Trade Marks and Brand Protection Group. He is qualified as a solicitor and as a registered trade mark attorney, and is nominated in the 2008 *Euromoney* Leading Trade Mark Law Practitioners. He manages the international trade mark portfolios of several household-name clients and has particular expertise in Community Trade Mark proceedings. He is a past chairman of the International Trade Mark Association's publications board and is editor of the INTA publication on the Community Trade Mark. He is a regular speaker on intellectual property issues at conferences around the world.

Maxwell Raison is a strategy director at Interbrand London, which he joined in 2002 after more than five years as a planner with an integrated advertising agency. He has over ten years' international experience and is responsible for the strategic direction of any project. He believes that the best results for any brand lie in the effective combination of rigour, insight and creativity. He has worked on projects with diverse clients, both national and international, including British Airways, Godrej, Inter-Continental Hotels and Resorts, Musgrave Group (winner Interbrand best work award 2006), McLaren (winner marketing research awards 2005), Procter & Gamble and the Royal Air Force. He has spoken at conferences and events and on radio and television, as well as writing articles in the marketing press and on brandchannel. A regular visitor to India, in 2007 he took a three-month break to explore the country.

John Simmons pioneered the discipline of verbal identity and has consulted for brands around the world such as Guinness, Unilever and Air Products. His books are valued as authoritative and engaging texts on the role of language in branding. He runs *Dark Angels* workshops in the UK and internationally. He is series editor of *Great Brand Stories*, and author of books in that series on Starbucks, Arsenal and Innocent Drinks. In 2007 John was writer-in-residence at King's Cross tube station in London. Previously a director of Newell and Sorrell and then of Interbrand, he is now an independent consultant and director of The Writer.

Shaun Smith is a leading expert in helping organisations create and deliver customer experiences that differentiate their brands. A consultant to a wide range of organisations covering many different industry sectors, he is also author of several best-selling books: *Managing the Customer Experience: Turning Customers into Advocates, Uncommon Practice: People Who Deliver a Great Brand Experience* and, most recently, *See, Feel, Think, Do: The Power of Instinct in Business.* Shaun speaks internationally on these subjects and was recently voted one of the UK's top business speakers.

Preface

The past few years have seen the apparent triumph of the brand concept; everyone from countries to political parties to individuals in organisations is now encouraged to think of themselves as a brand. At its best this means caring about, measuring and understanding how others see you, and adapting what you do to take account of it, without abandoning what you stand for. At its worst it means putting a cynical gloss or spin on your product or your actions to mislead or manipulate those you seek to exploit. These are hardly new ideas. What is new is the ubiquitous and often confused use of branding terminology to describe them.

This book aims to bring greater understanding into this complex and, to some, emotive area. Written by leading practitioners and analysts, it puts brands and branding into their historical context, describes current thinking and best practice, reviews the fast-changing patterns of brands in Asia and brands in an increasingly digital world, and ventures some thoughts about the future.

Brands are conceptually tricky. In the words of Jeremy Bullmore of WPP, they are "fiendishly complicated, elusive, slippery, half-real/half-virtual things. When CEOs try to think about brands, their brains hurt" ("Posh Spice and Persil", The Brands Lecture, British Brands Group, December 5th 2001). Part of the confusion comes from the fact that the word "brand", as a noun, is used in at least three separate but interrelated senses:

- In most everyday use (for example, "which brand did you buy?") a brand is a named product or service.
- In some contexts (for example, "which brand shall we use for this new product?") brands are trade marks.
- In other contexts (for example, "how will this strengthen or weaken our brand?"), brand refers to customers' and others' beliefs and expectations about products and services sold under a specific trade mark or about the company which provides them; the standard term for this is brand equity, although in a corporate or business-to-business context, the old-fashioned term "reputation" is almost synonymous.

The use of the same word to mean three categorically different things does not aid clear thinking; and the thinking gets muddier when the anti-globalisation movement refers to "brands as bullies", when really it is attacking the (mostly American) multinationals that own global consumer brands.

Brand valuation is an attempt to attribute part of the total value of a firm to brand equity. But brand equity – especially for a corporation, such as Microsoft, IBM or GE, as opposed to a product, such as Windows or Persil – is like reputation: it cannot be bought or sold. In contrast, a trade mark can be sold but has little inherent value apart from the associated brand equity.

This is not to deny that brands – that is, brand equity – can be an extremely important component of a firm's value. Most successful businesses today are valued by the market at far more than the value of their tangible assets; as Jan Lindemann shows in Chapter 3, the proportion of the market value of major companies accounted for by intangibles, including brand equity, increased from less than 20% in 1975 to 80% in 2005. Brand equity, whether or not it is a separable asset to which we can assign a single, precise and valid financial value, is often the most important of these intangible assets. The financial markets now understand this and are starting to require senior management to act as good stewards of this crucial aspect of business performance. In other words, the emphasis on brands, which started in the late 1980s, has proved to be more than a passing fad, although the issues are evolving, as several of the essays in this book explain.

If senior managers are becoming brand stewards, what, then, are the issues they should think about in today's market? As always in marketing, the specifics vary enormously, but there are a number of common themes.

Brand measurement, accountability and understanding

To manage brand equity (or anything) successfully requires current, valid data. This includes diagnostic data about why the brand is where it is. Few brand owners do this well. Customer/consumer insight can come from many sources, including direct customer contact ("immersion") as well as formal market research, customer database analysis, learning from operations (for example, complaints) and market intelligence. Of course, customer insights achieve nothing if they are not communicated openly – even when they challenge current assumptions and the resulting strategies – and then acted on. This is a big challenge in most organisations.

Another accountability issue relates to marketing metrics such as market share, customer loyalty, relative price and relative perceived quality. Managers should not only see these metrics regularly, and at a detailed level, but also report the main ones at a summary level to shareholders, apart from a few (such as customer complaints) which may be commercially sensitive. Resistance to accountability has been a systematic weakness of the marketing discipline, which is one of the reasons why finance tends to have more influence.

Brand support

Including a range of marketing metrics in performance measurement systems such as the balanced scorecard (to complement short-term financial measures) should make it easier to maintain investment in activities that will build and develop brand equity. The main trends are a shift of resources away from traditional media advertising towards digital marketing, and a gradual concentration of resources on fewer, bigger brands, each capable of supporting more products. Relating back to measurement and accountability, managers should insist on quantitative evaluations (post-audits) of all brand investments even though these are unlikely to pin down the full long-term effects. The three criteria in a post-audit should be effectiveness (did the campaign reach its objectives?), efficiency (was it good value for money?) and learning (what have we learned which will help us do better in future?).

The brand owner's social and ethical stance

There is no consensus about the net social impact of businesses, brands or branding either in general or in particular cases. Nor is there consensus about the implications for public policy (for example, regulation, investment incentives) or for businesses themselves; but because of attacks from diverse groups (both consumerist and anti-consumerist) brand owners need a viewpoint on these issues. They may rightly argue that many of the criticisms of them are confused and ill-informed; that, for instance, the labour and environmental standards of multinationals in developing countries are usually higher than those of local competitors; and that those who criticise their involvement in these countries rarely spell out the likely consequences if that involvement were to cease. These arguments, however, are insufficient either to address the substantive issues or to win the battle for hearts and minds.

Brand owners today need to take account of the fact that these issues are starting to affect not only the brand choices of some consumers but also areas such as graduate recruitment and government relations. Further, in a digitally connected world anti-brand websites and e-mail campaigns can have a dramatic impact within a few days. In other words, it is now even more important for companies to be clear about what they and their brands stand for.

Making the brand experience live up to the promise

A recurrent theme in this book is that successful brand management goes well beyond the cosmetics of branding (brand name, packaging, advertising and so on). All great brands are built on a bedrock of trust derived from customers' experience of buying and using products and services sold under the brand name. The resulting brand equity is then reinforced by brand communications in their mainly supporting role.

For some brands (mostly consumer packaged goods brands such as Coca-Cola and Marlboro), consumers find it hard to distinguish between different competing products in blind (unbranded) tests. In these cases, brand communications have a more central role, supported by great products and excellent distribution. A slightly different example is Intel, which owes some of its success to its Intel Inside "ingredient branding" strategy, but more to its products' price-performance, its strategic alliance with Microsoft and its dominance of standards. But for most top brands in most categories – IBM, GE, Nokia, Toyota, McDonald's, Google, Disney, American Express – brand equity comes primarily from customers' experience of buying and using products and services sold under the brand name. This is why Seán Meehan and I urged companies to focus first on delivering the generic category benefits "simply better" than the competition in our book *Simply Better: Winning and Keeping Customers by Delivering What Matters Most* (Harvard Business School Press, 2004).

This sounds unexciting but it represents the biggest opportunity for senior management as brand stewards in most companies. After 30 years of total quality management (TQM), customer relationship management (CRM) and other such management prescriptions, there is still a huge gap between promise and delivery for most brands, especially service brands. In today's increasingly digital world, consumers are more and more active and interconnected, so failure to deliver the brand promise is likely to be punished by the market faster and more toughly than ever. Technology can itself help companies reliably deliver, but the main issues are about the combination of human resources, operations, customer insight and marketing, company values and getting all the functions to work well together. This is extremely difficult and is why "simply better" companies such as Toyota and Procter & Gamble are sustainably successful. This challenge shows, however, why building a valuable brand can never be done by marketing people working alone.

Brands and branding

Brands create customer value because they reduce both the effort and the risk of buying things, and therefore give suppliers an incentive to invest in quality and innovation. Branding can also enhance the customer's experience aesthetically and psychologically. Today, there is far more interest in brands and recognition of their importance than there was 10 or 20 years ago, but there is still great ignorance and misunderstanding of many of the issues. This book is aimed at any open-minded person who seeks a better understanding of the social and financial value of brands, current best practice in branding, and some of the emerging issues around this important, complex and ever fascinating topic.

Patrick Barwise

PART 1
THE CASE FOR BRANDS

1 Introduction

Rita Clifton

In great part, this book, and its treatment of the subject of brands and branding, was originally inspired by a leader article, "Pro Logo", which appeared in *The Economist* on September 8th 2001. The date of publication may give some clue as to why the subject did not generate as much follow-up debate as it might have done.

But there were, and are, other factors which subdued the kind of support that the article advocated for brands. The title "Pro Logo" was a witty response to the title and arguments in Naomi Klein's 1999 book *No Logo*. That book had become an unofficial "bible" for the anti-capitalist and anti-globalisation movement, arguing that global brands had too much power and were the cause of a variety of evils and injustices in world society. *The Economist* article essentially advised Klein and her followers to grow up, and to recognise the importance of globalisation and brands to the economic and social development of all nations. Brands have been successful because people want them; and every organisation's need to protect its reputation (and so its corporate value) is a rather efficient stimulus for them to behave well.

If the "anti" fervour of that time died down in the mid-2000s, the momentous financial events of 2008, and the impact on the "real" economy, look likely to challenge people's views again about whether capitalism – and by implication the brands that symbolise it – should have the freedom to operate it has enjoyed.

This would be frustrating indeed. The problem is clearly not capitalism *per se*; without the energy and competition of markets, and the efficiency which professional businesses bring, there would be little relevant innovation and resources to help people's lives – and, of course, little money to pay for schools, hospitals and civil society. No, it is simply that capitalism needs to be run more sustainably, in all its senses: economically, socially and environmentally. It is not exaggerating to say that this means every organisation should pay more central attention to its brands. Brands – whether product, service, retail or corporate, consumer or business-to-business – are demonstrably the most important and sustainable asset any organisation has. While founding individuals might die, buildings fall down, and products and technologies become obsolete, brands live on if they are managed well – and are allowed to play the central managing and organising role that they justify. Being managed well extends as far as making sure that people understand and help to deliver the brand across all operations – including being appraised and given incentives in line with the brand values. As a topical example, had the errant bankers and financiers been measured by and given incentives to build long-term sustainable brand value rather than short-term financial targets – or at least a balance of the two – the outcome may well have been different.

Financial services has always been one of the most challenging sectors so far as branding is concerned. The structure of most banks and financial institutions is not focused on the company's brand promise to the customer, but rather on financial products and services. Even today, brand management, if it exists, is generally viewed as a separate activity, usually as the province of the marketing department and usually to do with advertising and communication materials. As an example of this, at a recent financial services conference for senior executives, there was a changeover from one speaker to the next. The first had talked about the short-term prospects for the financial markets, and the second was to talk about the value of branding. Before the second speaker had even started to speak, there was an exodus of around a quarter of the delegates. Clearly, many felt that the brand issue was either nothing to do with them or not important.

This echoed the sentiment of a recent letter from a FTSE company chief executive in response to an approach from a brand consultancy. No one could blame the CEO for rebuffing such an approach from a supplier, but it was the reason given that was illuminating: "Branding is not our main preoccupation at the moment." The letter was polite, but the implication was clear. Basically, in the face of difficult market conditions, the CEO was preoccupied with "more important" things such as, presumably, cutting costs and restructuring. In contrast, branding was, to him, a discretionary cost and most probably to do with expensive logo-twiddling. To equate "brand" with such superficial cosmetics is the equivalent of saying that people are really only the sum of their name, face and clothes – or, indeed, saying that "at the moment, we're not interested in our customers", or "we're not interested in generating sustainable wealth". Quite apart from anything else, a good understanding of where your brand adds most value ensures better decisions on where to make savings when necessary, as well as more efficient use of resources to keep the things that will keep any company going: a loyal customer, and some security of demand.

It is interesting that Warren Buffett, the world's most famous (and least sentimental) investor, told a group of investors in Germany that brand is the most important factor in deciding where to invest.[1] Traditionally, a strong balance sheet is the first criterion, but Buffett put that in third place. His second criterion was a good management team. But in first place he put brand. Even in hard times, brand is the key to protection and growth.

Yet even if that is accepted in theory, there is clearly still a strong need to explain and champion to a wider audience what brands and branding can really do, just how central they are to sustainable wealth creation – and, of course, how to achieve that in practice. As one chief executive noted, those who move from the traditional idea that the brand is about advertising and marketing to using the brand as the organising idea in their corporate strategy, to touch and inform everything they and their people make, do and say, may find that they "have made more progress as a business than we achieved in the previous ten years".

Recognising the different attitudes towards brands, and the different levels of understanding and practice, it seemed important for this book to air and explore a range of angles, both positive and negative, for a range of audiences. This is indeed what the book has set out to do, as is reflected in the chapter subjects and contributors.

However, we should be clear that there is a central tenet for this book, whether it is reflected in each individual contribution or not. The brand is the most important and sustainable asset of any organisation – whether a product- or service-based corporation or a not-for-profit concern – and it should be the central organising principle behind every decision and every action. Any organisation wanting to add value to day-to-day process and cost needs to think of itself as a brand.

The economic importance of brands

Certainly, all the hard economic evidence is there for the central importance of the brand. While the brand clearly belongs in the "intangible" assets of an organisation, this hardly makes its economic contribution and importance any less real. For example, the intangible element of the combined market capitalisation of Standard & Poor's 500 companies has increased to around 80%, compared with some 30% 20 years ago, and it is likely to grow even further as tangible distinctions between businesses become less sustainable. The brand element of that combined market value amounts to around one-third of the total, which confirms the brand as the most important single corporate asset. Globally, brands

5

are estimated to account for approximately one-third of all wealth; and that is just looking at their commercial definition. Some of the world's most recognised and influential brands are, of course, those of not-for-profit organisations, such as Oxfam and the Red Cross. This is an aspect of "global brands" all too rarely considered in the public debate about brands and branding.

The economic importance of brands on a national and international stage is undeniable. The 100 most valuable brands in 2008 were worth over $1.2 trillion, which would make them the 11th biggest "country" in the world in terms of GDP, ahead of India and just behind Brazil. If the financial clout wielded by these companies makes some commentators nervous, it should not. The owners of brands are also highly accountable institutions. If a brand delivers what it promises, behaves in a responsible fashion, and continues to innovate and add value, people will continue to vote for it with their wallets, their respect and even their affection. If, however, a brand begins to take its position for granted and becomes complacent, greedy or less scrupulous in its corporate practices, people will stop voting for it, with potentially disastrous effects for the brand and its owner.

In a word-processed, all-seeing digital world, where the ghosts of corporate malpractice are never laid to rest, there is every incentive for companies to behave well. One of the ironies of the anti-globalisation movement, in its original targeting of global brands, was the failure to acknowledge that the importance of brand reputation provides the strongest incentive for a company to do everything to protect the reputation of its brand, its most valuable corporate asset. If the ability to increase the value of that asset is the "carrot" for companies, then the "stick" is the knowledge of how worthless the once-proud names of companies such as Enron have now become.

From an investment perspective, the brand provides a more reliable and stable indicator of the future health of a business. Inspection of brand value, equity measures and audience relationships will give a more complete and realistic basis for underlying value than short-term financial results, which often reflect short-term priorities. A study by Harvard and South Carolina universities compared the financial performance of the world's most valuable 100 brands with the average of the Morgan Stanley Capital Index and the Standard & Poor's 500. The dramatic difference in performance gives further quantified substance to what is qualitatively obvious. Strong brands mean more return, for less risk.

The social and political aspects of brands

Brands, however, are not simply economic entities. Apart from the obvious social benefits of wealth creation in improvements in standards of living both nationally and internationally, there are less recognised social effects and benefits. Most of the world's most valuable brands have been around for more than 50 years. Brands are the most stable and sustainable assets in business, living on long after the passing of most management teams, offices, technological breakthroughs and short-term economic troughs. Clearly, to deliver this sustainable wealth, they need to be managed properly. But achieving sustainable wealth means more reliable income for companies, which means more reliable earnings. All this in turn leads to more security and stability of employment, which in itself is an important social benefit.

Related to the social perspective, there is also strong political significance in brands. Apart from the fact that political parties all over the world now employ some professional branding practices, there have been many articles and studies on issues such as "Brand America". These have looked at the role and global dominance of American brands, and at how these are being used as political symbols, for good or ill. Although initially the presence of McDonald's was greeted enthusiastically in the former Soviet Union as symbolic of Russia's new found "liberation", more recently McDonald's has been targeted for anti-American demonstrations, despite its best efforts at emphasising local management structures and locally sensitive approaches to tailoring product offers and practices.

An interesting development that goes beyond the idea of boycotting has been the launch of competitive initiatives such as Mecca-Cola, introduced in 2002 by Tawfik Mathlouthi, a French entrepreneur. This is another demonstration of the highest level of symbolic and economic importance of brands. The strongest brands have always worked at the level of personal identity. So even if Mecca-Cola has not been a substantial financial challenge to the $67 billion brand value of Coca-Cola, it highlighted new possibilities for actively expressing fundamental differences of view, with the nicely ironic touch that the "alternative statement" brand has almost exactly the same physical characteristics as the mainstream one. However, before commentators get too carried away in this area, the nature of competition in brands has always meant competition between product characteristics and broader brand values, image and associations. Whatever the motivation for launching a competitive brand, its long-term success will depend on its ability to satisfy a critical mass of customers on product, service and image grounds.

But a powerful political point about brands is their ability to cross borders, and potentially to bind people and cultures together more quickly and effectively than national governments, or the bureaucratic wheels of international law, ever could.

TV used to be called the second superpower; the internet is the new, alive and often mobile TV "screen" that has all but taken this role. Whereas it used to take decades and centuries for one culture to seep into another, now not only can lasting and transforming images of different cultures be transferred in seconds, but lasting connections can also be made. America's dominance of the TV, internet and media markets has ensured that American brands (and, indeed, Brand America) still dominate global markets in their turn; and although the production and servicing facilities for brands benefit from regional flexibility, those that own the brands own the greatest wealth. One of the reasons that China has not been satisfied with being the "factory of the world" is that it recognises that "he who owns the brand owns the wealth" and is busy trying to build its own world-class brands. However, any successful brand, of any provenance, must continue to understand and anticipate changes in its audiences to remain successful. It is beyond irony that the internet – essentially an American invention and "supplied" by America – has become such an instrument of challenge to its brands and its institutions and has helped to open a new world order.

This book will explore these and other issues, such as the changing power base between West and East, and how Asian brands are emerging as serious global players. What is certain, however, is that the strongest brands have, in their lifetime, already seen off seismic changes in political, social and economic circumstances, and continue to thrive through deserving trust and long-term relationships. Brands of all kinds do have extraordinary power: economic power, political power and social power. It is no exaggeration to say that brands have the power to change people's lives, and indeed the world. For this claim, think not just about the "one free world" images introduced by Coca-Cola advertising over the years, and the universality of the Red Cross, but also consider the more recent emergence of Microsoft, Nokia and Google as inspirers and enablers of social change.

Understanding the role of brands

If brands are so demonstrably powerful, and since the definition and benefit of brands embrace every type of business and organisation, the question to ask is why every business and organisation would not want to concentrate their resources, structure and financial accountability on this most important asset. Indeed, there is a clear need for organisations to be consistently preoccupied with maintaining the sustainable competitive advantage offered by the brand. The clarity of focus that a strong brand positioning gives organisations will always create more effectiveness, efficiency and competitive advantage across all operations; and from a pragmatic financial perspective, research among investment communities confirms that clarity of strategy is one of the first criteria for judging companies.

So why are brands sometimes not taken as seriously as the data, and even high-profile supporters, show us they should be? There seem to be several potential explanations.

Lack of understanding

Perhaps the first and most obvious is a lack of full understanding among some senior managers about what successful branding really is. If branding is treated as a cosmetic exercise only, and regarded merely as a new name/logo, stationery and possibly a new advertising campaign, it will have only a superficial effect at best. Indeed, if this "cosmetic" approach is applied in an effort to make a bad or confused business look more attractive, it is easy to see why these so-called "rebranding" exercises encourage such cynicism. Reputation is, after all, reality with a lag effect. Branding needs to start with a clear point of view on what an organisation should be about and how it will deliver sustainable competitive advantage; then it is about organising all product, service and corporate operations to deliver that. The visual (and verbal) elements of branding should, of course, then symbolise that difference, lodge it memorably in people's minds and protect it in law through the trade mark.

Terminology

The second explanation for why branding is sometimes not central in the corporate agenda seems to be to do with terminology. The term "brand" has now permeated just about every aspect of society, and can be as easily applied to utilities, charities, football teams and even government initiatives as it has been in the past to packaged goods. Yet there still seems to be a residual and stubborn belief that brands are relevant only to consumer goods and commerce. Clearly, this is nonsense when every organisation has "consumers" of some kind; furthermore, some of the world's most valuable brands are business to business, but that does not make them any less "consumers". However, rather than get deeply embroiled in the broader meanings of consumption, it is probably more helpful to talk about audiences for brands today. These can be consuming audiences, influencing audiences or internal audiences. All these audiences need to be engaged by the brand – again, whether it is a product, service, corporate or not-for-profit brand – for it to fulfil its potential.

If there are still those who would say "yes, but why does it have to be called brand?", it is worth remembering that every successful business and organisation needs to be set up and organised around a distinctive idea of some kind. To distinguish itself effectively and efficiently from other organisations, it is helpful to have some kind of shorthand: visual or verbal symbols, perhaps an icon that can be registered and protected. To make up another term for all this would seem perverse, as branding is already in existence. Rather, it is worth exploring why some people and organisations might have this aversion or misunderstanding and tackle the root cause.

In the case of some arts and charitable organisations, there can be a problem with commercial overtones; for commercial organisations working in the business-to-business arena, or in heavy or technical services, there may be concerns that branding feels too soft and intangible to be relevant. With the former, it is a harsh truth of the new arts and not-for-profit worlds that they are competing for talent, funding, supporters and audiences, and need to focus their efforts and investment with the effectiveness and efficiency that brand discipline brings. With the latter, there is nothing "soft" about the financial value that strong branding brings, in every and any sector; nor is it "soft" to use all possible competitive levers to gain every customer in a hypercompetitive international market. Price will always be a factor in choice. But acting like a commodity, rather than a trusted and differentiated brand, will eventually lead only to the lower-price road to perdition.

Ownership
The third area to examine is that of ownership within organisations. Whereas the more established consumer goods companies grew up around their individual brands, more complex and technical organisations may often be run by people who have little experience in marketing or selling. As a result, the brand may simply be regarded as the specialist province of the marketing team, or, since the visual aspects of brands are the most obvious manifestation, brand management may be delegated to the design manager. This is not to cast aspersions on the specialist marketing and design functions, since their skills are crucial in

maintaining the currency and aesthetics of the brand; however, unless the chief executive of the organisation is perceived to be the brand champion, the brand will remain a departmental province rather than the driving purpose of everyone in an organisation.

Although marketing is critical in shaping and presenting a brand to its audiences in the most powerful way, brands and marketing are not the same thing. And as far as the need for CEO attention is concerned, if the brand is the most important organisational asset, it makes rational sense for it to be the central management preoccupation. Business strategy is, or should be, brand strategy, and vice versa. Effective and efficient corporate governance is brand-driven governance. It is common for chief executives to say that people are their organisations' most important asset, but what matters is what they are organised to do. No matter how clever and talented a team is, unless the team members are united to create some kind of distinctive and sustainable brand offer, they will be just another group of talented people, working together for a while but not creating anything of lasting value.

Tangible and intangible elements

The last area to cover in explaining any remaining ambivalence about brands relates to their particular combination of tangible and intangible elements. The tangible area is always easier, since today's senior business culture is still often happier concentrating on the tangible, rational and quantifiable aspects of business. As far as quantification is concerned, brands can certainly now be measured, and it is critically important that they are. If their financial contribution is not already self-evident, there are many formally recognised ways to put a hard and quantifiable value on them.

It is the intangible, more creative, visual and verbal elements of brands that can sometimes be taken less seriously by senior management than they deserve. Yet it is these elements that will engage and inspire people, externally and internally, to the advantage of the organisation. When John McGrath, former CEO of Diageo, describes the creation of the Diageo corporate brand, and the vision and values to support it, he speaks warmly of the vision that clarified and inspired the company for a new future. He adds wryly that the £1m that was paid to brand consultants for helping the company create this was a high-profile topic of media discussion at the time. This was in contrast to the many more millions of pounds in fees and commissions that were reportedly paid to lawyers and financiers, and which passed with barely a murmur. Creativity and imagination are crucial to the success of a brand. It is the easiest thing in the world for people to approach new naming, product development, design and advertising ideas with an open mouth and a closed mind. In turn, brand practitioners need to have the courage of their convictions in publicly presenting new ideas, and to recognise that the most effective creative solution may even challenge their own professional conventions.

About this book

The following chapters in this book are divided into three parts.

Part 1 looks at the history and definition of brands, and their financial and social importance. Also examined are the world's most valuable brands and the lessons that can be learned from their experiences and the challenges they face.

Part 2 examines a number of crucial practice areas of brand management such as the disciplines of brand positioning and brand value management. This includes the need for brand alignment through all aspects of an organisation's operations, stretching across products and services, human resources practices and corporate behaviour, environments and communications. Also covered is the role of visual and verbal brand identity in engaging audiences and the ever more complex area of brand communications in the round. A chapter on public relations highlights the increasing need to make sure that internal and external messages are consistent in their representation of the brand. Another chapter looks at the importance of taking the necessary steps to ensure that a brand is legally protected.

Part 3 considers the future for brands of all kinds. It analyses the effects and opportunities of globalisation and examines the potential for Asian brands, and branding in China and India. One chapter considers the area of corporate social responsibility and its central future role; another puts the case for nations to take advantage of brand disciplines. There is also a discussion about branding in the digital age and its implications. The last chapter pulls together the trends that will shape the future of brands, business and society, and highlights what organisations need to focus on if they are to make the most of their most valuable asset: their brand.

Reference

1   Kuper, S., "The Jimmy Choo is on the other foot for the Wags", *Financial Times*, October 11th, 2008.

2 What is a brand?

Tom Blackett

Ancient and modern

The Oxford American Dictionary (1980) contains the following definition:

> **Brand** *(noun):* a trade mark, goods of a particular make: a mark
> of identification made with a hot iron, the iron used for this: a
> piece of burning or charred wood, *(verb):* to mark with a hot
> iron, or to label with a trade mark.

Similarly, *The Pocket Oxford Dictionary of Current English* (1934) says:

> **Brand.** 1. *n.* Piece of burning or smouldering wood, torch,
> *(literary);* sword *(poet.);* iron stamp used red-hot to leave an
> indelible mark, mark left by it, stigma, trade-mark, particular
> kind of goods. 2. *v.t.* Stamp *(mark, object, skin),* with b., impress
> indelibly *(is branded on my memory)*

These two entries, in the order in which they list the definitions and in the definitions themselves, illustrate how, over 50 years, the primary use of the word "brand" now has a commercial application. However, the definitions also underline a common origin. Almost irrespective of how the word is used today, it has always meant, in its passive form, the object by which an impression is formed, and in its active form the process of forming this impression.

The following pages develop the use of the word brand, both passive and active (albeit in human consciousness rather than on the flank of an animal), and explain how "branding" has become so important to business strategy. But first, there is a short history of brands.

A short history of brands

The word brand comes from the Old Norse *brandr*, meaning to burn, and from these origins made its way into Anglo-Saxon. It was of course by burning that early man stamped ownership on his livestock, and with the development of trade buyers would use brands as a means of distinguishing between the cattle of one farmer and another. A farmer with a particularly good reputation for the quality of his animals would find his brand much sought after, while the brands of farmers with a lesser reputation were to be avoided or treated with caution. Thus the utility of brands as a guide to choice was established, a role that has remained unchanged to the present day.

Some of the earliest manufactured goods in "mass" production were clay pots, the remains of which can be found in great abundance around the Mediterranean region, particularly in the ancient civilisations of Etruria, Greece and Rome. There is considerable evidence among these remains of the use of brands, which in their earliest form were the potter's mark. A potter would identify his pots by putting his thumbprint into the wet clay on the bottom of the pot or by making his mark: a fish, a star or cross, for example. From this we can safely say that symbols (rather than initials or names) were the earliest visual form of brands.

In Ancient Rome, principles of commercial law developed that acknowledged the origin and title of potters' marks, but this did not deter makers of inferior pots from imitating the marks of well-known makers in order to dupe the public. In the British Museum there are even examples of imitation Roman pottery bearing imitation Roman marks, which were made in Belgium and exported to Britain in the first century AD. Thus as trade followed the flag – or Roman Eagle – so the practice of unlawful imitation lurked close behind, a practice that remains common despite the strictures of our modern, highly developed legal systems.

With the fall of the Roman Empire, the elaborate and highly sophisticated system of trade that had bound together in mutual interdependence the Mediterranean and west European peoples gradually crumbled. Brands continued to be used but mainly on a local scale. The exceptions were the distinguishing marks used by kings, emperors and governments. The fleur-de-lis in France, the Hapsburg eagle in Austria–Hungary and the Imperial chrysanthemum in Japan indicated ownership or control. In a similar fashion the cockleshell, derived from the legend attached to the shrine of St James at Santiago de Compostela in north-west Spain, a favourite medieval centre of pilgrimage when the holy places of Palestine were closed to pilgrims by the Muslims, was widely used in pre-Renaissance Europe as a symbol of piety and faith.

In the 17th and 18th centuries, when the volume manufacture of fine porcelain, furniture and tapestries began in France and Belgium, largely because of royal patronage, factories increasingly used brands to indicate quality and origin. At the same time, laws relating to the hallmarking of gold and silver objects were enforced more rigidly to give the purchaser confidence in the product.

However, the widescale use of brands is essentially a phenomenon of the late 19th and early 20th centuries. The industrial revolution, with its improvements in manufacturing and communications, opened up the western world and allowed the mass-marketing of consumer products. Many of today's best-known consumer brands date from this period: Singer sewing-machines, Coca-Cola soft drinks, Bass beer, Quaker oats, Cook's tours, Sunlight soap, Shredded Wheat breakfast cereal, Kodak film, American Express travellers' cheques, Heinz baked beans and Prudential Insurance are just a few examples.

Hand in hand with the introduction of these brands came early trade mark legislation. This allowed the owners of these brands to protect them in law (indeed, the Bass "Red Triangle" trade mark was the very first registered in the UK in 1876, and the beaming Quaker, who adorns the pack of the eponymous oats, is now well into his second century). The birth of advertising agencies such as J Walter Thompson and NW Ayer in the late 19th century gave further impetus to the development of brands.

But it is the period since the end of the second world war that has seen the real explosion in the use of brands. Propelled by the collapse of communism, the arrival of the internet and mass broadcasting systems, and greatly improved transportation and communications, brands have come to symbolise the convergence of the world's economies on the demand-led rather than the command-led model.

Elements of the brand

The dictionary definitions quoted above suggest that brands are intrinsically striking and that their role is to create an indelible impression.

Intrinsically striking

The visual distinctiveness of a brand may be a combination of any of the following: name, letters, numbers, a symbol, a signature, a shape, a slogan, a colour, a particular typeface. But the name is the most important element of the brand as its use in language provides a universal reference point. The name is also the one element of the brand that should never change. All other elements can change over time (Shell's famous logo has evolved significantly from the early line drawing and Pepsi-Cola switched to all-blue livery a few years ago), but the brand name should be like Caesar: "as constant as the northern star".

This is not to say that brands achieve true visual distinctiveness through their names alone. Nike without its tick-like swoosh, Camel cigarettes without "Old Joe", the supercilious dromedary, Michelin without exuberant Monsieur Bibendum, McDonald's without its Golden Arches would be paler properties indeed. Brands like these – and many thousands of others – rely for their visual distinctiveness on the harmonious combination of these elements and the consistency with which this is maintained.

However, in certain markets where the use of branding is highly developed and consumers are particularly sophisticated, these rules are sometimes tested. In the fashion-clothing market, for example, brands like Mambo and Diesel have experimented with the use of completely different logos; Diesel even changed the name for a season (although all other visual aspects of the brand remained the same). The success of such tactics depends upon the awareness of the consumer. These two brands enjoy almost "cult" status, and the loyalty with which they are followed by their devotees has assured success.

Name changes of products and services are rare; they are uncommon too among companies, but perhaps a little more frequent. With products and services, the main reasons for change are either to extend the appeal of a brand to new markets where the original name may not be optimal, or to standardise the company's international trade mark portfolio. The Lucky Dog Phone Company, an AT&T subsidiary, changed its name to Lucky Guy in the United States because no counterpart to the lucky dog exists in the American Chinese, Japanese and Korean markets, all important targets. Mars changed the Marathon name to Snickers in the UK to bring the product's name into line with the rest of the world.

Companies generally change their names either because their function or their ownership has changed, or because their name is in some way misleading. Sometimes they revert to initials: Minnesota Mining and Manufacturing became 3M, a name that is both handier and more flexible strategically. Sometimes they combine the names of the merging companies: GlaxoSmithKline. Sometimes they opt for an entirely new name: Altria is now the name of the tobacco, beer and foods group once known as Philip Morris. There is no right or wrong way of renaming businesses; it is as much a matter of what the company feels comfortable with and what it feels it can make work. The key is commitment and good communications.

Sometimes these rules are not observed as faithfully as they should be. When Guinness merged with Grand Metropolitan the holding company adopted the name Diageo. Shareholders were not impressed, thinking that the decision to adopt a meaningless, foreign-sounding name, when perfectly good names like Grand Met or Guinness were available, amounted to corporate treachery. At the extraordinary general meeting held to approve the new name outbursts of booing enlivened the proceedings at each mention of "Diageo".

Name changes following mergers can be highly charged events, and closer communication with all stakeholder groups – particularly private shareholders, who may also be pensioners of the firms involved – may help ease the transition. In the case of Diageo, a name that has now "bedded down", the company should have explained why it had decided to adopt a neutral name for the new holding company and issued firm reassurances regarding the famous trading names – particularly Guinness – that it would continue to use.

Diageo, like Aviva, an insurance business, and Altria, mentioned above, is strictly a holding company name (as was the unfortunate Consignia, a name briefly adopted by the UK Post Office and now consigned to history). These names are not intended for "public consumption" – although a mischievous press made great play of post offices becoming "consignias" – so clarity is paramount; the rationale for change must be communicated to – and understood by – all stakeholder groups.

Creating an indelible impression

In developed economies consumers have an astonishing – often bewildering – array of choice. There are, for example, dozens of car manufacturers, hundreds of car models and thousands of different vehicle specifications to choose from; the days when Henry Ford offered "any colour you want as long as it's black" are long gone. This diversity of choice puts pressure on those making or selling products or services to offer high quality, excellent value and wide availability. It also puts pressure on them to find more potent ways of differentiating themselves and securing competitive advantage. According to *Fortune* magazine (in 1997):

> *In the twenty-first century, branding ultimately will be the only unique differentiator between companies. Brand equity is now a key asset.*

Much of the skill of marketing and branding nowadays is concerned with building "equity" for products whose characteristics, pricing, distribution and availability are really quite close to each other. Take cola drinks, for example: Coca-Cola and Pepsi-Cola are able to dominate the worldwide cola market. The power of their bottling and distribution systems no doubt plays a part in this, but the main factor is the strength and appeal of the two brands to consumers. The strong, instantly recognisable names, logos and colours of these two brands symbolise their makers' promise that consumers' expectations will be fulfilled, whatever the subtleties of these might be.

Brands allow the consumer to shop with confidence, and they provide a route map through a bewildering variety of choices. The customer does not have to be an expert on the complexities of mobile telecommunications to choose between one service supplier and another. The brand name, the tariff and the method of payment are all that is required to make an informed choice. And as tariffs and methods of payment are largely the same among competing companies, it is the brand – and consumers' appreciation of its underlying appeals – that will ultimately drive the purchase decision. It is the inculcation of these "underlying appeals" – the bedrock of brand equity – that concerns brand owners and has become the subject of unceasing attention and investment. Brands with strong equity embed themselves deeply in the hearts and minds of consumers.

The real power of successful brands is that they meet the expectations of those that buy them or, to put it another way, they represent a promise kept. As such they are a contract between a seller and a buyer: if the seller keeps to its side of the bargain, the buyer will be satisfied; if not, the buyer will in future look elsewhere.

Brands as business assets

The value to businesses of owning strong brands is incontestable. Brands that keep their promise attract loyal buyers who will return to them at regular intervals. The benefit to the brand owner is that forecasting cash flows becomes easier, and it becomes possible to plan and manage the development of the business with greater confidence. Thus brands, with their ability to secure income, can be classed as productive assets in exactly the same way as any other, more traditional assets of a business (plant, equipment, cash, investments and so on).

The asset value of brands is now widely recognised, not just by brand owners but by investors. Brands can generate high-quality earnings that can directly affect the overall performance of the business and thus influence the share price.

The stockmarket value of The Coca-Cola Company, for example, was around $136 billion in early 2008 and in late 2008 despite the eruption of the global financial crisis was still close to $140 billion, yet the book value (the net asset value) of the business was only $11.8 billion. A vast proportion of the value of the business is therefore dependent upon shareholders' confidence in the intangible assets of the business, and the ability of the company to manage these profitably. Coca-Cola owns few intangibles other than its "secret recipe", its contracts with its global network of bottlers and its brand names. An independent analysis (see Table 3.1 on page 28) estimated that the value of the Coca-Cola brand name in mid-2007 was almost $65 billion, over half of its intangible value at that time. Similarly, high-profile consumer brands like McDonald's can attribute a large proportion (around 50%) of their market value to their brands. At the other end of the scale, for two of the world's largest companies, General Electric and Intel, the ratio of brand values to intangible value is much lower. Both GE and Intel are rich in intangibles, but as these are linked to the technology in which these companies excel, they probably take the form of patents and know-how agreements.

It is not surprising that much of the merger and acquisition activity of the past 20 years or so has involved brand-owning businesses. The durability of brands, the quality of their earning power (unlike short-lived technology assets such as patents) and their widespread appeal make them highly desirable properties. The globalisation of trade is driving consolidation in many industries; an example is the purchase, for $21 billion, of Bestfoods by Unilever. Bestfoods owned many famous food brands, notably Knorr stock cubes and Hellmann's mayonnaise. These brands have truly global potential, which was more likely to be tapped by a company of the size and scale of Unilever than by Bestfoods, which was large but lacked Unilever's global resources.

Equally, in 1998 Volkswagen concluded a deal to acquire Rolls-Royce Motor Cars from Vickers, a UK engineering group, for around £400m. VW's interest was not in acquiring a pile of fully depreciated manufacturing assets in Derby, the home of Rolls-Royce, but in the famous Rolls-Royce and Bentley brands, crown jewels of the global automotive industry. However, although Vickers owned the Bentley name, it only had a licence for Rolls-Royce. In an interesting twist to this tale, Rolls-Royce Aero Engines, the owner of the Rolls-Royce brand name, refused to grant a licence in perpetuity to VW, handing this instead to BMW, VW's ancient German rival. Bentley and Rolls-Royce are now thriving under new ownership; both VW and BMW have kept manufacturing in the UK, realising the importance of the provenance of these two brands, and have invested heavily in state-of-the-art manufacturing.

The explosion of branding

The scale of adoption of branding has been breathtaking. An activity that for three-quarters of the 20th century was mainly confined to consumer goods and services now features in industrial and business-to-business sectors, the public and voluntary sectors, utilities and non-governmental organisations. Within the consumer sector, the development of technology has added thousands of new products and services: computer games, laptops, mobile telephones, the internet and the myriad services it distributes. Football teams, political parties and pop stars all now consider themselves brands; and the Church of England was recently urged in the media to adopt a more "branded" approach to the recruitment of clergy.

In parallel, we have seen the emergence of two new practices in branding: the application of branding techniques to corporations, and the "internalisation" of brands and their management, particularly within services businesses where the employee is pivotal in delivering customer satisfaction.

Corporate branding

Corporations have learned how important it is to be understood and appreciated, not just by investors, customers, suppliers and employees but also by opinion formers, activist groups and the general public. In shareholding societies there is intense interest in both the behaviour and the performance of quoted companies; and with the advent of the internet such companies find themselves increasingly in the "global fishbowl", where damaging news or opinions travel fast and wide. Reputation is paramount, and companies that are known for the quality of their products and services, their integrity and the transparency of their actions are the ones best placed to sustain a competitive advantage.

In the pharmaceuticals industry, for example, large corporations such as GlaxoSmithKline, Merck, Pfizer, Roche and Novartis all depend upon the development of successful new drugs for future profitability. With the declining productivity of in-house R&D, they compete fiercely for promising new products being developed by smaller, research-based organisations, such as those specialising in biotechnology. Here the reputation of the bidder is as critical as the price and the royalty terms being offered. The bidder must have a spotless record for the quality and effectiveness of its products, and for the way it conducts itself in the public arena. The reputations of several of the leading pharmaceuticals companies were damaged a few years ago through their involvement in the supply of HIV and AIDS drugs to southern Africa. The South African government threatened to overrule their patents and allow local manufacturers to produce the drugs, unless these companies reduced their prices, which – after negotiations that involved Oxfam, itself a conspicuous brand – they eventually did.

Starbucks was criticised for its opposition to an application by the Ethiopian government to register the Sidamo, Harar and Yirgacheffe names of coffee varieties as trade marks. The government planned to allow buyers of these beans – which include Starbucks – to take licences to use these names; however, it did not intend to charge a fee. Rather it argued that users should focus on promotional efforts to boost demand. Prices should then rise in response, a classic commodity branding strategy that would benefit both producers and their customers. Eventually an agreement was reached. In December 2007 it was announced that Starbucks had agreed to recognise Ethiopia's ownership of the three names and not to block Ethiopian attempts to win trade marks for them.

The companies referred to above have largely recovered the reputational ground they lost. The same cannot be said of such notorious casualties as Enron and WorldCom. Both these corporations were relative newcomers, but cheating your shareholders (your owners) so spectacularly represents a betrayal of trust that not even long-established brands can survive.

Services branding

The developed world has seen a huge shift in output from industry and manufacturing to services, and as demand for financial and leisure services increases, brands will play an increasing role in a "brand savvy" world in which people become more and more discriminating and difficult to please. Brand owners therefore need to ensure that they deliver high-quality services that are aligned with a compelling vision and delivered with a genuine commitment to customer satisfaction.

Thus the next journey for the brand is inside. Some of the most successful branded companies use the brand as their central organising principle. Richard Branson's determination to give the man in the street a better deal – whether it is in financial services, train services or air travel – animates the organisation and acts as a filter for corporate development. Not all of Branson's enterprises have been successful, notably Virgin Rail, but he is widely admired for his commitment and enthusiasm, even if these qualities are not always matched by service delivery. Fliers with Virgin Atlantic can readily sense the difference; not only is the flight cheaper, but the whole experience is different. It may not be to everyone's taste, but the friendliness and informality of the staff reflect the personality of Branson himself. The result is a well-managed customer experience, distinctive and memorable.

Contrast this with the financial services sector. Banks, in particular, have struggled to create and deliver a well-differentiated customer experience. Years of overclaiming in advertising – "the bank that likes to say 'yes'", "Come and talk to the listening bank" – have led to customer cynicism. Banks seem to lack a really big idea, which may be the result of over a century of trying not to be different. Some have experimented with telephone and internet banking, and it is notable that the most successful have been those that have adopted new names, such as First Direct and Egg, and have distanced themselves from their owners (respectively HSBC and Prudential, which sold Egg to Citigroup). But in truth it is exceptionally difficult for banks to differentiate; all have broadly the same products, premises and services, and all seek to recruit the same type of employee. Employees can make a difference, however, as anyone who has had a memorable experience when dealing with their bank branch will know. Employees can make or mar a long-standing relationship, and as banking has traditionally been the business of "relationships", investment in staff training is clearly one of the most important commitments to brand management that a bank can make.

But the biggest challenge that banks currently face is rebuilding trust after some had to be bailed out by governments and others had to find alternative ways to strengthen their balance sheets. The 2008 banking crisis placed the credibility of all bank brands in doubt, and it is questionable whether it is practical – or even desirable – for banks to consider themselves brands at all. After all, one of the key characteristics of a brand is continuity, whereas the system is endemically flawed. Who would wish to perpetuate this?

Other than our health, our wealth (or lack of it) is an aspect of life that is closest to most people's hearts. It is also an aspect of life where we frequently need advice and where "trust" carries a high premium. Brands have always been about trust, and it is instructive to reflect on how the level of trust we may have in our medical adviser contrasts with the level of trust we may have in our bank and other financial advisers. Financial institutions were once greatly esteemed by their customers but with the general drive towards greater operational efficiencies (downsizing) the personal contact with customers on which relationship-building depends is now greatly reduced. Automated teller machines (ATMs) and remote banking (via the internet) may be a boon in terms of banks' costs, but they remove the opportunity to help customers with the more complicated decisions they need to make in their lives, particularly those concerning investments and pensions. Increasing familiarity, and comfort, with the internet may eventually enable banks and other financial services providers to engage with customers at a more intimate level. But in the meantime, a return to good old-fashioned relationship-building, based on staff training that embraces business and social skills, will help restore some of the credibility these brands once had.

Overall, the best services brands are built around a unique business idea or a compelling vision. When employees are excited by the proposition they will help to sustain it and communicate it to customers, suppliers and others through their enthusiasm and commitment.

Guidelines for good brand management

Some of the guidelines given below are eternal truths that apply equally to products, services and corporate brands, and some apply particularly to one category of brand or another.

- **Protect your brand.** Trade mark law offers provision for the protection of your brand and corporate names, your logo and colours, the shape of your packaging, smells and the advertising jingle you use. This protection can last indefinitely, subject to payment of a fee and the observation of some none too onerous rules of use. Patent law allows you to protect your product for periods of up to 20 years, provided the product is your invention and is a novel or non-obvious idea. Copyrights allow you to protect artistic, literary, dramatic and musical works for up to 70 years after the death of the author or originator. Protect these elements of your brand on a wide geographical scale: you may not yet be an international player, but the real opportunities are for brands whose appeals are potentially universal.
- **Honour your stakeholders.** Your customers expect attractive, well-differentiated products and services that will live up to their expectations and are well priced. Your employees want to work for a company with a compelling business idea, where they feel engaged and where they can make a difference. Your shareholders expect sound corporate governance and a well-managed company with a commitment to growing shareholder value. Your trade partners want fairness and respect in their dealings with you, and they want your reputation to enhance their own. Opinion leaders and industry commentators expect performance, innovation,

transparency and a sense of social responsibility. Interest groups want you to listen and to act.

◿ **Treat your brand as an investment, not a cost.** Brands are among the most important assets that a business can own, and strong brands can ensure business continuity in times of difficulty. Brands must remain relevant to their customers, contemporary and appealing. This means that sufficient investment must be made in advertising and marketing as well as in new product development. For many businesses active in mature markets, brand support and development is often the single biggest item of overhead cost. Investors and analysts will, quite rightly, expect the management of the business to account for the effectiveness of this expenditure; but they will look in vain at the balance sheet for evidence of this. Periodic valuations of the brands in the business will help explain how successfully management is steering the brands for the benefit of shareholders.

◿ **Exploit the financial potential of your brand.** As well as seeking ways to extend the brand through new product development, companies should look at opportunities to exploit the equity in their brands through co-branding, licensing and franchising. Co-branding can be a highly cost-effective way of entering new markets and geographical areas; the art is in finding a suitably compatible partner. Licensing is the granting of a right to use a brand in relation to similar goods or services. However, the licensor must retain control over the quality of the goods and services produced by the licensee and marketed under the brand (the practice is common in the brewing industry). Franchising is the granting of a right to a number of licensees in different geographical areas to use the brand together with a business system developed by the licensor (this practice is common in fast foods, print shops, florists and so on). Co-branding, licensing and franchising can be highly lucrative ways of exploiting a brand, broadening its exposure and enhancing its message.

◿ **Understand that successful brand management is a complex task.** It requires skills not normally associated with the traditional marketing function. The ability to brief market-research companies, advertising agencies and designers, to liaise with the sales and distribution people and to survive the odd skirmish with the "bean counters" is no longer enough. Brand managers certainly need to be adept in all these areas, but they also need to understand how a brand can be managed for the benefit of shareholders. This requires an understanding of how, in financial terms, a brand contributes to the success of a business and the creation of shareholder value. Managers of services brands need to become adept at internal communication and training, to ensure that customer satisfaction is delivered consistently in support of their brand's promise. And if the brand is the corporation, the brand manager needs to understand not just the subtle art of corporate communications but the infinitely more demanding role of stakeholder accountability.

Conclusion

The last few years of the 20th century saw a dramatic reappraisal of the role of brands in business and society, and this continues. No doubt much of this was prompted by the frenzy of merger and acquisition activity involving brand-owning companies in the late 1980s and early 1990s. The escalating bid premiums involved in these contests alerted the interest of investors and analysts, who could find no justification for these in either the share prices or in the accounts of the businesses in play. The first brand valuations did much to explain where these hidden values lay and to expose the inadequacy of (then) current goodwill accounting. They also gave organisations serious cause to consider how well these assets were being managed, and in many cases to change fundamentally the nature of their businesses.

Unlike the so-called dotcom revolution a decade later, when similar enthusiasm was shown by investors, the brand revolution was built on solid assets, with well-established and proven track records. As was said at the time, brands may be intangible in nature but successful brands produce earnings that are tangible indeed.

Now we are seeing the extension of branding techniques to almost every corner of commerce and society. The more alarming forecasts of the "global village" seem not to have been realised; the public at large, with great good sense, has administered timely warnings to overweening brand owners with inappropriate ambitions. In societies that permit free choice the success of brands will always depend on how well their owners can build and maintain trust. As long as trust remains the central guiding principle of brand-owning organisations, this can only be in the general interest.

3 The financial value of brands

Jan Lindemann

If this business were split up, I would give you the land and bricks and mortar, and I would take the brands and trade marks, and I would fare better than you.

John Stuart, chairman of Quaker (circa 1900)

In the last quarter of the 20th century there was a dramatic shift in the understanding of the creation of shareholder value. For most of the century, tangible assets were regarded as the main source of business value. These included manufacturing assets, land and buildings or financial assets such as receivables and investments. They would be valued at cost or outstanding value as shown in the balance sheet. The market was aware of intangibles, but their specific value remained unclear and was not specifically quantified. Even today, the evaluation of profitability and performance of businesses focuses on indicators such as return on investment, assets or equity that exclude intangibles from the denominator. Measures of price relatives (for example, price-to-book ratio) also exclude the value of intangible assets as these are absent from accounting book values.

This does not mean that management failed to recognise the importance of intangibles. Brands, technology, patents and employees were always at the heart of corporate success, but rarely explicitly valued. Their value was subsumed in the overall asset value. Major brand owners like The Coca-Cola Company, Procter & Gamble, Unilever and Nestlé were aware of the importance of their brands, as indicated by their creation of brand managers, but on the stockmarket investors focused their value assessment on the exploitation of tangible assets.

Evidence of brand value

The increasing recognition of the value of intangibles came with the continuous increase in the gap between companies' book values and their stockmarket valuations, as well as sharp increases in premiums above the stockmarket value that were paid in mergers and acquisitions in the late 1980s. A study on the relationship between intangible and tangible assets of the companies included in the s&p 500 index (see Figure 3.1) showed

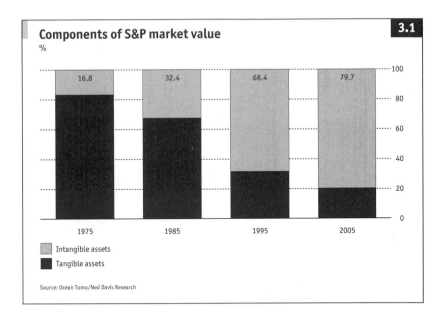

Components of S&P market value 3.1

%

Intangible assets

Tangible assets

Source: Ocean Tomo/Ned Davis Research

that over the 30-year period between 1975 and 2005 the contribution of intangibles to overall corporate value increased from 17% to 80%.

Today it is therefore possible to argue that in general most business value is derived from intangibles. Management attention to these assets has certainly increased substantially.

The brand is a special intangible that in many businesses is the most important asset. This is because of the economic impact that brands have. They influence the choices of customers, employees, investors and government authorities. In a world of abundant choices, such influence is crucial for commercial success and creation of shareholder value. Even non-profit organisations have started embracing the brand as a key asset for obtaining donations, sponsorships and volunteers.

Some brands have also demonstrated an astonishing durability. The world's most valuable brand,[1] Coca-Cola, is more than 120 years old; and the majority of the world's most valuable brands have been around for more than 60 years. This compares with an estimated average life span for a corporation of 25 years or so.[2] Many brands have survived a string of different corporate owners.

Several studies have tried to estimate the contribution that brands make to shareholder value. A study by *BusinessWeek* (see Table 3.1 overleaf) concluded that on average brands account for more than one-third of shareholder value. The study reveals that brands create significant value as either consumer or corporate brands or as a combination of both. This is matched by a survey of the world's leading CEOs and organisation leaders who estimated that corporate brand or reputation represents more than 40% of a company's market capitalisation.[3]

Table 3.1 **The contribution of brands to shareholder value**

Company	2007 brand value ($bn)	Market cap of parent company (%)	2006 brand value ($bn)
Coca-Cola	65.3	54	67.0
Microsoft	58.7	20	56.9
IBM	57.1	36	56.2
GE	51.6	13	48.9
Nokia	33.7	29	30.1
Toyota	32.1	16	27.9
Intel	30.9	24	32.3
McDonald's	29.3	48	27.5
Disney	29.2	42	27.8
Mercedes-Benz	23.6	25	21.8

Source: *BusinessWeek*/Interbrand, Best Global Brands, 2007

Table 3.1 shows how big the economic contribution made by brands to companies can be. The Coca-Cola brand alone accounted for 54% of the stockmarket value of The Coca-Cola Company in 2007. This is despite the fact that the company owns a large portfolio of other drinks brands such as Sprite and Fanta. The impact of brands on shareholder value is not confined to consumer-facing businesses. Even brands that focus purely on business customers can make a significant contribution to shareholder value as demonstrated by the IBM brand, which in 2007 accounted for 36% of the company's stockmarket value.

Studies by academics[4] and by Interbrand[5] of the companies featured in the "best global brands" league table indicate that companies with strong brands outperform the market in respect of several indices. It has also been shown that a portfolio weighted by the brand values of the best global brands performs significantly better than Morgan Stanley's global

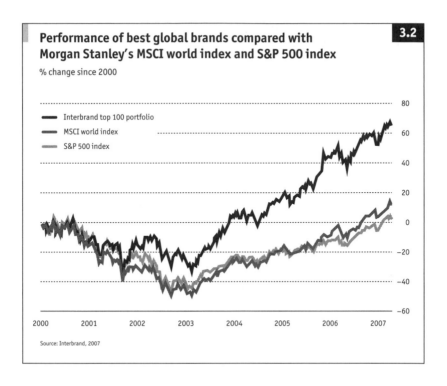

Performance of best global brands compared with Morgan Stanley's MSCI world index and S&P 500 index

3.2

% change since 2000

- Interbrand top 100 portfolio
- MSCI world index
- S&P 500 index

Source: Interbrand, 2007

MSCI index and the American-focused S&P 500 index (Figure 3.2).

Today leading companies focus their management efforts on intangible assets. For example, in January 2005, Procter & Gamble invested $57 billion to buy Gillette and other consumer brands including Duracell, Braun and Oral-B.[6] Companies such as Unilever and Pearson have become potential targets for private equity groups because of their attractive brand portfolios.[7] Samsung, one of the most successful electronics groups, invests heavily in its intangibles, spending about 7.5% of annual revenues on R&D and another 5% on communications.[8] In packaged consumer goods, companies spend about 14% of annual revenues on marketing support.[9] As John Akasie wrote in an article in *Forbes*:[10]

> It's about brands and brand building and consumer relationships
> ... Decapitalised, brand owning companies can earn huge returns
> on their capital and grow faster, unencumbered by factories
> and masses of manual workers. Those are the things that the
> stockmarket rewards with high price/earnings ratios.

Brands on the balance sheet

A wave of brand acquisitions in the late 1980s resulted in large amounts of goodwill that most accounting standards could not deal with in an economically sensible way. Transactions that sparked the debate about accounting for goodwill on the balance sheet included Nestlé's purchase of Rowntree, United Biscuits' acquisition and later divestiture of Keebler, Grand Metropolitan acquiring Pillsbury and Danone buying Nabisco's European businesses.

Accounting practice for so-called goodwill did not deal with the increasing importance of intangible assets, with the result that companies were penalised for making what they believed to be value-enhancing acquisitions. They either had to suffer massive amortisation charges on their profit and loss accounts (income statements), or they had to write off the amount to reserves and in many cases ended up with a lower asset base than before the acquisition.

In countries such as the UK, France, Australia and New Zealand it was, and still is, possible to recognise the value of acquired brands as "identifiable intangible assets" and to put these on the balance sheet of the acquiring company. This helped to resolve the problem of goodwill. Then the recognition of brands as intangible assets made use of a grey area of accounting, at least in the UK and France, whereby companies were not encouraged to include brands on the balance sheet but nor were they prevented from doing so. In the mid-1980s, Reckitt & Colman, a UK-based company, put a value on its balance sheet for the Airwick brand that it had recently bought; Grand Metropolitan did the same with the Smirnoff brand, which it had acquired as part of Heublein. At the same time, some newspaper groups put the value of their acquired mastheads on their balance sheets.

By the late 1980s, the recognition of the value of acquired brands on the balance sheet prompted a similar recognition of internally generated brands as valuable financial assets within a company. In 1988, Rank Hovis McDougall (RHM), a leading UK food conglomerate, played heavily on the power of its brands to successfully defend a hostile takeover bid by Goodman Fielder Wattie (GFW). RHM's defence strategy involved carrying out an exercise that demonstrated the value of RHM's brand portfolio. This was the first independent brand valuation establishing that it was possible to value brands not only when they had been acquired, but also when they had been created by the company itself. After successfully fending off the GFW bid, RHM included in its 1988 financial accounts the value of both the internally generated and acquired brands under "intangible assets" on the balance sheet.

In 1989, the London Stock Exchange endorsed the concept of brand valuation as used by RHM by allowing the inclusion of intangible assets in the class tests for shareholder approvals during takeovers. This proved to be the impetus for a wave of major branded-goods companies to recognise the value of brands as intangible assets on their balance sheets. In the UK, these included Cadbury Schweppes, Grand Metropolitan (when it bought Pillsbury for $5 billion), Guinness, Ladbrokes (when it acquired Hilton) and United Biscuits (including the Smith's brand).

Today, many companies including LVMH, L'Oréal, Gucci, Prada and PPR have recognised acquired brands on their balance sheets. For example, after the acquisition of Puma, PPR's intangible assets, which were mainly made up of acquired brands such as Gucci and Puma, accounted for about one-third of the company's total assets.[11] Some companies have used the balance-sheet recognition of their brands as an investor-relations tool by providing historic brand values and using brand value as a financial performance indicator.

In terms of accounting standards, the UK, Australia and New Zealand led the way by allowing acquired brands to appear on the balance sheet and providing detailed guidelines on how to deal with acquired goodwill. In 1999, the UK Accounting Standards Board introduced FRS 10 and 11 on the treatment of acquired goodwill on the balance sheet. The International Accounting Standards Board followed suit with IAS 38. And in 2002 the US Accounting Standards Board introduced FASB 141 and 142, abandoning pooling accounting and laying out detailed rules about recognising acquired goodwill on the balance sheet. In 2007, the International Valuation Standards Committee (IVSC) published a discussion paper on determining the fair value of intangible assets for IFRS reporting, providing a more detailed approach to intangible assets and their valuation.

The principal stipulations of all these accounting standards are that acquired goodwill needs to be capitalised on the balance sheet and amortised according to its useful life. However, intangible assets such as brands that can claim infinite life do not have to be subjected to amortisation. Instead, companies need to perform annual impairment tests. If the value is the same or higher than the initial valuation, the asset value on the balance sheet remains the same. If the impairment value is lower, the asset needs to be written down to the lower value. Recommended valuation methods are discounted cash flow (DCF) and market value approaches. The valuations need to be performed on the business unit (or subsidiary) that generates the revenues and profit.

The accounting treatment of goodwill upon acquisition is an important step in improving the financial reporting of intangibles such as brands. It is still insufficient, as only acquired goodwill is recognised and the detail of the reporting is reduced to a minor footnote in the accounts. This leads to the distortion that the McDonald's brand does not appear on the company's balance sheet, even though it was estimated in 2007 to account for almost 50% of the firm's stockmarket value (see Table 3.1 on page 28), yet the Burger King brand is recognised on the balance sheet of Burger King Holdings because of its acquistion by a private equity consortium in 2002. There is also still a problem with the quality of brand valuations for balance-sheet recognition. Although some companies use a brand-specific valuation approach, others use less sophisticated valuation techniques that often produce questionable values. The debate about bringing financial reporting more in line with the reality of long-term corporate value is likely to continue, but if there is greater consistency in brand-valuation approaches and greater reporting of brand values, corporate asset values will become much more transparent.

Brands and society

The economic value of brands to their owners is now widely accepted, but do brands create value for anyone other than their owners, and is the value they create at the expense of society at large?[12] The ubiquity of global mega-brands has made branding the focus of discontent for many people around the world. They see a direct link between brands and such issues as the exploitation of workers in developing countries and the homogenisation of cultures. Furthermore, brands are accused of stifling competition and tarnishing the virtues of the capitalist system by encouraging monopoly and limiting consumer choice. The opposing argument is that brands create substantial social as well as economic value as a result of increased competition, improved product performance and the pressure on brand owners to behave in socially responsible ways as the following chapter discusses in detail.

Competition on the basis of performance as well as price, which is the nature of brand competition, fosters product development and improvement. And there is evidence that companies that promote their brands more heavily than others in their categories are also more innovative in their categories. A study by PIMS Europe for the European Brands Association[13] revealed that less-branded businesses launch fewer products, invest significantly less in development and have fewer product advantages than their branded counterparts. Almost half of the "non-branded" sample spent nothing on product R&D compared with less than a quarter of the "branded" sample. And although 26% of non-branded producers never introduced significant new products, this figure was far lower at 7% for the branded set.

The need to keep brands relevant promotes increased investments in R&D, which in turn leads to a continuous process of product improvement and development. Brand owners are accountable for both the quality and the performance of their branded products and services and for their ethical practices. Given the direct link between brand value and both sales and share price, the potential costs of behaving unethically far outweigh any benefits, and outweigh the monitoring costs associated with an ethical business.

A number of high-profile brands have been accused of unethical practices. Interestingly, among these are some of the brands that have been pioneering the use of voluntary codes of conduct and internal monitoring systems. This is not to say that these brands have successfully eradicated unethical business practices, but at least they are demonstrating the will to deal with the problem.

The more honest companies are in admitting the gap they have to bridge in terms of ethical behaviour, the more credible they will seem. Nike, a company once criticised for the employment practices of some of its suppliers in developing countries, now posts results of external audits and interviews with factory workers at www.nikebiz.com. The concern of multinational companies is understandable, considering that a 5% drop in sales could result in a loss of brand value exceeding $1 billion. It is clearly in their economic interests to behave ethically.

Approaches to brand valuation

Financial values have to some extent always been attached to brands and to other intangible assets, but as indicated earlier it was only in the late 1980s that valuation approaches were established that could fairly claim to understand and assess the specific value of brands. The idea of putting a separate value on brands is now widely accepted. Indeed, for those concerned with accounting, transfer pricing and licensing agreements, mergers and acquisitions and value-based management, brand valuation is crucial in business today.

Unlike other assets such as stocks, bonds, commodities and real estate, there is no active market in brands that would provide "comparable" values. So to arrive at an authoritative and valid approach, a number of brand evaluation models have been developed. Most have fallen into two categories:

◪ research-based brand equity evaluations;
◪ purely financially driven approaches.

Research-based approaches

There are numerous brand equity models that use consumer research to assess the relative performance of brands. These do not put a financial value on brands; instead, they measure consumer behaviour and attitudes that have an impact on the economic performance of brands. Although the sophistication and complexity of such models vary, they all try to explain, interpret and measure consumers' perceptions that influence purchase behaviour. They include a wide range of perceptive measures such as different levels of awareness (unaided, aided, top of mind), knowledge, familiarity, relevance, specific image attributes, purchase consideration, preference, satisfaction and recommendation. Some models add behavioural measures such as market share and relative price.

Through different stages and depths of statistical modelling, these measures are arranged either in hierarchic order, to provide hurdles that lead from awareness to preference and purchase, or relative to their impact on overall consumer perception, to provide an overall brand equity score or measure. A change in one or a combination of indicators is expected to influence consumers' purchasing behaviour, which in turn will affect the financial value of the brand in question. However, these approaches do not differentiate between the effects of other influential factors such as R&D and design and the brand. They therefore do not provide a clear link between the specific marketing indicators and the financial performance of the brand. A brand can perform strongly according to these indicators but still fail to create financial and shareholder value.

The understanding, interpretation and measurement of brand equity indicators are crucial for assessing the financial value of brands. After all, they are key measures of consumers' purchasing behaviour upon which the success of the brand depends. However, unless they are integrated into an economic model, they are insufficient for assessing the economic value of brands.

Financially driven approaches

Cost-based approaches

These define the value of a brand as the aggregation of all historic costs incurred or replacement costs required in bringing the brand to its current state: that is, the sum of the development costs, marketing costs, advertising and other communication costs, and so on. These approaches fail because there is no direct correlation between the financial investment made and the value added by a brand. Financial investment is an important component in building brand value, provided it is effectively targeted. If it isn't, it may not make a bean of difference. The investment needs to go beyond the obvious advertising and promotion and include R&D, employee training, packaging and product design, retail design and so on.

Comparables
Another approach is to arrive at a value for a brand on the basis of something comparable. But comparability is difficult in the case of brands as by definition they should be differentiated and thus not comparable. Furthermore, the value creation of brands in the same category can be very different, even if most other aspects of the underlying business such as target groups, advertising spend, price promotions and distribution channel are similar or identical. Comparables can provide an interesting cross-check, however, even though they should never be relied on solely for valuing brands.

Premium price
In the premium price method, the value is calculated as the net present value of future price premiums that a branded product would command over an unbranded or generic equivalent. However, the primary purpose of many brands is not necessarily to obtain a price premium but rather to secure the highest level of future demand. The value generation of these brands therefore lies in securing future volumes rather than a premium price. This is true for many durable and non-durable consumer goods categories.

This method is flawed because there are rarely generic equivalents to which the premium price of a branded product can be compared. Today, almost everything is branded, and in some cases store brands can be as strong as producer brands charging the same or similar prices. The price difference between a brand and competing products can be an indicator of its strength, but it does not represent the only and most important value contribution a brand makes to the underlying business.

Economic use
Approaches that are driven exclusively by brand equity measures or financial measures lack either the financial or the marketing component to provide a complete and robust assessment of the economic value of brands.

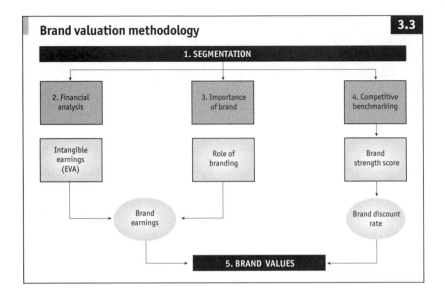

Brand valuation methodology 3.3

The economic use approach, which was developed in 1988, combines brand equity and financial measures, and has become the most widely recognised and accepted methodology for brand valuation. It has been used in more than 5,000 brand valuations worldwide. The economic use approach is based on fundamental marketing and financial principles:

◪ The marketing principle relates to the commercial function that brands perform within businesses. First, brands help generate customer demand; customers can be individual consumers as well as corporate consumers depending on the nature of the business and the purchase situation. Customer demand translates into revenues through purchase volume, price and frequency. Second, brands secure customer demand for the long term through repurchase and loyalty.

◪ The financial principle relates to the net present value of future expected earnings, a concept widely used in business. The brand's future earnings are identified and then discounted to a net present value using a discount rate that reflects the risk of those earnings being realised.

To capture the complex value creation of a brand, take the following five steps (Figure 3.3):

1 **Market segmentation.** Brands influence customer choice, but the influence varies depending on the market in which the brand operates. Split the brand's markets into non-overlapping and homogeneous groups of consumers according to applicable criteria such as product or service, distribution channels, consumption patterns, purchase sophistication, geography, existing and new customers and so on. The brand is valued in each segment and the sum of the segment valuations constitutes the total value of the brand.

2 **Financial analysis.** Identify and forecast revenues and "earnings from intangibles" generated by the brand for each of the distinct segments determined in step 1. Intangible earnings are defined as brand revenue less operating costs, applicable taxes and a charge for the capital employed. The concept is similar to the notion of economic profit.

3 **Demand analysis.** Assess the role that the brand plays in driving demand for products and services in the markets in which it operates, and determine what proportion of intangible earnings is attributable to the brand measured by an indicator referred to as the "role of branding index". This is done by first identifying the various drivers of demand for the branded business, then determining the degree to which each driver is directly influenced by the brand. The role of branding index represents the percentage of intangible earnings that are generated by the brand. Brand earnings are calculated by multiplying the role of branding index by intangible earnings.

4 **Competitive benchmarking.** Determine the competitive strengths and weaknesses of the brand to derive the specific brand discount rate that reflects the risk profile of its expected future earnings (this is measured by an indicator referred to as the "brand strength score"). This comprises extensive competitive benchmarking and a structured evaluation of the brand's market, stability, leadership, relevance, support, diversification and protectability.

5 **Brand value calculation.** Brand value is the net present value (NPV) of the forecast brand earnings, discounted by the brand discount rate. The NPV calculation comprises both the forecast period and the period beyond, reflecting the ability of brands to continue generating future earnings.

An example of a hypothetical valuation of a brand in one market segment is shown in Table 3.2 on the next page.

Table 3.2 **Sample brand value calculation**

	Year 1
Market (units)	250,000,000
Market growth rate	
Market share (volume)	15%
Volume	37,500,000
Price ($)	10
Price change	
Branded revenues	**375,000,000**
Cost of sales	150,000,000
Gross margin	225,000,000
Marketing costs	67,500,000
Depreciation	2,812,500
Other overheads	18,750,000
Central cost allocation	3,750,000
EBITA (earnings before interest, tax and amortisation)	**132,187,500**
Applicable taxes 35%	46,265,625
NOPAT (net operating profit after tax)	**85,921,875**
Capital employed	**131,250,000**
Working capital	112,500,000
Net PPE	18,750,000
Capital charge 8%	**10,500,000**
Intangible earnings	**75,421,875**
Role of branding index 79%	
Brand earnings	**59,583,281**
Brand strength score 66	
Brand discount rate 7.4%	
Discounted brand earnings	**55,477,916**
NPV of discounted brand earnings (Years 1–5)	329,546,442
Long-term growth rate	2.5%
NPV of terminal brand value (beyond Year 5)	1,454,475,639
Brand value	**1,784,022,082**

Year 2	Year 3	Year 4	Year 5
258,750,000	267,806,250	277,179,469	286,880,750
4%	4%	4%	4%
17%	19%	21%	20%
43,987,500	50,883,188	58,207,688	57,376,150
10	10	11	11
3%	2%	2%	2%
450,871,875	531,983,725	621,341,172	625,326,631
180,348,750	212,793,490	248,536,469	250,130,653
270,523,125	319,190,235	372,804,703	375,195,979
81,156,938	95,757,071	111,841,411	112,558,794
3,381,539	3,989,878	4,660,059	4,689,950
22,543,594	26,599,186	31,067,059	31,266,332
4,508,719	5,319,837	6,213,412	6,253,266
158,932,336	187,524,263	219,022,763	220,427,638
55,626,318	65,633,492	76,657,967	77,149,673
103,306,018	121,890,771	142,364,796	143,277,964
157,805,156	186,194,304	217,469,410	218,864,321
135,261,563	159,595,118	186,402,351	187,597,989
22,543,594	26,599,186	31,067,059	31,266,332
12,624,413	14,895,544	17,397,553	17,509,146
90,681,606	106,995,227	124,967,243	125,768,819
71,638,469	84,526,229	98,724,122	99,357,367
62,106,597	68,230,515	74,200,384	69,531,031

This calculation is useful for brand value modelling in a wide range of situations, such as:

◪ predicting the effect of marketing and investment strategies;
◪ determining and assessing communication budgets;
◪ calculating the return on brand investment;
◪ assessing opportunities in new or underexploited markets;
◪ tracking brand value management.

Applications

The range of applications for brand valuation has widened considerably since its creation by Interbrand in 1988, and it is now used in most strategic marketing and financial decisions. There are two main categories of applications:

◪ Strategic brand management, where brand valuation focuses mainly on internal audiences by providing tools and processes to manage and increase the economic value of brands.
◪ Financial transactions, where brand valuation helps in a variety of brand-related transactions with external parties.

Strategic brand management

Recognition of the economic value of brands has increased the demand for effective management of the brand asset. In the pursuit of increasing shareholder value, companies are keen to establish procedures for the management of brands that are aligned with those for other business assets, as well as for the company as a whole. As traditional purely research-based measurements proved insufficient for understanding and managing the economic value of brands, companies have adopted brand valuation as a brand management tool. Brand valuation helps them establish value-based systems for brand management. Economic value creation becomes the focus of brand management and all brand-related investment decisions. Companies as diverse as American Express, IBM, Samsung Electronics, Accenture, United Way of America, BP, Philips and Duke Energy have used brand valuation to help them refocus their businesses on their brands and to create an economic rationale for branding decisions and investments. Many companies have made brand value creation part of the remuneration criteria for senior marketing executives. These companies find brand valuation helpful for the following:

◪ Making decisions on business investments. By making the brand asset comparable to other intangible and tangible company assets, resource allocation between the different asset types can follow the same economic criteria and rationale, for example capital allocation and return requirements.

◪ Measuring the return on brand investments based on brand value to arrive at a return on investment (ROI) that can be directly compared with other investments. Brand management and marketing service providers can be measured against clearly identified performance targets related to the value of the brand asset.

◪ Making decisions on brand investments. By prioritising them by brand, customer segment, geographic market, product or service, distribution channel and so on, brand investments can be assessed for cost and impact and judged on which will produce the highest returns.

◪ Making decisions on licensing the brand to subsidiary companies. Under a licence the subsidiaries will be accountable for the brand's management and use, and an asset that has to be paid for will be managed more rigorously than one that is free.

◪ Reassessing marketing expenditures as investments in the brand aimed at increasing its asset value. The relationship between investments in and returns from the brand becomes transparent and manageable. Remuneration and career development of marketing staff can be linked to and measured by brand value development.

◪ Allocating marketing expenditures according to the benefit each business unit derives from the brand asset.

◪ Organising and optimising the use of different brands in the business (for example, corporate, product and subsidiary brands) according to their respective economic value contribution.

◪ Assessing co-branding initiatives according to their economic benefits and risks to the value of the company's brand.

◪ Deciding the appropriate branding after a merger according to a clear economic rationale.

◪ Managing brand migration more successfully as a result of a better understanding of the value of different brands, and therefore of what can be lost or gained if brand migration occurs.

◪ Establishing brand value scorecards based on the understanding of the drivers of brand value that provide focused and actionable measures for optimal brand performance.

◪ Managing a portfolio of brands across a variety of markets. Brand performance and brand investments can be assessed on a comparable basis to enhance the overall return from the brand portfolio.

◪ Communicating where appropriate the economic value creation of the brand to the capital markets in order to support share prices and obtain funding.

Financial transactions

The financial uses of brand valuation include the following:

◪ Assessing fair transfer prices for the use of brands in subsidiary companies. Brand royalties can be repatriated as income to corporate headquarters in a tax-effective way. Brands can be licensed to international subsidiaries and, in the United States, to subsidiaries in different states.

◪ Determining brand royalty rates for optimal exploitation of the brand asset through licensing the brand to third parties.

◪ Capitalising brand assets on the balance sheet according to generally accepted accounting principles (GAAP), International Financial Reporting Standards (IFRS) and many country-specific accounting standards. Brand valuation is used for both the initial valuation and the periodical impairment tests for the derived values.

◪ Determining a price for brand assets in mergers and acquisitions as well as clearly identifying the value that brands add to a transaction.

◪ Determining the contribution of brands to joint ventures to establish profit share, investment requirements and shareholding in the venture.

◪ Using brands for securitisation of debt facilities in which the rights for the economic exploitations of brands are used as collateral.

Conclusion

As global competition becomes tougher and many competitive advantages, such as technology, become more short-lived, the brand's contribution to shareholder value will increase. The brand is one of the few assets that can provide long-term competitive advantage.

Despite the commercial importance of brands, the management of them still lags behind that of their tangible counterparts. Even though measurement has become the mantra of modern management, it is astonishing how few agreed systems and processes exist to manage the brand asset. When it comes to managing and measuring factory output the choice of measures is staggering, as are the investments in sophisticated computer systems that measure and analyse every detail of the manufacturing process. The same is true for financial controlling. But, strangely, this cannot be said for the management of the brand asset. Although many brand measures are available, few can link the brand to long-term financial value creation. Nor has investment in brand management reached a level of sophistication comparable with other controlling measures. As the importance of intangibles to companies increases, managers will want to install more value-based brand management systems that can align the management of the brand asset with that of other corporate assets.

There is a similar lack of detail about the contribution of brands in the financial reporting of company results. Investments in and returns from tangible assets are reported at sophisticated and detailed levels, but this is not true for intangible assets. For example, Coca-Cola's balance sheet, income statement and cash flow calculation tell us about working capital, net fixed assets and financial investments, but little about the performance of the most important company asset, the Coca-Cola brand. The same is true for most other brand-owning companies. Current accounting regulations are deficient in their treatment of intangible assets. The increasing value placed on intangibles through mergers and acquisitions over the past two decades has forced accounting standards to acknowledge and deal with intangible assets on the balance sheet. However, the standards deal only with the bare minimum accounting for acquired intangibles, formerly known as goodwill. As a bizarre consequence, the value of acquired brands is included in companies' balance sheets but the value of internally generated brands remains unaccounted for.

Overall, there is an increasing need for brand valuation from both a management and transactional point of view. With the development of the economic use approach, there is at last a standard that can be used for brand valuation. This may well become the most important brand management tool in the future.

Notes and references

1 "The Best Global Brands", *BusinessWeek*, August 6th 2007.
2 Foster, R. and Kaplan, S., *Creative Destruction: Why Companies That Are Built to Last Underperform the Market – And How to Successfully Transform Them*, Doubleday, 2001.

3 The World Economic Forum, Voice of the Leaders survey, Fleishman Hillard, January 22nd 2004.

4 Madden, T.J. (University of South Carolina), Fehle, F. (University of South Carolina) and Fournier, S.M. (Harvard University), "Brands Matter: An Empirical Investigation of the Creation of Shareholder Value through Branding", *Journal of the Academy of Marketing Science*, No. 34, 2006, pp. 224–34.

5 Interbrand, *Brand Valuation*, March 2003, p. 3.

6 CNN, January 28th 2005.

7 *The Independent*, February 6th 2007.

8 K.W. Suh, manager, global marketing, Samsung Electronics, interview, August 6th 2003.

9 Marketing Leadership Council, Corporate Executive Board, Washington, DC, 2004.

10 Akasie, J.F., "Ford's Model E", *Forbes*, July 17th 2000, pp. 30–34.

11 PPR, press release, Paris, August 31st 2007.

12 Examples are Klein, N., *No Logo*, Picador, 1999; Philip Kotler, interview in the *Financial Times*, May 31st 2003.

13 PIMS (Profit Impact of Marketing Strategy), "Evidence on the contribution of branded consumer business to economic growth", *PIMS Europe*, London, September 1998.

4 The social value of brands

Giles Gibbons

The rise of the consumer society is frequently blamed for many ills but rarely praised for its principal social contribution: generating the wealth that pays for and sustains social progress. Long-term improvements in health, education, living standards and opportunities depend on wealth creation. Strong economic growth goes hand-in-hand with strong, recognisable brands. No brand: no way to create mass customer loyalty; no customer loyalty: no guarantee of reliable earnings; no reliable earnings: less investment and employment; less investment and employment: less wealth created; less wealth created: lower government receipts to spend on social goods (see Figure 4.1 on the next page). This is the most basic, and arguably the most valuable, social contribution that brands make. But the ways in which brands create social value are considerably more nuanced and sophisticated than this.

Brands are the promise of something. Historically, brands have promised quality – the quality of the product, service or experience. Now, increasingly, consumers expect more of brands. As the spotlight on the social and environmental behaviour of corporations intensifies, and consumer interest in ethical issues grows, brands need to meet expectations. Whether or not they actively seek to do so, brands act as guardians, making sure companies are doing the right thing. They keep businesses on track, delivering on their promises, because companies know that if they fail to do this, they will not have a business. Brands are a form of social insurance.

This social value is, to a certain extent, inherent in all brands. But some brands have recognised that there is another way of creating social value, if they are prepared to seize the opportunity. As consumers, we trust brands, and listen to what they say. Why? Because brands have made promises to us before, and we have found them to be true. Brands can, if they choose, use this trust to change the way that we see the world and the way that we act. They can use their expertise to create social value through innovation. Moreover, they can use their position of trust to campaign to create social change.

This power inherent in brands is not restricted to commercial

Brands and social progress 4.1

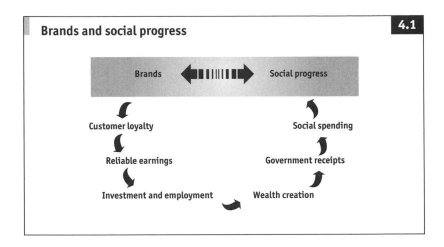

institutions. Non-government organisations (NGOS) are increasingly focusing on building up their brands and boosting levels of trust and credibility. This raises the bar in terms of what consumers expect from NGOS: how they spend donations and how they conduct themselves. But the increased trust and credibility that a brand brings also gives them the platform to be much more effective as organisations that can influence governments, corporations and individuals for the better.

This chapter aims to offer a positive re-evaluation of the role of brands in society. It would be misguided to suggest that brands' social role is consistently and universally positive. Brands have had a bad press in recent years, but the "No Logo" furore has abated somewhat as consumers have come to realise that brands are not necessarily the villains; in fact, they have been the solution. They have responded to the challenge and have become the means of addressing the corporate irresponsibility against which No Logo and its ilk railed. Brands have taken up the challenge and have become the way to guarantee higher business standards.

Brands: a societal insurance policy

Brands act as a powerful mechanism for consumer protection. Regulation is often assumed to be the consumer's best protection against poor-quality goods and services. It is true that regulation plays a crucial role in enforcing and raising standards in this field, as in many others, but even without a regulatory constraint, brands provide an inbuilt market mechanism for consumer protection. The need for brands to create and maintain customer loyalty is a powerful incentive for them to guarantee quality and reliability. For example, Sony endeavours to ensure that its televisions do not malfunction so that those who buy them might subsequently return to the Sony brand for a video-games console that they know will work. When something does go wrong – as in well-known instances such as Johnson & Johnson discovering that bottles of its Tylenol painkiller capsules had been laced with cyanide, or Coca-Cola in the UK finding that its Dasani spring water was contaminated with bromates – consumers are best protected when a brand is involved. The company that owns the brand will want to put things right as a matter of urgency, not just to safeguard consumers, but also to protect its own reputation.

In the digital age, there is nowhere to hide. The rise of the internet has intensified the pressure on brands to get it right. Consumers have an unprecedented level of access to information about a company – not just from the company itself but from bulletin boards, blogs, the media, NGO statements – and their concerns about the social and environmental impacts of the brands they buy have risen in tandem with this flood of information.

In this way, famous brands perform a naturally positive social role. Brands are a mark of standards, of quality and reliability as powerful as any kitemark or stamp of approval. In the industrial age, a brand served as a mark of trust, to assure consumers of what was in the tin. This essential aspect of what brands are about – giving you trust – has not gone away. When we choose a branded product, we know what we are getting. Duracell black and gold means the batteries will work; Coca-Cola red means the drink will quench your thirst and not poison you; Nivea blue means the cream will not give you a rash. These are not trivial advantages, and they are guaranteed by brands.

Brands are an inbuilt mechanism to guarantee that promises are kept in order to maintain reputation and loyalty. They can be seen not just as mechanisms for consumer protection but as wider guardians of society as a whole when it comes to a business's practices. Brands provide a powerful driver for companies to deliver on their brands' promises in the way that is expected of them – knowing that there is a high risk that their businesses will suffer if they do not.

So much for the brands themselves. What of the businesses that lie behind the brands? There are plenty of examples of companies large and small which have behaved in ways that deserve condemnation – for despoiling the environment, damaging local communities, covering up health risks associated with their products, exploiting their workers and misleading their customers in search of a quick buck. A greater focus on corporate responsibility (CR) is designed to reduce such harmful business activity, and brands now serve as a shorthand for the social and environmental credentials of a product – something that matters more than ever to today's consumer. For example, the Fairtrade brand means suppliers were paid a fair price for the raw product; an Innocent logo means the contents of the drink are 100% natural; The Body Shop sign means the products are fairly produced and are not tested on animals.

Consumers choose brands because the brands make a promise about the provenance of the product they are buying: where it was produced, what it is made from, who made it and the conditions they worked in, and how it was brought from its place of manufacture to the place of sale. When we buy a coat from Marks and Spencer, we expect that the buttons will stay on and the seams will not unravel. But we also assume that it was not sewn by small children, and that the people who did make it were paid a living wage. Even if we do not consciously articulate these expectations, the Marks and Spencer brand stands as shorthand for all these assumptions.

The need to behave responsibly is felt most keenly by companies that have brand reputations they want to build and/or protect because they will feel the wrath of the consumer if they do not demonstrate that they are behaving responsibly. These companies are the ones under the most pressure to improve their practices and show consumers, through their brands, that they can be trusted – not only to deliver the product they promise, but also to deliver it in the right way.

McDonald's provides a compelling example of a company that was pressurised to change its practices fairly comprehensively in response to pressure from the media, from governments, from NGOs and campaigners and, crucially, from consumers. Concerns about rising rates of obesity, the company's treatment of its employees and the provenance of its ingredients led to a barrage of negative headlines. Consumers turned against a brand that they felt had let them down and the company was forced to address its working and supply chain practices, and its menu. It was not just McDonald's that was in the firing line with regard to such issues, but it was McDonald's that took much of the flak. And it is McDonald's that has arguably gone furthest in addressing the concerns of its customers and other audiences. The rehabilitation of the brand may not be complete, but it has come a long way from the dark days when commentators were forecasting its demise.

Global brands make the connection on a mass scale between consumer choices "here" and economic and social realities "there". Brands are the transmission mechanism through which we can most clearly understand the consequences – good and bad – of business behaviour, and work to eliminate the bad in favour of the good. The smartest companies are improving their practices throughout the business and communicating this to consumers through their various brands.

Contrary to the traditional anti-globalisation and anti-capitalist dogma, far from causing bad outcomes for society, brands are revealing them. Brands do not lead to social and environmental damage; they are helping to deal with it in their capacity as the public face of private-sector activity.

It is easy to criticise big brands: they are visible and they are vulnerable if they let standards slip. But when we understand how they drive businesses to improve their ethical standards, it becomes clear that they play a powerful role in ensuring that businesses bring us what they promise, in the right way. Conversely, the absence of trusted branding carries no such promise, just uncertainty. It is not well-known brand-name companies we should be worried about, but the little-known or unbranded ones.

But in addition to providing a mechanism for complying with society's expectations, brands can be a springboard for social innovation and change.

Brands as agents of change

As well as helping to create wealth, protect consumers and drive improvements in the standards of business practices, some brands are creating social value through the way they design their products and the way they communicate with consumers. For a business that is willing to take the risk, and recognise the opportunity, brands can be a powerful tool for positive social change.

Brands have to innovate constantly to keep their appeal. Many of the innovations may be subtle and hardly noticeable but some have distinctly positive outcomes for society, such as better quality health products, more convenient ways to purchase services, or more effective communications technology. Procter & Gamble's Pampers brand of nappies bases all its innovation and marketing on a simple proposition: a dry baby is a happy baby. As a result, millions of mothers all over the world have happier babies thanks to Pampers products. Take away the Pampers brand, and you take away any incentive for Procter & Gamble to develop new products that make babies (and mothers) happy. Innovations such as these have positive value, but a more interesting consideration is how brands pursue new ideas that can lead to positive social outcomes by directly tackling social issues.

It is important to remember that the brand, not the company or its innovation department, is the essential component. Without a brand, companies would not risk innovating, since they would not be able to ₊ ₊ociate new products and services with their own efforts and investments, and would therefore not be able to capture the benefits of innovation. However, with the benefit of a strong brand, companies can innovate and take risks because they can rely upon their consumers trying a new product, since they already trust the brand. Gillette can produce and sell ever more advanced (and expensive) varieties of razor blade because consumers trust it to deliver products that meet their needs reliably and efficiently. This trust plays out in the arena of social innovation as well – we trust Philips when it tells us that its Green Flagship TVs will use 15% less energy and 29% less packaging than the alternative, because of its reputation and track record.

This is how brands can innovate socially; but why do they? As before, the desire to protect and enhance their reputation drives companies to act. Consumers today care more about issues such as social justice and climate change, and they want to see companies playing their part in tackling these areas. The rise of these "concerned consumers" has been mirrored in brand activity, and not just in niche brands. There are, of course, plenty of ethical and new brands that are leading the way in social innovation. Innocent has enjoyed huge success as a brand that is all about healthy, 100% natural smoothies that are "good" – both for you and for the planet. It gives 10% of profits to charity and has established strong links with Fairtrade suppliers, while continually innovating for social benefit. It was one of the first manufacturers to "carbon footprint" its product and communicate this to consumers on the bottle, and it uses 100% recycled plastic in its bottles.

Established brands are also going to great lengths to capture the imagination of consumers with products and services that will make a real difference to the issues of the day. Think of Timberland's "nutrition label", which all its products carry, setting out the energy used to make its shoes and boots, the percentage of renewable energy used, and the labour record of the factory where they were made. Or Unilever – a long-established company that innovates through its brands to achieve real social benefits. This is demonstrated by its Lifebuoy soap brand, whose mission has always been to make people safer through raising hygiene standards. In 2002 Lifebuoy set a five-year goal to educate 200m Indians to wash their hands with soap after using the toilet. "Safe Hands" has developed into a sophisticated education programme, which runs alongside product innovation – a low-cost 18-gram bar of Lifebuoy soap was introduced, enough for one person to wash their hands daily for ten weeks. Unilever is clear that Lifebuoy's work in India is not philanthropy: it is brand marketing and innovation with social benefits.

Vodafone is another brand that has used innovation to help tackle social challenges, most notably with its M-Pesa mobile banking service in Kenya. Some 80% of adults in Kenya do not have a bank account, but many have a mobile phone. With M-Pesa, users can transfer money to friends or family via text message, and pay in and withdraw money at a variety of outlets. Some 18 months after its launch in 2007, M-Pesa had in the region of 1.8m subscribers, whose average transactions are $15 or less. The service was seed funded by the UK government's Department for International Development, but the driving force behind it was Vodafone, which in 2008 expanded the programme into Afghanistan and Tanzania.

Lifebuoy and M-Pesa's initiatives are focused on challenges in developing markets and, while they are unquestionably about profit rather than philanthropy, they are more focused on addressing a social need and establishing the brands in new marketplaces than on yielding huge profits. But that is not to suggest that social innovation cannot sit at the heart of a business strategy, as GE's Ecomagination business demonstrates.

Ecomagination represents GE's commitment to developing products and services that tackle environmental issues, from solar energy to fuel cells to energy-efficient lighting. Ecomagination has been highly successful for GE. In 2007, just two years after its launch, a 15% growth in revenue saw Ecomagination's value to the business rise to around $14 billion. This represented 8% of GE's overall revenue of $173 billion. It has significantly outpaced total GE revenue growth, and the company is aiming for $25 billion in sales by 2010. Social innovation can be big business.

All these companies have an understanding of the importance of brand innovation and how it can bring benefits to the business, to consumers and to society. Value, choice, effectiveness, taste, functionality, convenience: in order to prosper, businesses have to innovate to offer consumers these benefits. Increasingly, they also have to show how they are using their powerful positions to develop products and services that directly bring about real social benefits.

This is the ultimate win-win for brands, innovating to delight consumers and to have a positive social impact. It is not easy to see why companies would fail to factor social considerations into their innovation processes. Of course this has to take place within the realistic bounds of cost, function and quality. But, with all else being equal, if brand managers can help tackle a global issue and sell more products at the same time, why wouldn't they? Consumers certainly have the appetite for responsible products and, when price and quality are comparable, they will opt for the product that also does a little more to improve the world around them. This is common sense. Many brands understand this, and some have successfully built it into their innovation processes. However, there are still a vast number of brands which need to take a step forward and recognise that it is absolutely logical for them to be making products that serve a dual purpose; products that the consumer wants, and that society needs. It is not just the right thing to do; it is simply good business sense.

Brands as a social campaigning tool

We have seen how companies respond to reputational pressures to deliver on the promises they make to consumers, and how, increasingly, they are doing so in a way that takes into account their social and environmental impacts.

Using brands for social campaigning, however, represents a step into new territory, beyond their roles as societal insurance policies and agents of change (see Figure 4.2). Companies that take this path recognise the opportunity that they have to exceed consumers' expectations of their brands and to bring about real social benefits in doing so.

The two most important ways in which brands are creating social campaigning opportunities for corporations are by harnessing the cultural power of brands for positive social change, and by applying brand power to the urgent task of spreading the benefits of globalisation more widely.

Elsewhere in this book, readers will gain an understanding of the economic value of brands; how many calculate their worth with forensic actuarial rigour so they can be included on corporations' balance sheets; how these valuations often place the brand way above tangible assets as a source of long-term value. Marketing people treat their brands' customer relationships with the greatest respect, often going to extraordinary lengths to understand consumer needs and desires. More often than not, they seek to imbue brands with a sense of meaning that conveys more than just the functional benefits of whatever is being promoted. Brands lay claim to a social role too. However, it is rare to see these claims backed up by concrete social action. More usually, they are artificial constructs designed solely to identify with consumers' social concerns, rather than to do anything about them.

When communicating to consumers, companies invest far more time, effort and money in building a positive image for their brands than they do

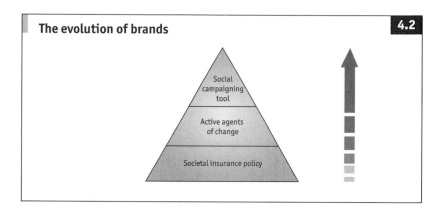

The evolution of brands — 4.2

Social campaigning tool

Active agents of change

Societal insurance policy

in promoting their reputation as a corporation. Indeed, one of the primary aims of anti-globalisation campaigners is to expose what they see as the vast gulf between the wholesome, upbeat images that companies develop for their brands, and the allegedly destructive, irresponsible behaviour of the brands' corporate parents. But consumers listen when brands talk; and this trust gives corporations a readymade tool for social leadership. Consumer trust in brands can become a valuable asset in campaigns for social change, and campaigning for social change can become an additional source of value for the corporations behind the brands.

Many of the social issues that governments and not-for-profit organisations wrestle with on a daily basis are hard to deal with using the conventional tools of passing laws and spending money. For example, to improve literacy in rich societies the greatest need is not for more books, but for more parents to read with their children from an early age. On health, what is needed are more informed and positive lifestyle choices, rather than more effective (and expensive) treatments. For these and more, the social policy requirement is for a change of attitude and a change of behaviour. It is the same in the developing world: governments and aid agencies can pump billions into disease-eradication programmes, but these will work only if attitudes and behaviours also change.

It is brands that are best placed to help change people's attitudes and behaviour. This is why brands' cultural power, as well as their economic power, is potentially such a huge component of their social value. Using their brands to bring about social change is one of the most effective ways in which corporations can demonstrate both corporate responsibility and real leadership. This is emphatically not the same as brands linking up with charities or good causes for mutually beneficial promotional campaigns.

This is about a corporation using its brand's ability to change consumer behaviour as a way of changing social behaviour, thereby strengthening that brand's reputation.

Dove's Campaign For Real Beauty did just that. In 2004 Unilever began using Dove's powerful position as a trusted, widely used brand to tackle the issue of self-esteem among women. The campaign arose from market research that showed that 90% of women were unhappy with the way they looked. Dove used powerful advertising campaigns, digital and print, to challenge narrow perceptions of beauty, and railed against the way the media and advertising worlds portray women. And it went further than marketing. It also launched the Dove Self-Esteem Fund to provide educational materials for young women and tied the campaigns to product ranges such as "Pro-Age" and "Firming", which used real women, with normal body shapes, in their advertising, in place of models. The campaign, and its impact on the brand's reputation, was hugely successful. Sales of Dove products increased by around 600% in the first two months, with an overall sales increase across the entire brand of 20% in the year after the campaign began.

A marketing campaign that packs a strong social punch is a powerful tool. But a brand that can take a new or existing product or innovation and build a campaign around the social or environmental benefits of this product can go further still.

Fiat has done much to reduce its carbon footprint. It has cut the carbon emissions from its manufacturing process and developed the lowest average emission fleet in Europe. Its new initiative eco:Drive, launched in 2008, seeks to go further and change the way that people drive. This is not just about telling people to drive in a more fuel-efficient way. In-car eco:Drive technology gives personal feedback on Fiat drivers' driving style and helps them improve their efficiency and reduce CO_2 emissions. eco:Drive is about Fiat using its position to help change the way people think about how they drive, rather than just what they drive.

As social campaigners, brands can have far-reaching impacts by helping to spread the positive benefits of globalisation. Just as brands have become instrumental in raising awareness of issues such as sweatshops and child labour, so too could they raise awareness and spur action on the reason why globalisation's benefits are not spread more widely. This is the division of the global economy between the formal and informal sectors. This division is rarely one between countries; rather it is one that is present within all countries, the proportions varying depending on whether you happen to be in the developed or developing world.

In the formal economy, most things work: rights to physical and intellectual property can be enforced; assets can be used to borrow money and generate wealth; taxes are collected; and utility and other essential business services are provided. But in the informal economy (which represents most of the global economy), many or all of these preconditions for a successful and prosperous consumer society are absent.

Brands are well placed to help tackle the challenge of reducing this division, since they are often the only entities present on both sides of the divide. Coca-Cola, for example, is as much a part of life in the slums as in the skyscrapers. Brands could use their grass-roots presence to foster local institutions that start to break down the barriers between these divided worlds. They could use their media and cultural power to argue more firmly and more publicly for good governance and commercial infrastructure. Through their trading relationships, they could forge closer links between the two divided sectors of the world economy, enabling more and more people to enjoy the benefits of globalisation. Most of all, brands could take on a campaigning role: raising awareness, mobilising opinion and forcing the pace of change.

These dimensions of corporate social campaigning – harnessing cultural power and campaigning for social change – are often best demonstrated by the brands that have used a social or environmental platform to define and differentiate themselves in the marketplace. For example, the Co-operative Bank raising awareness of ethical investment; Microsoft tackling the digital divide through its Unlimited Potential campaign; and Café Direct demonstrating through Fairtrade that an inclusive global business model is achievable. With consumers increasingly interested in the social and environmental consequences of their purchasing decisions, the most successful brands of the future are likely to be those that embrace social leadership as a core component of their strategy.

Social brands

So far, we have focused on the social value created by brands in the commercial sector. But in the not-for-profit sector too, brands create value for society by enabling charities, NGOs and multilateral institutions to accomplish their goals more effectively. Indeed, some activists have remarked with chagrin that with their professional logos and identities, their wristbands and globally screened entertainment events, their sophisticated communications strategies and partnerships with multinationals, leading NGOs are themselves beginning to resemble the big corporations that they have traditionally seen as their enemies. That this should be a

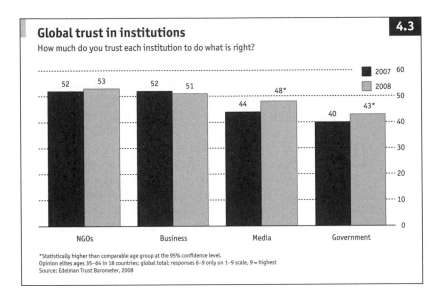

Global trust in institutions

4.3

How much do you trust each institution to do what is right?

NGOs — 52 (2007), 53 (2008)
Business — 52 (2007), 51 (2008)
Media — 44 (2007), 48* (2008)
Government — 40 (2007), 43* (2008)

2007
2008

*Statistically higher than comparable age group at the 95% confidence level.
Opinion elites ages 35–64 in 18 countries; global total; responses 6–9 only on 1–9 scale, 9 = highest
Source: Edelman Trust Barometer, 2008

cause for regret probably says more about the prejudices of such activists than their commitment to social progress, since polling evidence shows that the public's trust in and respect for NGOs – crucial factors in their ability to create positive social change – has risen enormously in recent years as NGOs have embraced the benefits of branding. In the 2008 Edelman Trust Barometer, NGOs maintain their position as trust leaders, in joint first place with businesses (see Figure 4.3). The trust trend away from governments continues; they are at the bottom of the poll for the second year running, with the media just ahead.

The authors' analysis of the ways in which commercial brands have social value suggests that brands act as an insurance policy and, in some cases, as social campaigners. As in the commercial sector, so in the NGO world. The importance of delivering on expectations is as important for Oxfam as it is for McDonald's. When we donate to Oxfam, we expect that our donation will be used properly and responsibly to deliver a socially valuable service. This expectation comes with a risk for the organisation should it fail to deliver on the promises it makes, just as McDonald's faces risks if it fails to deliver on its promises about the burgers it sells. Similarly, brands of all types can take the opportunity to go further, through leadership and campaigning, to create social value. Oxfam goes beyond its day-to-day activity of receiving and distributing donations, extending its reach through branded campaigns such as Make Trade Fair and Make Poverty

History. It takes the opportunities afforded to it as a strong brand to exceed expectations, to educate and spread messages, and to create even greater social value.

Just as trust in commercial brands gives them an important role in upholding business practices and a responsibility to deliver on their promises, so too the public's trust gives NGOs a powerful role as arbiters in complex social and environmental issues where competing claims are being made.

Global brands such as the Red Cross, Médecins Sans Frontières and the UN are increasingly called upon to make sense of international events where trust is in short supply. This may be either because information is scarce and these organisations have first-hand, on-the-ground knowledge and expertise, or because other organisations (such as governments or private-sector companies) have a vested interest in one particular outcome, whereas these social brands are assumed to be motivated by the best interests of society. This independent, arbiter role is essential in a world of instant information and opinion, and is only made possible by the brand. A report or comment by the Red Cross on a particular humanitarian situation is more likely to be believed, and acted upon, than that of, say, a famous academic. The credibility of the Red Cross derives not from the qualifications or expertise of individual Red Cross employees, but from global trust in the Red Cross brand. Of course, this high degree of trust comes with significant responsibilities, and NGOs that fail to deliver on their promises to, say, spend our donations in the proper way will find their brands irreparably damaged.

Another important manifestation of the role of social brands as an arbiter is in their interactions with the private sector. Commercial brands seeking to thread their way through the minefields of CR are increasingly turning to trusted NGO brands to serve as their guide. Shell pioneered this approach, entering into constructive dialogue with formerly implacable NGO critics such as Greenpeace and Amnesty International in order to better understand the social and environmental issues connected with its business and to seek advice on how to deal with them. This trend towards constructive engagement and open dialogue is now recognised as best practice in the private sector. It extends to companies seeking the public endorsement of trusted NGO brands for their activities. Many company social and environmental reports now feature commentary, some of it critical, from social brands. The proliferation of cause-related marketing schemes, whereby charities and NGOs establish fundraising or public education campaigns in partnership with leading commercial brands, is another example. These developments are an implicit recognition by large corporations of the higher levels of trust that reside in the not-for-profit sector when it comes to social and environmental matters.

Clearly, this changing relationship between companies and not-for-profit organisations needs to be nurtured carefully. NGOs need to ensure that their trusted status is not compromised by sacrificing their independence and credibility for a seat at the boardroom table or a sizeable corporate donation.

Equally, businesses need to make sure that in an effort to accommodate their critics, they do not lurch into an unthinking acceptance of often highly partisan, unrepresentative points of view. But overall, there can be no doubt that real social value is being created by the application of social brands' experience and expertise to the social and environmental challenges faced by businesses.

The second way in which social brands deliver social value is through their campaigning platform. Just as commercial brands can use the trust of their consumers to innovate and campaign for social benefits, so too NGOs can use their trust and credibility to raise awareness of important public issues, thus making a vital contribution to tackling those issues. This may involve a direct appeal to citizens, such as the NSPCC's Full Stop campaign, designed to raise public awareness of child abuse. But it also encompasses less direct campaigning activity, where the objective is to change public policy (or the policy of corporations) in order to advance social or environmental objectives. Examples include Oxfam's Make Poverty History campaign, which raised public awareness while lobbying hard behind the scenes to change government policy and corporate behaviour to improve the lives of millions of people in developing countries. Again, it is the platform provided by the brands associated with these causes that ensures the effectiveness of the campaigns. A lone scientist, however well qualified, might struggle to make an impact on public consciousness, regardless of the merits of his or her case. Backed by the Greenpeace brand, however, the impact would be transformed.

This is how traditional social brands build on their trust, credibility and ability to use their position to campaign for social change. The similarities between the ways non-profit and commercial brands operate have arisen as traditional NGOs have started to learn from some of the lessons from the commercial sector. Some have done this successfully; others have a way to go. However, in recent years, there has been a move away from the traditional NGO model into a new territory – that of social enterprise. Profits from a social enterprise are ploughed back into the business to tackle the social issue that the business was set up to address. These new "hybrid" brands set out purposely to achieve social benefit by modelling themselves on commercial brands, and they have often achieved great success in doing so.

British chef Jamie Oliver set up his London restaurant, Fifteen, in 2002 with a view to providing training and employment for disadvantaged and long-term unemployed young people in the catering industry. Trainee chefs serve one-year apprenticeships in the restaurants, learning on the job and in college. All profits go straight back into the Fifteen Foundation, which funds and manages the Fifteen apprenticeships, supports graduates of the system and invests in their business ideas, and looks for new ways to spread the Fifteen concept. The success of the enterprise is demonstrated by the fact that there are now Fifteen restaurants in Australia and the Netherlands, as well as elsewhere in the UK.

The growth of the social enterprise sector demonstrates the power of brands to capture the imagination of consumers and to change the way they think about an issue. Few social enterprises epitomise this belief more clearly than the UK-based movement We Are What We Do (WAWWD). WAWWD was born out of an explicit desire on the part of its founders to use the power of a brand to create social change, using commercial tools to generate significant social action. WAWWD has a clear identity and philosophy – small actions x lots of people = big change – which helps it to achieve its mission of encouraging people to help change the world in small steps. From a series of books suggesting ways to change the world (tips include "read a book to a child" and "turn your thermostat down by 1°C") to high-profile campaigns such as its collaboration with designer Anya Hindmarch on the hugely successful "I'm Not A Plastic Bag" bag, all WAWWD activities use the strength of its brand to campaign, inform and ultimately influence the way people think about their role in society.

A social role for brands in the 21st century

Not all brands are equally socially valuable. We cannot pretend that brands never market their products inappropriately, that they always treat their employees, and their suppliers, fairly and equitably, or that they are all focused on campaigning vigorously for our social well-being while improving environmental standards. Brands are not an unambiguous force for good in the world. But while accepting this fact, it is important not to overlook the many ways in which they can, and do, contribute to our well-being and happiness, through raising levels of trust in business, through valuable innovation and through changing attitudes. Without brands, reputation means nothing and many of the incentives for businesses to perform to high social and environmental standards are lost. With brands, businesses have so much more to lose if they fail to meet our expectations.

As brands become more adept at managing their social and environmental impacts, at innovating and at changing consumer attitudes, there is a bigger challenge that is yet to be addressed. In the years ahead, we are going to have to face up to the reality of a changing climate and a growing population. We are going to need to adapt the way we live and the way we consume. This is not about tinkering around the edges of modern life, but about a fundamental reassessment of how we live.

Some brands, especially new brands, understand this and are enjoying the benefits that come as a result. But many others are yet to take up this challenge, and it remains for them to instigate a change in the way they think about their role in society. Brand managers will rightly continue to ask themselves the question: do consumers want this product? But there are two further questions they should now be asking: is the product creating maximum social benefit? And are we minimising its negative impact? These must be the fundamentals of brand management in the 21st century, and if all three can be achieved without compromise on cost or quality, it makes no sense to operate in any other way. It is the brands that rise to this challenge – that can answer "yes" to all three of these fundamental questions – that will prosper, and it is society that will reap the rewards.

5 What makes brands great

Jez Frampton

Over the course of the past decade, the environments in which brands operate, and the challenges and opportunities they face, have changed dramatically. Brands serve as a route map for purchasing behaviour and, when managed properly, generally accrue significant value to their owners. But how do you evaluate a brand and understand what makes it special?

This chapter examines what makes brands great, but first it is helpful to briefly review valuation and evaluation approaches. For years, most brand owners relied on marketing-oriented measures such as awareness, esteem and equity. Today, as explained in Chapter 3, they use more innovative and financially driven techniques to better quantify the value that brands represent.

These new techniques draw from a mix of traditional business valuation models and economic tools that measure brand performance in terms of monetary quantification, historical benchmarking, competitive assessment and return-on-investment analyses. This has enabled companies to evaluate their brands more rigorously and to establish criteria with which to govern their development in the future.

But what is the right answer for evaluating brand performance? Some would argue that financial models in isolation are unreliable, given fluctuations in corporate profitability. Some would contend that marketing measures alone are unsuited to the realities of today's management needs. Others would argue that no single methodology is credible enough to encompass all the dimensions and complexities of a full evaluation of a brand. These different points of view mean that there has been a proliferation of measurement approaches that attempt to bridge the traditionally separate considerations of finance and marketing needed to provide a more holistic view of brand performance.

For the purposes of this chapter, 23 models that assessed the value and benefits of brands were examined (see list on pages 69–70). Some were more financially driven and others employed traditional marketing techniques. Many offered brand rankings based on their methodologies. From those rankings, the brands that repeatedly appear at the top of the different lists of rankings (see Table 5.1) were identified in order to determine why they come out on top regardless of the criteria used to rank them.

Table 5.1 **Brands most often cited as leading or great**

Coca-Cola	Citi
Microsoft	Hewlett-Packard
IBM	BMW
GE	Marlboro
Nokia	American Express
Toyota	Gillette
Intel	Louis Vuitton
McDonald's	Cisco
Disney	Honda

That they do is perhaps no surprise, as they are widely recognised as being leaders in best practices in brand investment and management. These "usual suspects" among brand leaders appear to perform consistently well against a broad range of factors, including tangible equity, customer purchasing habits and market stature. The reason is that they share certain characteristics and approaches that contribute to their success as a brand and as a business.

What great brands share

Great brands are defined by their relevance and distinctiveness, by that single-minded proposition that places them in the hearts and minds of consumers. What can we extrapolate, then, as the underlying principles that great brands can be seen to share?

A compelling idea

Behind every brand is a compelling idea, which captures customers' attention and loyalty by filling an unmet or unsatisfied need, or by doing it better than the competition. Such is the magnetism of the consumer demand and desire they create, that the choice of that brand over another is often unquestioned and rarely compromised by an alternative.

The promises and verifications of a brand 5.1

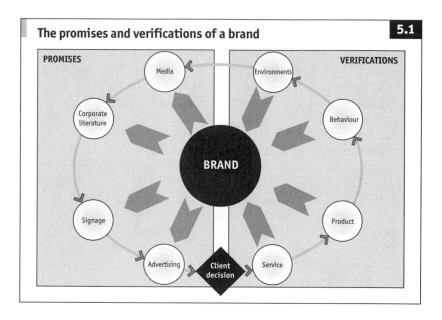

Consistency in delivering on their promise

Leading brands communicate their promise to the market, encouraging customers to purchase the product or service. At the time of customer decision, they must do everything within their power to deliver on the promise. Everything the customer experiences in the process of evaluation, trial, purchase and adoption is a verification of the original promise (see Figure 5.1).

By observing the habits of the 18 leading brands listed in Table 5.1, it is clear that to deliver on their individual promises requires taking a stand and not wavering for short-term benefit. It demands that consistency and clarity within the organisation remain constant, even though the business strategy and tactics will need to be revised regularly to address and take advantage of the circumstances of a changing, and often largely unanticipated, world and business environment.

Expression of the brand through every experience

When we think about the organisations that form an intrinsic part of our daily routine it is not their logos that spring to mind. Our experience of a brand is defined and shaped every time we interact with it, and with every manifestation of what the brand stands for. These are the touch points that make or break the brand experience. Brands are built second by second, experience by experience. Brand leaders capture what is special about their offering, communicate it with an uncompromising consistency to the desired audience and allow customers to experience it.

Effective experience development is about branding the customer experience. For example, Ikea has opened up the furniture showroom to create an experience. Unlike many retailers, the company has developed an emotional connection with its customers. Most large retail environments are confusing, noisy and impersonal, yet Ikea has created a shopping experience that is highly customer-centric and personal. It has managed to customise the experience even though the product is mass-produced. Chairs are pounded with machinery to demonstrate durability and product-knowledge sessions are run in-store. Themed spaces, restaurants and kids' areas further communicate and amplify the Ikea brand proposition. That level of touch is about to be taken one step further, with the opening of the Ikea hostel in Norway, born out of the recognition that for many customers, a trip to Ikea is a "destination day". Customers will be able to stay overnight, making the shopping experience less pressurised and more enjoyable. Ikea is more than a store – it's a way of life, an attitude, a brand.

Starbucks is another emblematic example of the importance of connecting with the customer at every level of the brand experience. As an integral part of CEO Howard Schultz's "back to the future" strategy, he will re-instigate the grinding of coffee in the stores, fuelling their hallmark "third space" with the authentic aroma at the very heart of the brand.

Alignment of internal and external commitment to the brand

Many businesses focus their marketing and brand strategies only on the customer. Leading brands understand that an internal culture supportive of the brand strategy has a far better chance of delivering a consistent, relevant, yet differentiated experience. The internal values are aligned with brand values to shape the organisation's culture and embed the core purpose. The true test of a leading brand is whether employees' commitment to the brand is high, as that will help keep customer commitment high. If those who make and sell the brand are not committed to it, why should anyone else be? In other words, those who live the brand will deliver the brand.

Harley-Davidson has created a cult following because of the consistency between its internal beliefs and practices and what it communicates and delivers externally. Both Harley customers and Harley employees embody the basic attitudes of freedom, individualism, enjoyment, self-expression and self-confidence. This has resulted in an enviable loyalty rate where 45% of current owners have previously owned a Harley. The brand is also popular with non-bike-owners as a significant component of revenue is derived from the licensing of merchandise and clothing.

If branding is about belonging to a club, then Harley-Davidson has established an active and loyal membership largely because of the connection that employees and customers make and maintain. John Russell, vice-president and managing director of Harley-Davidson Europe, says:

> We actively engage with our customers; we encourage our people to spend time with our customers, riding with our customers, being with our customers whenever the opportunity arises.

This marriage of the internal employee experience and the external customer experience strengthens brand loyalty, as Russell confirms:

> If you move from being a commodity product to an emotional product, through to the real attachment and engagement that comes from creating an experience, the degree of differences might appear to be quite small but the results are going to be much greater.

Relevance

Leading brands constantly maintain their relevance to a targeted set of customers, ensuring ownership of clear points of difference compared with the competition. They sustain their credibility by increasing customers' trust of and loyalty to them.

However, for every great brand there are scores of underperforming brands. Even once-successful brands lose their way, and in most cases the causes are obvious but are recognised too late.

The Ford brand is an illustration of this. Once a great brand, it now fails to define itself meaningfully in the marketplace. BMW stands for precision and driving experience. Toyota has become synonymous with quality, reliability and, more recently, for "sustainability". By comparison, the sense of Ford's identity, of what the brand stands for and who it should appeal to, is notably absent.

There is no magic formula for creating a successful brand. However, brands that lose their sparkle should compare their past with their present and look to the future with regard to three things: relevance, differentiation and credibility. Once a brand loses touch with its customer or ignores a potential new audience, it has lost relevance. Successful brands understand the wants and needs of their stakeholders and tailor their offering to maintain its relevance. Differentiation is a critical component of the branding process. And, because brands are based on promises and trust, they must be credible. Customers grant companies the right to provide them with what they need. As Adam Smith wrote many, many years ago in *The Wealth of Nations*: "Money is merely a claim on goods and services." Today we know that customers who experience a breach in trust will take that claim elsewhere.

Recovering lost ground

Jim Collins says in his book *Good to be Great* that to build a great company you "have to have a strong set of core values" that you never compromise:

> *If you are not willing to sacrifice your profits, if you're not willing to endure the pain for those values, then you will not build a great company.*

Brands that lose direction often do so because they depart from their core values. Thus it follows that they can recover by returning to them and by asking and answering such questions as: what is our lasting influence? What void will exist if we were to disappear? A frank appraisal of what made the brand great in the first place, coupled with an innovative reinvention of it, can make it as relevant and great as it used to be.

IBM is an example of a great brand bouncing back. The company dominated the mainframe computer market but was outflanked in the personal computer age by companies such as Compaq and Dell. It has since reinvented itself as an IT services provider of "creative" solutions. It was a high-risk strategy and a challenging journey, during which IBM invented and pioneered large-scale brand management. It centralised brand strategy and focused the marketing spend for overall leverage of the brand. It used the brand as a central management tool to drive behaviour internally and communicate consistently. It provided enough flexibility to be nimble in the fast-moving technologies segments but maintained control and discipline to ensure integrity. Brand equity was measured to gauge performance and ensure a brand-driven culture, which would never again take the customer for granted.

As a result, IBM has become the largest IT services provider in the world, and the brand communicates both innovation and reliability. When it claims that it can provide "deeper" services to clients, IBM comes across as highly credible.

The world's leading brands

Having defined a core set of qualities possessed by great brands, there are also some observations that can be made about the world's leading brands.

Most leading brands are American

Of the 20 leading brands, 14 are American. Does this mean that although a leading brand can originate from anywhere, the United States is better at the practice of branding than other countries? Its dominance of the list of leading brands may be attributed to the nature of American society. The American entrepreneurial culture – which recognises and rewards those successful in business – the size of the economy and the worldwide acceptance of the English language encourage risk-taking and the kind of innovation that produces the big idea from which a leading brand may develop. In effect, the United States has an established and natural incubator for business innovation rooted in the core purpose and values of American society.

Americans are also credited if not with inventing the practice of branding, certainly with embracing it as a management discipline. The rise of consumer-product brands in the United States after the second world war was simultaneously a response to prosperous times and a signal to consumers to spend because times were indeed better. Goods were plentiful and choice, in the form of brands, was apparent on shelves across the country.

Brands and branding practices within the United States became more sophisticated through product and line extensions, corporate identity programmes and advertising wars that were waged throughout the 50 states and the world. American companies recognised that to succeed in business they needed to differentiate themselves in ways that could not be copied by other companies. Management books of the last 30 years reflect this primary tenet. Whether it is a differentiated strategy, product, service, technology or process, it will have been based on "what we have" versus "what they don't have" or the fact that "we just do it better".

If differentiation is the goal, branding is the process. And if a brand is a major source of value, it requires investment and dedicated management. This is precisely what the mostly American firms that own the leading brands do: they nurture their brands in order to increase their value – and they evaluate their performance.

Most leading brands are in highly competitive markets

The products and services of Coca-Cola, Pepsi and Starbucks are easily substituted; BMW, Toyota and Harley-Davidson face plenty of competition; and there are many mobile phone alternatives to Nokia. Brands are about choice, and these brands have to compete in a crowded and noisy space. Brand owners have therefore had to continually search out what makes their brands special to so many people and how they can innovate in order to meet these people's needs. They know that customers have a choice, and that if the benefits of their product or service are not readily apparent and consistently delivered, people will choose something else.

The strategic imperative is clear. Continually search out what makes the brand unique. Renew and refresh the brand to ensure continuing relevance, differentiation and credibility.

Brand-building skills

Brands are important assets. The greatest brands are created with a vision of the valuable assets that they have the potential to be, and once they begin to achieve that potential, great brands become greater by being managed as the valuable assets that they have become. Anyone with responsibility for building and managing a brand needs to act on two guiding principles: proactive management of the brand as an asset and consistent leverage of brand value as a guiding force.

Manage the brand as an asset

As noted in Chapter 3, by 2005 intangible assets accounted for 80% of the market value of major companies (see Figure 3.1 on page 27). And the greatest brands continually outperform such leading market indicators as the MSCI World Index and the S&P 500 Index (Figure 3.2 on page 29). Strong brands provide a security of return. The owners of great brands make sure that the brand lives and breathes throughout the organisation and not just in the marketing department. They embrace and embed the brand as an asset of the whole organisation, recognising it not just as a planning tool or theory but as a central organising principle, so that every activity the business undertakes reinforces the brand.

Brand position, purpose and values are employed as management levers to guide decision-making. This becomes so ingrained in leading organisations that they consciously ask themselves: "How will this decision impact upon the brand?" or "Is this on-brand?" According to Shelly Lazarus, chairman of Ogilvy & Mather:

Once the enterprise understands what the brand is all about, it gives direction to the whole enterprise. You know what products you're supposed to make and not make. You know how you're supposed to answer your telephone. You know how you're going to package things. It gives a set of principles to an entire enterprise.

Use brand value as a guiding force

Great brands are founded on hard numbers as well as imagination. Brand value offers a powerful framework of measurement for an organisation, and in the early stages of defining the brand opportunity, valuation metrics play a crucial role in determining the optimum space for the brand. Such an approach roots the brand in the precision and incision of commercial reality, establishing a robust and rigorous platform on which value-building actions may be defined and implemented. Over the years, valuation has had a critical role to play in monitoring the brand: assessing the value achieved through the strategy and identifying areas and opportunities through which that value may be maintained and increased.

Markets, customer preferences and competitive frameworks are dynamic and brands must respond to remain relevant. For great brands to maintain their position in the market and in customers' hearts and minds there has to be an understanding that brand management is a continuous process.

Specific rankings

Brandchannel.com, Brand of the Year
BrandEconomics, Valuation Model
Interbrand, World's Most Valuable Brands
Semion, Brand Evaluation
Young & Rubicam, Brand Asset Valuator
Wunderman, Brand Experience Scorecard

Brand valuation models, rankings and surveys

The A.C. Nielson Brand Balance Sheet
The A.C. Nielson Brand Performance
Aker, Brand Equity Approach
BBDO, Brand Equitation Evaluation Systems (BEES) ranking

BBDO, Brand Equity Evaluator
BBDO, Five-level Model
Brandchannel.com, Brand of the Year Survey
Consor, Licence-based Brand Valuation
Emnin/Horiont, Brand Barometer
Emnin/Horiont, Brand Positioning Models
icon, Brand Trek Approach
Interbrand, Brand Valuation
Kapferer, Brand Equity Model
Keller, Brand Equity Approach
Kern, Brand valuation based on the concept of enterprise value
McKinsey Consulting, Brand Valuation System
Repenn, Brand valuation based on the concept of enterprise value
Sander, Crimmins and Herp, Price Premium-oriented Brand Valuation
The Sattler Brand Value Approach
The Semion Brand Value Approach
Simon and Sullivan, Capital Market-oriented Brand Valuation
Wunderman, Brand Experience Scorecard
Young & Rubicam, Brand Asset Valuator

Bibliography

BBDO, *Brand Equity Evaluation*, November 2001.
BBDO, *Brand Equity Analysis*, September 2002.
Brandchannel, www.brandchannel.com
BrandEconomics, www.brandeconomics.com
"Famous Brands – Half Off!", *Fortune Magazine*, August 13th 2002.
"The Brand Report Card", *Harvard Business Review*, January–February 2000.
Interbrand, *Brands – The New Wealth Creators*, 1998.
Interbrand, *Brand Valuation*, 1997.
Interbrand, *The Future of Brands*, 2000.
Interbrand, *The World's Greatest Brands*, 1997.
Interbrand, *Uncommon Practice*, 2002.
"AC Puts Number of Global Brands at 43", *Wall Street Journal*, November 1st 2001.
Wunderman, www.wunderman.com

PART 2
BEST PRACTICE IN BRANDING

6 Brand strategy

Iain Ellwood

Building a strong brand

Truly great brands own a superior brand positioning that is consistently executed for their target audience. Merely good brands do one or the other well, they either have a superior brand positioning with less than stellar execution or they have a good brand positioning outstandingly executed. Great ones are not a compromise – they have both the best brand positioning and the best execution in the marketplace. In great brands, the organisation is galvanised around the power of the central brand positioning. Rather than just using the brand as a marketing communications brief, senior management use it as a guide that drives virtually every decision the company makes.

Brands like Nike, Amazon, Intel and BMW exude their brand positioning through everything they do. They are able to translate their brand positioning into meaningful actions at each point where the organisation comes into direct contact with a client or customer. It is the integration of positioning with customer-facing operations that generates tangible results – superior business performance and brand value creation. But they also go further by taking care to align the points where the organisation interacts with its employees and business partners with the brand positioning. Thus brand execution is greatly improved by the employee experience being aligned with the customer experience in a seamless way.

The result is an organisation that is fully engaged emotionally, intellectually and behaviourally around a single clear, relevant and distinctive brand positioning. This gives it a powerful wealth-creating business asset – a competitive advantage that is difficult for others to replicate.

Clarity starts with a powerful brand positioning

Behind any great brand is usually a crystal clear positioning – Starbucks' "third place", Apple's "tools for creative minds" or Ritz-Carlton's "ladies and gentlemen serving ladies and gentlemen". If the brand positioning is not inherently clear, succinct and easily communicated, potential customers will find it hard if not impossible to understand it and will be unlikely to buy it. But creating clear positioning is a challenging process. In most organisations many people influence the process and what starts out as a simple positioning often becomes overburdened, overcomplicated and compromised. This is because it is easier to accumulate ideas on positioning than to simplify them. Simplification requires decisions be made about what not to do – arguably the most important aspect of strategy and business.

What is a powerful brand positioning?

A powerful brand positioning is credible, relevant and differentiated; it stretches the organisation, enabling it to grow and increase its competitiveness. But for the idea to have a tangible impact it also must be perfectly executed in a way that is clear and consistent. Brand positioning is owning a territory in people's minds and the marketplace.

A powerful positioning articulates why a customer should choose a specific brand over another.

The brand positioning process

The positioning process requires a blend of analytical, creative and strategic skills. Analytical tools and techniques are required to establish a fact-based foundation to guide and underpin decisions about the overall thematic territory for the positioning. But within that territory there could be a number of potential positionings. Creative strategic thinking is required to go beyond the facts to identify the optimal positioning and the crafting of the positioning statement. Without a combination of both, the positioning will either simply reflect the functional needs or be a random idea not based on the business and customer preferences. The process illustrated in Figure 6.1 ensures a powerful positioning.

Step 1 Define the market and customer target

To identify the functional and emotional benefits that a brand should offer, it is essential to define the target market and customer audience. This requires tough decisions about which types of market and customers are most important for the business and the brand. Once a target group of customers has been selected, a thorough understanding needs to be gained of what drives their purchases by looking closely at their attitudes, motivations and behaviours. As well as doing a traditional analysis of their demographics and which products or services they buy, it is important to understand the broader context of their lives. Great brands are built on insights about a target audience that are gained from having a deep

The brand positioning process

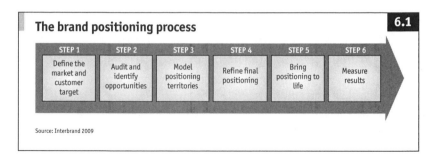

6.1

STEP 1	STEP 2	STEP 3	STEP 4	STEP 5	STEP 6
Define the market and customer target	Audit and identify opportunities	Model positioning territories	Refine final positioning	Bring positioning to life	Measure results

Source: Interbrand 2009

understanding of it. Apple's "think different" (the advertising articulation of its brand idea) demonstrates an insight that its target customers believe in and desire a better way for humans to interact with technology. Similarly, Orange, a mobile phone business, built its brand around the idea of optimism because it understood that its customers wanted to create a better world through stronger communications between their families and friends.

Techniques include:

- ◩ Demographic outline – to understand what type of people are buying your brand including their age, education, gender, and income.
- ◩ Usage and behavioural research – to understand how frequently and in what type of stores, size of pack and format customers prefer to purchase a brand.
- ◩ Psychographic and attitudinal profiling – to understand why they are more likely to choose a brand based on their attitudes to things like the environment, quality and value; on their hedonism, status and individuality; and on how group oriented they are.

Step 2 Audit the current situation to identify potential opportunities

To gain insights about the market and the opportunities that it presents, it is crucial again to begin by gathering a fact-based foundation of knowledge about the business opportunity and customer needs and purchase decision drivers. Without these facts, the brand may be built on myths or simply replicate competitors' product functions without having anything that differentiates it for the customer. Armed with the facts and more qualitative insights, it is possible to identify specific brand positioning territories.

Techniques include:

▣ Management interviews to identify internal business views. These are confidential 40-minute discussions to draw on the personal experience of internal management on the nature of the problem and potential solutions.
▣ Broader stakeholder interviews to gain a 360 degree view of opportunities. These are similar to the management interviews but draw on the experience of people outside the company.
▣ Qualitative customer insight research on preferences about the brand. This is non-statistical research that provides insights and ideas rather than proven facts. It can be done with a small number, that is, less than 100 potential customers.
▣ Quantitative research on needs, perceptions of the current brand and purchase decisions factors. This is statistically robust research and therefore a reliable fact-based foundation for business decision-making. It requires a large number of target customers to be accurate.
▣ Benchmark in category and out of category best in class examples. It is often valuable to learn lessons from other brands that have undertaken similar issues. Case studies of brands in the same category or a different category can therefore provide benchmarks of the best way an issue has been tackled in the past.

Step 3 Model potential brand positioning territories

Defining appropriate territories requires exploring each of the four elements of the opportunity model (see Figure 6.2). This ensures that the brand position is compelling and credible yet differentiating and stretching for the organisation.

Techniques include:

▣ Opportunity modelling. This structures the research information and insights from many of the above research techniques to help identify the most likely solution scenarios for the brand positioning.
▣ Competitive mapping techniques. Competitors' positioning statements are plotted against customer purchase criteria to identify whether they are all targeting the same or different customer needs.

The opportunity model

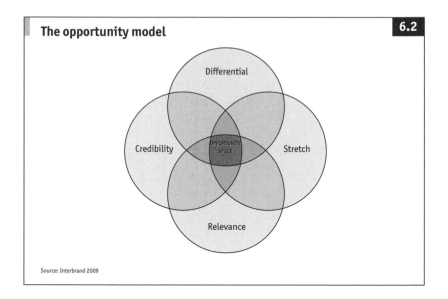

Credibility · Differential · Stretch · Relevance · OPPORTUNITY SPACE

Source: Interbrand 2009

Relevance

A great brand must be relevant at both a functional and an emotional level. Functional relevance is easy to understand; Starbucks coffee, for example, has to taste good. Emotional relevance is harder to define and attain. But it is crucial in building a strongly appealing positioning with a target audience and for engaging and energising employees who shape the brand. It is often suggested that people make decisions largely based on emotions and then justify them afterwards with logical reasons. Emotions clearly do play a major role in decisions and a great brand evokes precisely the types of emotions that its target audience desire and that drive their purchase decision. One common technique is to attach aspiration or hope to the brand. Charles Revlon was famously quoted as saying: "We don't sell jars of make-up, we sell jars of hope." People are generally optimistic about themselves – in surveys the vast majority consider themselves to be above average. Brands that affirm this optimism are far more successful than those that fail to do so and are far more likely to create a strong emotional bond with their customers. They must, however, beware of taking it to an extreme by overpromising and underdelivering.

Credibility

Any positioning needs to align with the underlying internal capabilities, culture and personality of an organisation otherwise it will not be credible. A positioning that overclaims inevitably leads to customer disappointment. Employees have to deal with the customer backlash as the experience and offer fail to live up to the promise, and this reduces morale within the organisation. This risk is especially acute for brands in transition. It is all too easy to misalign customer expectations with the experience because communications, brand names and the visual identity can be changed far more quickly than the customer experience, the offer and the organisation. So while a brand positioning should be aspirational to evoke a stronger emotional connection with customers, it must be genuine, or at least come close to the brand promise.

Differentiation
The brand positioning needs to clearly distinguish itself from other competition in the marketplace. That sharpness is needed to help polarise customers so they either clearly love the brand (the target audience) or are not attracted to it. One of the worst things a brand can be is so bland that no one has any passion for it. In mobile phones, for example, too many firms describe themselves as "connecting people", leading to identical looking brands and marketing communications that reduce customer loyalty. This often results in management behaviours and attitudes that offer no clue to employees as to what they need to do to stand out and succeed in the marketplace.

Strong brands such as Apple are brave enough to stand for something unique and in doing so end up creating entirely new categories of products or force the evolution of an existing one. For example, Apple took a basic memory technology storage device such as a hard drive and solid state memory and turned it into a portable and desirable way to store an entire music collection – something that no one before had thought would be compelling to customers.

Distinguishing a brand can be done in many different ways: by offering distinctive product and service features; by offering new combinations of existing products and services; by using a different tone or attitude; by making changes in production and/or delivery that allow reductions in price or expanded features and benefits. And of course a brand can become distinctive by doing some combination of these. However, competitors will inevitably copy anything that works well. McDonald's adoption of premium coffee, healthier food and upgraded stores has taken business away from Starbucks in the United States. To stay one step ahead, what distinguishes a brand must be constantly reviewed in the light of competitors' activities as well as emerging trends.

Stretch

Business growth comes from driving and energising the organisation around the positioning, which therefore needs to stretch the organisation to increase performance and ensure that the brand will continue to be relevant in the future. This means understanding what future customer needs will be and how the organisation can develop its products and services to retain and sell more to current customers and attract future customers. The strategy adopted should not stretch the organisation too much as this may result in overpromising and underdelivering and thus a loss of credibility. However, not stretching the organisation enough means that it will not be re-energised and is likely to lose ground to competitors in the future.

Step 4 Refine final positioning

Territories can be researched with the target audience to identify the most compelling territory. Then the final positioning statement needs to be crafted to become a galvanising message which can be simply expressed for all audiences and which encapsulates and strengthens the brand. This statement should be a maximum of two or three words, supported by a longer phrase that explains each element. If the positioning statement is longer than a few words it is unlikely to be adopted by the organisation because it is not easy to memorise. For example, the positioning of Inter-Continental Hotels focuses on the company being the insider knowledge expert in each city. The statement is therefore:

In the Know

This is further explained by the fuller statement:

For people who want to be in the know,
InterContinental is the brand that goes out of its way
to deliver authentic and enriching experiences
that make your world feel bigger.

Initially, there may be several versions of the statement; for example, insider knowledge, in the know or city guide. Each should emphasise a different aspect of the positioning. Refining the final positioning can take weeks or even months to ensure it truly crystallises the benefit. It also needs to be checked against cultural and international filters to make sure that it means the same thing throughout the world.

Techniques include:

⬛ Word crafting. This is used to explore variants and synonyms of words to ensure that the words chosen have the precise, desired meaning; for example, choosing between clever, smart and knowledgeable.
⬛ Cultural and regional nuance sense checks. Often words have slightly different meanings in different countries and these can sometimes have negative associations. "Direct" can mean a person is straightforward but in some cultures it can also mean "rude".
⬛ Identifying memorable phrases. For example, "first class service", "one step ahead".
⬛ Using power words, those that are loaded with rich meaning. "Gold Standard", for example, has an evocative meaning and associations beyond the pure words.

Step 5 Bring positioning to life

Consistently executing the positioning across internal and external touch points is another critical aspect of successful brands. One of the fundamental reasons that people buy a brand is that they know what to expect, and so the brand reduces the risk associated with a purchase. You will be loyal to – and may be willing to pay more for – a brand that has served you consistently well in the past. Singapore Airlines is consistently ranked as a five-star airline built on components such as "consistency of staff service". One of the reasons attributed to the weak performance of McDonald's a few years ago was that it had stopped rigorously enforcing quality standards on franchisees in order to grow more quickly. Indeed, once the old tough programme was put back into place, the business quickly perked up. Codifying the brand positioning into processes and operating procedures, policies, systems, staffing and training is essential to ensuring brand consistency. Initially, the simplest way to put the positioning into operation is to use the quadrant model to identify key changes to the brand experience. The InterContinental hotel brand positioning "In the Know" has been successfully translated across all the four quadrants in Figure 6.3.

Techniques include:

⬛ Quadrant model (see Figure 6.3). Translating the positioning into meaningful people behaviours, communications, environmental designs and products and services is a good way to check that the

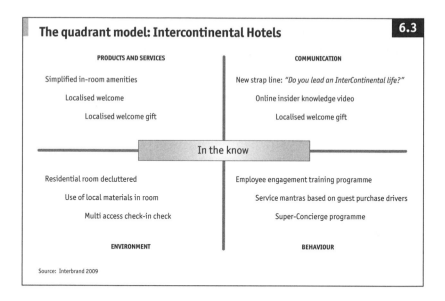

The quadrant model: Intercontinental Hotels   6.3

PRODUCTS AND SERVICES	COMMUNICATION
Simplified in-room amenities	New strap line: *"Do you lead an InterContinental life?"*
Localised welcome	Online insider knowledge video
Localised welcome gift	Localised welcome gift

In the know

Residential room decluttered	Employee engagement training programme
Use of local materials in room	Service mantras based on guest purchase drivers
Multi access check-in check	Super-Concierge programme
ENVIRONMENT	BEHAVIOUR

Source: Interbrand 2009

positioning statement will drive real change in the business.

◪ Employee engagement programme. In service businesses it is particularly important to ensure that staff adapt their behaviour to reflect the brand consistently. For example, the Avis brand is all about "We try harder"; it would denigrate the brand if the customer experience was that Avis staff were unhelpful or lazy.

◪ Brand experience design. Often customers will experience the brand through touch points such as packaging or retail stores. It is crucial that the experience is designed rather than just badged with the logo. This means designing the ambience, music, lighting and service behaviour as well as the visual elements.

◪ Customer service design. Customers have to go on a journey when they interact with a brand. For a hotel that includes the arrivals process, finding the bedroom, eating in the restaurant. This journey needs to have the right kind of service design to match the brand positioning which could be friendly and easy-going, formal and conservative or funky and playful depending on the brand.

Step 6 Measuring results

Measuring the performance of the brand positioning can be done through three metrics: employees, customers and business performance (see Figure 6.4 overleaf). There is a hard linkage between these three, and depending

Brand positioning metrics 6.4

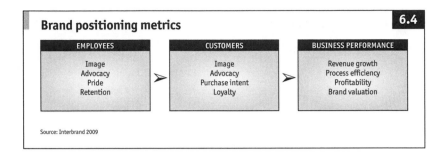

EMPLOYEES		CUSTOMERS		BUSINESS PERFORMANCE
Image Advocacy Pride Retention	>	Image Advocacy Purchase intent Loyalty	>	Revenue growth Process efficiency Profitability Brand valuation

Source: Interbrand 2009

on the type of business they should be measured and reported monthly, quarterly and annually.

Employees

High levels of employee understanding and motivation around the brand feed through to high levels of service and product quality. These in turn will increase customer satisfaction and drive purchase intent and loyalty which lead to higher revenue growth, profits and brand value. Measuring the performance of brands can be done by measuring employee attitudes and behaviours.

Employee metrics:

- Image. Are employees projecting the brand image – playful, formal, professional, for example?
- Advocacy. Are employees advocates for the brand to their family and friends?
- Pride. How much pride do employees have in their employer? This links strongly to their overall commitment to their job and therefore customer satisfaction levels.
- Retention. What level of employee turnover does the brand have? Is it above or below the sector average?

Customers

Measuring customer attitudes and behaviours provides invaluable information about the performance of brands and improves understanding of how to create value through consumer purchase process/choice. Data can be measured for customers, non-customers and/or competitors' customers depending on the customer strategy.

Customer metrics:

◪ Image. What image perceptions do customers have of the brand? And how close are these perceptions to the desired brand positioning?

◪ Advocacy. How strongly do customers recommend the brand to others?

◪ Purchase intent. How likely are customers to try the brand, or buy more of the brand, more frequently?

◪ Loyalty. How loyal are customers to the brand? If it is not available in their usual store, how far will they go to get it? Have they bought the brand for a long period of time?

Business performance

The performance of brands needs to be measured in relation to the business strategy. This helps improve understanding of how the brand drives the business most effectively and efficiently.

Business metrics:

◪ Revenue growth. This is typically tracked as part of the monthly business management accounts.

◪ Process efficiency. This can be measured by the reduction or addition of resources required to deliver a product or service. Typically, this will include people, cost and time measurement.

◪ Profitability. This is typically tracked as part of the monthly business management accounts.

◪ Brand valuation. This can be measured using proprietary methods that identify the brand-related earnings (or reasons for purchase). This is then linked to the competitive strength of the brand in its market and the likelihood of sustaining those earnings over the coming five years. Research has shown that many businesses in the FTSE and Dow Jones indices have substantial brand-related earnings (on average approximately 30% of total earnings).

Repositioning InterContinental Hotels

InterContinental Hotels is a traditional brand that has reinvigorated itself by developing a new brand positioning then executing it perfectly by embedding it in the customer experience and offer. The following is a brief summary of the repositioning of InterContinental Hotels to bring the brand positioning process to life.

PRIMARY BUSINESS OBJECTIVE
Increase ADR (average daily room rate).

TARGET AUDIENCE
A mixture of quantitative and qualitative insights:

- Upmarket travellers
- Usage more than five business trips and two leisure trips annually
- Income above $100,000
- Attitudinal belief that travel improves the world

CORE INSIGHT
Knowledge is the social currency of these travellers and therefore highly valuable to them.

BRAND POSITIONING
"In the Know"
For these luxury travellers it is no longer the softness of the beds or the power shower that differentiates and adds value to their stay experience. They want the additional value of authentic, insider knowledge about the places they visit. They are prepared to pay a premium for gaining this social currency and the priceless stories they can share with their family and friends.

Relevant
The target audience value local knowledge because it makes them feel enriched. They like to share this insider knowledge with their family and friends.

Credible
This is a brand that draws on its long heritage. InterContinental grew alongside Pan-American Airways. It created the world of luxury international travel as the airline developed new routes to new, exotic locations. InterContinental unlocked the world for these adventurous travellers.

Differentiation
These guests want to associate with a brand that stands for a way of life not just a hotel. The focus of the brand positioning and implementation is the knowledge, interaction and service style of the employees. It goes beyond the functional attributes; the towels, showers and menus of the competition.

Stretch
While fitting with its heritage, it was crucial to modernise the hotel experience. The challenge was to educate and motivate large numbers of migrant or part-time staff to deliver on this promise consistently around the world. It was a fundamental shift to move from hiding the staff to making them the heroes and encouraging them to interact with guests.

BRING THE BRAND TO LIFE
Employee behaviour
InterContinental's implementation of the idea affected employees, the environment, the offer and communications. For employees, this new positioning was translated into an insider knowledge programme. The phrase "To you it's just a walk to work; to our guest it's a great view of local culture" was used to educate and empower all staff to share their local knowledge with guests.

Environments
InterContinental used a core insight into its guests' lives to redesign its rooms: it recognised that they were experienced and sophisticated travellers. This was translated into a more residential look and feel to its rooms to demonstrate that the brand acknowledged their experience and would not patronise them. It stripped out much of the usual hotel ephemera, such as cards explaining how to use the safe or bathrobe, because it knew that its guests already knew how to use hotels. It provided local touches to its rooms to emphasise the flavour of each location. This created stronger relationships with guests because they felt treated as individuals rather than objects to be processed by the system.

Products and services
InterContinental built a new online local knowledge guide. Guests can download a video tour of the city by the local concierge, either before the trip or once they have checked into their room.

Communications
The new brand positioning was communicated through a new strap line and advertising campaign: "Do you lead an InterContinental life?" The line, tone of voice and imagery clearly differentiate InterContinental hotels from other hotels that typically focus only on the room or property. One advertising line was "Always have plenty to declare", with an image of local Balinese crafts. It encourages and celebrates the opportunity to enrich your life with local experiences rather than just the sandy beaches of the competition. InterContinental specifically avoids using shots of its rooms or buildings as travellers expect these to be world class.

It cleverly advertises the additional value that InterContinental offers above the competition.

RESULTS

As part of its development programme, InterContinental used a brand return on investment (ROI) model to test the impact and costs of radically changing its brand positioning and experience. This helped it build a detailed business case to convince owners as well as focus brand investments where they could achieve the highest returns. In 2007, following the rebrand, IHG.com reported an increase in positive brand perception of 10% and an increase in revenue per room of 12%. The rebranding put the brand positioning "In the Know" at the heart of the company's operations and then translated this across the entire business.

The brand name as a signal of a powerful positioning

One crucial dimension of brand clarity is picking the right brand name either to launch a new brand or to signal a revamping of an existing one. Broadly, a name can say only one or two things about your brand: what it does functionally (for example, British Airways) or what it is like through its personality and values (for example, Google). In recent years descriptive names have become increasingly difficult to use since virtually all common English and Latin-root words are already trademarked in one or more countries and their internet URLs are already registered. It is becoming harder and harder to use a "real" word, even in a new context.

Moreover, descriptive names often become too constraining as the business and brand evolve. For instance, Carphone Warehouse is no longer just about car phones and the stores no longer look anything like warehouses. This does not matter in the UK, where the company has built a strong and broad set of service associations around the brand name, but it will require some explanation when expanding internationally. Equally, AOL originally meant America OnLine, which became far too limiting as the internet went global. Although the company has established the initials AOL as the "new" brand name over time, names abbreviated to sets of initials risk losing personality and distinctiveness. But companies like AOL have little choice short of developing a completely new name and must make this change because they have extended beyond their core business. Keeping to their full name limits the credibility of their offering.

Although abstract names are becoming more and more common

because of the limits of registering and expanding the meaning of descriptive ones, they bring with them considerable challenges. Abstract names require substantial investment in communicating what they are about. They are an empty vessel that needs to be filled with meaning before anyone will consider purchasing the brand. Not surprisingly, many companies settle somewhere in the middle of this spectrum with a name that suggests the right associations but goes beyond a straightforward description, such as the Ford Mondeo, one of the company's European cars, with its associations of "world" through the word "Mondeo". Significantly, some of the strongest names are those that dramatically break out of existing category conventions. Contrast the launch of the Nintendo Wii – connoting togetherness, fun (think 'weeeeee!'), positivity (from the French *oui*) as well as wireless internet – with the comparatively prosaic names of its gaming competitors Xbox and Sony PlayStation.

Abstract (and sometimes even associative) names can be the subject of criticism, even ridicule, when they are announced, and this can make an organisation fearful of taking this route. But unusual names are often more memorable than more predictable ones, and even those that are lampooned at first can become accepted and even admired in time. Orange and Accenture are names that had their fair share of criticism when first launched but nevertheless have become familiar and provide great brand clarity. Some brand names have failed to become established. PricewaterhouseCoopers, for example, tried to rename its consulting offer "Monday" but reverted after a week because of international scepticism.

Brand portfolio management

Many companies today – both large and small – have more than one brand. And some companies have a portfolio of hundreds; for example, Procter & Gamble has over 300 brands and Unilever has over 400 brands, though it has been trying to reduce the number. When multiple brands exist two major issues arise, one external and the other internal. The external issue is to establish the optimal economic balance between maintenance of the current brand portfolio and its evolution for future growth. The internal issue is how to allocate investments across the portfolio of brands to maximise economic return. This then requires managing those brands to retain their individuality.

Brand portfolio strategy is the process of managing the linkages between the masterbrand and product brands (see Figure 6.5 overleaf) to achieve higher economic returns and thereby increase the long-term brand equity. There are five guiding principles to successful portfolio strategy:

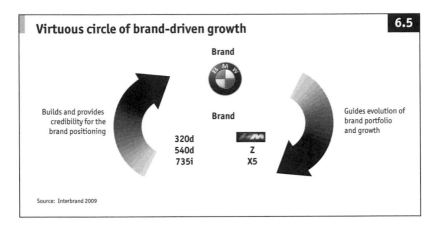

Virtuous circle of brand-driven growth — 6.5

Brand

Builds and provides credibility for the brand positioning

Brand

320d
540d
735i

Z
X5

Guides evolution of brand portfolio and growth

Source: Interbrand 2009

- ◪ Accelerate investment of resources in the essential parts of the portfolio.
- ◪ Build stronger connections with the master brand.
- ◪ Identify growth opportunities.
- ◪ Realign brand and product names with customer needs.
- ◪ Create a strong visual system.

Brand portfolios typically fit into a brand portfolio spectrum (see Figure 6.6). At one end is the branded house where most brands have the same distinctive brand name and are distinguished, if at all, by basic functional descriptors. General Electric (GE) is one organisation that follows this convention with GE Capital, GE Lighting, GE Healthcare, GE Aviation, GE Security and GE appliances covering most of its lines of business. This is also referred to as a master brand strategy. At the other end is a house of brands, such as Procter & Gamble (P&G), where the product or service brands have little explicit relationship to the overall P&G brand or to one another. Tide, Cheer, Era and Dreft sit together on the retail shelves in the United States trying to be the consumer's choice to clean their clothes. In Europe, P&G does the same but with a different stable of brands: Ariel, Bold, Daz and Fairy.

Many companies adopt a hybrid position. They have a strong master brand that stretches across most of their business but also use other brands for different audiences or products. Nestlé, for example, uses its full corporate brand where it can optimise value with audiences while using strong sub-brands such as Twix or Yorkie that are subtly endorsed by the Nestlé mark of quality. It has a third group of brands such as Nescafé and Nesquik that

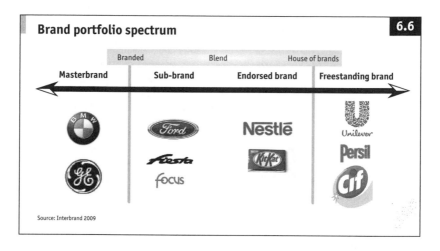

Brand portfolio spectrum　　6.6

Source: Interbrand 2009

strongly reflect the master brand name. By using a combination of master brand, endorsed brands and sub-brands, companies maximise the value of their brand asset across all their audiences and markets.

Economic factors often drive companies towards either end of the brand portfolio spectrum. In addition to cost savings or greater scale, factors that commonly encourage companies to embrace a master brand approach include:

- Common needs or desires among different customer segments.
- A business strategy that prioritises some degree of either cross-selling or operational integration.

There are also factors that push companies such as P&G to have a house of brands or Nestlé to maintain some brands as independent of the master brand. These include:

- Customer segments with different needs.
- Brand ideas that are in opposition or contradictory in a way that cannot be resolved.
- Large amounts of existing equity in brands that would be expensive and/or risky to migrate.
- Decentralised organisation or management philosophy.
- Desire to possibly sell brands in the future – merger and acquisition flexibility.

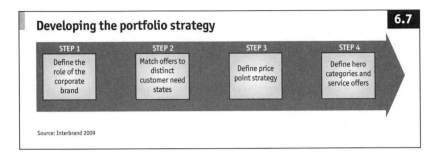

Developing the portfolio strategy

6.7

STEP 1	STEP 2	STEP 3	STEP 4
Define the role of the corporate brand	Match offers to distinct customer need states	Define price point strategy	Define hero categories and service offers

Source: Interbrand 2009

Portfolio strategy process

There are four steps to developing the portfolio strategy (see Figure 6.7).

Step 1 Define the role of the corporate brand

The corporate brand needs to play different roles with different stakeholders. There are generally two roles:

- Investor, employee and community. The corporate brand must reinforce the message of assured business performance, strong corporate ethics and working practices for these audiences. These include managed business performance, corporate social responsibility (CSR), employee working conditions and environmental concerns.
- Customer. The corporate brand must reinforce a clear customer centricity and dedication to customer responsiveness. This might include new product development, research and development, and improvements in product or service offer.

Step 2 Match offers to distinct customer needs

Building a systematic portfolio strategy requires matching customer needs to the offers. Clustering types of customers by their needs helps establish the primary and secondary benefits that customers find valuable and encourages the business to become more customer-centric in the process. Tesco has clustered its orange juice offering into indulgence, value, regular and health sub-brands. Each of these targets different needs and several of them may be bought by a customer at the same time. A parent might buy a large multi-value pack for daily use, a healthy pack with added vitamins for the children and an indulgence pack for the weekend breakfast in bed. Sub-branding the portfolio helps customers to navigate the offer and focus on specific customer benefits.

Step 3 Define price point strategy

It is critical to establish which price points are most effective against the competition. "Tesco Finest" is Tesco's premium product range and is designed to compete against "A" brands like Heinz. Its regular range "Tesco" offers a balance between value and quality, and its budget range "Tesco Value" offers competitively low-priced benefits. Tesco is very clear about where it can compete at the top and bottom price points. So there is no need for a Tesco Finest toilet tissue, but Tesco Value brands play strongly where the company sees no need to compete at the top. Conversely, a Tesco Finest Parma ham is consistent with establishing it as an authority on food, whereas a Tesco Value pack of Parma ham would undermine it. Wal-Mart's price point strategy follows similar lines, with "Sam's Choice" for its premium offer and "Great Value" for its value range. It also has a number of targeted brands such as "Athletic Works" for gym clothing, "Metro-7" for women's clothing and "Equate" for consumable pharmacy items.

Step 4 Define hero categories and service offers

The final part of the strategy is to define hero categories and service offers – ones that accelerate recognition of the brand positioning and cast a valuable halo across the rest of the range. Tesco has cleverly used its banking and insurance comparison sites to demonstrate its brand idea that "Every little helps". This portfolio strategy has been extremely successful in competing against premium and value players in the market, and by 2005, according to tesco.com, Tesco's sales accounted for an incredible one-eighth of the total UK grocery spend.

A brand portfolio must evolve. Competitors change, trends emerge, fads fade, customers change their preferences over time, and so changes must be made to the portfolio if it is to enjoy continuing success. New brands must be added, existing brands repositioned and ineffective brands dropped. Investment decisions have to be made: which brands should be funded and by how much both to deliver short-term results and to drive longer-term value. In other words, brand portfolios have to be managed as a portfolio of both independent entities and interrelated ones. Even at P&G, which has many brands within the laundry category with no apparent external relationship to the customer since they share the same shelf in the store, considerable time and effort have been invested to carve out distinct positionings for each in order to maximise the overall economic value of the portfolio, by targeting different purchase drivers for each brand and reducing cannibalisation of sales across the portfolio.

AT&T

AT&T is an iconic American brand. It once provided voice and data services to the vast majority of Americans and developed or pioneered such ground-breaking technologies as the transistor. However, by the late 1990s this once proud and powerful brand was weak, brought down by deregulation and divestitures, new competitors, acquisitions such as in cable that failed to produce expected benefits, new technologies such as the internet and massive internal change as the organisation downsized.

Primary business objective
AT&T's acquisition by SBC Communications created a need to define an optimal brand and business portfolio.

Target audience
Large corporations, small and medium-sized enterprises, personal mobile phone users.

Core insight
The AT&T brand had greater brand equity with the majority of core audiences than the SBC brand.

Brand portfolio strategy
Brand analytics provided a fact-based approach to decision-making about the future portfolio of brands. This identified a true brand equity measure for each brand with each individual target audience. This was then statistically modelled to provide the real dollar value of each brand as a business asset as well as the potential risks associated with migrating any of the brands. These quantitative insights helped the management team build the optimal value portfolio focused on a master brand strategy based on the acquired AT&T brand. This needed to be reinvigorated and repositioned and was successfully relaunched in 2007. SBC defied the sceptics, relaunching AT&T across its traditional services and, more controversially, dropping the Cingular brand, arguably one of the strongest brands in mobile phones.

Bring the brand to life
AT&T not only invested in new communications and visual representation of the brand, it also revamped its stores, retrained its employees and revitalised its product assortment through the launch with Apple of the iPhone in the United States in 2007.

Results
AT&T once again is one of the most powerful brands in the United States, successfully gaining traction in numerous studies against a host of hyper-competitive cable and telecommunications brands.

Competitive growth strategies

For an individual brand or a portfolio of brands there must be a strategy for dealing with the competition in order to build or maintain a successful position in the market. There are three competitive strategies (see Figure 6.8).

Direct competition

With direct competition the primary goal of an existing brand is to steal another brand's customers. This involves developing a thorough under-standing of a competitor brand, incorporating anything that appears to be working better for the competitor and identifying incremental improve-ments that provide an advantage. This sort of competition is often found in low-growth categories of products with a few large competitors. It is mainly an endurance battle to maintain parity and gain a slight advantage.

In the case of new entrants to a market, direct competition takes the form of a challenger brand strategy. Here a new entrant directly challenges an entrenched and often stale incumbent by pointing out its flaws, typically much to its irritation. If the first approach is more about a battle among equals, this has more in common with David and Goliath. But as before the goal is to steal the customers of the larger incumbent brand. Virgin chal-lenged British Airways directly as a cheeky underdog and successfully estab-lished a profitable business and brand for itself largely at BA's expense.

Competitive growth strategies — 6.8

	COMPETITIVE STRATEGY	NEW CUSTOMER SOURCE
Business and brand growth strategy?	Direct competition	Market share gain
	Indirect competition	New customers to the category
	Avoid competition	Redefine category

Source: Interbrand 2009

Indirect competition

A strategy for indirect competition has a few variations too. One approach is to grow the overall category. By not focusing on stealing customers from other brands, but attracting entirely new customers to the brand or getting existing customers to increase overall usage, the brand avoids direct competition. Typically only brands with high market share find that growing the category is economically viable; this is because a brand with low market share would run a disproportionate risk that the new customers it entices into the category will end up with the larger players. For Cisco, a company which dominates the market for networking gear, it made sense to invest many years and millions of dollars to develop new uses such as VOIP phone calling. This is because the additional network load that this creates translates into new sales of networking gear, in most cases for Cisco as the category leader.

Avoid competition

Lastly, a highly effective growth strategy is to avoid competition entirely. This can be done but not easily, otherwise everyone would do so. A brand can avoid competition in two ways: advance the customer experience and offer so dramatically that no one can match them, or define an entirely new category. Toyota and Honda in the 1980s introduced cars that were so dramatically superior to the product offer of the established American brands that they now dominate the market. Other companies such as Starbucks, Apple, IKEA and Target (an American retailer) created new categories. Starbucks did it by creating a "third place" between work and home. Apple did it with the iPod by moving digital music off the computer. IKEA and Target brought inexpensive design and style to customers. All these companies created a new category by combining two existing ideas in a new and interesting way. With Starbucks it was work and home; with the iPod it was digital music and mobility; and with IKEA and Target it was inexpensive great design.

The effects of growth strategies

Each of these growth strategies influences individual brands and the brand portfolio. In the case of direct competition between equals, the brands are generally broadly similar in appearance, offer and customer experience. However, if one is a challenger, it will frequently go to great lengths to make its brand's visual and verbal identity, customer experience and offer very different from the established brand.

When a brand leapfrogs the competition the offer often looks dramatically different – just as the Hondas and Toyotas of the 1980s looked and handled very differently from the American brands. When a new category is created there is usually a mix of old and new: old to reassure people, giving them a point of reference as they experience the new brand, and new things to signal that something is unique. At Starbucks the logo is classic yet at the same time mystical. Within the stores the tables and chairs were familiar; the couches and padded chairs were both familiar and unfamiliar in that they were not in the right setting – your home; and ordering a "venti" or "grande" was not at all familiar. This approach is necessary because of a fundamental human factor: people have immense difficulty seeing and understanding anything that does not meet their expectations. It can be so severe that individuals will disregard clear factual information that fails to meet what they expect to see or what they believe. As a result, the adoption of a radically new brand is highly dependent on how it is presented. The easiest way to make people switch brands is to start with the familiar and take them to the unfamiliar.

Conclusion

The greatest brands have a superior brand strategy, perfectly executed. They often exist within a portfolio of brands that are proactively managed. They have a clear growth strategy of how they will beat the competition and when it all works the impact can be truly remarkable.

The seven lessons on building the world's best global brands are as follows:

- ◪ Actively manage the brand as a business asset.
- ◪ Build the brand from a customer perspective and insight.
- ◪ Gather enough facts and do enough analysis to inform decision-making.
- ◪ Use the brand positioning as a central organising principle.
- ◪ Use the portfolio strategy to drive the brand positioning and innovation.
- ◪ Gain stakeholder buy-in through education, motivation and engagement.
- ◪ Use value-based tracking to manage growth – that is, define measurements that link management actions from product creation to sales and profitability to identify true value creators across that chain of events rather than in only one part of the chain.

7 Brand experience

Shaun Smith

Part 1 of this book argued for making the brand the central organising principle of an organisation. Why, then, do so few companies do this? In *Uncommon Practice: People Who Deliver a Great Brand Experience,*[1] it is found that although the notion of organising around the brand is accepted and becoming a strategic aim for many companies, it remains uncommon in practice because it is so hard to implement without a guiding framework. It requires leaders to take a holistic view of the brand that transcends the marketing function and makes it the rallying cry for the whole organisation. More importantly, it requires the organisation to align its people, processes and products with its proposition in order to deliver the promise it makes to customers every day.

Delivering the promise your brand makes may not be easy but it is very satisfying. Researchers at Satmetrix Systems conducted a study in 2002 to determine if there was a link between improved customer satisfaction and higher price/earnings ratios. They discovered that the P/E ratios of global companies with above-average brand loyalty scores were almost double those of their competitors.

So what is it that drives customer loyalty? For many years we have been told that a brand's success is a result of skilfully applying the "4 Ps" of the marketing mix: product, price, promotion and place. Gallup, a research company, conducted a poll of 6,000 consumers between November 1999 and January 2000 and found that the fifth "p", people, is by far the most important driver of brand loyalty. In motor vehicle retailing, Gallup found that customers who feel their dealer representative "stands out from all others" were 10–15 times more likely to choose the same brand for their next purchase. The same ratio holds true for the airline industry, and in the banking sector the influence of people on the brand is even greater, with customers saying they were 10–20 times more likely to repurchase from those organisations with outstanding employees.[2]

Stelios Haji-Ioannou, chairman of easyGroup and founder of easyJet, makes this clear by saying:

> *You can spend £15m on advertising, go bankrupt and your name*

can still mean nothing to people. Your brand is created out of customer contact and the experience your customers have of you.

Taking a broad view of branding has important and far-reaching implications for organisations. It places the responsibility squarely on the shoulders of the whole executive team, particularly the CEO, and it means that the "product" cannot simply be mass-produced, quality-assured and packaged. Customers experience the brand in many ways – through the people who sell it, the product itself, the people who provide after-sales service, the reactions to it of friends and colleagues and so on – and customers are sometimes irrational, inconsistent and difficult to manage.

The holistic view of brands

Brands traditionally have been the province of the marketing department. The main focus has been on communicating a brand in a distinctive way to target customers and managing their expectations. The result of a brand positioning exercise was often a thick book that carefully specified a number of design rules that had to be adhered to, such as pantone numbers and type faces. Soon, company vehicles would be seen sporting the new logo and signage would appear on office buildings and warehouses announcing the new tag line.

In the case of an airline, the rebranding process can take years as aircraft wait for their turn to be repainted in the new livery. But for customers and employees not much else changes: the service levels are no better, the planes are delayed as often, and management is as remote from customers and employees as it was before. In other words, the experience of the brand does not change. The exercise is often cosmetic and fails to deliver any lasting benefit. The UK's nationally owned Post Office spent millions of pounds re-branding itself as Consignia, yet failed to tackle the underlying performance problems that were driving customers away. The result was consumer derision over the choice of name, public criticism over the expense involved and widespread scepticism that the rebranding would make any difference. The organisation subsequently rebranded itself as the Royal Mail Group. The Post Office logo continues to adorn every outlet.

Another example of how not to do it is Abbey, a UK-based bank. In a blaze of publicity in September 2003 the bank launched a £11m branding campaign intended to "turn banking on its head". The bank's 700 or so branches were rebranded with a new, softer image and new advertising was launched promising customers: "Abbey's straightforward attitude and simplified accounts will help you get on top of your money." Unfortunately, the bank did not seem able to get on top of its own. It reported losses of £686m for the year ending December 31st 2003, a year when most of its competitors reported record profits. It also failed to communicate the new strategy clearly to its employees or put in place the new behaviours necessary to execute it. It lost the confidence of its people and as a result experienced staff turnover 17% higher than the industry average. Abbey was acquired by Banco Santander Central Hispano, a Spanish bank that quickly rebranded it once again.

No wonder consumers and employees have seen branding exercises as the corporate equivalent of rearranging deck chairs on the *Titanic*. This analogy is particularly apt as traditional branding exercises concentrate on the tip of the iceberg, changing what is visible, while below the surface the organisation functions much as before.

The Carlson Marketing Group conducts an annual survey that quantifies the quality of the relationship between a consumer (or employee or channel partner) and the brand. These surveys have found a direct relationship between the strength of the relationship and profitability. Customer spend, retention and their willingness to recommend the brand to others are all influenced by the strength of the relationship. In the 2007 financial services survey those organisations rated "high" for relationship had retention levels 75% higher than those brands with the weakest relationship scores and their customers had a 57% greater propensity to spend. So what is relationship strength? The researchers defined this as:

- Trust – consumers believe that the brand will deliver its promise, respect them, and be open and honest with them.
- Commitment – consumers feel some longer-term emotional attachment to their relationship with the brand.
- Alignment and mutuality – a two-way affinity between consumers and the brand, with mutual respect, shared values and expectations met, which results in a continually rewarding experience.

Tom Lacki, Carlson's senior director for knowledge management, sums it up:[3]

The consistency of the customer experience is key, because consistency enables trust, and trust is a fundamental enabling condition for the development of productive and authentic relationships.

A holistic view of brands carries the implication that the brand is, or should be, no less than the DNA of the organisation, the fundamental building block and expression of its existence. In an ideal world, the customer should be able to experience any customer process, talk to any employee, examine any product and the essence of the brand should shine through. All Nippon Airways (ANA), a Japanese airline, understands this. A widely seen ANA advertisement read:

> *Attention to detail isn't written in our training manuals, it's in our DNA.*

Southwest Airlines, Amazon, The Carphone Warehouse, Harley-Davidson, First Direct and Starbucks all have the same clarity of purpose and holistic approach to managing their brand, even though they are all in very different markets. What they have in common is a leading position, enthusiastic customers and exceptional growth rates.

The brand management iceberg

Subsequent chapters look at how to position and create brands. This chapter focuses on the management of brands according to a holistic approach that requires aligning the traditional marketing activities that lie "above the water" with the organisational capabilities that lie "below the water", as in the brand management iceberg illustrated in Figure 7.1 overleaf.

Clear proposition

Successful brands begin with a clear proposition. Unless a brand has a clear idea of the value it brings and to whom, it will have difficulty in ever making the brand stand for anything distinctive.

First Direct is a UK telephone and internet bank that is part of the HSBC group. If you visit its website, www.firstdirect.com/whyjoinus, you will find the following statement:

> *The real difference about First Direct is simple, most banks are about money. First Direct is about people. Simple but revolutionary.*

Unlike most retail banks First Direct then proceeds to deliver this simple

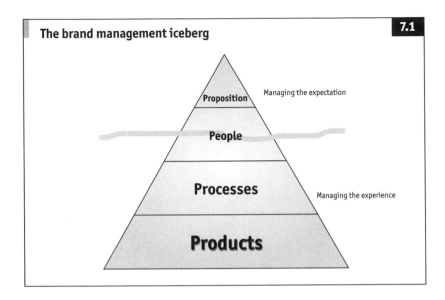

The brand management iceberg   `7.1`

Proposition — Managing the expectation

People

Processes — Managing the experience

Products

proposition every day. No wonder it has the highest customer satisfaction ratings of any bank, with 96% of customers being willing to recommend the bank to others.[4] According to the bank's website, it attracts a new customer every eight seconds through direct referral. First Direct was rated number one in the Top 50 Call Centres for Customer Service in 2008.[5] Peter Simpson, the bank's former commercial director, describes it thus:

> What First Direct did was to realise that people were changing their habits and would want to bank 24 hours a day, seven days a week.

As a result, the brand conceived the idea of centralised telephone banking built around an intimate knowledge of the customer backed up by simple processes and exceptionally friendly people. Paradoxically, First Direct is able to provide better customer service on the telephone than its competitors are providing face-to-face in branches.

So why is it that some organisations are able to deliver on their brand promise and others fall short? The answer lies in having a rigorous process for designing and delivering a customer experience that consistently delivers the brand promise. The simple model shown in Figure 7.2 on page 108 is used to achieve this.

People

Research has shown that there is a strong correlation between the way employees feel about the brand and the way customers view it.[6] For this reason some companies are paying as much attention to their employee experience as their customer experience. The *Sunday Times* said this about First Direct:

> With on-site masseur, concierge, car servicing and laundry to name but a few of the services provided to employees based both at Leeds and Hamilton, it's little wonder that First Direct, the UK's most recommended bank, has won a coveted place in the prestigious Sunday Times 100 Best Companies to Work for 2006 list.

As Simpson says:

> You can't pretend to be one style of brand to your consumers if you're a different style of brand to your people. People are at the waterline level because, for most companies, they represent the point at which customers finally interact with the brand. Customers have seen the advertisements or promotional activity and are interested – they have an expectation – now it is all about the experience. It is at this point that the brand delivers or not. Employees are the conduit through which all the careful product design, manufacturing, packaging and processes are finally delivered to customers; they are the means to bring the brand alive.

In *Managing the Customer Experience: Turning Customers into Advocates*,[7] four steps are suggested to bring brands alive through people:

- Hire people with competencies to satisfy customer expectations.
- Train employees to deliver experiences that uniquely fit your brand promise.
- Reward them for the right behaviours.
- Most importantly, drive the behaviours from the very top of the organisation.

Take, for example, The Carphone Warehouse. The brand started out with the simple proposition of offering "simple, impartial advice" to consumers wishing to navigate the minefield of mobile phone contracts. The company is now offering value-added services and is competing in the fixed-line and broadband market. However, what has not changed is its focus on differentiating the brand on the basis of the customer experience. Fundamental to the brand is the performance of its people. The company philosophy is summed up in five simple operating principles:

- If we don't look after the customer, someone else will.
- Nothing is gained by winning an argument but losing a customer.
- Always deliver what we promise. If in doubt, underpromise and overdeliver.
- Always treat customers as we ourselves would like to be treated.
- The reputation of the whole company is in the hands of each individual.

These principles are unusual in that they focus people on behaviours rather than high-level values such as "trustworthy, valued or responsive". The way in which The Carphone Warehouse applies them also sets it apart. For example, it invests four times the industry average in training. New employees must undergo two weeks of intensive training and a rigorous assessment before they are allowed in front of a customer. In April 2006 Charles Dunstone, the company's CEO, announced that customers would enjoy "free broadband". Within 24 hours 20,000 new customers signed up, five times more than anticipated. Despite having tripled call-centre capacity The Carphone Warehouse was unprepared, leading to widespread customer criticism. By the end of 2006 2.6m customers had subscribed to TalkTalk, the new fixed-line product. Dunstone's December 2006 blog entry read:

> Our focus for the year ahead is to rebuild people's confidence in our product and in our ability to deliver it.

That is exactly what he did. The message here is that successful brands focus less on brand image and more on brand action.

There is probably not a large organisation that does not train its staff or have recognition systems of some kind, yet the fact remains that for most brands the experience that their customers have is largely undifferentiated. The reason for this is simple: companies' training and recognition schemes are generic, that is, they are much the same as their competitors' schemes and insufficiently tied to their brand proposition. This is particularly true when companies go to the same large consultancies for essentially repackaged service training or reward systems. The answer is to provide a learning experience designed to bring the brand to life for employees.

Waterstone's, a UK book retailer, is training all the "colleagues" in its 340 stores using a series of specially designed modules built into the rhythm of the operation and delivered by store and departmental managers. Each of the modules focuses on delivery of Waterstone's brand promise and the behaviours necessary to bring it alive for customers. The desired behaviour is reinforced by aligning its mystery shopper survey with the new customer experience.

Recruitment also needs to be "on-brand". Most organisations use the same generic interview processes for hiring staff, yet their brands may require very different interpersonal qualities. Contrast this with Southwest Airlines, one of the few consistently profitable airlines in the United States. The company has won an enviable reputation for its fun-loving, friendly cabin attendants. The airline does not recruit; it holds auditions where would-be employees are encouraged to sing, act or anything else they choose. The process is designed to allow candidates to demonstrate their ability to bring their personalities to work. Would this recruitment process be appropriate for anyone else? Probably not, which is exactly the point.

Pret A Manger, a fast-growing international sandwich chain, takes a very different approach. Prospective employees are asked to work in a store for a day, at the end of which the store's employees are asked to vote on whether they should be hired or not. Only 5% of the people who apply for jobs at Pret are accepted. The reason for this unusual recruitment method is that the company believes that one of the biggest responsibilities of management is to look after the corporate "DNA".

For a brand to mean something different to customers it must behave differently internally, and that includes its processes.

Process

One recurring fad is the attention that organisations give to their processes. We have seen total quality management (TQM), business process re-engineering (BPR), customer relationship management (CRM), customer managed relationships (CMR) and the re-emergence of the Six-Sigma Way. There is nothing inherently wrong with any of these concepts as they encourage companies to focus on improving those processes that create the most value. Unfortunately, all too often these approaches are used simply as a means to take cost (or rather frontline people) out of the system without really examining whether the revised process is adding value to the brand and delivering the promise to customers. So UK high-street banks now have impersonal call and processing centres, often located somewhere in India, and customers can no longer phone their friendly bank manager directly. The banks may argue that this is to improve service, but their customers know that the main reason for the change is to cut costs.

CRM has been said to be the management tool that most often fails to meet management expectations. This is because it is essentially a "dumb" technology that is used to capture more and more information about customers without thinking about how it can be used to create value for them or how it will improve their experience of the brand. Lengthy voice-activated response systems and more targeted direct mailshots are a poor substitute for processes that truly add value to the customer.

Amazon is one of the most widely recognised and respected brands in the world. Jeff Bezos, the company's CEO, has said:

> It has always seemed to me that your brand is formed, primarily, not by what your company says about itself, but by what the company does.

An example is Amazon's "One-Click" ordering process. The Amazon brand promises reliability and simplicity, and to demonstrate these values the ordering process was reviewed. Amazon's web designers came up with the idea of One-Click, a system which remembers customers' payment and shipping details so that subsequent items can be purchased with literally one mouse click. When it was tested, customers were sceptical because of concerns about security and confidentiality. However, Bezos insisted on introducing One-Click because he felt that the simplified process was on-brand for Amazon and that his customers' trust in the Amazon brand would overcome their reservations. He was right and it has proved extremely successful.

Likewise, First Direct has helped turn its brand promise into reality through simple processes. Switching banks used to involve a lot of hassle so that customers who were dissatisfied with their bank could rarely be bothered to move their accounts. First Direct tells its prospective customers:

> We can now transfer your standing orders and direct debits for you – so transferring bank accounts has never been easier.

And it does. With one simple click on the "I agree" button, it swings into action and contacts your current bank to arrange everything on your behalf.

These examples raise another interesting question about this notion of holistic branding. What is the product? It used to be easy: it was the can of cola or the airline seat or perhaps the pair of jeans. But the expanded definition of brand means that the product is now much broader. It is the totality of the experience.

Product

It used to be said that the difference between a product and a service is that customers are actively engaged in experiencing a service but they acquire and use a product. Customers experience a restaurant but cannot take it home; they buy a doughnut and consume it, but the doughnut does not provide a service. If this is true, what is the Starbucks product? Is it the coffee or the service experience? Howard Schultz, the company's chairman, believes that the advantage Starbucks has over traditional brands is that "our customers see themselves inside our company, inside our brand, because they're part of the Starbucks experience". Starbucks' customers seem happy to pay a premium for that privilege.

This is true too for many other sectors, including professional services. Clifford Chance, one of the world's largest law firms, sees the legal expertise that it provides as vital but expected and that the true differentiator for its brand is the relationship it builds with its clients. Clifford Chance is investing in training to help its lawyers deliver a more seamless and client-focused experience.

Some years ago the Greater China division of Leo Burnett, an advertising agency, was under threat from other agencies and was losing clients and employees. By taking a holistic view of the brand and working on improving the creative processes and upgrading the skills of its people, the division's products steadily improved. Leo Burnett cut employee turnover by 40%, raised new account profitability by 63% and rose from sixth to first place in total billings. Two years later it was voted agency of the year.[8]

Brands are now emerging that create experiences connected to the purchase or the use of a product, but they offer value to the customer that goes beyond the product alone and becomes synonymous with the brand.

The brand promise of Harley-Davidson, an American motorcycle-maker, is "We Fulfil Dreams". It expands on this by saying:

Fulfilling dreams for people from all walks of life who cherish the common values of freedom, adventure and individual expression, involves much more than building and selling motorcycles. The secret to our enduring brand lies in delivering an experience rather than just a collection of products and services.

If you think that this is just PR spin, Harley-Davidson has over 1m active members in its Harley Owners Group (HOG), and these enthusiasts typically spend 30% more than Harley owners who are non-members. This increased expenditure is on clothing, holidays and events – in other words, the experience. According to one estimate, nearly 20% of the company's sales are derived from non-motorcycle-related sales.[9] Harley's bundling of customer experiences with product and direct involvement with customers have led to over 20 years of financial growth and a 50% share of the big bike market in the United States and 30% world wide. A shareholder who invested $10,000 when the organisation went public in 1986 would now be a millionaire.

Redefine

When you think of Harley-Davidson, do you think of grizzly, tattooed, Hells Angels? Think again. Of the 4,000 people who went through Harley's "Riders Edge" programme, a motorcycling safety course designed to attract new riders, in 2002, nearly 45% were female and half of these were aged under 35. Of course the reality is that a Harley-Davidson is more likely to be ridden by a professional than by a tearaway. The average purchaser of a Harley motorcycle is a married male in his 40s with a median household income of $81,700. Harley has redefined itself.

At a typical weekend rally 25,000 people will show up, including all the company's senior managers. Harley-Davidson management refers to these events as "super-engagement" because the leaders are all active participants in HOG activities. In this way the leaders keep tuned in to the changing needs of their customers and combat competitive threats. This has meant new processes and new products, including the V-Rod motorcycle that embodies all the traditional Harley-Davidson brand values in a state-of-the-art bike for which customers were clamouring.

Perhaps this is why Harley-Davidson celebrated its centenary in 2003 with huge events around the world while so many other famous motorcycle brands have died.

Contrast this with another icon that has even higher brand recognition:

McDonald's. Although it is one of the best-known brands in the world, it has been through a turbulent period, shutting some of its stores and reporting losses. It came last in a 2002 *Wall Street Journal* customer satisfaction survey and achieved a lower customer satisfaction index than the US Internal Revenue Service in a survey conducted by the University of Michigan.[10]

Pick up any management textbook published during the last decade and the chances are that you will find a reference to McDonald's and its promise to provide consistent quality, service and value. These values are still there, but the problem is that consistency is now the entry price for any brand that wants to do business. McDonald's is trying out new propositions under its "We're Lovin' it" tag line. It seems that the renewed focus on customers has put the brand, once again, on a growth curve, with annual sales increases of nearly 8% across its operations.[11]

Consumers want brands to offer products and experiences that complement their lifestyles. Pret A Manger, in which McDonald's had a stake between 2001 and 2008, is consistent but also offers wholesome food with great service. Its proposition "Passionate about food" is evident in every detail. The brand has responded to customers who are now looking for fast food that is healthy and served in a pleasant environment by friendly employees. The message here is that tastes change, and unless brands can be dynamic and move quickly to meet emerging and changing needs they will decline. Mounting a new advertising or promotional campaign, launching a revised logo or even changing the brand promise is not enough. The response can and should include these activities, but unless it is accompanied by fundamental changes to the processes, upgraded products and employees who are briefed and trained to be able to deliver the revised proposition, the marketing effort will be worthless.

A consequence of this concept is that the marketing department may still lead but no longer wholly own the brand. It has to be jointly owned by marketing, human resources and operations because each has a vital role to play in delivering the brand to consumers. The word "marketing" should describe an attitude, a holistic approach to business, not a specific function or series of processes. The role of the chief executive is crucial in setting this agenda and ensuring that the three functions work together. This kind of alignment is called "Triad Power" and it will define how organisations will function in the future. What is needed now is a simple framework or tool for facilitating this alignment. The brand management process (see Figure 7.2 on the next page) answers this need.

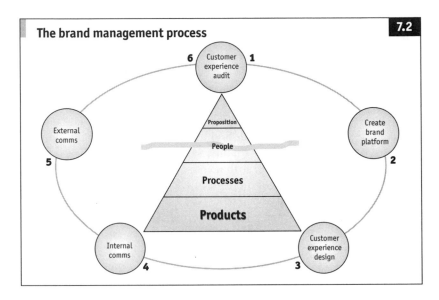

The brand management process `7.2`

Using the brand management iceberg

Although the process will vary according to the nature and needs of the brand, Figure 7.2 represents a logical framework for managing the activities that align both the expectation and the experience that customers have of the brand.

Customer experience audit

Begin by measuring the current experience of the brand. What is the total experience customers have of the organisation and the brand in terms of the following:

- **Proposition.** How clear is the offer and what does the brand promise? Is this valuable to target customers?
- **People.** To what extent do people behave in a way that meets customer expectations and delivers the brand promise?
- **Processes.** Do processes create value for customers and deliver the brand promise?
- **Products.** Are products differentiated and valuable to target customers?

Creating the brand platform

Some of this work is usually already in place, but make sure that it is absolutely clear and fully effective, as without clarity around the brand platform the following phases cannot be undertaken. It involves the following:

- **Brand positioning.** How can you position your brand with clarity and precision?
- **Brand naming.** Choosing a name for the brand that is distinctive and creates the right emotional associations.
- **Brand architecture.** How should the brand or sub-brands work together to communicate the proposition?
- **Brand identity.** How best can the brand be portrayed visually and verbally?

Customer experience design

Having audited the current situation and created clarity around the brand positioning and values, you can design the new experience that will consistently deliver the brand to target customers. Attention should be given to the same dimensions as in the customer experience audit:

- **Proposition.** What can the brand promise in specific terms to target customers that will create competitive advantage?
- **People.** How must people behave to bring this promise to life at every point where the organisation interacts with the customer?
- **Processes.** What processes need to be improved, eliminated or added to enable employees to behave in this way?
- **Products.** How can products be improved to highlight or demonstrate the brand values?

Communicating the brand internally

Having designed the new experience, you are ready to communicate it internally. At this point, many organisations rush out a new advertising campaign and end up overpromising and underdelivering because their people are not fully prepared. As much effort must go into marketing internally as into marketing externally:

- **Communication.** Make sure everyone knows who the target customers are, what they expect, what the brand stands for and what it promises.
- **Leadership.** Prepare managers to lead the brand and demonstrate their own commitment to the promise.

◪ **Training.** Develop "on-brand" training that will emotionally engage managers and employees and equip them with the knowledge, attitude and skills to deliver the brand promise.

◪ **Measurement.** Align measurement systems so that everyone is aware of the extent to which the organisation is meeting customer needs and is rewarded for delivering the promise.

Communicating the brand externally

Now, and only now, are you ready to communicate the proposition externally. Much of this work may have been done in preparation, but you will want to make sure the organisation is ready to deliver the experience before you raise the expectation by going live. The focus needs to be on:

◪ **Brand communication.** How best can the brand be communicated to its intended audience? This includes advertising, promotion, packaging, and so on.

Continuing management, audits and redefinition

Lastly, the brand must be protected and refreshed over time to keep it current with target customer needs and competitively strong. This requires the following:

◪ **Management.** Cross-functional sponsorship and leadership to ensure all the activities that support the brand are aligned and managed.

◪ **Audits.** Regular measurement of brand image, reputation and the customer experience against the desired proposition.

◪ **Redefinition.** Periodic refreshing and upgrades to ensure that the offer stays current with target customer expectations and combats competitive threats.

Using the brand management iceberg allows senior managers to align an organisation's people, processes and products with the brand proposition to create value for target customers. As was said at the start of this chapter, this is common sense but still uncommon practice.

Notes and references

1 Smith, S. and Milligan, A., *Uncommon Practice: People Who Deliver a Great Brand Experience*, Financial Times Prentice Hall, 2002.
2 McEwen, B., "All Brands are the same", www.gallup.com.

3 Lacki, T.D., "Achieving the Promise of CRM", *Interactive Marketing*, Vol. 4, No. 4, 2003, pp. 355–75.

4 Research International, November–December 2006.

5 *Call Centre Focus Magazine*, November 2008.

6 shaunsmith+co, Customer Experience Management Survey, Organisational Alignment Survey, 2007.

7 Smith, S. and Wheeler, J., *Managing the Customer Experience: Turning Customers into Advocates*, Financial Times Prentice Hall, 2002.

8 1995 Asian Ad Awards.

9 www.wikinvest.com/stock/Harley-Davidson_(HOG)

10 *Sunday Times*, April 6th 2003.

11 *McDonald's Delivers Another Month of Strong Global Comparable Sales – November up 7.7%*, press release, December 12th 2008.

8 Visual and verbal identity

Tony Allen and John Simmons

In 1955, the president of IBM, Thomas Watson Jr, asked the following question:

> *Do you think it's possible that IBM could look like the kind of company it really is?*

The question was put to Eliot Noyes, IBM's industrial design consultant. Watson and Noyes realised that IBM was at that time about to be eclipsed by the good looks of Olivetti. That was the conclusion you would have reached if you had looked at the two companies side by side. Both of them were vying to be recognised as "leader of the modern world", but IBM looked more like the leader of Caxton's world. So a programme was born to introduce the discipline of corporate identity to IBM, spurred on by the man described by *Fortune* magazine as "the greatest capitalist who ever lived".

"Visual identity" is a recent term that was probably coined to avoid lengthy arguments about the meaning of "brand" versus "corporate identity". In the 1980s, the term brand migrated from soap powders and came to mean virtually anything on the planet with an ability to sustain an attraction or influence among people. Politics, countries, movements, artists, celebrities and educational establishments as well as companies and chocolate bars all became brands. So brand came to mean more or less what had been described as corporate identity: the total experience offered by a company to its staff, customers and others, a heady and distinctive concoction of intangible promises and tangible attributes and benefits.

Visual identity is a component in branding – the part you see, obviously. As such it is an important part because what you see is more likely to influence you than what you are told or what you comprehend from a deck of 80 word slides.

Visual identity

Visual identity comprises the graphic components that together provide a system for identifying and representing a brand. The "basic elements" of a brand's visual identity might comprise distinctive versions of the following:

- Logotypes
- Symbols
- Colours
- Typefaces

Think of the way IBM consistently reproduces its name in its logotype; the McDonald's arches symbol; the Royal Mail's use of pillar-box red; the Johnson typeface created exclusively for London Underground. These basic elements are often supplemented by other graphic elements such as patterns, approaches to illustration and photography, and a range of icons.

BMW uses the visual design and styling of its cars, key-rings, graphics, showrooms and communications to express its now powerful and easily recognised global brand identity. BMW's visual expression is clear, attractive, distinctive and noticeably consistent wherever you see it. Each part of a customer's journey to purchase or experience owning or driving a BMW is carefully orchestrated to send the same messages about the brand. The BMW brand is an often-quoted example of an exceptionally high standard in visual identity expression.

By contrast, despite being a truly mighty automotive brand, Ford made visual and verbal errors with the Edsel in 1957. A car whose visual quirkiness might work well now, the Edsel had an unpopular "horse-collar" grille, designed to stand out from other cars but described by one customer as looking like "a vagina with teeth". Moreover, the name (after Edsel Ford, son of Henry Ford and a former company president) lacked appeal as the public thought it sounded odd, and, indeed, the Ford family is thought to have disapproved of the use of it. These two factors were not the only ones to bring the Edsel to an early end, but they were crucial in sealing the unpopularity of the car and the brand, leading to discontinued production after 1960.

This chapter is also about verbal identity. This is another recent term that was coined to make it clear that identity is also expressed through words and language, whether we mean it to be or not. Some organisations have changed their language to be more "customer friendly" (tax offices, government agencies and charities). Some organisations still cling to powerfully bad verbal identities, so bad on occasion that you can only navigate them with a professional guide. For example, IT firms often still befuddle their audiences with technical terms, jargon and bad English, and many lawyers continue to intimidate their clients with arcane phrases and technical (sometimes Latin) terms.

Verbal identity

Verbal identity's "basic elements" aim to make a brand's language distinctive. These might comprise the following:

◪ The name
◪ A naming system for products, sub-brands and groups
◪ A strapline
◪ Tone of voice principles
◪ The use of stories

Combining the visual and the verbal provides the means to make brands that really work. Ben & Jerry's ice creams, for example, have self-indulgent and tasty names like Phish Food, Chunky Monkey and Cherry Garcia, an edible tribute to the late Jerry Garcia of the Grateful Dead, a famous American rock band. Such carefully orchestrated naivety takes more effort to do well than, say, achieving the gleaming polish of Häagen-Dazs (a made-up name). It is strange that the "soul" of Ben & Jerry's was thought to be at risk when it was bought by one of the most careful consumer branding companies of all – Unilever – which understands that brands need to have souls.

Any company, product, service or anything else will make little progress if it cannot show what it is about and why it is different. Showing this means having a purpose behind the way names are created and used, the creation of logos and symbols, the uses of colours and typography, illustration and photography, pattern, style and the use of language.

This chapter examines the tactics and strategy of identity using examples of well-known companies and brands, several of which are featured in the colour plate section which appears in the book. But to put the subject in context, where does the idea of identity come from?

From *brandr* to today

As explained in Chapter 2, the word brand comes from the Old Norse *brandr*, meaning to burn, and mass branding existed in the ancient civilisations of Etruria, Greece and Rome, where potters made their marks on the pots they made. Today in Texas there are some 230,000 registered cattle brands, many of them showing a fusion between the visual and the verbal – see the symbol, read the name and vice versa – in the same way as the brands of organisations such as the Red Cross, Shell, Penguin Books and "3", a mobile telecommunications company. Since the 1930s there have been certain identifiable trends relating to the creation of brand identities.

Designer-driven identity

In the 1950s and 1960s, especially in the United States, corporate bosses put their faith in the creative skills of a number of unusually talented designers. These included, among others, Paul Rand, designer of the IBM and UPS corporate identities; Saul Bass, designer of the AT&T, United Airlines, Minolta, General Foods, Rockwell International identities; Raymond Loewy, designer of "Lucky Strike" in 1940 and Shell in 1967; and Milton Glaser, designer of the "I love New York" logo. But one of the earliest notable grand-scale visual projects was Egbert Jacobsen's 1930s design of nearly "every surface" of Walter P. Paepcke's company, the Container Corporation of America (CCA), including its factories, vehicles, packaging, invoices, brochures and advertising. Paepcke was convinced that good design was an integral component of corporate culture, taking the view that just as national culture is shaped by its use of visual symbols and icons, so too are corporations by the symbols and icons they use. Jacobsen's work for CCA, William Golden's famous late-1940s "eye" identity for the Columbia Broadcasting System (CBS) and Rand's original design for UPS played an important role in establishing the importance of design in creating powerful visual logos and brand ownership symbols. It is also at this time that we see the beginnings of associations between corporations and the colours they used to identify their products and services, for instance yellow belonging to Kodak, red to Coca-Cola, green to BP, brown to UPS and blue to IBM and AT&T.

American corporations were largely responsible for establishing the professional role of corporate design, but the nature of the work often owed more to a relationship between the company owner and the designer than the intervention of the marketing department. This was partly because "marketing" was seen as more or less interchangeable with "sales" and therefore had a lower status. Similarly, the notion of corporate identity as a strategic tool was in its infancy.

One of the most famous examples of an owner-designer relationship is that of Thomas J. Watson Jr, son of the founder of IBM. In 1955, Watson recognised, partly as a result of prompts from a colleague in Europe, that IBM's designs and buildings were substantially "off the pace" for a company then entering the electronic era. At that time it was Olivetti, not IBM, that had an ultra-contemporary New York City showroom. Watson visited Adriano Olivetti in Milan and saw at first hand the extent and ingenuity of the identity programme which had been started by Olivetti and which included buildings, offices, employee housing, products, brochures and advertisements. Olivetti was even involved in bringing new functional and aesthetic designs to urban planning. Watson wrote that it was then that he decided to "improve IBM design, not only in architecture and typography, but colour, interiors, the whole spectrum". The experience of seeing Olivetti's work in Milan resulted in one of the most succinct quotations on the subject of identity and its meaning, included at the beginning of this chapter.

The landmarks that followed included a series of changes to the famous IBM logotype masterminded by Rand, who had been brought into IBM and had quietly got on with redesigning the company's brochures and printed material. Rand was also responsible for building up IBM's design capacity, bringing new talent into the monolithic business and helping to spark a golden era of expressive identity design, matched by a vast array of building and architectural projects, notably IBM's pavilion at the New York World Fair in 1964.

IBM's story is an impressive illustration of visual identity. More recently, while remaining true to the principles of a consistent visual identity, the company has negotiated a transition from stolid and solid hardware manufacturer to cerebral "creative" solutions provider. Its visual identity has evolved seamlessly. Its verbal identity has changed subtly too, perhaps exemplified by the advertising line "I think therefore IBM". IBM's language has become less technologically obsessed, less to do with bits and bytes and more to do with having an interesting way of thinking. Indeed, in terms of verbal identity, it drew the response from Apple "Think different", which was a blow aimed at IBM's supposed weak spot: its association with "blue suit" conformity.

Strategy-driven identity

In the 1970s, as a result of the boom in marketing, particularly market and customer research, and the vogue for change management initiatives, the ownership of corporate identity was transferred to the marketing department as one of an armoury of tools to be used and linked to other tools. Identity had to mature and be measured and accountable. It was not enough to say that the logo was the signature of the company. Was the logo the right logo for the customer?

Arguably, this was a time when designers, who formerly had free rein to work with corporate bosses on anything they wanted, looked for new creative opportunities in the growing non-mainstream areas, such as publishing, music and entertainment, where graphic design enjoyed boom times, especially with punk towards the end of the 1970s. Visual identity moved into a different kind of creative period as designers and marketers began to understand and play with new possibilities. Having established that the logo itself was the basis for a consistent visual identity, questions started to be asked about the memorability or recognisability of the mark. If this was to represent the company's business strategy, could it really be achieved by a "dynamic typographic rendition"? Or would more creative visual symbols help companies to express their strategies with a clearer sense of energy and novelty?

In this context, some visual identities stand out as landmarks. The Bovis identity, with its use of the humming bird as a symbol, was a breakthrough in the early 1970s. The humming bird itself was, from the advantage of hindsight, easy to justify as "nimble" and "industrious". But, more importantly, in the context of its time, it made a statement about the company's belief in aesthetic principles and its focus on the customer. After all, Bovis was aiming not to be just any old construction company; it was carefully creating the modern environments in which people would live and work.

From the 1970s until the mid-1980s, a new benchmark became apparent. It was about creating a visual symbol that had "artistic" quality while representing a clear commercial articulation of business strategy. This strand of visual identity continues today, but perhaps reached its pinnacle in Michael Wolff's work for 3i in the early to mid-1980s. Here the mark itself was a thing of beauty – a watercolour painting of the numeral 3 with an eye – but the logo became almost irrelevant in the overall scheme of the company's new identity.

First, it was a bold piece of renaming. The Industrial and Commercial Finance Corporation became Investors in Industry, known as 3i. This

117

set the tone for a radical approach to marketing financial services and venture capital. Using illustrations by Jeff Fisher, the new 3i advertising burst out of the pages of business magazines, proclaiming through its visual and verbal style "we are different and we will support ventures that are different too". The challenge then was to maintain this sense of difference. The annual 3i calendar, using cartoons, helped to do this. Poetry by Christopher Logue, for example, reinforced the effect. But "being different" is a hard act to sustain, even if it is the goal of every identity programme. 3i survives, and prospers, with the basics of its 1980s identity intact, even if nowadays nobody speaks of it in quite the same hushed tones as they did then. Its market positioning, as well as its identity, is no longer as pioneering as it once was.

At the same time as being both strategic and creative, companies became more proficient at running identity programmes, which presented fresh problems.

Controlling and category identity: the "CI manual" and the lookalikes

During the 1970s, 1980s and 1990s a vast number of powerful international identities were launched for companies such as Akzo Nobel, BT, ICI, BP and Unisys, and with them came weighty corporate identity manuals. These valuable management tools or "dead-hands", according to your point of view, were often to be found propping open a door instead of being pored over for their timely and topical advice.

Interestingly, this "professionalising" of visual identity probably did more to reduce differentiation between companies than at any other time. Professional standards were rapidly shared and copied, and many companies started to share similar visual cues. But in its way, the lookalike factor helped spur the rapid expansion of branding and identity in the past 30 years. This is because there has been a tendency to react in two ways to new breakthrough identities within a particular business category. The first is to acknowledge a rival's success in differentiation through identity by creating a completely different approach to the task. The second is to recognise success by saying "we'll have some of the same". So, for example, the 3i identity led to a plethora of illustration-based visual identities. Not all of them were bad, and because they found something new to say, they were not purely imitative. But, as ever, there were fashionable trends in design and identity, and sometimes these trends became more entrenched than the one-off, copycat, flash-in-the-pan reactions. In many cases, companies from one sector or category of business ended up "borrowing" ideas and learning from others; and often the borrowing was creative and catalytic for a different sector of business. Commercialisation of the public sector in the UK has created many branding opportunities. One category could be called the lookalike higher education sector. In the late 1980s, polytechnics were able to become universities, but to succeed they had to look like a university. Dozens of former polytechnics marched into corporate identity programmes to emerge looking the same. Category identity had taken off by the late 1980s, but it reached its zenith during the late 1990s as dotcom companies raced to portray the ethereal nature of their services and excited possibly the biggest spate of lookalike identities ever seen. There were endless flowing, single-line "swooshes" usually accompanied by a mad name and intended to convey a sense of energy and dynamism. But Nike's swoosh design mark has stayed the course, perhaps because of its sheer omnipresence.

Diversifying identities

The history of corporate identity is littered with examples of powerful structural identities that labelled every department and every function in the same way. By the 1990s, such an approach was considered to be overcontrolling and was even compared by some to the identities of Hitler's national socialism and Russia's communism. For many, the corporate identity manual, intended to be a vibrant source of inspiration for company-to-customer communication, became associated with negative regulation or a police-state environment. The unofficial job title "logo cop" came into being.

The explosive nature of the digital age, the recognition that a job was no longer for life and the concept that quality of work was more important than financial reward, promoted by magazines such as *Fast Company*, *Wired* and even *Fortune*, meant that identity, if it was going to succeed, had to be tackled differently, more intelligently and creatively than before.

In 1997, British Airways launched a new identity that took the idea of diversity to a height not seen before, at least not in the airline world. The reaction to it was mixed and often critical. The old BA identity had been classically "British", heraldic and sober, and the image-tracking studies carried out by the company in the mid-1990s had picked this up. Certainly, BA had an image of being global but hardly caring. The British-ness exemplified by the silver-grey crest on the tailfin said more about a cool and possibly unforgiving attitude to customer service than it did about a top-notch travelling experience for millions of economy-class passengers.

To combat this, the new identity was designed to make a highly visible display of the company's real interest in serving customers from all over the world. This was symbolised through a ground-breaking project: artists from different world communities were invited to display their work as an integral part of BA's visual identity, including placing artworks on the tailfins themselves, the traditional branding space reserved for only the most formal of identifiers.

What might have appeared as a surface treatment, possibly even a shock tactic, had serious ambitions in the area of employee retraining and behaviour. BA rightly observed that a change in perception in the minds of its customers would come only through a change in the experience they enjoyed from the beginning to the end of their encounter with the airline. The identity, with its obvious message of diversity, was a catalyst in significant internal change and, perhaps, a reflection of internal change that was already taking place and becoming visible. As a result, BA people would master more languages in the future; they would be encouraged to be themselves with passengers; they would strive for the highest standards in service; and they would make this a self-fulfilling prophecy.

Interestingly, the reaction to the new identity included as much opposition to the loss of British uniformity as praise for the globally diverse perspective taken by a British company. The visual identity, itself an expression of a radical change of business direction, became an easy target for those, internally and externally, who were unhappy about the company's new direction. This was exacerbated by the fact that airlines are, inevitably, partly representatives of national identities. Those who attacked the new BA identity most bitterly were also those who defended most stoutly the established view of the British national identity. Other airlines, in other parts of the world, have found themselves in a similar position to BA when considering their identity. A changing identity reflects a company, organisation or even a nation in a state of flux and forces the question: "Are you comfortable with the way you are going?" Inevitably, in some cases, the answer has been "No". BA backtracked on the diversity of the new identity and the chief executive stood down not long after. The basic elements of the visual identity remained but the tailfins used the version of the Union Jack flag originally intended for use only on Concorde. A diverse identity had become monolithic.

Non-corporate identities: the new generation

Being "corporate" took a knock in the mid 2000s. Perhaps this was caused by business scandals like Enron. Perhaps it was fuelled by the massive growth in social networking sites, which are anti-corporate by nature. Perhaps it was fanned by the near-worldwide condemnation of President George W. Bush and American policies in Iraq, which were seen to have a corporate agenda. Perhaps it was all these and more, linked to an anti-American feeling, as the "corporation" itself is an American concept. Looking "corporate" became a byword for looking dull, straight, insensitive and uncaring about the real issues in life. Even worse, looking corporate, flashy and omnipotent (as Enron did) reminded people of corporate crime and injustice, as if just by clothing themselves in the icons, colours and patterns of serious-suited corporate life businesses were sneakily trying to hide something. Non-corporate celebrities such as Bono, Richard Branson and Bob Geldof annually flew the flag for anti-corporatisation, becoming regular faces at World Economic Forum meetings at Davos. Hope seemed to spring more readily from their ideas than from established corporations such as IBM and UBS. Visually and verbally, big new businesses such as Google and Facebook, which were collectively worth more than many average-sized countries, looked and sounded like friends to confide in and spend time with as an alternative to going to the pub or watching TV.

The visual identities of early 21st-century digital businesses – Facebook, iTunes, YouTube, Google, Bebo, Flickr and so on – were not fashioned using the old templates of letterhead and business-card designs, vehicle liveries, beverage bottles or factory signs. These identities sprang out of no barriers, globally accessible, spontaneous, individual participation on the internet. In a way they are nothing identities. Facebook does not have a strong logo and the site has no extraneous decoration; the user's content, supplied without brand intervention, is all there is.

Taking their cue from the successes of the internet generation, some bricks and mortar businesses have become befuddled. Should they look like a friend with whom the customer senses trust and reassurance? Or should they look like leaders who can dispense advice with the certainty that their expertise is of unique value? Should they be so casual in the portrayal of their identity that they look unstructured and not really like a business, or should they find another way? Brands that live solely on the internet have brought new ideas in communication and a wealth of visual references to the conventional economy.

Apple, surely the most talked about case study in the world of brands, has succeeded in pulling off the ultimate performance of being the corporation for the individual. Apple's design innovation from 2000 onwards has helped turn its business from being a small, delectable, trendy stock into one of the most influential companies in the world in terms of style, communication and originality.

But in other sectors there are embarrassing sights to be seen. For years banks tried to win customers by not looking or sounding like banks. Banking is a tough retail category. At least if you are in clothing you can make products in synthetic, natural or organically grown fibres; and fashion allows you to swap flares for drainpipes and recycle them both at regular intervals. In retail financial services, the dynamic is always the same no matter how hard you try to repackage it. To differentiate themselves, banks need to develop strong visual identities, but since it is ingrained that no one apart from shareholders actually likes banks, the problem of visual identity is a conundrum for the average bank. Should it look strong and diligent enough to fine, supervise and admonish wayward customers, or like a caring, cosy partner in a world where everything is always rosy?

The banking crisis of 2008 probably made the question easier to answer in the future. Indeed, the projection of banks as friendly businesses that have a "hole in the wall" rather than an ATM was part of the problem that led to the crash. Banks need to say no sometimes even if that seems less friendly. When the market returns to stability banks will focus more on their traditional values – solidity, prudence, trustworthiness – and play down the values that led to them being portrayed as villains with big egos and big bonuses. But they will still face the fundamental branding issue of differentiation, a difficult notion in an industry that is essentially undifferentiated at its core.

From the recent trend towards anti-corporate design comes one of the best examples of non-corporate identity: the logo for the London Olympics in 2012 created by Wolff Olins. This logo firmly breaks the tradition of all Olympic identity design and opens the door for an "anything goes" policy in the future. What is interesting about the 2012 logo is that its design is a conscious underlining of the fact that in 2007, when the logo was launched, it was acceptable to look a bit ugly, a bit real and not at all heroic. Perhaps it makes us think differently about the role of the Olympics. In itself it becomes a powerful endorsement for the transforming effect of a simple piece of graphic design.

Some of the issues touched on above, particularly the growing ambition for identities to influence the behaviour of customers and employees, brought language into the identity mix more prominently. Perhaps for the first time language, or tone of voice, was identified as a "basic element" of identity. As such it was seen as a way to differentiate a brand and to reach out to audiences with a message about its diversity. Orange, a UK mobile telecommunications company, was much admired in the 1990s for doing this. So the logic of visual and verbal identity supporting each other to create a more engaging, rounded identity became accepted.

Like its visual companion, verbal identity has a number of possible elements which can be used separately or in isolation. Its equivalents to logo, colours, typography and photographic or illustrative style include name(s), straplines, stories and tone of voice. The identity mix becomes richer, while allowing individual elements of it to stand out. Arguably, the line "Just do it" became an identity element for Nike that was just as important as its swoosh design mark.

As with visual identity, corporations are keen to own and control their verbal identity. McDonald's has gone to the trouble and expense of registering ownership of more than 100 phrases. It is as if to say "this is our linguistic territory, no one else can enter it". Such a legalistic approach, though, is limited and limiting, because it also means that a brand's own language does not stray far outside those narrow borders. Brands such as Guinness have discovered that by being expansive rather than restrictive, by telling stories, they can connect more emotionally with audiences (see the example in the colour plate section). This might be with customers and potential customers, particularly through advertising, or with their own employees, suppliers and partners through a range of communications, including books, videos and e-mails. In doing so, they establish a storytelling approach that is verbally and emotionally rich. Indeed, to return to the Olympics, Sebastian Coe's personal story was cited as the clinching factor behind London's successful presentation and bid.

Innocent Drinks

From Innocent's *Company Rule Book*

Always ask an expert
What's the answer? We don't know. Most of the time we don't even know the question. But there's always someone we can turn to. And that's you, dear reader. We couldn't have done it without you ...

In the summer of '98, we bought £500 worth of fruit, turned it into smoothies and sold them from a stall at a little music festival in London. We put up a big sign saying "Do you think we should give up our jobs to make these smoothies?" and put out a bin saying "YES" and a bin saying "NO". At the end of the weekend the "YES" bin was full so we went in the next day and resigned.

It is this desire for emotional connection that is encouraging brands to be more creative and adventurous with the words they use to express their personalities. Increasingly, humour can be employed as a deliberate strategy rather than a one-off campaign tactic. Brands like Innocent Drinks in the UK and Tazo in the United States take risks with humour and language that would have been unimaginable to serious marketers a few years ago. The logo cops would be making wholesale arrests. But if your brand name is Innocent, which expresses an innocent personality and approach to life, then that personality should be expressed consistently through an innocent visual and verbal identity.

Conclusion

So what next? What are the conclusions that can be made about visual and verbal identity and their relationship to brands in the future?

There are a few easy pointers:

- There will be a continued greater emphasis on using visual identity systems to deliver truly differentiated content rather than just existence for its own sake.
- The growth of luxury brands will eventually influence how non-luxury brands portray themselves. This will result in a general upgrading of the presentation of all services, even at the discount ends of markets.
- Sensitivity to using environmentally friendly building materials and less energy will result in retail innovation among the large global retail brands. This will have a positive knock-on effect and will revive good architectural design on high streets as the best way to differentiate in the absence of flashy lighting schemes and extruded plastic fascias.
- America will rebrand itself in the process of changing from one president to another. The new look, new sound America will encourage the removal of old-style corporate branding and replace it with less showy work. Bragging graphics will be exchanged for

a plainer, more responsible look. But of course this will not last for ever, as change is inevitable.

◼ Verbal identity will become a more important tool for brand expression as brands realise that their stories are a rich, differentiating and motivating resource, containing the truth of a company's identity.

◼ Management of an existing visual identity will become a real concern. Brand owners will increasingly look for better integration between the languages of identity and advertising.

◼ Naming will undergo a regenerative period following years of cynical jibes from the media. Names will be sensible or extreme, but "manufactured" Latinate names (such as Consignia) have had their heyday.

◼ Photography and illustration will also go through a period of rethinking. The past ten years have been dominated by a noticeable style to show "real people in real situations", but this will reach saturation point. Even the image banks will start to baulk at the trend. Illustration with all its magical self-gratifying and artistic qualities will resume its place in the identity palette.

◼ Controlling identities will reappear, not in the same way as in the 1970s and 1980s but in a practical, no-nonsense way. They will be implemented using simple automating technology so that the mechanics are swept out of the way of people's daily lives.

◼ The economies of Asia, Russia, China and Africa will leapfrog the branding learning curve. The result will challenge the most staid patterns of our established markets, raising issues of intellectual property, trademark protection and ethics between the developing and developed worlds.

◼ There will be a renewed emphasis on honesty, practicality and cost of implementation. But alongside this, perhaps, will be the realisation that brands and branding have not had the best deal recently and now it is time to fly a flag for originality and freshness.

Visual identity and verbal identity are part and parcel of brands and branding. They exist and will make a statement even if brand owners choose to ignore them. When not controlled they can do damage, so it is better to lock them firmly into the brand management of a business.

An identity should be reviewed frequently and maintained like any other asset. Unlike pure science, identity is a triumph of opinion backed up by assertion. Its subjectivity is the very property that allows you to be bold and get away with it. The world's greatest identities are irrational, just like brands. Create them in this way and you will not go far wrong. Indeed, you might find the whole world casting admiring glances at you and hanging on your every word.

Recommended reading

If you would like to read further around the subject of this chapter, you may find the following books interesting and useful.

Fletcher, A., *The Art of Looking Sideways*, Phaidon Press, 2001.

Haig, M., *Brand Failures*, Kogan Page, 2003.

Heller, S., *Paul Rand*, Phaidon Press, 1999.

McKenzie, G., *Orbiting the Giant Hairball*, Penguin Putnam, 1998.

Ogilvy, D., *Ogilvy on Advertising*, Orbis, 1983.

Olins, W., *Corporate Identity*, Thames & Hudson, 1989.

Olins, W., *Wally Olins on Brand*, Thames & Hudson, 2003.

Pentagram, *Ideas on Design*, Faber and Faber, 1986.

Simmons, J., *The Invisible Grail: How Brands Can Use Words to Engage with Audiences*, Cyan, 2006.

Simmons, J., *We, Me, Them & It: How to Write Powerfully for Business*, Cyan, 2006.

Vincent, L., *Legendary Brands: Unleashing the Power of Storytelling to Create a Winning Market Strategy*, Dearborn, 2002.

Whyte, D., *Crossing the Unknown Sea: Work and the Shaping of Identity*, Penguin Books, 2002.

BMW has one of the world's most immaculate and consistently powerful visual identities which is a benchmark not just for automotive companies.

Ben Cohen and Jerry Green created a living identity for their ice-cream brand by apparently not trying. Names of flavours were sensical and non-sensical at the same time.

Who could possibly miss the lead guitarist of the *Grateful Dead* as the inspiration for Ben & Jerry's cherry concoction?

Woody Jackson cows are an integral part of Ben & Jerry's visual identity – you can buy t-shirts of the cows as an indirect tribute to the ice-cream makers themselves.

Branding irons started the brand ball rolling. There are 260,000 registered variations of simple shapes like these in Texas today.

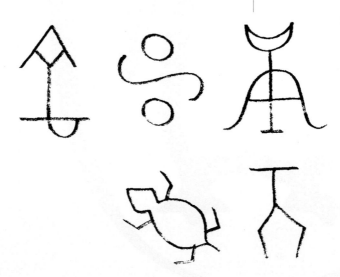

See the symbol, read the name:
Penguin Books.

3, Shell and Red Cross.

The Penguin logo is a registered trademark of Penguin Books Limited

Shell trade mark reproduced with the permission of Shell International Petroleum Company Limited

Some brands are associated with colours.

Artist Haddon Sundblom created the universally recognised image of Santa Claus for Coca-Cola's advertising in 1931, dressed for the first time in red to match the company's corporate colours.

UPS and BP both retained strong colour associations when they rebranded.

You can't think of Kodak without visualising yellow and red.

IBM®

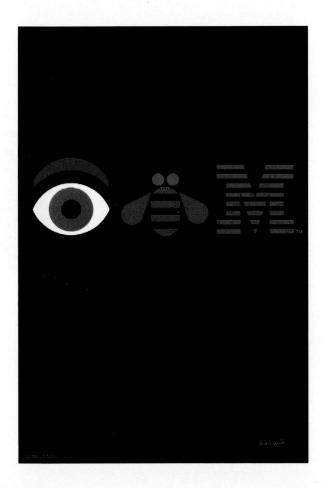

The Bovis Hummingbird,
a beautiful escape from the
predictability of company
logos in the 1970s.

The 3i logo inspired
countless tributes during
the 1980s and was restyled
in 2003. 3i calendar cartoon
by Charles Barsotti.

Lumino, also in the 1980s,
shows new possibilities
with the illustration style
made famous by 3i.

LUMINO

" YOU DAMN STUPID DUCK, EVERY
MORNING IT'S A BRAND-NEW
WORLD FOR YOU, ISN'T IT?"

London fashion shop Jones
followed suit.

London's Natural History
Museum logo (1989) rounds off
a great ten-year era in soft,
communicative identity styles.

Around 60% of BA's customers live outside the UK. An important aspect of the controversial 1997 identity was to project the airline's global reach through tailfins decorated with artists' work from around the world. But departing from the convention of using a national flag met with disapproval from the country's former prime minister, Margaret Thatcher, who is seen here trying to cover up the new design with her handkerchief.

Thou shalt not commit adultery.
You said it big guy. That's one guideline we follow religiously; our smoothies are 100% pure fruit. We call them innocent because we refuse to adulterate them in anyway.

Wherever you see the dude ☺ you have got our cross-your-heart-hope-to-die promise that the drink will be completely pure, natural and delicious. If it isn't, you can ring us on the banana phone and make us beg for forgiveness.

Amen.

Why not say hello?
Drop a line or pop around to Fruit Towers, 6 The Buspace, Conlan Street, London W10 5AP

Call the banana phone on **020 8969 7080** or visit our online gym at **www.beinnocent.co.uk**

® = Religious-experience

The story starts with

The Founder's Tale

We don't need to sanctify the memory of our founder

but no one ever recorded the swear words Arthur Guinness

flung across the barricades at the gentlemen

from the Dublin Corporation in 1775

But fling them he did

The temptation is to describe Arthur Guinness as a stout gentleman. Well, we make no point about his girth but we do know that Arthur Guinness took his time before he came around to brewing porter. When he finally did it, it was worth waiting for.

But it was water that did it. The whole history of Guinness is built on water.

Think of that the next time you sink a pint. If Arthur hadn't made his first stand against the bureaucrats and stood up for his commercial rights we wouldn't be here now thinking of new ways to fight the Guinness cause.

I did a deal **dammit** so let's stick to it!

Arthur Guinness stuck to it. It took him twelve years to win his fight for the Dublin water rights, but he won. And that was the first crucial turning point in the story of Guinness.

It takes strength to do it. Not necessarily the girder-lifting strength of a strongman, but the commitment that comes with an inner certainty.

Think about it

Savour it

And lift your glass to Arthur

We owe it to him

The visual identities of early 21st-century
digital businesses sprang out of
no barriers, globally accessible,
spontaneous, individual participation
on the internet.

Facebook is a registered trademark of Facebook, Inc.

Google celebrates its everyday appeal by changing its
own logo to mark famous anniversaries and
contemporary events.

Google™

Leonardo da Vinci's birthday

Louis Braille's birthday

50th anniversary of understanding of DNA

Through its inspiring step change from traditional Games logos, London's 2012 logo shows how powerful a simple graphic can be in communicating the broad and exciting vision of the 2012 Olympic and Paralympic Games.

9 Brand communications

Paul Feldwick

Everything a brand does is communication. As Paul Watzlawick, a communications theorist, wrote: "It is impossible not to communicate."[1] The way the packs are designed, the way words are used, the way phones are answered (or not), the products the name is put to, the shops in which these are sold, the experience of interacting with a brand on the internet: these are all aspects of brand communication and are more or less under the control of the brand managers. But we should remember that people also receive other signals about a brand which are not directly under the control of its marketers. These include the contexts in which the brand is encountered in daily life, who is seen to use it and where, and what others say or write about it, whether in the pub or an internet chatroom. All these things together help form the network of mental and emotional associations which any individual has with a brand, and so influence the relationship between the individual and the brand.

It is the strength of these associations, and the nature of this relationship, which can lead to stability and profitability for a brand and hence increase its value. How a brand communicates is therefore of central importance in its long-term business success. And communication here means more than simple one-way transmission of explicit messages. Much of the communication that matters is implicit and often unconscious; much of it, too, is only indirectly influenced by marketers, if at all. A mechanistic message transmission model will therefore be inadequate in planning successful brand communications.

Chapter 8 deals with the important areas of verbal and visual identity. But as well as managing the brand's design and language in a general sense, brand managers communicate with the brand's various stakeholders through many specific channels. These include direct mail, PR, telemarketing, the internet, events, sponsorship and – by no means least, despite the complex changes in the media landscape – the established advertising media of TV, print, cinema and radio.

From their beginnings as mass phenomena in the 19th century, brands and advertising (in the broadest sense of that word) have evolved together. Early mass-market brands, from Pear's Soap to Kodak to Coca-Cola, built their business on heavy advertising investments (by 1912 Coca-Cola was spending over $1m a year on advertising). Right up to the present day, it is exceptional to find a large or successful brand that does not continue to invest heavily in communications.

Traditionally, brand communications have been segregated into categories known as "above the line" and "below the line", terms originally connected with agency accounting procedures. The media paid commission for activities above the line but not for those below the line (an advertising agency's clients did not pay directly for its services; the agency made its money as sales agent for the media). Press, TV, outdoor, radio and cinema were above the line; direct mail, PR, sales promotions of various sorts, events and sponsorships were generally below.

Originally, advertising agencies would offer all these services and could subsidise the below-the-line activities with the commissions from the others. Over time, below-the-line activities became more specialised and separate agencies grew up to deal with them, and as advertisers negotiated to have commissions rebated or to switch to fee payment, the economics of the old-style full service became unsustainable. Today a wide range of communications agencies offer specialised services, so that a brand's communications are normally fragmented among a number of different suppliers. The expressions above and below the line linger on, but there is now much talk about the importance of "integrated marketing", or "through the line", which is about how best to manage together the fragmented pattern of activities in the better interests of the client.

The past decade has seen various predictions of the "death of advertising", meaning the classic above-the-line media. This is unlikely to happen. While acknowledging some of the major changes taking place in the media/marketing landscape, we should also be careful to keep track of what remains consistent.

Technology, media supply and marketing technology have undergone substantial changes and are continually evolving. Some well-known examples are as follows:

- It is no longer possible, in general, to obtain the huge, monolithic mass-market audiences that UK or American network television delivered until the 1970s.
- Entertainment and information are increasingly accessed not only through broadcast media or high-street shops, but also via downloads to computers and mobile phones.
- Advances in technology have led to systems for collecting

and using data about individual consumers which a previous generation of marketers could hardly have dreamt of, giving a new impetus to direct marketing, both online and offline.

◪ Increasingly large proportions of populations throughout the world now have access to the internet, many of them via broadband. (In late 2008, according to www.internetworldstats.com, 73% of North Americans and 48% of Europeans had access to the internet.) This has transformed many people's daily activities, such as buying or selling, booking travel, finding or sharing information, socialising, accessing entertainment. It has also created massive opportunities for new forms of advertising. Online advertising is growing rapidly and accounts for a significant share of total advertising expenditure. Online strategies and tactics for advertising are evolving as fast as the medium is growing, and it is too early to predict which will prove to be most effective in the long term. At present the fastest growing area, which also has the largest share of the category, is search marketing – the ability to target messages to individuals searching for specific words.

There is no reason, however, to assume that the growth of the internet and of internet advertising is creating a decline in television viewing or the effectiveness of TV advertising. The evidence so far suggests that the two media not only address significantly different needs, but also increasingly complement and support each other:

◪ Television is still one of the world's fastest-growing media. The worldwide number of TV homes has trebled in the past 20 years (more than a quarter are now in China).
◪ In established marketplaces such as the UK, people in all demographic groups are watching more hours of television, and more of this is commercial television. Total numbers of commercial impacts delivered through TV have grown every year since 2002.
◪ Although technology has increasingly made it possible for viewers to avoid commercials, research shows that few use it for this purpose.
◪ Large-screen and high-definition (HD) TVs have enhanced the watching experience, and programming content from *The Sopranos* to *Big Brother* shows how producers can still seize the public imagination in a big way.

◪ Analysis of successful campaigns by Binet and Field (see "Measuring the value of advertising" below) shows that TV continues to be the backbone of most effective campaigns.

Measuring the value of advertising

In a provocative but evidence-based analysis of IPA Effectiveness Award winning papers, two British researchers, Les Binet and Peter Field, have argued that most marketers pay too much attention to intermediate attitudinal measures, and too little to behavioural and business outcomes.

They also concluded, among other things, that:

◪ when marketers do focus on business measures, they focus on the wrong ones – sales rather than market share, and volume rather than value;
◪ the need for accountability often makes marketers focus on rational product messages. In fact, emotional campaigns are more powerful, even in "rational" categories;
◪ marketers often focus on absolute levels of spend or ad to sales ratio when setting budgets. In fact, share of voice is a better KPI [key performance indicator].
◪ there is little evidence that TV is becoming less effective. In fact, TV effectiveness may be increasing.

Source: Binet, L. and Field, P., *Marketing in the Era of Accountability*,
World Advertising Research Center, 2007

It may be a mistake to see different channels such as TV and the internet as being in competition with each other. From the consumer's point of view they are more likely to be complementary and even symbiotic. For example, the internet offers the ability to watch *Big Brother* live 24 hours a day; or a site like BitTorrent allows you to download an episode of *Neighbours* a month before it appears on local TV; or you can just browse through classic commercials of the 1970s on YouTube.

Similar points could be made about print media. While the economics and business models of online versus offline continue to evolve, from the consumer's point of view the two play valuable roles, and when managed together support each other. So-called "new media" do not, on the whole, put existing media out of business. People text each other on their mobile phones and throw sheep at each other on Facebook, but they also continue to read newspapers, browse through glossy magazines at the dentist, and stand on station platforms staring at cross-track posters. The smart way to deal with the new complexity of media channels is not to be fixated by novelty or resistant to it, but to recognise that people are using a wider variety of media in more complex ways. This means more opportunities for campaigns that can work across different media in ways which link them together (see "The story of O2" below).

However the media landscape changes, the principles of how communications build brand relationships are unlikely to change.

The story of O_2

O_2 is an example of how integrated brand communications can build brand value. In 2001 BT Cellnet was a struggling brand in the UK mobile phone service category. When it was demerged from BT and relaunched as O_2, most analysts had little hope for its success.

Right from the start O_2 had a clear brand vision reflected in consistent brand communications. The visual identity is a deep blue enlivened by oxygen bubbles. The feeling evoked by TV commercials, with the help of ambient music, is of relaxation and peace, a contrast to the usual association of mobile phones with hectic activity. Promotional activity has consistently put the customer first and levels of personal service have been high. Promotional messages have been communicated through consistent use of the visual identity, using a whole range of media including interactive use of phone texting.

By 2005, against initial expectations, O_2 had built the biggest user base in the UK and scored most highly on a range of key brand affiliation measures. The business was bought that year by Telefonica for £18 billion, four times the share price at the date the brand was launched. As demonstrated in two effectiveness-award-winning cases, this increase in shareholder value can be in large part attributed to the consistent and integrated brand communications.

Since then O_2 has sponsored the former Millennium Dome in London's docklands, now rated the world's best venue for popular music[2] – a bold move which has further increased O_2's stature, linked the brand to the important territory of music and created a total brand experience for visitors to the venue. The brand is also moving into new markets, such as broadband. The brand vision and identity, however, still remain consistent and fully integrated across all channels.

Source: IPA Effectiveness Awards, 2004, 2006

How do communications build brands?

Certain types of brand communication give information or are aimed at leading directly to a transaction: brochures, coupons, mailshots, direct-response ads and most websites. But a great deal of brand communication neither offers information nor directly involves a transaction. When a company sponsors a Rolling Stones tour, or puts out a TV commercial for a chocolate brand which shows nothing but a man in a gorilla suit playing the drums, how do such promotional strategies influence behaviour and create value? Some marketers may believe that any communication not directly involved in selling must be an indulgence, but history shows that, with few exceptions, strong brands are not built on this kind of thinking.

Communications with an immediate selling aim may appear more productive. Being linked to sales, their direct results may be more easily measurable, but in terms of the long-term health of the brand it may be others that create more competitive advantage. Brand strength is about more than volume sales. It is about the ability of a brand to resist competition, to support a premium price, to weather negative publicity and thus to offer shareholders a more reliable promise of future cash flows. Brand owners should ensure that their communications not only stimulate sales, but also enhance the underlying value of the brand.

How brand communications influence behaviour

What do we know about the effects of advertising on short-term buying behaviour and on long-term business results?

Stimulating short-term behaviour

Single-source panels are research sources that record both individual buying behaviour and individual exposure to specific advertisements. Analyses of single-source panel data have shown that in about 45–50% of cases, exposure to even one advertisement in a short period before buying measurably increases the probability of buying the advertised brand, sometimes by a considerable degree. Thus advertising gives a real short-term nudge towards increased choice of the brand. Interestingly, one such analysis shows that the most effective communications are not only biased towards information, but also seek to play on emotions and to entertain.[3]

Longer-term effects on brand behaviour

There is some evidence that the probability of choosing a brand is increased if, first, the same brand has been chosen before (habit), and if, second, it is seen to be chosen by other people (conformity). If, as single-source panels show, exposure to an advertisement can also increase the probability of the brand being bought, this single "nudge" repeated over time should increase patterns of both habitual purchase and social endorsement, thus having a cumulative knock-on effect that builds into a more established behaviour. Memories of and repeated exposure to the advertising will also provide continuing cues to reinforce and reward the purchase behaviour that has taken place, further strengthening the pattern of brand choice.

It is in this longer-term behaviour that advertising usually becomes economic. In the short term – say within a year – advertising for all but the largest brands seldom pays for itself in short-term increases in profit. Over the longer term, however, it can frequently be shown that a brand without advertising will find its volumes and margins eroded by competitive pressure from advertised brands, or cheaper brands, or both. As a result, though cutting advertising within one year may often improve immediate profitability, advertising over time can be shown to build future cash flows and therefore shareholder value.[4]

How brand communications create mental models

The above explanation is deliberately behaviourist, treating advertising as a stimulus and buying behaviour as the response. In creating and judging advertisements, however, it is hard to avoid making certain assumptions about the intervening mental processes that link stimulus and response. Although this area is more problematic, there is now considerable evidence that some of the most common assumptions made by advertisers are likely to be wrong.

Any attempt to explain mental processes inevitably oversimplifies, but three common strands of thinking can be used to explain the process by which communications about brands have an influence on people's behaviour. These are loosely based on a 1990 study by Mike Hall and Doug Maclay, two British researchers.

1 By communicating information

Claude Hopkins, an early and influential theorist, claimed that this was what really mattered. "Give people facts ... the more you tell, the more you sell," he thundered in 1922. In Hopkins's view, humour, unusual visuals, even white space, were all wasteful or counterproductive.

Within the limits of his own experience, Hopkins was more right than wrong. His experience was writing what were then called "mail order" ads, those with a coupon for the reader to make a purchase, or at least send for more information. By careful measurement of responses, Hopkins and his contemporaries learnt from experience exactly what worked most efficiently.

Hopkins's rules are still good ones for most direct-response advertising, and for any situation when, in Hopkins's words, you want to "hail a few people only" and give them information that will be of interest to them. However, not all brand communications work this way. Hopkins wrote:

> The sole purpose of advertising is to sell ... it is not to keep your name before the public. It is not to help your other salesmen.

But why not? Much advertising, perhaps most, does precisely these things. To say that the purpose of advertising is to sell is as helpful as saying that the purpose of a football team is to score goals. In one sense, this is absolutely correct, but it is misleading in so far as actual shots at the goal form a tiny part of what footballers actually do on the pitch (and indeed, off it) which is necessary to make those goals possible. In the words of Stephen King, the founder of account planning at the J Walter Thompson agency in the 1960s, the most important role of advertising is not to sell, but to create "sale-ability".[5] This begins to explain why much effective advertising not only contains no factual information, but also can break any or all of Hopkins's other rules.

2 By creating awareness, fame, familiarity or "salience"
This cluster of ideas is based on the fact that we have a general tendency, other things being equal, to choose things that we are more familiar with, or recognise or think of first.

We know this works at the individual level, from both advertising examples and psychological experiments. There is a social dimension to it as well. If a brand is famous, people generally assume it is popular and has the endorsement of others. DDB's Brand Capital survey has shown the power of this "contagious demand", in that brands with more "friends" almost invariably have a higher proportion of those friends as "lovers"; in other words, they have a stronger average attachment to the brand. In view of these findings it is important to think of brand communications not just as one-to-one messages from the brand to an individual, but also as public rituals creating shared meanings. Not only do I see an advertisement, but I know everyone else sees it too, and in many cases I am aware of how they react to it.[6]

There is such strong evidence to support the importance of this "salience" model (in Hall and Maclay's term) that some theorists believe this is all that is necessary to explain communication effects. Andrew Ehrenberg of South Bank Business School in London argues that this is all that advertising does. The role that creativity or distinct brand properties play in the process is simply to enhance the salience effect, rather than to attach distinct meanings to brands. This may be an extreme view, but there is no doubt that the role that fame and publicity play in advertising effect, quite independently of advertising content, is often underestimated.

Evaluating brand communications

Broadly, there are two types of measurable outcomes of brand communications: effects on sales or business and consumer responses. Both are important.

It used to be thought that sales effects of advertising could never be satisfactorily separated from other factors affecting a business. However, the problem is not such a great one, as long as reliable data exist, especially with the use of modern modelling techniques.

Consumer responses include reactions to the advertising itself – recall, liking – and attitudes to the brand. Of these, brand responses are ultimately the more important.

Longer-term effects of brand communications on the strength of a brand may be seen through attitudinal questions and by the brand's marketplace performance, such as its ability to command a price premium or resist competitive pressures.

Source: Feldwick, P., *What is Brand Equity, Anyway?*, WARC Publications, 2002

3 By creating "involvement"

As well as these simple ideas, which could be called facts and fame, there is also a third strand, often recognised but more difficult to put into words. Hall and Maclay christened this "involvement". James Webb Young of J Walter Thompson, in 1960, talked of how advertising "creates a value not in the product". Ernest Dichter and other Freud-influenced advertising psychologists of the 1960s wrote about "motivation" and stressed the importance of symbol and metaphor in communication. Others have used the words "enhancement" and "transformation". If you look at any selection of successful campaigns you will probably agree that there is an

.

element of persuasive communication which is not based just on information or salience. Can we get closer to defining what this is?

This would be useful because this third strand is the one most likely to be overruled in practice. As the hardest to define and analyse, and therefore hardest to measure, it often has least force in the world of corporate decision-making. It is often subsumed under such unbusiness-like terms as emotion, intuition or artistry, resulting in frequent dialogues of the deaf between those who demand clarity and proof and those who "just know what feels right" (often, but not always, the client and the creative department respectively).

Other ideas about how brand communications influence behaviour

Some of the following ideas, which have their roots in neuroscience and communications theory, are recent, some less so, but generally they have not been applied enough to thinking about brand communications.

1 By creating associations that will influence behaviour

One idea that may help dates back about 100 years to the first serious academic study of how advertising works: *The Psychology of Advertising* by Walter Dill Scott of Northwestern University published in 1903. Scott's theory, formulated long before Hopkins's model of information transfer had achieved its hegemony, was based on the simple and long-established idea of associations. As a psychological theory this goes back to Aristotle, and it was an important concept for 18th-century philosophers such as David Hume and John Locke. It states that any idea or sense experience automatically triggers connections in the mind to other ideas and feelings, and that although these connections may not always be conscious ones, they can be powerful enough to influence our behaviour.

Scott thought that advertising works by creating the right kind of associations for the brand. This process does not have to be conscious or verbal. He writes about the effects of pictures in advertisements, criticising a picture of a frog in a coffee advertisement because coffee should not be associated with a "disgusting, slimy reptile". He also quotes examples of how advertising can influence people's attitudes to brands without them being able to consciously recall seeing the advertising itself:

> One young lady asserted that she had never looked at any of the cards in the [street]cars in which she had been riding for years. When questioned further, it appeared that she knew by heart

every advertisement appearing on the line ... and that the goods advertised won her highest esteem. She was not aware of the fact that she had been studying the advertisements, and flatly resented the suggestion that she had been influenced by them.

These ideas, which were subsequently sidelined in most advertising thinking for almost a century, are now strengthened by some recent findings in the study of the brain. Antonio Damasio in his book *Descartes' Error*[7] writes of neural connections called "engrams" and links between thoughts and feelings which he calls "somatic markers", thus founding our whole decision-making process not in reason but in our emotions and unconscious memories. Daniel Schacter in *Searching for Memory*[8] confirms Scott's observation (one that most advertising researchers have been inclined to ignore or deny):

You may think that because you pay little attention to commercials on television or newspapers, your judgements about products are unaffected by them. But a recent experiment showed that people tend to prefer products featured in ads they barely glanced at several minutes earlier – even when they had no explicit memory for having seen the ad.

We can develop this third model, then, by arguing with Scott that advertising works by creating associations that will influence behaviour. These associations may well be non-verbal and also non-conscious. We now understand from recent research (well summarised by Robert Heath in his book *The Hidden Power of Advertising*[9]) that such implicit learning, far from being weak, can be extremely powerful.

Integration

Effective brand communications can be integrated in three different ways:

- Functional integration
- Brand integration
- Thematic integration

Functional integration
Thinking about how the brand's different actions relate in real time and space to

each other and to (for instance) the purchase decision process. So to encourage employees to sign up for a health care plan, they might need to go through a process of:

- recognising their need for health care;
- being aware of a particular brand;
- requesting information;
- reading the brochure;
- making an appointment for a sales meeting;
- keeping the appointment;
- concluding the agreement.

Moreover, the general effect of the brand's mass communications on "sale-ability" is likely to have a significant effect on conversion at each step of the process (though measuring response rates to each communication separately is unlikely to show this).

This level of planning requires a good understanding of the prospect's "road to purchase", and the practical or mental barriers at each step. It should acknowledge that creating sale-ability may be as important as closing a sale.

Brand integration
Ensuring that everything the brand does in some way reflects and contributes to its unique identity as a brand: its values, its tone of voice, the kind of relationship it aspires to have with others. This is broader and deeper than a visual identity manual, although at a practical level this would also reflect the brand's identity in a tangible way.

If a brand's sense of identity is strong, this may be enough to ensure that any of its communications will be unmistakably linked to the brand. (Early Volkswagen advertisements were unlike other American car advertising – simple black and white photographs of the car in white space, when everyone else was using coloured drawings, propped with glamorous people and surroundings.) The use of visual or other brand cues – the Dulux dog, the Pillsbury doughboy, the colours of Mastercard – is another common and more tangible way of linking a brand's communications together, without necessarily going quite as far as thematic integration.

Thematic integration
Unlike the first two, thematic integration should be regarded as optional, but it nevertheless has powerful effects. This is when a specific creative idea is developed through multiple channels or multiple messages: TV, outdoor, direct mail, internet promotions. The Bud Light Institute (see page 142) is a good example of this.

Theoretically, the creative idea that links this kind of campaign together could originate in any communication channel, from sponsorship to direct mail. In reality, however, it is hard to find examples of such big ideas that did not start in TV or print. This suggests that the greater creative freedom of these channels, when they are used fully, will continue to be a crucial ingredient in effective brand communications.

2 Digital and analog communications

Communication that is non-verbal or non-conscious is very different from the conscious, verbal – and therefore transparent – sort of communication. But it is not something dreamt up by evil scientists or "hidden persuaders" in the advertising business: it is simply the way we communicate most of the time in all our lives. In everyday interactions between people, according to Albert Mehrabian, a psychologist, between 55% and 95% of communication is non-verbal. We respond to gestures, tone of voice, physical appearance, clothes and context rather more than to what may be being said, and most of the time we do this without being consciously aware of it. Brands are no different.

We also interpret this non-verbal communication in a different way. Watzlawick makes an important distinction between what he called "digital" and "analog" communications (writing in the 1960s, he used an analogy between different types of computers; today we should not confuse this sense with talk of "digital media"). Other terms for the same idea are "denotative/connotative", or even "explicit/implicit". Digital communication aims to be precise; a word or symbol stands for one, unambiguous idea, almost as in a code. In analog communication, meanings are not fixed; they may vary from one recipient to the next, or in context, or simply show a multiplicity of possible interpretations. (John Hartley Williams, a poet, has written about "one dimensional and three dimensional language", the latter including poetry.)

In business we are often conditioned to believe that digital (precision) is good and that analog (ambiguity or vagueness) is bad. Yet all non-verbal communication, according to Watzlawick, is essentially analogic. This explains both the powerful effect that images, gestures or music can have and the unease that they can create in a business environment.

What is more, the function of analog communication is often different. For Watzlawick, every act of communication is about two things: the actual content and the relationship between the parties communicating.

If we stop to think about much of our everyday conversation, for instance (to say nothing of body language), small talk about weather, sports or fashion has more to do with our relationships with each other than with its ostensible content.

This applies to brand communications too. If an advertisement, event or mailshot is entertaining, shocking or informative, these effects, quite independent of content, modify the relationship between the brand and the viewer. Looked at through this lens, many ads that seem pointless when considered in terms of content take on a whole new level of meaning, one which the audience has no difficulty intuitively responding to.

Watzlawick makes a further point of great relevance: it is impossible to translate analog communication into digital. We need only to discuss any successful advertisement with a group of people to see this in action. Ask a simple question such as "What makes this advertisement work?" and you will get a multiplicity of answers. Many will contain some truthful element, but none will be the truth. Yet marketers continually struggle to translate the visual or audiovisual language of advertisements and brands into a digital, verbal language of analysis. We look at Budweiser's well-known TV commercial "Whassup" and say it's about "camaraderie"; we look at the Michelin baby and say it's about "trust". Those formulations may, or may not, say something useful. But in the process we have lost everything that made those campaigns successful.

This is why Scott was not necessarily right when he complained about the "disgusting slimy frog" in a coffee ad. That was only one possible reading of the image. It might equally have been seen as, for instance, playful, friendly, natural, organic, lively, jumping or fresh. Yet these too are just words, none of which fully does justice to the image. Images like this are powerful precisely because they are volatile and multifaceted, so their interpretation in decision-making is never simple. Many people might have wondered why chimpanzees were an appropriate vehicle to promote tea, as in the UK PG Tips campaign that ran for 35 years, or why frogs and lizards were an effective way to sell Budweiser in the United States. One answer in both these cases is that because the creatures were strongly anthropomorphised, their human characteristics predominated over what might have been negative animal associations. But such rational analysis has its limitations when talking about successful brand communications.

Businesses that aspire to "rational", accountable decision-making will always be uncomfortable with the analog side of brand communications.[10] But it would be a mistake to think that brands can do without this high-octane fuel, and equally wrong to think that the same results can be obtained by acknowledging only those aspects of communication that can be safely digitised and analysed. This does not mean we are powerless to make good decisions about creative work. We are all capable of making intuitive judgments as long as we are allowed to, and as long as we develop our intuition rather than suppress it. We also have a useful, if not infallible, guide in the voices of the target audience, as long as we know what kind of questions to ask them and how to make sense of their responses.

But if we acknowledge this level of communication is important in advertising, it also explains why much that is important defies simple analysis. Bill Bernbach, voted the most influential ad person of the 20th century by *Ad Age*, once said:

> *Logic and overanalysis can immobilise and sterilise an idea. It's like love – the more you analyse it, the more it disappears.*

He also said:

> *Is creativity some obscure, esoteric art form? Not on your life. It's the most practical thing a businessman can employ.*

Referring to a famous and successful mail-order advertisement for a correspondence course that ran for years from the 1920s onwards under the headline "They laughed when I sat down at the piano ...", Bernbach remarked:

> *What if this ad had been written in different language? Would it have been as effective? What if it had said, "They admired my piano playing", which also plays to the instinct of being admired? Would that have been enough? Or was it the talented, imaginative expression of the thought that did the job? That wonderful feeling of revenge.*
>
> *Suppose Winston Churchill had said "We owe a lot to the RAF" instead of "Never was so much owed by so many to so few". Do you think the impact would have been the same?*

The Bud Light Institute

To promote Bud Light beer in Canada, Anheuser-Busch's agency DDB invented the (fictitious) Bud Light Institute. Its purpose is to help men spend more time with their male friends, preferably drinking Bud Light, by creating elaborate strategies to help them escape from their wives or girlfriends.

TV commercials launched the institute by showing how, for instance, they could provide a horde of Vikings to break up a family barbecue, or create the first 48-hour romantic movie that would keep women occupied for an entire weekend. Another commercial was a spoof ad for a compilation of romantic songs with titles such as "I love you because you let me go out with my friends on a weekly basis". (The interest in this was so great that real CD called *Ulterior Emotions* was made available through the Bud Light Institute website, and at one point this became the second best selling CD in Canada.)

Bud Light also covered a new office building in Vancouver with a huge hoarding announcing that this was to be the headquarters of the Bud Light Institute. It advertised for a director, held interviews and eventually announced the "appointment" of a real applicant.

In these and other ways the idea originally created for TV was developed into an elaborate joke through many different channels and devices. (As jokes are by their nature analogic, this digital summary totally fails to reflect the fact that the campaign is also very funny.)

The content of this campaign says nothing about the product, and indeed beer is featured only peripherally or not at all. The campaign works by a witty sharing of men's feelings about women, creating a sense of complicity and a friendly relationship with the brand.

Although one-to-one communications (website, promotions, direct mail) work well as part of this campaign, its overall effect depends entirely on the public, shared nature of the joke.

Conclusion

Brand communications may do three things for a brand:

- provide information about the brand;
- make a brand famous and familiar;
- create distinctive patterns of associations and meanings which make the brand more attractive and saleable.

These associations and meanings may be non-verbal and non-conscious. The communication will be analog as well as digital and its purpose is about creating a relationship with the brand as well as about its actual content.

This may sound theoretical, but it is simply trying to find words to bring into consciousness things that we all experience every day in all types of communication. These ideas may not be ones we could ever objectively call right or wrong, but they may be more useful in conceptualising the ways in which communications build brands. Certainly, these ideas help make sense of many aspects of successful advertising which are poorly explained by the models of information/persuasion or simple saliency. They also have big implications in practice:

- The return on communications budgets should not be measured only in the short term or in sales responses that can be directly linked to specific activities. For many brands, investment in communications, at a level comparable with that of competitors, should be regarded as a continuing cost of doing business and ensuring the future cash flows of the brand.
- Not all effective brand communications can be intellectualised in terms of content. Rational decision-making processes may destroy the analog communications that could become a major source of added value. Organisations need to find better strategies for handling these kinds of decisions.
- Research techniques for evaluating advertising or other communications, whether before or after exposure, can easily become biased towards things that are easy to measure, such as verbal understanding of information or conscious memory. These do not necessarily reflect the effectiveness of communications.
- Advertisers should never lose sight of the business goals of their brand communications and should concentrate research resources on linking these to creative executions.
- There is no reason to suppose that the basic frameworks of brand communication change whenever patterns of media consumption or media technologies change. The initial response to the internet as an advertising medium was to use its power to make ads literally "pop up" between the user and the page they wanted to look at. If advertising is imagined as a war for attention, such tactics seem to make sense. In any relationship, however, it is better to understand that interrupting someone unless you

have an extremely good excuse for doing so is not likely to make them feel warmer towards you, or to associate you with a good feeling. Similarly, the fact that it is now easy to wrap buses and buildings in enormous brand liveries does not improve the brand relationship if this is experienced as invasive or crass. Different individuals will of course respond differently, but if your brand is seen as violating either private or public space, it should not be surprising if people are less positive towards it. This is not just a question of social or political restrictions on advertising's licence to operate, though it is interesting that in 2007 the city of São Paulo voted to ban all outdoor advertising. It should be obvious in any case that irritating people or defacing their environment does not enhance the associations they make with a brand or the relationship they have with it.

Lastly, there are two caveats:

◪ To be clear, this chapter does not mean to argue that "analog" communication is good and "digital" is bad. Human beings communicate in both ways. Sometimes precise information is the most persuasive thing to offer, and offering information in itself creates a certain kind of relationship. With the current decline of the "long copy" ad, there are undoubtedly many missed opportunities in such categories as IT and finance for brands to differentiate themselves positively by having an intelligent dialogue with their customers, rather than paying for yet another full page in a broadsheet newspaper containing a picture of a flower and a portentous phrase like "inventing the future".

◪ Effective communication frequently defies simple analysis, but this does not mean that the process of planning brand communications should be without any discipline. Important questions should always be asked, such as what is the objective of the communication, who are the target audience, what action does the communication seek to influence? And they should always be answered on the basis of the best and most sensitive understanding of the people you are seeking to communicate with. Consumer understanding and insight are essential starting points, but effective communication at some point needs to take a leap into the realm of intuition and artistry.

To quote Bill Bernbach again:

There are two attitudes you can wear: that of cold arithmetic or that of warm human persuasion. I will urge the latter on you. For there is evidence that in the field of communications the more intellectual you grow, the more you lose the great intuitive skills that make for the greatest persuasion – the things that really touch and move people.

Notes and references

1 Watzlawick, P., *Pragmatics of Human Communication*, W.W. Norton, 1967.
2 "The O₂ arena has been voted both best new concert venue and best international arena of the year at the 2008 Pollstar Concert Industry Awards." *Music Week*, February 11th 2008.
3 Jones, J.P., *When Ads Work*, Lexington Books, 1995.
4 Doyle, P., *Value Based Marketing*, John Wiley & Sons, 2000.
5 Lannon, J. and Baskin, M., *A Master Class in Brand Planning: The Timeless Works of Stephen King*, John Wiley & Sons, 2007.
6 Crimmins, J. and Anschuetz, N., "Contagious Demand", Market Research Society Conference, 2003.
7 Damasio, A., *Descartes' Error: Emotion, Reason, and the Human Brain*, Putnam, 1944.
8 Schacter, D., *Searching for Memory: The Brain, The Mind, and The Past*, Basic Books, 1997.
9 Heath, R., *The Hidden Power of Advertising*, WARC, 2002.
10 Heath, R. and Feldwick, P., "Fifty Years Using the Wrong Model of Advertising", *International Journal of Market Research*, Vol. 50, No.1, January 2008.

10 The public relations perspective on branding

Deborah Bowker

Brand equity is built upon a carefully managed balance of performance and perception. Perceptions, accurate or not, are often the basis of decision-making whether the decision is that of a customer choosing a product or service, an employee remaining with a company, or a shareowner continuing to invest. The power to shape the perceptions of an organisation is contingent on leadership credibility, which only too quickly disappears when corporate executives are seen to be behaving in ways that undermine trust in their ethics or operations. Public relations is increasingly about closing the "communication gap" among leadership actions, brand promise, operational and financial performance and the perceptions of key influencers and stakeholders. These influencers and stakeholders include media, industry and financial analysts, policymakers, customers, shareholders, and employees.

Enhancing the awareness, understanding and commitment to a brand through a PR/communications strategy is an essential part of any overall strategy aimed at sustaining and raising brand value. Public relations is an important element in supporting the power and value of an organisation's brand for all stakeholders. All the elements of a corporate brand, from tone and personality, functional and emotional benefits to core message and essential reputation – if fully leveraged with internal and external audiences – can help raise performance and credibility.

Putting the brand in context

A brand is far more than a visual symbol and memorable tag line; it anchors the mission and vision, operating principles and tactics of an organisation. Internally, the brand is central to all decisions, actions and values, enabling employees to deliver the brand promise. The internal and external messages about the brand must tell a consistent story and be seen as part of the same narrative, and they should relate to the following:

- Values – the organisation's core beliefs; what it and the brand stand for.
- Behaviours – how the organisation interacts with internal and external stakeholders.
- Positioning – what the organisation wants stakeholders to think about a brand.
- Identity – names, logos, visual standards, verbal themes.

A brand's value can be judged by an organisation's performance and that depends on interconnections. Recognising and reinforcing a brand's interconnections with an organisation's culture and performance through a communications campaign focused on employee alignment with business results and reputation can have powerful effects.

Brand identity must be built from within, across geographies, levels and functions. The notion of a winning culture is reinforced over time through recruitment, training, structure, reward and recognition aligned with the brand dimensions of values, employee behaviours, external positioning and symbols.

Brand-based values rather than empty slogans help people to "walk the talk", and defined behaviours, relevant to individual employees' day-to-day life, bring these brand-based values to life. Creating a community of employees who share an understanding of these values and behaviours brings vibrancy and momentum to an organisation and helps focus people on the need for consistently high standards of performance. This is the source of customer satisfaction and corporate reputation.

The linkage with performance and reputation

High-performance organisations share certain characteristics at every location and level:

- Focus – a few key measures of success are clearly understood.
- Unity of purpose – a "one company" mentality with everyone pulling together.
- Energy – a sense of urgency in fulfilling customer expectations.
- Agility – an ability to adapt to a changing business environment.
- Learning –a desire to share knowledge and the organisational infrastructure to enable knowledge to be shared.
- Identity – an individual and collective identification with an organisation's mission, values, business strategy, competitive advantage and brand promise.

If all the above characteristics are fostered, high standards of perform-ance can be sustained even in the face of fierce competition or times of crisis.

High-reputation organisations share certain robust drivers of repu-tation. For example, companies on *Fortune*'s most admired companies list are rated by surveying perceptions of their reputation drivers among industry analysts, directors and managers. These include:

- quality of management;
- quality of products and services;
- capacity to innovate;
- value as a long-term investment;
- soundness of financial position;
- wise use of corporate assets;
- ability to attract, develop and keep talented people;
- community, social and environmental responsibility.

These drivers are given different weight and priority in different indus-tries. But it is fair to say that they are perceived as strong or weak in a particular corporation based not only on actual financial performance, but also on perceptions of leadership reputation and credibility, and commitment to human assets and community relationships. A brand that is consistently perceived as representing high standards of quality and integrity is a strong and valuable brand.

Brand-owning organisations that are highly regarded share certain things:

- Leadership – a recognition that the brand is personified by the CEO and the whole senior management team in their accountability to multiple stakeholders.
- Transparency – an acceptance that stakeholders must understand the decisions driving risk and reward.
- Pride – an appreciation that individual employee pride leads to collective quality.
- Innovation – evidence that sharing of ideas and the responsibility for taking risks is encouraged and rewarded.
- Long-term view – a focus on what is right in the longer term rather than what is expedient in the short term.
- Citizenship – an organisational commitment to acting as a good citizen.

◪ Talent – a recognition that talent must be valued and nurtured.

A brand can embody all of the above if there is a conscious choice to broaden its meaning beyond product benefits or quarterly earnings in order to connect with stakeholders in a holistic way. Espousing a more holistic leadership model in the wake of global financial downturn and depressed consumer confidence, Carly Fiorina, former CEO of Hewlett-Packard, in an October 2008 address to the Detroit Economic Club, urged businesses to take a balanced approach to customers, communities, employees and shareholders and institute measurable accountability to each stakeholder group.

Public relations can help underscore a multifaceted, brand-enhancing strategy and this is critically important in today's harsh PR environment. A consensus among top brand and PR practitioners from such diverse organisations as The Coca-Cola Company, VISA, the US Postal Service and Intel confirms that they are operating in a business environment with:

◪ exploding choice and accessibility of communications channels;
◪ diminishing stakeholders' time and attention;
◪ declining levels of trust in corporations and government;
◪ shareholders and employees at the focal point of corporate perceptions;
◪ CEOs as drivers of reputation.

Given this environment, every effort must be made to offer consistency and clarity of message with a focus on both shareholder value and corporate values.

A brand and its legacy of values: The Coca-Cola Company

The Coca-Cola Company, a global beverages company which owns one of the world's most famous brands, has successfully faced a number of challenges to its reputation as a result of increased antagonism to global brands, especially those so strongly identified with the United States, as well as the issues that emanate from this, including environmental impact and health concerns.

The company has taken steps to maintain its position as a top global brand. Through changes in leadership and economic ups and downs, Coca-Cola has increased its focus on global citizenship, communicating its commitment to environment and water stewardship through its campaign "Make Every Drop Count". This appealed to all stakeholder groups, including employees with its commitment to their communities and bottling partners with its focus on environmentally sound operations.

On obesity, which some have attempted to link to soft drinks, the company and its bottling partners have emphasised the full array of choice from "diet" and other soft drinks to juices, water and sports drinks. Its advertising often underscores the range of choice to suit every preference. Its guidelines say that there should be no overt marketing of soft drinks to children who are 12 or under. Vending machines offer a "portfolio" of beverages (soft drinks, water, fruit juice), and the company sponsors a variety of programmes in schools reinforcing an active lifestyle.

As far as anti-Americanism is concerned, Coca-Cola may be an American brand, but its philosophy and the way it operates are international. Outside the United States it has local managers and employees who are encouraged to actively and consistently demonstrate good local citizenship.

CEOs have focused on its legacy of values in their words, actions and marketing dollars. As one recent annual report expressed:

> The values that underpin our success are integrity, quality, accountability, diversity, and relationships based on our respect for each other, for the communities where we do business and for the environment. People know what to expect from the Coca-Cola Company precisely because we have always lived by our values. When a consumer enjoys a bottle of Coke, when people invest in us, when partners do business with us, or when we operate in a community, we keep our promise to benefit and refresh them. We create value – economic and social – reliably and predictably.

A robust corporate brand should:

- inform public policy and corporate positioning;
- support change initiatives;
- stand for credibility in difficult times;
- underscore employee values and guide behaviours.

This happens when the corporate communications function assumes its responsibilities in championing the brand, protecting its reputation and demonstrating its values.

If a financial services organisation's goal is to be positioned as a financially empowering, positive force, questions of corporate transparency must be weighed from many different viewpoints. What will be the short- and longer-term impact on the organisation's financial position, assets, values, and so on?

If a technology company is moving from selling chips, boxes or applications to selling solutions, the brand needs to take into account how the change enhances core assets, strengthens functional benefits and aligns with evolved values and adapt accordingly.

As companies contemplate choices confronting them – for example, executive remuneration packages, sponsorships, reaction to a newsworthy issue or a major change in company structure – focusing on the core brand values can help in making the right decisions.

A brand undergoing transformational change: VISA

With a change in leadership and global structure (as a result of moving from being a private to a public company in 2008), one of VISA's biggest challenges was to maintain consistency of message and a commitment to brand assets with stakeholders and employees. A priority was the restructuring of the public affairs and communications function and a realignment of resources across all regions. These resources needed to be aligned to successfully communicate industry leadership, technology superiority and system/product innovation in ways relevant to each region in which VISA operates. On day one of the change the new, public VISA focused employees on employee ownership while bolstering their understanding of what it means to be a public company through business literacy education and business growth information. Executives such as chief operating officer Hans Morris understood employees were a priority in the transformation of VISA and spent time in direct, open and honest communication with them.

At the same time, VISA maintained a commitment to its worldwide sports sponsorships – the Olympics and worldwide soccer – using them to convey important messages. VISA was able to communicate global industry leadership and local financial empowerment in emerging markets. It was able to underscore its technology and operational value together with its values of trust, transparency and empowerment. VISA's marketing initiatives and sponsorships underscored both product relevance and corporate citizenship. Its advertising and PR programmes emphasised an interconnected world coming together to celebrate through the world of sports. PR programmes also enabled banks, merchants, cardholders and employees to take part in the excitement and fun.

To get the most value out of a brand, it must be:

◪ defined by behaviours that will bring the brand to life;
◪ interconnected with elements driving organisational performance;
◪ recognised by leadership as a source of strategic focus;
◪ launched internally with a sustaining plan;
◪ reinforced by PR efforts in times of crisis or celebration.

To leverage the value of their brands, organisations need to recognise and communicate with the full range of stakeholders. Public relations can play a crucial role in this.

PR is not simply about making statements and issuing press releases. Today's best corporate communications functions recognise that accurately assessing and strategically shaping corporate perceptions must take account of the full array of influencers who motivate, shape perceptions and have an impact on media coverage, and ultimately corporate reputation.

An affirmation of "who this corporation is and what we promise our customers, our shareholders, our employees, our communities" serves any organisation in times of crisis or celebration.

Sustaining brand value in crisis: US Postal Service

The US Postal Service (USPS) as a brand has been tested over time, from "going postal", referring to violence in the workplace, to "the mail moment", representing the anticipation and value of the mix of mail in a mailbox. Through the decades, the "We Deliver" tag line has neatly encapsulated both the delivery of the mail and the brand promise.

Measures of the USPS brand reveal that it has enduring relevance and value to consumers, despite negative images of "snail mail" that attach to the medium itself. The brand attributes of traditional, reliable, trustworthy, and "cares about customers" served it particularly well throughout the memorable anthrax crisis that followed the September 11th 2001 terrorist attacks in the United States.

Letters containing the deadly anthrax virus were delivered through the mail to the US Senate in Washington, DC, and to news media offices in New York and Florida. Some 800,000 employees were potentially at risk and 28,000 facilities were potentially contaminated. The safety of the mail was in question.

The challenge was to restore confidence and trust in the postal system among employees, who were handling and delivering the mail; major businesses and other organisational users of the mail system; and the public, who were continuing to receive their mail each day. Every stakeholder had to be reassured.

Tactically, the USPS managed the crisis in innovative ways, including:

- A special mailing for every American household with safety guidelines for mail handling.
- A redesigned internet site, created in just days, with a dedicated section on "keeping the mail safe and moving" with audience-tailored facts, videos, questions and answers, posters and mail service updates.
- A daily or twice daily facts update posted on the website and sent via e-mail and fax, eliminating thousands of customer and media calls.
- A daily update for local postmasters with facts and messages for their discussions with employees, customers and communities.
- A three-tiered cadre of spokespeople and press briefings with major media daily and later when needed.
- Mandatory meetings for the 800,000 employees at which supervisors would discuss the crisis and how to handle it. Toolkits were provided to help them do this.
- An employee hotline for illness reports and general information.
- A summit with executives of major customers to discuss ways to keep the mail safe and moving.

The USPS moved through the crisis with its credibility intact and even enhanced. It demonstrated a communications function that was capable of effectively managing information and stakeholder relations. Two surveys carried out immediately after the crisis showed that the brand's reputation was intact:

- A public opinion poll indicated 97% of respondents approved of its overall handling of the crisis; 96% said it was doing everything within reason to protect against future terrorism.
- Of the 90,000 employee respondents to a "Voice of the Employee" survey, 71% responded favourably to the statement: "I am proud to work for the Postal Service."

The strength of the USPS brand had given it a reservoir of public trust. The decision to be completely transparent and provide continuously updated, reliable information reinforced that trust. By continuously providing reporters with facts and the public with consistent advice, ill-founded rumours were quickly quashed. Competence, caring and common sense prevailed.

PR gives "legs" and life to brand attributes and the essential brand promise by enabling credible leadership communication and corporate transparency and providing support for the truth of a brand's advertising images. This is all the more important in an evolving media and business environment.

A brand with competitive advantage: Intel

No brand has more consistently symbolised and reinforced consumer confidence than the longstanding "Intel Inside", meaning of course Intel's chips powering computers manufactured by Hewlett-Packard and others. Average consumers know little about the inner workings of a computer, but many consumers look for that tiny slogan of reassurance. To be sure, withstanding the onslaught of competition in the highly competitive technology industry is about more than brand. It is about technology superiority, agile innovation and financial performance. At the same time, it remains true in a media environment of fast-increasing sources of information that actively monitoring and managing stakeholder perceptions, reputation and brand is a crucial element of competitive success.

Intel invests in the management of both performance and perception. The company globally monitors a vast array of media commentary and coverage on a daily basis and rapidly responds to competitive attack in every region of the world. It pushes its continuous product innovation through advertising, events, analyst relations, customer relations and PR. But this is baseline activity in the global technology industry.

Intel's brand-enhancing activities also include significant financial and human asset investment in its community relations and corporate social responsibility. This serves as the foundation for Intel's operations around the world and enables the company to enjoy favourable status in countries which are financially critical to cost competitiveness. Intel invests in markets as far apart as Ireland and India and publicises its community support focusing on environmental stewardship, computer access and affordability, and education. Mathematics and science education has been a decades-long commitment that Intel has supported in most markets in which it operates, encouraging its employees to contribute time locally and sponsoring maths and science student competitions globally. This activity is not the latest fad of the current year, but has been a sustained commitment serving as the basis for fundamental community and public affairs credibility and earning Intel governmental trust and business community recognition. As a result, Intel has weathered many a competitive attack that might have more severely threatened a company without strong relationships with its stakeholders and such brand strength.

Conclusion

In an era in which corporate motives are continuously questioned and executives are frequently viewed as greedy and lacking in accountability, legitimate reputational enhancement is crucial to success. As information sources have multiplied, consumers have become increasingly sceptical and weighed down by information overload and journalists increasingly seek to "protect" shareholders and consumers from questionable corporate information and motives. Yet there are opportunities to execute brand-based PR and enhance reputation. A 2006 Burson-Marsteller survey of premier global media outlets confirmed a negative media skew towards corporations while at the same time offering a few insights on sources of positive perception. The survey found that CEOs conveying transparent business strategy externally and clear strategic direction internally have a positive halo effect on a corporate brand. At the same time, journalists, when consistently provided with solid evidence of an innovation culture and innovation investment, will give corporate brands positive coverage. Last but not least, a CEO's reputation as a good steward of corporate finances and corporate citizenship enhances corporate reputation among all stakeholders.

The proliferation of television channels and niche magazines, the easy availability of 24-hour news and the exponential growth of the internet mean that an organisation has no choice but to manage the perceptions people have of it, and its brand reputation, through PR. It has to be up to the mark, ready to rebut damaging stories, and it must always make sure that it gets its message across. The reality is that, according to Thomas L. Harris research, companies in the top 200 of Fortune's most admired companies list spend twice as much on PR as those in the bottom 200.

All this illustrates how important PR is to brand strategy and to building and sustaining corporate reputation. The development of a successful PR strategy involves four elements:

◼ Identification of the various attributes and characteristics of the brand; for example, its values and supporting behaviours, its positioning and identity. Once these have been identified an assessment must be made of their implications with regard to an organisation's culture and opportunities for motivating performance. Then a public relations platform can be built on the alignment of brand, culture and performance.

◪ The perceptions of all external stakeholders must be assessed. This should extend beyond perceptions about products to include such drivers of reputation as leadership, innovation, financial value, quality of management and corporate citizenship. It is fundamental to understand who your key stakeholders are, what they expect from you and who influences them.

◪ The corporate communications function should use the brand's attributes and characteristics internally to inform employees of the company's positioning on different issues to support change initiatives, to underscore credibility in crisis and to guide behaviour. Essentially, employees must understand how to deliver on the brand promise.

◪ An annual, measurable PR plan should be created, anchored by the brand promise, with the objective of shaping key audiences' perceptions of leadership, customer connections, marketplace innovation and corporate responsibility.

The execution of strategic PR is dependent on a public affairs and communications function capable of and dedicated to supporting corporate leadership in aligning brand promise and corporate actions and communicating accountable performance to a range of stakeholders with clarity and consistency.

11 Brand protection

Allan Poulter

How do we go about protecting this valuable yet intangible asset known as a brand? This chapter is not concerned with how the brand's values are retained and developed from a commercial perspective (which is more than adequately covered elsewhere), but rather how we can use the law to protect certain physical manifestations of the brand from misuse or unauthorised use by third parties. In other words how to maintain the exclusivity in the use of the distinctive features of the brand.

The first task is to identify the features of a business that serve to distinguish that business from its competitors or, indeed, any other business. The most obvious example is the brand name. But there are many other features that make up or represent the brand: logos, slogans, colours, sounds, the shape of a product, the "get-up" of packaging or "trade dress", layout of retail outlets, and so on. Which of these features would brand owners want to prevent other traders from adopting and how would they go about it? Then there is the question of the current geographical presence and future aspirations of a business (and any local variations of the distinctive features that have been identified). Once these questions have been addressed it should be possible to identify what protection may be available in each relevant country.

Another crucial factor is, of course, cost. What budget is available to protect the features that have been identified as important? It is unlikely that the allotted funds will be sufficient to allow for all possible available protection to be sought in all the countries of interest. It will be necessary to prioritise and determine what gives the best value in terms of the extent of protection afforded.

The area of law that is most useful in providing protection to the brand owner is that of intellectual property. There has been a fair degree of harmonisation of intellectual property laws throughout the world, and many of the principles discussed below are of general application in many of the major commercial jurisdictions. The need for a consistent approach to the protection of intellectual property rights on an international scale has long been recognised through a number of international initiatives that have supported the concept of reciprocal protection for such rights between countries. Although there may be local variations (particularly in procedure), the principles of protection are broadly the same. The position is continually evolving, but the trend is certainly towards further harmonisation. This chapter concentrates on the general principles that apply in common law jurisdictions such as the UK and the United States, referring also to EU and international initiatives.

Trade marks

By far the most important weapon in a brand owner's armoury is a comprehensive portfolio of trade mark registrations. Trade mark rights are territorial and it is possible to file applications for registration in just about

every country of the world. The first application filed in the UK for trade mark registration was in 1876 for the Bass "Red Triangle" label mark and it remains on the register today. Indeed, many trade marks still on the UK register have celebrated their centenary, including household names such as Kodak, Coca-Cola and Wedgwood, to name but a few.

The legislation relating to trade mark registration has attempted to keep pace with changes in commercial practices, and there has been a fair degree of harmonisation of trade mark laws, particularly within the EU. For example, the UK Trade Marks Act 1994 reflects and implements provisions of the European Trade Mark Harmonisation Directive. Its definition of a trade mark is very broad:

A trade mark is any sign which is both
(a) capable of being represented graphically; and
(b) capable of distinguishing goods or services of one
undertaking from those of other undertakings.

It goes on to state – and this is not an exhaustive list – that a trade mark may consist of

... words (including personal names), designs, letters, numerals,
or the shape of goods or their packaging.

This marked a significant extension to what would constitute a trade mark. For example, under the previous legislation (Trade Marks Act 1938) an application had been filed for registration of the shape of the Coca-Cola bottle as a trade mark. The application was refused and the decision was upheld on appeal at the highest level. The basis of the refusal was that what was being sought to be registered was the product itself rather than something that was applied to the product. Following the implementation of the 1994 act, a new application was filed for the shape of the bottle and this went through without difficulty. Indeed, many shapes have now been registered as well as the colours, sounds and even smells that form part of the "get-up" of products.

The European Harmonisation Directive has served as a model for many other countries that have adopted new legislation governing trade mark rights in recent years.

What should be registered?

When considering what should be the subject of trade mark protection, the first step is to identify the features of a business that serve to denote the origin of the goods produced and/or services provided by that business. For example:

- Nike has protected, among other things, its word mark Nike, the swoosh design mark and the strapline "Just do it".
- The Intel Corporation has registered its name Intel and the distinctive jingle that features prominently in its advertising and promotional campaigns. Sounds are becoming increasingly important in commerce and sonic branding is an area where further developments are likely.
- Orange Personal Communications has registered both the name Orange and the colour orange for telecommunications services and related goods.

There are also examples of smells being registered, including "the strong smell of bitter beer applied to flights for darts". However, a decision of the European Court of Justice has called into the question the registrability of smell marks having regard to the difficulty in representing such marks graphically with sufficient clarity to define the scope of the protection afforded. The US Patent Office has accepted smell mark registrations, including the smell of plumeria blossom applied to thread.

Registrations have been secured for the shape and get-up of products, holograms, animated marks, the distinctive layout of retail outlets and even gestures.

Classification of goods and services

Once the relevant distinctive features have been identified, the next step is to decide on the range of goods and services for which protection is required. This is, predominantly, a commercial decision based on the nature of the business being conducted and any likely expansion or diversification of its commercial activities.

Most trade mark registries have adopted the Nice classification system, which divides the register into 45 classes. When the range of goods and services for which registration is to be sought have been identified, it is necessary to determine the specific classes within which these goods or services fall. In many countries it is possible to file a single application covering any number of classes, paying an additional fee for each class, whereas other countries still require separate applications to be filed for each class. This can be costly.

Different countries take different positions on what is an acceptable specification. For example, the United States requires specifications to be restricted to those goods or services for which use of the mark can be established. The UK, however, allows for broad specifications as long as the applicant has an intention to use the mark for the goods and services claimed. In many other countries it is possible to file for all goods and services.

To avoid registers becoming cluttered with registrations of marks that are not being used, there is usually provision within the local legislation for the possibility of a registration being attacked on the grounds of (usually five years) non-use.

Where should registration be sought?

Having identified the mark or marks for which protection is required and the relevant goods and services to be covered, consideration has to be given to the geographical extent of protection that should be sought. This will normally be governed by a company's current activities and its short- to medium-term ambitions. Of course, it may be that different marks will be used in different jurisdictions and the range of goods or services provided may also differ. However, once a decision has been made as to what protection is required and where, the next step is to identify how best to obtain appropriate protection in the most cost-effective manner.

One possibility is to file applications in each of the countries of interest directly through the national registration system of that country. This would normally require the instruction of lawyers in each country to file the application. However, an international registration system (the Madrid Agreement and Madrid Protocol) allows for a single application to be filed at the World Intellectual Property Organisation (WIPO) in Geneva, nominating the member countries for which registrations are required. Where this is possible it can result in significant savings, as local lawyers will need to be instructed only if there is opposition or an objection to the application. A list of member countries of both the agreement and protocol can be found at www.wipo.org/madrid/en/index.htm.

Within the EU it is also now possible to file a single application for a Community trade mark registration through the Office for Harmonisation in the Internal Market (OHIM), which is based in Alicante, Spain (colloquially known as the Community Trade Mark Office). This is not a system for filing national applications within EU countries; it is a unitary system resulting in a single registration that is enforceable throughout the EU, effectively recognising the EU as a single market. As well as being significantly cheaper than filing separate applications in each of the EU countries (either directly or through the international system), there are other significant substantive advantages of using the Community trade marks system. For example, it is possible to get an EU-wide injunction against the use of an infringing trade mark, and the genuine use of the mark in any of the EU countries should be sufficient to protect the registration from an attack on the grounds of non-use. This is particularly useful for companies that have current trading activity in a limited number of EU countries but intend gradually to expand their commercial activities across the region.

Why register?

A registered trade mark provides its owner with the right to prevent the unauthorised use of the mark by a third party in circumstances where such use is not justified. Again, in most countries, the rights conferred by registration extend beyond merely being able to prevent use of the mark in respect of the goods covered by the registration. In certain circumstances, they may allow the proprietor to prevent the use of "similar marks" being used in respect of "similar" goods or services and, in some cases, the use of the mark even in respect of "dissimilar" goods. The remedies that are normally available include the grant of an injunction to prevent the continued use of the mark and an award of damages to compensate for the loss attributable to the unauthorised use.

A registration is also a property right which can be assigned or used as security, and can underpin any licensing activity. This is particularly important for businesses involved in merchandising or franchising activities.

Maintaining a trade mark portfolio

The phrase "use it or lose it" is relevant to trade mark protection. If a mark is not used within a country for the goods or services covered by the registration, it is likely to become vulnerable to an attack. Furthermore, token use designed solely to maintain the validity of a registration will normally be disregarded. Only genuine use of the mark within the relevant territory is likely to be sufficient. It is also important to police and take action against unauthorised use by third parties.

Renewals

Trade mark registrations last for a defined period, usually ten years, and have to be renewed if they are to be retained. It is, therefore, imperative that effective mechanisms are put in place to ensure that renewal deadlines are not missed. One important advantage of registered trade mark protection over other intellectual property rights is its potentially perpetual nature.

Watching services/reporting lines

It is, of course, only possible to take action against potential infringements if and when you become aware of them. It is important that employees, local distributors and other parties involved in the company's business are made aware of the need to report instances of potentially infringing activities, and that there is in place a reporting line that enables such information to reach the desk of the person or department within the organisation responsible for handling these issues. It is certainly worthwhile subscribing to a watching service so that notification is received of any attempt by a third party to register a mark that is similar to your mark. You can then take appropriate action to prevent registration and the use of the mark by the applicant.

Record keeping

It is essential to keep comprehensive records of the use of the mark in each country as well as copies of promotional and marketing materials and evidence of sales in each country. The first line of defence in an infringement action is for the defendant to attack the validity of the registration on the grounds of non-use. It is not uncommon for companies to have difficulty in obtaining evidence of their use of marks even where such use may have been extensive. This information will also be relevant in infringement proceedings or passing off (see below) or unfair competition actions where it is necessary to establish goodwill or reputation within a particular jurisdiction.

Creating a new mark: searching

There is no point in selecting a new mark where, because of earlier conflicting rights, the use of the mark is likely to be prevented by the owner of the earlier right. As well as ensuring that the new mark satisfies the commercial demands of the company and does not have any unfortunate linguistic or cultural connotations, sufficient legal clearance searches have to be conducted. Although the cost of these searches may seem daunting, they can represent a fraction of the cost of having to change the name or defend infringement proceedings following a rebranding project or the launch of a new product or service.

It is possible to reduce the cost of clearance searches by allowing sufficient time in the name creation process for straightforward searches for identical (or almost identical) names and marks before embarking on the more comprehensive full-clearance searches that are required to enable legal advisers to make an informed decision about the availability of the chosen mark.

Searching is a form of risk assessment or insurance. The more comprehensive the searches conducted, the less likely it will be that significant problems will be faced. A properly conducted search programme will help avoid both the embarrassment of launching a brand that cannot then be used and the cost of withdrawing it and rebranding.

The legal aspects of clearing a new brand name should never be underestimated. There are more than 500,000 registrations on the UK register alone with over 35,000 new applications being filed each year. Since its launch in 1996, over 400,000 trade marks have been registered at the Community Trade Mark Office. The procedure is even more difficult in the United States, where there are well over 1m current trade mark registrations.

It is rare for an initial search report to conclude that there are no risks associated with the proposed adoption of a new mark. However, this does not necessarily mean that such a mark should be disregarded. Many options may be available to overcome any conflicting rights identified by the searches. Earlier trade mark registrations may no longer be in use for all or even any of the goods or services covered by the registration and may be open to a challenge on the grounds of non-use. In other circumstances, where a technical legal risk has been identified, it may be that further investigations could establish that there is no commercial overlap with the activities of the proprietor of the earlier right and that a coexistence agreement can be negotiated to avoid or reduce any potential conflict between the parties. Earlier rights can also be purchased or licences negotiated. It has even been known for the proprietor company to be purchased in order to secure the rights in a name.

Within any name clearance project, you should provide sufficient time and budget for any further investigations or negotiations that may be necessary.

In general, the less distinctive the chosen mark, the more likely it is to run into problems. Furthermore, rights conferred on marks that are of a descriptive nature are likely to be construed narrowly. Indeed, most registries refuse to register a mark that consists exclusively of words that are descriptive of the goods or services or their characteristics unless it can be established that the mark has become distinctive as a result of its use by its owner. The more descriptive the mark is, the harder it is to establish this acquired distinctiveness.

The failure to conduct appropriate clearance searches can have expensive consequences. Although trade mark infringement claims following the launch of a new brand or company name do not often come to the public's attention (usually because any subsequent settlement agreement will include a confidentiality clause), it is not uncommon for such claims to be made. Substantial payments have been made within the context of a coexistence agreement to avoid the need to cancel a launch, remove a product or rebrand. There are examples of seven-figure sums being paid to avoid the possibility of a negative result within litigation, even where the alleged infringement claim has had little prospect of success, thereby removing the slight risk of the additional expense, inconvenience and embarrassment associated with an aborted rebranding exercise.

Trade mark portfolio audit

An audit of a company's existing portfolio of trade mark registrations will almost certainly reveal gaps in protection, inaccuracies in details recorded on the register and possibly vulnerable, unnecessary or redundant registrations. As organisations become larger, particularly where growth has been by merger or acquisition, it is likely that these deficiencies will be even more significant. Multi-brand and international organisations are also more likely to have large and complex portfolios, increasing the likelihood of records being incomplete or containing inaccuracies.

The "clearing up" of such a portfolio should be seen not as an administrative problem but as an essential process to ensure that the protection required to maintain the value of a brand is kept in place. Such an audit will also invariably identify opportunities for cost savings.

Passing off and unfair competition

In many jurisdictions it is possible, in certain circumstances, to bring an action to prevent the unauthorised use of a mark even in the absence of a trade mark registration. The elements of such an action vary from country to country, but common features include the necessity to establish goodwill in the mark within the country and a likelihood of confusion arising from the defendant's activities. Such an action (called passing off in the UK) allows the owner of goodwill in a mark to prevent another party from benefiting from or damaging that goodwill through misrepresenting that its business or goods are in some relevant commercial way connected.

Lord Halsbury stated the principle in the case of Reddaway vs Banham (1896) as "nobody has any right to represent his goods as the goods of somebody else".

Bringing proceedings for passing off can be expensive as it is usually necessary to establish not only that goodwill exists but also that there has been a relevant misrepresentation that is likely to cause confusion and lead to damage. It is not uncommon for survey evidence to have to be obtained to help substantiate such a charge.

Copyright

The law of copyright is designed to protect original works (the most relevant to branding being artistic works and, in respect of sonic branding, musical works) against unauthorised copying. Copyright arises automatically upon creation of the work and, with certain exceptions, it will initially belong to the creator of that work. The main exception is a work created by an employee in the course of his or her employment, in which case the copyright is normally vested in the employer.

There is no requirement to register copyright, although in the United States and some other countries it is possible to register it. This is important from an evidentiary viewpoint should there be any dispute about ownership of a copyright.

The obvious relevance of copyright to branding is where an original logo or get-up has been created specifically for a brand. The required level of "artistic" merit for copyright to exist is low, and the principal factor in establishing copyright in a work is that of originality.

The rights conferred by copyright are more limited than registered trade mark rights to the extent, as suggested by the term, that copyright provides the owner with the right to prevent copying of the work. If the alleged infringing work has been created independently, there will be no grounds for a breach of copyright action. However, unlike trade mark rights, a copyright in an artistic or musical work is not specific to any goods or services to which it is applied but extends to any copying, subject to certain defences.

Unlike registered trade mark rights, which subject to certain conditions being met can be renewed in perpetuity, copyright in an artistic or musical work is of a defined and limited duration, usually the life of the author plus a further 70 years.

Where the "work" has been created by someone who is not an employee of the company, such as an independent design contractor, it is important to secure an assignment of the copyright. This requirement should be covered in the contract with the design contractor.

Copyright should not be seen as a substitute for trade mark registration, but it can provide a useful additional basis for attacking unauthorised use of visual and sound marks.

Registered and unregistered designs

As an intellectual property right, design rights have been considered something of a poor cousin to the other rights discussed above. However, recent changes in the legislation governing registered designs within the EU have raised their profile and their potential significance in the area of branding. Following the implementation of the EU's Design Harmonisation Directive and the introduction of a new European Registered Community Design right, the scope of what can be registered as a design has been extended significantly. It now includes such things as logos, get-up and packaging, which traditionally would have been protected through trade mark registration or copyright.

As with copyright, registered designs do not limit the scope of protection to specific goods, and the registration process is reasonably cheap and quick. The rights conferred by registration are also not restricted to the prevention of copying. However, the period of protection for registered designs is limited to an initial period of five years, which can be renewed for subsequent five-year periods up to a total of 25 years. Protection may also be afforded albeit to a lesser extent in unregistered designs.

Domain names and the internet

Although undoubtedly a valuable commercial asset, the ownership of a domain name does not of itself give any rights in the name (other than the fact that it will prevent a third party from obtaining the identical domain name). For example, the ability of Amazon to prevent third parties from using "Amazon" or any confusingly similar name for online retailing does not arise from its ownership of the top-level domain www.Amazon.com. It will be dependent upon its having secured appropriate trade mark registrations as well as the goodwill in the Amazon name acquired as a result of extensive use and promotional activities.

The internet has had a significant impact on trade mark legal practice as a result of the dichotomy between the territorial nature of trade mark protection and the unconstrained geographical boundaries of the internet. This has raised some interesting issues in terms of the location of the "use" of a mark within infringement proceedings. In countries where the question of use has been considered by the courts, there seems to be a degree of conformity in treating the internet merely as a medium for communication. This requires an analysis of the facts of each case to determine where use of the mark has actually taken place (notwithstanding that any website can potentially be accessed from anywhere in the world).

There are other questions relating to trade mark law arising from the use of marks on the internet. For example, is it possible to infringe a trade mark registration where the alleged infringement is in the form of a meta-tag which can be picked up by a search engine but is not visible to potential customers? Courts in several jurisdictions have held that such use can constitute an infringement.

It has become clear that the ownership of relevant trade mark registrations has played a significant role in allowing the proprietors of such registrations to secure the removal or transfer of relevant domain names incorporating the registered mark through procedures operated by domain-name registries such as ICANN and Nominet.

Conclusion

So what does the future hold for brand protection? From a trading perspective, the world is shrinking and brand owners are increasingly having to consider protecting their brands beyond their traditional geographic boundaries. Careful thought needs to be given to the appropriate nature and extent of protection sought.

Starting from the viewpoint that a brand is a valuable asset of a company and is worth protecting, this exercise should not merely be treated as an administrative inconvenience. A company's legal advisers on brand protection should be actively involved in devising and implementing a strategy for securing, maintaining and enforcing appropriate intellectual property rights in a cost-effective manner. The protection secured should be reviewed on a regular basis to ensure that it retains its relevance to the business as it develops. Too much effort is expended in creating and developing a brand to risk jeopardising the value created through failure to secure adequate legal protection.

The following are some of the questions that should be addressed:

- What are the identifiable distinctive features of the brand?
- For what range of goods or services is brand protection required?
- In which countries does the brand have or is likely to have a commercial presence?
- Have appropriate trade mark registrations been secured?
- Has ownership of copyright been established in any artistic or musical work that underpins any element of the brand?
- If outside contractors are being used to create a mark, have they agreed in writing to assign any rights in it?
- Are the identified features of the brand covered by a watching service?
- Is there a mechanism in place to report instances of unauthorised use or misuse of the brand?
- Is there a mechanism in place for the central collection of evidence to establish use, goodwill, promotional activities, and so on?
- How are renewals of registered rights dealt with?
- Has an audit of the portfolio of intellectual rights been conducted recently?

PART 3
THE FUTURE FOR BRANDS

12 Globalisation and brands

Sameena Ahmad

Globalisation is once again under attack. For most of the first decade of the new millennium, the benefits of open markets, free trade and internationalisation were indisputable. Riding the crest of one of the biggest peacetime economic expansions the world has seen (between 2003 and 2007), liberal market capitalism reigned supreme. Widespread prosperity was created in the West and millions of people were lifted out of poverty in emerging markets – particularly in the so-called BRIC economies of Brazil, Russia, India and China. Multinational corporations, with their vast resources and international presence, were both the proponents and the beneficiaries of this expansion. Many of their chieftains became unimaginably rich.

A portion of that boom was built on shaky foundations, however: on a series of economic imbalances between the overconsuming and over-borrowed West, particularly the United States, and an excess of savings in Asia and the Middle East. A series of asset bubbles inflated, first in equities, then in housing and lastly in credit. When the last and most damaging of these popped in the autumn of 2007 it led to a financial crisis that threatened to turn into a global depression and to damage much of our current economic infrastructure.

As a consequence, companies – and brands, their public face – are back in the dock as easy scapegoats for the worst excesses of global capitalism. Following the financial crisis that erupted in 2008, public fury was directed primarily at financial brands: the investment banks, brokers and hedge funds whose irresponsible embrace of debt and creation of opaque financial instruments have littered the world with what are regarded as toxic assets. But as financial deleveraging on Wall Street leads to recession on Main Street, as retailers and manufacturers shutter shops and factories, companies across the board will come under attack. The critics of globalisation and capitalism will once more blame brands and their creators for job losses, for social inequality, for spoiling the environment and for homogenising our culture.

It will then be up to the guardians of brands, mostly those same large and largely western multinational corporations, to make a better fist of defending themselves than they have done so far. At the same time, they face a second challenge from the slow but steady rise of brands in emerging markets.

The case for brands

Though many in the West worry that dominance of brands globally reflects unprecedented levels of consumerism,[1] the absence of brands signals something far more unhealthy. The existence of brands is, in fact, one indicator of a well-functioning economy. At its core, a successful brand is the culmination of efforts by a company to distinguish its products or services from those of its rivals. Becoming an established brand is no easy matter, particularly now that a proliferation of products has given consumers vast choice. Brand creators work hard and spend huge sums on marketing and product innovation to tempt consumers with something new, improved or with some intangible benefit such as exclusivity. The more brands there are and the more ferociously they compete for our attention, the more consumers benefit. Competition between products results in cheaper or better quality or more innovative things. Lower prices and innovation both lead to improved consumption and economic growth. An economy in which companies can freely compete to offer a wide choice of goods, and where consumer behaviour, rather than the state, dictates the existence and success of a product, is a competitive economy with open markets. As studies from the World Bank[2] and the Fraser Institute[3] show, economic openness is one of the best predictors of future prosperity.

Critics like to claim that big brands stifle competition and reduce choice – making cultures homogeneous as people switch from distinctive local offerings to mass-produced and globally distributed goods. But brands are an indicator of a healthy level of choice: the existence of brands is synonymous with the existence of competition. In the Soviet Union, companies had no reason to create brands because they faced no competition. Everything was supplied by state-owned companies and sold at set prices – the public had little choice in what they could buy. There was no incentive for suppliers to improve quality or innovate, leading to economic stagnation and falling living standards.

It is worth comparing a world of no brands with one where brands are highly visible. In the United States, Wal-Mart stores,[4] the world's biggest retailer, is commonly used to point to everything that seems wrong with big brands: the destruction of small competitors, reduced choice, the spread of dull homogeneity. But the discount store giant's impact on the United States has been impressively positive. Wal-Mart has been responsible for boosting economic growth, raising global standards in retailing and supply chain logistics, and increasing consumer choice and spending power. A report by McKinsey, a management consultancy, in 2001[5] concluded that Wal-Mart probably played a bigger role in America's productivity miracle of the late 1990s than the huge surge in investment in information technology. The report found that almost one-quarter of the increase in productivity growth – from 1.4% a year between 1972 and 1995 to 2.5% between 1995 and 2000 – came from the retail sector, most of it as a result of huge gains at Wal-Mart, whose emphasis on low prices and big stores increased its efficiency and sales and forced other companies to follow its lead.

Through cheap prices, Wal-Mart has boosted the spending power of a large number of people not just in the United States but also globally (for instance by forcing German retailers to open for longer hours and sell more cheaply), further stimulating consumption. In his autobiography, Sam Walton, the retail group's founder, calculated that between 1982 and 1992 alone, operating efficiencies had saved its customers in the United States a "very conservative" $13 billion, or 10% of sales, over the decade:[6]

Wal-Mart has been a powerful force for improving the standard of living in our mostly rural trade areas.

Wal-Mart's "productivity miracle" can be partly credited to the fact that its presence forced rivals to raise their game. A good brand will raise standards in an industry. Only weak, overpriced or poor-quality competitors suffer in competition with successful brands. Walton devotes a chapter in his book to explaining how rival retailers can compete with it: not by trying to beat Wal-Mart on price (impossible without its hefty buying power), but by offering what it does not – specialist product know-how or a sophisticated and pleasant shopping ambience.

Who really holds the power?

While brands both reflect and bolster healthy economies, individually they are surprisingly weak. Critics argue that big brands have an unstoppable influence, wiping out local culture as they spread globally. They claim that big brands are bigger and more powerful than governments, able to skew political decisions in their favour and manipulate a gullible public into buying them. Yet brands have become less powerful over time, not more so. When just a few big brands existed, they had enormous influence with the buying public. As people have been given more choice, as they have become less naive about marketing tactics and more demanding about what they want, and as advertising media have fragmented, consumers have become less accessible to marketers. The modern marketing tactics of big brands look aggressive when they raise prices, bombard the media with their monikers or retreat behind automated telephone systems to avoid grumbling customers. But all of this reflects desperation: as media fragment, many brands are using more and more resources to reach fewer and fewer people, unable to distinguish themselves from an increasing number of equally desperate rivals.

Wal-Mart has faced numerous hurdles in its attempt to sell cheap goods to people. Planning constraints and political and public opposition in the United States have often tripped it up. It has stumbled in its international expansion, withdrawing from the German market after years of heavy losses, and is well behind the UK's Tesco and France's Carrefour in Asia and eastern Europe. As the seesawing fortunes of brands such as McDonald's, Coca-Cola and British retailer Marks & Spencer show, a brand whose success was born in an era of no competition can be highly vulnerable to the emergence of new rivals and changing consumer tastes. Complacent management and the inability to respond nimbly to change have meant that all these brands have fallen hard at various times. McDonald's, for example, though it has recently produced good growth in both sales and profits, failed in the early 2000s to react to a proliferation of stylish chains that were serving better-quality food in more sophisticated surroundings and stealing its market share. Only after changes in senior management did the world's biggest restaurant company fight back by improving service, sprucing up its menu and ensuring basic standards in its outlets such as clean toilets. Coca-Cola is still trying to cope with the rise of healthier alternatives to its carbonated drinks – a challenge it has dealt with less well than its smaller rival PepsiCo. Marks & Spencer, after shrinking itself back to health in the early 2000s, appears to have overexpanded once again – and its current chairman and chief executive, Stuart Rose, hailed for a recovery that saw Marks & Spencer voted the UK's most admired company in 2007, found himself under fire for lacklustre sales and falling profits less than a year later.

In truth, the power of a brand is determined not by its size, but by the presence of competition. In the 1950s the three biggest companies in the media and automotive markets in the United States were much smaller in absolute size than they are today. However, they had far more power since competition was limited and they controlled some 90% of their markets. Today, few brands have anything like that market share. Competition is too fierce, unpredictable and global for market dominance to last long. Banks, for example, now face rivals from unexpected sectors as supermarket chains such as the UK's Tesco and Sainsbury and Japan's Seven-Eleven move into financial services. Marks & Spencer, once alone in providing quality clothes in the UK, now faces a host of rivals from around the world including Zara (Spain), The Gap (America), Uniqlo (Japan) and Hennes & Mauritz (Sweden).

Nor are brands and the companies that market them more powerful than governments, as critics of brands often suggest. The profits of companies are tiny compared with the "profits" (that is the GDP) of countries, the correct basis of comparison. Governments have the power to tax, imprison and change laws. Companies use their size and importance to lobby governments, but so do unions, non-governmental organisations (NGOs) and consumer groups. And financial resources are only one source of influence; media pressure and votes matter too. Anyone worried about the influence of drug companies on academic research or Coca-Cola on lessons in schools should note how effective America's huge steel and textile unions have been at persuading politicians to protect their domestic markets from cheap imports and how NGOs such as Greenpeace and Oxfam influence the political and social agenda and hence the activities of corporations. Lobbying reflects a healthy democracy, and in a healthy democracy commercial interests will always be weighed against others.

Power in the consumer industry rests with consumers not brands. Brands ensure that companies are accountable for the products they make. If our Gap jeans fray or our Toyota car breaks down, we know who to blame and where to go to get things fixed, down to the address of the company's headquarters and the name of the chief executive. In the unbranded Soviet Union, customers had no recourse if a product failed. Indeed, the quality of goods and services fell so much as a result that in the 1950s, Soviet planners in central office decided to artificially introduce brands on some goods to make their producers more accountable and force them to improve.

Goodness and guilt

Even if they are not that powerful after all, argue the critics, companies behave badly, act ruthlessly and can damage society. They are inherently self-interested and consider only their profits. Companies have to be forced to do good, say their detractors. They must compensate and

175

apologise for the damaging effects of their commercial activities and the huge sums they pay their directors by "giving back" to society somehow: by helping good causes or funding research into environmentally sound products. This is to misunderstand the essence of free-market capitalism. Companies are neither good nor evil – they are not moral entities at all. Companies are structures designed to look after other people's money: that of their owners or shareholders. And through mutual funds and pension plans, we are all shareholders.

Companies do not need to be and, in fundamental ways, should not aim to be moral entities. The virtue of free markets is that simply by existing, a business, which is serious and sound enough to be around for year after year, does enormous good. Companies with freedom to focus on their long-term financial health can secure a long-term source of jobs, investments and tax revenue for society and generate more growth. A company with a view to the future and acting within the law will naturally (not because of external pressure for some artificial code of ethics) treat employees, suppliers and customers well and fairly. That will not mean offering jobs for life or paying suppliers more generously than they can afford – that would be bad business. By trying to keep their business healthy, profitable and competitive, companies are naturally acting for the good of the majority of those that depend on it.

As non-moral entities, some companies will of course be tempted to break the law or stretch it to boost their stock prices and profits. Others pay their management more than is sensible for a job poorly done. But those companies, though they grab the headlines, are a minority. As we saw in the cases of WorldCom and Enron, free markets governed by democratically elected politicians and underpinned by carefully crafted, relevant corporate regulation are the best methods for rooting out bad behaviour and punishing it.

One of the big lessons from the financial crisis that followed the credit crunch is that regulators, governments and even the senior managers of most financial institutions did not keep up with innovation on the trading floors of banks. The deregulation of financial services that began in the mid 1980s was correct in principle, but with hindsight it was done in a clumsy, piecemeal fashion. In the United States, for example, banks were answerable to four different regulators for various parts of their business, while large sections of the derivatives industry, particularly those traded "over the counter", were not subject to any oversight. That the credit ratings agencies, whose assessments underpinned the gigantic securitisation industry, were paid by the issuers of the bonds and not the investors in them created a huge conflict of interest. But the conclusion to draw from this is that the financial system needs smarter, better-paid regulators rather than an avalanche of new rules that will simply stifle innovation and thereby delay recovery.

That critics of business have lost sight of the essential role of free-market capitalism in building long-term wealth partly reflects a western middle class ill at ease with itself. People in developed countries enjoy comfort, leisure, security and a long life – things that did not exist for their grandparents and great grandparents. Progress in information technology, engineering and medicine is a result of the free movement of goods, people and money. Much of this is now taken for granted. Few young people know, and many older ones have forgotten, the excitement and pride when the family acquired its first colour television set or the years of saving by their parents or grandparents for a new bicycle or a foreign holiday. Many in the West complain that materialism has made us less caring. Yet there is little evidence for this. Concern – for people and the environment – is a feature of economically well-off societies. People who have enough food in their mouths can afford to give their money to charities or sympathise with the poor. Others say that consumerism has made us unhappy. That may be true, but being unable to resist an overpriced handbag or a child insisting on having an electronic games machine is far more indicative of poor self control and problems in parenting than unfair marketing tactics. High levels of unhappiness expressed by people in the West may also reflect that they have the leisure to ponder spiritual contentment: a luxury made possible by economic success.

Yet the West often feels a need to protect people in the developing world from becoming consumers of brands and the products of global companies. Aspiring middle classes in India and China are not listening: they are hungry to acquire western brands as a mark of their personal economic success, just as western consumers were in the middle of the 20th century. They are also creating their own desirable brands. Westerners claim to be sated by consumerism, but those still climbing the economic ladder are unembarrassed by it.

What globalisation can do for you

In fighting globalisation, its critics are opposing the very mechanism that can deliver greater wealth to poorer people. Globalisation offers a way out of poverty. Countries that open themselves up to trading their products and ideas freely with other countries raise the standard of living for everyone. Rich countries are forced to shift out of manufacturing and build new, more productive, more advanced industries to make room for countries that can make goods more cheaply. Poor countries get a leg up out of poverty, moving their economies from farming to manufacturing and eventually services as happened in Hong Kong and has been happening across Asia from China and Vietnam to Malaysia and South Korea. Developing countries that open their markets to foreign investment are seeing their income per head grow fast; at some 5%, even faster than western countries that are growing at some 2%. Those countries that are not globalising (mainly African and Arab countries) are slowing down.[7] Their economic malaise makes them dissatisfied and unstable.

One of the most effective tools for promoting globalisation is foreign direct investment (FDI). When established western multinationals move into the developing world, it is often assumed that they exploit workers, who are forced to toil in sweatshop conditions. Yet exploitation happens most at faceless, unbranded local companies, which can treat workers badly without fear of detection. Their brands and their public share listings make multinationals visible and accountable. As such, they make ready targets for activists. Yet it is multinationals that set the highest standards in pay, benefits and conditions. By attacking them, western activists are threatening some of the best jobs available to foreign workers.

Nike, a sports shoemaker, which has been criticised for its operations in the developing world, is one case. Indirectly, it employs nearly 800,000 workers in its global supply chain. An Australian survey found that Nike factories in Indonesia paid women factory workers 40% higher wages than rival local companies. Another report by the University of Michigan found that Nike paid above-average wages in its foreign-owned export factories in Vietnam (above five times the legal minimum wage) and Indonesia (about three times the legal minimum). In Vietnam, Nike is the country's second-largest exporter and is credited with helping to cut poverty in half in the past decade or so. Since Nike set up a third-party-run factory in Samyang, near Ho Chi Minh City, employing 5,200 people in 1995, it has helped to create an economic hot spot, which has spread beyond its own factory as other local companies have been forced to compete for workers. Samyang currently pays three times the wages paid by state-owned factories and twice the local wage. Four times more residents in the area have telephones than when Nike moved in; two in three have motorbikes (compared with one in three before); 8% are earning less than $10 a month compared with 20% before; and 75% own televisions compared with 30% in 1995.[8]

Think about intentions

Certainly big international companies do not always behave well in emerging markets, particularly if they are operating in countries where politicians encourage and protect unethical behaviour. However, as Daniel Litvin's account of multinationals in developing markets describes,[9] throughout history western observers have exaggerated or misjudged the role that western corporations play in the problems of developing countries, with serious consequences for how those problems were subsequently dealt with. Shell's oil operations in Nigeria during the 1990s are an example. Though the world held Shell responsible for destroying tribal lands and for the murder of a tribal leader, Nigeria's corrupt government was far more culpable. The government resisted attempts by Shell to share the profits of its oil exploration with those living on the land. Yet for the tribes affected who wanted help from the West, drawing attention to a publicly listed company, rather than battling Nigeria's government, got them striking results. The undesirable result was that Shell felt stung enough to help Nigeria in ways that let its government off the hook: Shell assumed the role of the government by funding and running schools and other social institutions. As Litvin makes clear, companies are more often just clumsy and incompetent when they enter a new market, rather than setting out with an intent to exploit. Their mistakes at least result in them trying to change, which is not the case for most of the world's nastiest political regimes.

The example of Shell also illustrates the dangers of grafting the West's moral certitude onto developing countries. The $40m a year that the oil group spends on good causes in Nigeria might have led to far greater long-term prosperity if Shell had been allowed to plough it into its core business, creating permanent jobs through long-term investment. Similarly, in Pakistan, the western campaign that urged consumers to boycott Nike products in the 1980s, because the sports firm was using children to stitch footballs, cost thousands of children jobs that their families depended on, forced them into more dangerous, more poorly paid employment and did nothing to change the fact that over 20m children in Pakistan work and probably will until the country becomes richer. The campaign had another unintended side effect, costing many women their economic independence, since the boycotts forced Nike to take the stitching work out of homes, where women could work, and into dedicated factories to which they were unable to travel because their husbands forbade it. Although branded multinationals are easy targets compared with governments, western activists often fail to see that their campaigns can have consequences that hurt the very poor people that they claim to want to help.

Time for a new approach

Is there anything that companies can do to change what is becoming a renewed and damaging antipathy to business practices and free-market capitalism? Certainly many need to get better at their core business of selling things. Many multinationals can no longer find easy ways to make their products appealing and many have been slow to respond to change. Fierce competition and increasingly fragmented media have made it more difficult for brands to reach potential customers. Decades ago, when there were fewer advertisements, fewer television channels and few other places to advertise, marketing campaigns could readily become embedded in our popular culture. Now the public is exposed to thousands of advertising messages a day, not just through television, but on computers, on billboards, on the streets and through product placement. Around a quarter of American college students now take marketing courses. Young people understand how big companies are trying to reach them.

Much has been written about how companies like McDonald's[10] or Wal-Mart try to persuade us and many people are insensitive to or suspicious of marketing messages. Though consumers have become more sophisticated, a lot of advertising is still based on surprisingly old-fashioned methods. Marketing departments can be surprisingly conservative and wedded to blunt tools such as focus groups or crude software to predict shopping habits. Meanwhile, though marketing remains a soft subject, finance directors increasingly want hard proof that the money spent on it is paying off. In many cases, marketers find it difficult to justify what they are spending. While marketing departments are more closely linked to core business functions such as strategy, many marketers are failing to understand human psychology well enough to effectively sell.

The need for honest answers

Times are difficult for brands. Gloomy titles abound: *The End of Advertising as We Know It*[11], *Big Brands, Big Trouble*[12] and *Brand Failures*[13]. Most big branded consumer-goods companies, from Procter & Gamble and Coca-Cola in the United States to Unilever and Nestlé in Europe and Sony in Japan, are facing slowing growth, declining market share or worse. As well as facing renewed attack from the anti-corporate brigade as global economies slow, the current economic downturn is putting pressure on corporate profits and share prices. Marketers are expected to produce better results with fewer resources and must demonstrate the true value of marketing to chief executives and the board or face further cuts. Company managements, meanwhile, are questioning the effectiveness of advertising and are busy streamlining marketing departments. Many marketers are desperately trying to hang on to the customers they have, tempting them with price cuts, free offers and loyalty programmes. But chasing short-term sales at the expense of brand building may prove to be a short-sighted strategy.

To regain appeal for their brands, marketers must find better tactics: guerrilla campaigns, sponsoring events and product placement in films and television shows are becoming popular. The internet offers a new way to reach younger consumers – it can be a cheap means of creating a buzz. BMW's series of mini-movies featuring its cars and shot by famous directors worked well. Companies will also need to overhaul their recruiting procedures, pay and career structures to improve the quality of people that choose marketing as a career. None of this will be easy as the world moves into recession.

Western brands also face competition from companies in the developing world. So far, most of the biggest companies from emerging markets such as China are resource groups or utilities. But technology and consumer groups such as Lenovo, Huawei and Haier from China or India's Tata group are trying to expand internationally (partly to escape rough markets at home) and some are already competing on quality as well as price. Huawei's basic telecoms gear can now compete with that of Ericsson and Alcatel, and Tata's cheap Nano car is worrying the established auto manufacturers. If Chinese and Indian consumers can start to trust some of their home-grown brands, patriotism may well prompt them to choose their goods over those of an arrogant (yet floundering) America.

At a time when globalisation and icons of business are facing intense criticism, the companies behind brands need to understand how to respond. Many have given their products an "environmentally friendly" slant, but not all are credible. Moreover, firms that buy into environmentalism are in many ways handing a stick to those who decry capitalism by agreeing that they must compensate for being in business. If firms are going to spend time and resources outside their core business, it would be better to find ways to explain to a new generation of potential consumers why business, brands and free markets are good for society, particularly the world's poorest people. They might sponsor debates about economics or globalisation in schools or help pay those able to explain economics to go into schools to talk about these subjects. Companies could also consider ways they might help parents and teachers cope with raising young people in a world filled with choice. Blaming fast-food brands or soft drinks in schools for childhood obesity or games companies for a child obsessed by a PlayStation is easy, but unhelpful. While it may be a challenge for some parents to teach a child why reading a book rather than surfing a website is time well spent, it can be done. Parents and teachers need to understand their job better – and it is not inconceivable for companies to find ways to help. Brands also need to make sure what they sell is what consumers want. Innovation is in pitifully short supply among branded companies. Rather than continuing to sell a sugar-loaded cereal that parents are eschewing, a food brand may have to take the difficult decision to shed product lines and move into new, more appealing areas, even if it means a few years of bad profit news for its shareholders.

It will not be easy for brands to engage in the defence of business at a time when people feel that capitalism has failed them. But companies need to be robust and confident enough to understand the arguments and give honest answers. Many could more openly stress the benefits of what they make in terms of lower prices, higher quality and innovation for consumers in the West and jobs for those in the developing world. It should be possible for consumers of Nike shoes to understand that their purchase is not just about being cool but is also providing someone in Indonesia with a secure wage. Companies should take the chance to help people understand why business and the brands that they create are good for the world. Particularly now, those arguments are sorely needed.

Notes and references

1 Frank, R.H., *Luxury Fever: Why Money Fails to Satisfy in an Era of Excess*, Free Press, 1999.
2 Dollar, D. and Kray, A., *Trade, Growth, and Poverty*, World Bank Working Paper, June 2001.
3 Gwartney, J. and Lawson, R., *Economic Freedom of the World: 2002 Annual Report*, The Fraser Institute, June 2002.
4 Ortega, R., *In Sam We Trust. The Untold Story of Sam Walton and How Wal-Mart is Devouring America*, Times Books, 1998.
5 McKinsey Global Institute, *U.S. Productivity Growth, 1995–2000*, October 2001.
6 Walton, S. with Huey, J., *Sam Walton. Made in America. My Story*, Doubleday, 1992.
7 Dollar, D. and Collier, P., *Globalization, Growth and Poverty: Building an Inclusive World Economy*, World Bank Policy Research Report, December 2001.

8 Legrain, P., *Open World: The Truth About Globalisation*, Abacus, 2002.

9 Litvin, D., *Empires of Profit: Commerce, Conquest and Corporate Responsibility*, Texere, 2003.

10 Schlosser, E., *Fast Food Nation: The Dark Side of the All-American Meal*, Harper Perennial, 2002.

11 Zyman, S., *The End of Advertising as We Know It*, John Wiley & Sons, 2002.

12 Trout, J., *Big Brands, Big Trouble. Lessons Learned the Hard Way*, John Wiley & Sons, 2001.

13 Haig, M., *Brand Failures*, Kogan Page, 2005.

13 Branding in Asia

Jonathan Chajet

Asia is home to half the world's population and spans 12,000km at its widest point. It is wonderfully complex, with thousands of languages, hundreds of subcultures and dozens of political systems. Thus there is no such thing as the "Asian consumer". Indeed, it could be argued that the only thing Asian countries share is their borders (and even these are occasionally in dispute).

Few have as much experience with the diversity of Asia as multinational companies. Although many have headquarters in Asia, pan-Asian marketing campaigns are extremely rare. It is impossible to buy media in bulk. There are virtually no retailers with a region-wide footprint. Consumers range from the world's wealthiest to the world's poorest. In some markets, religion is a part of daily life; in others, it is discouraged. Marketers simply cannot address the range of consumer needs under a single brand, in a single language, with a single customer experience. But when they embark on customer segmentation, what is it useful, as is the case around the world, is not similarities in demographics, but similarities in values. Confucianism forms the foundation of many Asian societies. But what do such traditional notions mean to today's consumers? Asian or otherwise, great brands connect to their audiences on an emotional level first and foremost. If Asian consumers share so little culturally, how can marketers hope to create pan-Asian brands?

A new chapter

Kofi Annan, former secretary-general of the UN, once said that arguing against globalisation is like arguing against the law of gravity. There is little doubt that the single greatest economic force in the world today is globalisation. Some would argue the environment is next, but it most certainly will be "brought to you by globalisation". The economic miracle of Asia is a direct result of globalisation. Western marketers, encouraged by declining import/export barriers, have found manufacturers in the farthest corners of China, Indonesia, Taiwan, India, Malaysia and now Vietnam eager to offer the lowest-cost goods. Cash in, products out.

For most East Asian consumers, living standards have improved significantly. Average life expectancy is now 50% longer than it was in the 1950s, and the infant mortality rate has declined by almost 75% since the 1960s. Today, the average literacy rate is over 90% (compared with 50% in the 1970s). And in China in the past quarter of a century, more than 200m have been lifted out of poverty. Consumers are now able to afford more than the basic necessities of life. They are eager to spend their new-found wealth, and they use brands as signposts to guide their spending.

Globalisation is having a secondary effect as well. The rise of the internet and global entertainment is giving Asian consumers a taste of western lifestyles. Online social networks, camera-enabled mobile phones, high-definition streaming media: each innovation is a window on what is possible for even a dollar-a-day garment worker.

Goods are not just flowing from East to West. Today, western marketers are competing fiercely for shelf space and store locations, not just in the top tier cities of Shanghai, Delhi and Kuala Lumpur, but in the second, third and fourth tier cities that are home to hundreds of millions of consumers. Governments are frantically building the airports, highways and rail tracks that will enable deeper distribution and greater growth. These potential markets are the primary reason China is projected to be the world's largest economy in the next 20 years. Moreover, Asia's insatiable appetite for new technology gives savvy marketers more and more tools to help reach consumers – for example, mobile phone SMS text messaging for brand promotions by breweries in Thailand, carmakers in Malaysia, or travel operators in Taiwan.

This combination of increasing disposable income, access to global media and improving infrastructure is paving the way for mass brand building in Asia. Just look at how fashion trends spread in Asia. Copies of new looks in Europe and the United States hit the shops of Tokyo's Aoyama and Roppongi districts in no time, quickly spreading to Seoul, Hong Kong and Singapore, being adapted to local tastes along the way. Celebrities don the fashions on teledramas, which are subtitled and rerun across the region. Consumers download images from the internet, then visit their local stores or tailors seeking an approximate copy they can wear to school or work the next day. New centres of influence like Shanghai, Bangkok and Mumbai and local designer brands like Shanghai Tang may change the direction of the fashion trade winds, but Asia as a market is growing more connected by the day.

The role of branding

Some question whether brands are really that important yet in Asia. The answer is yes and no.

Affluent consumers in Japan, South Korea, Hong Kong and Singapore are already avid brand loyalists, with little difference from their counterparts in North America or western Europe. They are connected to media and entertainment seemingly 24 hours a day, travel overseas frequently and are eager to sample what is new and different. They see western brands as higher quality, even though they are largely manufactured in Asia. They will cheerfully pay a premium to demonstrate (through beautiful – and well-branded – packaging) that a purchase was made at a leading department store in the Ginza in Tokyo and not at a store where they could have bought exactly the same item at a considerable saving. They can afford the best, and they have the opportunity to buy it.

But the large majority of consumers in Asia are not affluent. Middle-class people may like to visit air-conditioned stores but they are extremely price conscious and many prefer to buy goods at discount prices, usually online or in tax-free zones such as Hong Kong. They are not yet familiar with many of the western brands just entering the market (although the internet is paving the way). They will consider knock-offs for the basic necessities of life. And they are deeply nationalistic, preferring to buy local brands if they feel the quality is good enough.

The majority of sales in Asia take place not in gleaming shopping malls, such as the Mall of Asia in Manila (among the largest in the world), but in local "mom and pop" shops that are often the front half of the shop owner's home. Here there is little room for product variety, and a branded experience involves the scent of tonight's dinner and a micron-thin plastic bag to carry your purchase home. So, to influence most Asian consumers, brands must rely on the promises they make before the point of purchase if they are to affect the consumer's decision.

Rich or poor, what these segments share, in direct contrast to their western counterparts, is a different hierarchy of needs. Figure 13.1 is a classic illustration of Maslow's pyramid. In the West, self-actualisation is at the top of the pyramid. In marketing terms, consumers seek brands that help them feel better about themselves. Hence the popularity of sports-utility vehicles and Timberland boots: "I may never get into the outdoors, but at least I feel like I could." In Asia, the top two layers of the pyramid are reversed. Group before individual, we before me, needs of superiors before needs of self – these values are the result of thousands of years of social and family norms. In marketing terms, Asian consumers seek

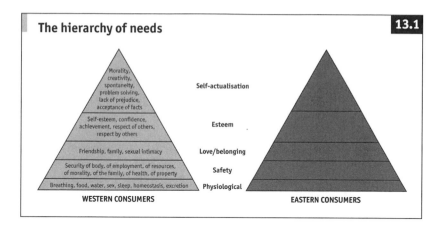

The hierarchy of needs **13.1**

Self-actualisation

Esteem

Love/belonging

Safety

Physiological

Morality, creativity, spontaneity, problem solving, lack of prejudice, acceptance of facts

Self-esteem, confidence, achievement, respect of others, respect by others

Friendship, family, sexual intimacy

Security of body, of employment, of resources, of morality, of the family, of health, of property

Breathing, food, water, sex, sleep, homeostasis, excretion

WESTERN CONSUMERS

EASTERN CONSUMERS

brands that give them "face": "What does this brand make others think about me?" Hermes, Häagen-Dazs and Johnnie Walker are extraordinarily popular in Asia – even if consumers make the purchase for others as often as they do for themselves.

Theoretically, as luxury goods become more democratised and consumers become accustomed to a higher standard of living, status-seeking will diminish in importance in Asia. But in wealthier countries such as Japan and South Korea, which have been modernised for decades, there is little evidence that this hierarchy is changing, and the luxury product boom continues unabated. So for the time being, status-seeking is the playground of modern branding in Asia.

The China factor

China is significant not only because of its central role in globalisation, but also as an encapsulation of how branding in Asia is evolving. China's economy is developing at an amazing rate – there has been double-digit growth in GDP for over ten years. However, the country is not immune to the economic slowdown, and the consensus among economists is that there will be more modest growth of 7–8% in the future – still a figure that most countries can only dream about.

China's sustained growth has created a golden age for the study of social science. Better educated and facing greater opportunities, children are often paid salaries ten times higher than those of their parents, and they still live together. Imagine the discussions around the dinner table: "I remember when we would have to line up for hours for a loaf of bread" versus "Should I spend one month's salary on that new Coach handbag?" Chinese parents seem to be taking this in their stride. They are enormously proud of their children's accomplishments but concerned about the erosion of traditional values.

Interestingly, censorship has not slowed down the understanding that Chinese consumers have of western brands or their access to them. China is now the biggest luxury market in the world. It is estimated that in 2007 more iPhones were bought in China than in the United States – even though Apple had yet to sell them there. Even today, they are manufactured in China, shipped to the United States, and then illegally shipped back to China for resale (at a hefty premium). And because they are not officially sold in China, Apple has no defence against competing products that look identical and are quite popular.

The Chinese government is investing heavily in infrastructure: roads, bridges, hotels, high-speed trains, shopping malls. With so many enterprises owned by the state, economic development is a matter of government policy rather than return on investment. This is one major reason why China's economy is advancing more rapidly than India's, despite India's distinct advantages in education, technology and language.

But although China is developing quickly, values are not changing as quickly as buying power. Older consumers are still highly price conscious; they have the time and the willingness to travel on a public bus across town for a modest promotion on cooking oil. Younger consumers may not have so much time to spare, but for more expensive items, they will browse in stores and surf online for hours to find the best deal on a brand they love.

Brands are playing a significant social role in China, where standing out in a country of 1.3 billion people can be difficult. The majority of the population live in some of the world's largest and most densely populated cities, so personal space is at a premium. If you are a fresh out of university, you are competing with millions of other graduates for the same jobs. The intense pressure to put group before self discourages you from setting yourself apart from the crowd.

Brands give consumers the chance to talk about themselves without speaking a word. Bergstrom Trends, a research consultancy that reports on youth trends in China, describes this as the birth of individuality. Young Chinese consumers are eager to find ways to express themselves. They accessorise their mobile phones, create elaborate online alter-egos and assimilate fashions from around the world into a personal style that is uniquely their own. Brands, whether global or local, are part of the colour palette that Chinese consumers are using to decorate their lives.

The rise of local brands

After more than ten years of careful management and continuous innovation, some Chinese brands have succeeded in building high awareness and preference among consumers. With the increasing consumer appetite for brands, local Chinese companies are beginning to realise their great potential. In 2007, Interbrand conducted a study of the top brands in China based on their financial value (see Table 13.1 on the next page).

Table 13.1 shows that most of the top brands are large-scale, state-owned enterprises which have historically dominated China's economy. These organisations have special advantages: protection from competition, dominant market share, easier access to capital and consumer recognition accumulated through a long history.

Today, several highly market-oriented, competitive brands such as Li Ning and Baidu (see "David versus Goliath" below) are growing in popularity. These brands spent their early days studying the success of foreign brands and now that they are well established, they are migrating from learning and following to creating and exploring their own paths. They are taking the lead in management innovation and brand-building in their industries, including reorganising their marketing departments, appointing chief marketing officers, increasing brand-building budgets, tracking results, and so on. They are searching for their own brand principles in China in order to create localised best practices and redefine their industries.

David versus Goliath

Sports brand Li Ning is competing head-to-head with world-famous brands Nike and Adidas in the Chinese market. Under strong pressure, Chinese search expert Baidu has outmanoeuvred Google with better localisation, brand communication and understanding of the Chinese language. In 2006, Baidu's market share had risen to 60%, giving the company the lead position in China's market. Young and highly market-oriented companies such as Li Ning and Baidu are listening carefully to the market, gradually accumulating brand value and taking their place alongside China's advantage-rich enterprises.

Compared with global brands, the value of the top Chinese brands is still a smaller proportion of their company's market capitalisation. This

Table 13.1 **The best Chinese brands, 2007**

Rank 2007	Rank 2006	Brand	Industry	Brand value (Rmb '000)	% change 2006/2007
1	1	China Mobile	Telecommunications	313,000	11
2	3	China Construction Bank	Financial services	83,000	22
3	2	Bank of China	Financial services	82,000	0
4	5	China Life	Insurance	64,000	100
5	–	ICBC	Financial services	46,000	–
6	4	China Telecom	Telecommunications	30,000	–6
7	6	Ping An	Insurance	21,000	62
8	7	China Merchants Bank	Financial services	13,000	0
9	8	Moutai	Alcohol	13,000	24
10	–	China Unicom	Telecommunications	12,000	–
11	10	Lenovo	IT	9,700	59
12	9	Bank of Communication	Financial services	9,300	56
13	11	Netease	Internet	5,500	22
14	–	CITIC Bank	Financial services	5,300	–
15	–	PICC	Insurance	5,300	–
16	–	Minsheng Bank	Financial services	4,700	–
17	14	Wuliangye	Alcohol	3,500	30
18	16	Changyu	Alcohol	2,800	22
19	17	Vanke	Real estate	2,100	31
20	–	Suning	Retail	1,800	–
21	18	Gree	Electronics	1,700	13
22	–	Mengniu	Dairy	1,700	–
23	–	Li Ning	Apparel	1,400	–
24	20	China Overseas Property	Real estate	1,200	20
25	–	Baidu	Internet	1,100	–

Source: Interbrand

is primarily because the role of the brand – a key metric in the methodology used to assess how important brands are in a consumer's purchase decision – is generally less important in China than it is globally, as Table 13.2 shows.

Table 13.2 **Brand value as a proportion of market capitalisation (%)**

Industry	China	Global	
		High	Low
Airline	20		
Alcohol	50	50	65
Automotive	40	55	70
Computer hardware/IT	30	25	60
Consumer electronics	50	50	80
Financial services	20	9	30
Food	40	10	80
Insurance	22		
Internet services	35	30	50
Pharmaceuticals	25	4	10
Property	28		
Telecoms: fixed and mobile lines	25		
Telecoms: equipment	35	35	35
Telecoms: mobile handsets	25		

Source: Interbrand

However, the values of the top Chinese brands are quite high; for example, China Mobile would be sixth in Interbrand's ranking of the best global brands if more than 30% of its sales were outside China. This is because Chinese brands still have enormous room for growth. For example, China Mobile owns 80% of China's mobile telephony market, but less than 50% of the population has a mobile phone. China Life already accounts for almost 50% of China's life insurance market, but only about 20% of the population is insured.

To grow their value, one of the trends that both local and global brands are tapping into is national pride. As China grows in importance economically and politically, so does its confidence. Chinese consumers bond with brands that celebrate China's success, or are a product of it. For example, many brands, both foreign and domestic, are incorporating traditional Chinese visual and verbal elements in their advertising, packaging and retail stores. There is also a resurgence of *lao zi hao*, or time-honoured brands, which have survived for centuries and are being revitalised for pro-China audiences.

Local challenges

There are some areas where local brands have yet to establish a foothold. China lacks its own knowledge-intensive brands to compete with the likes of Microsoft, SAP and Intel. However, there are a few, such as Lenovo and Huawei, which have earned their brand images through business acumen, cost competitiveness and speed to market. Knowledge-intensive brands build equity by investing in R&D, protecting intellectual property and customising products to meet consumer preferences.

China also lacks its own luxury brands to compete with, for example, Rolex and Louis Vuitton. However, in traditional luxury categories such as tea, wine, herbal remedies and antiques a few Chinese brands are emerging. Local alcohol brands such as Wuliangye and Moutai have a long history and classical heritage, but they lack the profit margins needed to invest in the marketing that a luxury brand requires. To become lifestyle brand symbols, Chinese luxury brands will need to focus on relevant aspects of Chinese culture.

The lesson many local Chinese companies have yet to fully learn is the importance of brand experience in building long-term relationships with consumers. Successful global brands deliver their core idea to the consumer at every touch point, using advanced technology to create a powerful experience. Deeper brand experiences mean more customer-oriented interactions that lead to deeper reflection and action by the consumer. The banking industry is a good example; for local Chinese brands to take their business to the next stage, they must gather insights of different customer groups, deliver more focused services and design more distinctive business environments. Chinese banks could learn from Vanke, China's largest real estate developer, which has rewritten the rules of its industry (see "Redefining the rules" opposite).

Redefining the rules

Typically, real estate companies around the world diminish the role of the corporate brand in favour of property brands. But in China, where mixed developer quality has tested consumer confidence, China's largest real estate developer, Vanke, treats its corporate brand as a strategic resource and has cultivated it for long-term development. In a real estate market where developers are often criticised and questioned, Vanke is respected and loved as a brand with moral integrity.

Looking to the future, once Chinese brands have built a lead in their domestic markets, they must continue to invest to maintain that lead. A warning sign can be seen in what the Japanese call *gaiatsu*, or outside pressure. Strong global brands are exerting a new kind of *gaiatsu* in Japan, forcing local brands to fight for their lives. An example is the hospitality industry. For years, the Okura Hotel and Imperial Hotel in Tokyo set the high mark in service quality that hotels across the region aspired to. That is history now. Global hotel brands led first by Westin, and more recently Ritz-Carlton, Conrad (Hilton), Grand Hyatt and Mandarin Oriental, have built five-star properties that have transformed the Tokyo skyline and redefined the playing field. Second-tier brands ANA and PRINCE Hotels have sold many of their properties to global operators in the past year.

Going global

While multinational brands are entering China, many Chinese enterprises such as Haier (white goods), Lenovo (computers), TCL (televisions) and Huawei (high technology) are ready to compete on a global stage. There is no doubt this crucial step will be difficult, and for every Samsung and Sony there are hundreds of other Asian companies that have failed to make the leap. Chinese brands must learn to adapt to global consumer demands, market environments, business models, languages, cultures and staff values. But some Chinese brands are breaking through. Lenovo's merger with IBM's PC business and its sponsorship of the 2008 Olympics are leading to global brand awareness. According to a 2007 Interbrand survey among 700 business executives living outside China, Lenovo's brand awareness reached 59%, ranking it first among Chinese brands, and already exceeding some international brands (see Figure 13.2 overleaf).

As China takes its place on the global stage, a handful of Chinese

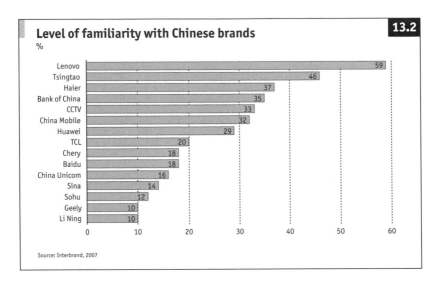

Level of familiarity with Chinese brands `13.2`

%

Lenovo	59
Tsingtao	46
Haier	37
Bank of China	35
CCTV	33
China Mobile	32
Huawei	29
TCL	20
Chery	18
Baidu	18
China Unicom	16
Sina	14
Sohu	12
Geely	10
Li Ning	10

Source: Interbrand, 2007

companies are beginning to establish their own brands overseas, and even more have said they intend to do so in the next few years. Although few Chinese companies are selling direct to overseas consumers under their own brands, many are already reaching foreign markets as OEMS (original equipment manufacturers). Others, such as television manufacturer TCL and telecommunications operator China Mobile, have acquired foreign companies and retained or licensed the use of local brands.

The establishment of Chinese global brands, carrying the torch passed on by other Asian brands such as Toyota, Sony and Samsung, which are now global household names, is inevitable. It is interesting to note that Japan was the first economic powerhouse to emerge out of Asia in the post-war era, but it was not branding and marketing acumen that put it on the map – it was sensational product quality and design. Moreover, many of the Japanese brands that led the early invasion of overseas markets have not performed as well over the past decade.

Challenges in going overseas

Many Chinese companies are still building the capabilities to take their brands global. Today, the primary competitive advantage for most Chinese companies is low-cost manufacturing, leading to low prices in the marketplace. As other countries such as India, Vietnam and Africa try to replicate the Chinese economic miracle, this advantage is likely to diminish. A related factor is the ability of Chinese companies to generate sufficient margins to support long-term brand-building efforts. Many are first looking to consolidate strengths at home and build sufficient scale to achieve higher margins before attacking markets overseas.

Another barrier for Chinese brands in going global is their lack of marketing experience. Some companies do not have a marketing department or even a manager whose sole responsibility is marketing. Branding is often treated as a "special project" led by the CEO. Top-down initiatives must start the branding process, but bottom-up support is crucial for long-term success.

Even when they are organisationally ready, Chinese companies still face some formidable hurdles. Many focus their efforts on "prestige" markets such as the United States and western Europe. Although these markets are lucrative, competitors are substantially stronger and more entrenched, and marketing costs are significantly more expensive.

Chinese brands must also find ways to make themselves relevant and compelling to consumers outside China. This will require appealing to different tastes, purchase drivers and cultural cues. Many Chinese brand names are difficult to pronounce in Latin-based languages, and communications touch points such as websites must be reformulated for local markets.

Perhaps the biggest challenge is brand awareness. For some, the 2008 Olympics was a defining moment. A few companies sponsored the Beijing Olympics at various levels, including Lenovo, which was a global sponsor. But sustained overseas investment will be necessary for Chinese brands to pierce the global consciousness.

The latest hurdle: Made in China

A series of highly publicised quality issues for Chinese exports has raised questions about the potential for Chinese brands in overseas markets. According to the Consumer Product Safety Commission, over 40% of recalls in the United States in 2007 were for products from China. The "Made in China" brand has suffered a serious setback; those consumers who know or check the country of origin of a product will think twice for the next few years. This is probably more significant in categories where safety and hygiene are primary purchase drivers such as food, beverages, cosmetics, automobiles and toys.

Several factors may mitigate the challenge to a "Made in China" label. Most consumers do not consistently check for the country of origin label (survey data seem to support this; see Figure 13.3 on the next page). With so many western companies outsourcing manufacturing to China, and

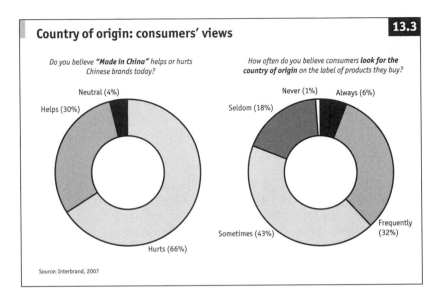

Country of origin: consumers' views `13.3`

Do you believe "Made in China" helps or hurts Chinese brands today?

Neutral (4%)
Helps (30%)
Hurts (66%)

How often do you believe consumers look for the country of origin on the label of products they buy?

Never (1%) Always (6%)
Seldom (18%)
Sometimes (43%)
Frequently (32%)

Source: Interbrand, 2007

the high costs of shifting production to another country, consumers are left with little choice in the short term. According to the Consumer Product Safety Commission, 40% of consumer products imported to the United States in 2006 came from China.

Over time, consumer trust in a product brand may counterbalance concerns about the country of origin. For example, the Crest brand may give consumers confidence in the quality of the toothpaste, even if it is made in China. Modern brands can also be nationality-neutral. Most consumers do not know that Häagen-Dazs is manufactured in New Jersey. Effective brand development and management can help emerging Chinese brands navigate lingering negative consumer sentiment about the "Made in China" label.

Conclusion

Branding in Asia is entering a new era. As local consumers enjoy a higher standard of living their appetite for brands will grow. In boardrooms on Wall Street and in the City of London the question is no longer when they will enter China, but rather how it will increase market share (and earn better margins). For many companies Asia already represents a substantial portion of their revenue and profits. And local brands are getting much more savvy about how to compete against global competitors.

Given the diversity across the region, it is hard to identify a common set of values and preferences that marketers can use to target a pan-Asian consumer. Western brands still largely dominate the luxury landscape of "premium", "high quality" and "innovative" products. But for basic consumables, are wealthy consumers in Tokyo so different from their counterparts in Shanghai, New York or Paris? Even in an age of intense nationalism, the differences may be less dramatic than most would readily admit.

Media and technology are carrying the latest trends across the Pacific and Indian oceans to the far reaches of Asia and have been influencing consumer preferences for years. But as Asian economies grow in importance, so does their ability to reverse the flow of influence. Brands from Japan and South Korea are already household names in the West. The next waves are sure to come from China and India. In this ebb and flow of the global economy, brands are playing a critical role in bringing consumers – and the world – closer together.

14 From elephant to tiger: brands and branding in India

Max Raison

A s anyone who has visited India will know, it is full of surprises, delight, intrigue, frustration and the downright bizarre. Nowhere else can you sit in a traffic jam, surrounded by a cacophony of car horns, debating the merits of proportional representation with a cab driver only to gaze out of the window and spot a stark naked *sadhu* (a holy man who has renounced all material wealth and possessions) sauntering along the side of the road.

India's economy has been growing at a fast pace, and as with all countries its particular path to industrialisation and its social and economic structure have had a profound influence on the way that brands have been created and the way consumers relate to them.

Jaguar, Land Rover, White & MacKay and Tetley Tea are all well-known international brands, but what is less well-known is that they are owned by Indian companies – Jaguar, Land Rover and Tetley Tea by Tata Group[1] and White & MacKay by United Breweries.[2] Home-grown Indian brands have also become powerful on the world stage. ArcelorMittal is the world's number one steel company, with over 326,000 employees in more than 60 countries producing 10% of the world's steel. Wipro and Infosys are giants of IT, outsourcing their expertise to companies like Sony, Goldman Sachs, CISCO, UBS and Honda.

These brands and businesses got to where they are today as a result of unbridled ambition. Tata, still a family-run business, created headlines not only with the purchase of Jaguar and Land Rover, but also with the announcement of the production of the Nano, a 3-metre-long, four-seater, 65mph people's car priced at only Rs100,000 ($2,000). This car could become the Ford "Model T" of India and the developing world, bringing with it the social and economic transformation that Ford enabled in the United States.

India is the largest democracy in the world with a population of 1.12 billion that is likely to overtake China's by 2030 and grow to 1.59 billion by 2050. There are 18 languages, 844 dialects and gods too numerous to count. It is an ancient civilisation dating back over 4,500 years. European influence began when Vasco da Gama's voyage to India in 1497 led to a century-long monopoly on trade with Europe by Portugal, until in the 17th century Holland, Britain and France began to compete. The British East India Company emerged triumphant. It established settlements from 1600 onwards, including a formal government for Bengal in 1700. By 1757 it had defeated the Mughals, and in 1784 Britain decided to bring the company under its formal control. Two years later, Britain appointed the first governor-general. When Britain finally conceded independence, on August 15th 1947, its Indian Empire was partitioned between the new Muslim country of Pakistan and the rest of India.

Following independence a series of five-year plans were drawn up by economists who were imbued with the liberal socialism of the London School of Economics and who also saw the Soviet Union as a model for the development of a vast, heavily populated land mass. Added to this was the Gandhian philosophy of self-sufficiency. In retrospect, however, it can be seen that India suffered badly from this autarkic approach. While the countries of South-East Asia enjoyed decades of fast growth, India's economic growth rate dawdled at 3.4% a year from 1950 to 1973, equal to only 1.2% per head.

The dawdling was an inevitable consequence of some of the world's most protectionist policies. For example, imports of all but the most essential items were forbidden, or subject to high tariffs; licences were required for virtually any form of production, including the right to change it or increase it; and it was made almost impossible to close a loss-making factory or sack a redundant workforce. On top of this came the collapse of the Soviet Union, with which India had enjoyed subsidised trading links.

Only in the 1990s was the economy slowly and reluctantly liberalised and foreign investment allowed. The result has been a substantial increase in economic growth which in the decade to 2008 averaged around 8% a year. This has presented huge opportunities for businesses and brands. But what are the keys to success? The consumers are there, but how can they be reached profitably?

Indian consumers

The profile of the Indian consumer is changing, creating new dynamics in the markets in which brands have to compete. Middle-class Indians are revelling in their new-found wealth and have become avid consumers. Figure 14.1 on the next page shows just how dramatic the social transition has been, in particular the rise of the "consuming class", which has grown to over 400m consumers today. Some paint an even more

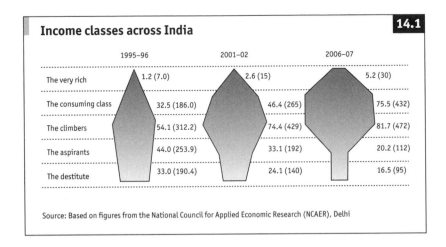

14.1

Income classes across India

	1995–96	2001–02	2006–07
The very rich	1.2 (7.0)	2.6 (15)	5.2 (30)
The consuming class	32.5 (186.0)	46.4 (265)	75.5 (432)
The climbers	54.1 (312.2)	74.4 (429)	81.7 (472)
The aspirants	44.0 (253.9)	33.1 (192)	20.2 (112)
The destitute	33.0 (190.4)	24.1 (140)	16.5 (95)

Source: Based on figures from the National Council for Applied Economic Research (NCAER), Delhi

extreme picture; McKinsey & Co, a management consulting firm, predicts that India's middle class, currently around 50m, will reach 583m by 2025 if high economic growth continues. These are the primary target for brands today. Many are young consumers, who work hard (50 hours a week on average, compared with 42 hours in the United States and under 40 hours in Europe[3]) and have developed a strong appetite for spending.

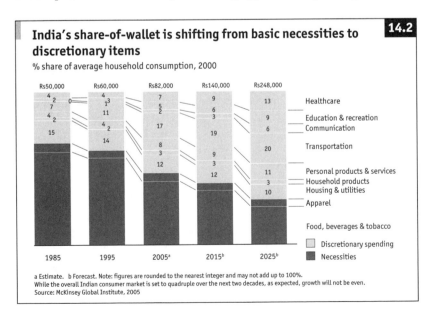

14.2

India's share-of-wallet is shifting from basic necessities to discretionary items

% share of average household consumption, 2000

Legend: Healthcare; Education & recreation; Communication; Transportation; Personal products & services; Household products; Housing & utilities; Apparel; Food, beverages & tobacco

Discretionary spending / Necessities

1985 — 1995 — 2005ᵃ — 2015ᵇ — 2025ᵇ

a Estimate. b Forecast. Note: figures are rounded to the nearest integer and may not add up to 100%.
While the overall Indian consumer market is set to quadruple over the next two decades, as expected, growth will not be even.
Source: McKinsey Global Institute, 2005

The new middle classes are unlike their parents, preferring not to save but to spend their money on Nokia phones and ProVogue jeans, in Café Coffee Day bars and on holidays. Some have developed a taste for borrowing, leveraging their income based on their future earning opportunities. Figure 14.2 highlights how spending is shifting from necessity to discretionary purchases, fuelling the growth of new categories and brands.

Changing brandscape – "Hindustan zindabad" (long live India)

These new consumers believe in themselves and in India. They have a thirst for education and a first-world mentality. This strong belief and confidence in India have raised confidence in Indian companies and brands, as research by Ashok Gopal and Rajesh Srinivasan shows.[4] In 1996 only 34% of respondents in their survey expressed confidence in Indian companies; ten years later the figure had risen to 56%. It will undoubtedly be higher today, making it harder for new foreign brands to establish a foothold in India.

The brandscape is made up of four principal groups of brands. Groups 1–3 are strong domestic brands such as Tata, Bajaj and Godrej (see below), which are often multicategory, family-run, long-established companies; established multinational brands such as Hero Honda, which pursued a joint-venture strategy with a local partner in the years of protectionism; and new foreign brands such as Vodafone and Nokia.

Godrej: 112 years young

Godrej was founded in 1897. It is one of the largest industrial powerhouses in India and is involved in an array of businesses that include construction, furniture, space technology, typewriters, cosmetics and detergents. Worried that the brand was losing resonance with a changing India and younger consumers, it undertook an extensive programme of qualitative and quantitative research, across its customer base, into attitudes to and perceptions of its brand.

The findings indicated that Godrej needed to shift its brand positioning to one that captured India's new mood of optimism and that placed the group at the heart of its progress. The positioning concept of "Brighter living" went down well with both employees and customers. A visual campaign that transcended language barriers was created to associate the brand with the energy, vibrancy, confidence, pride and optimism of the new India, and to appeal to consumers of all ages.

Source: www.godrej.com

The fourth group consists of the domestic brands that are now exploiting their "Indian-ness" in overseas markets. Kingfisher is an example. Owned by United Breweries, the Kingfisher brand, which started as a regional domestic beer, now includes an international airline and various sporting interests. The company's charismatic chairman, Vijay Mallya, master-minded the entrance of Team India into the highly competitive world of Formula One.

Another UK-based example is Cobra Beer, a company started by Karan Bilimoria to pay off his student loan which brewed Indian beer in Bangalore for the British curry house market. Cobra is now available in over 50 countries around the world. Bilimoria became a British life peer in 2006 and in 2008 announced his intention to sell Cobra.

The intergenerational gulf

By 2010, 50% of the population will be under the age of 25. These new consumers are challenging the foundations on which many brands are built, creating dramatic differences between the young and the old. The young expect first-world brands and their associated experiences and standards, and the lifestyle marketing associated with them. The older generations are more functional in their demands and needs and rely on word of mouth for their information. This intergenerational gap results in surprise and confusion for the old and frustration for the young. For example, in the past, having a telephone installed in a private home would be a long-drawn-out process involving numerous government departments, applications and a long and often frustrating wait; now a mobile phone can be purchased in a matter of minutes from a street vendor and a tariff selected to meet an individual's needs, switched on and used instantly

Changing values – balancing yesterday with tomorrow

There has also been a powerful shift in the values of younger consumers, modern living being balanced with the past and tradition. Young professionals, educated abroad and holding down high-profile IT jobs, may still have an arranged marriage. They try to balance the values of yesterday and tomorrow. The rise of coffee bars in India has just as much to do with these changing social patterns as with the skill of the barista. They provide a way for youngsters to meet away from their parents' watchful eyes.

Meeting the new consumer needs

There are a number of elements that brands must understand to be successful in India.

The retail structure

There is little organised retailing in India, creating a huge challenge in distribution. In 2006 Verdict[6] showed that a staggering 96.9% of retail expenditure is through street markets and small convenience stores (*kiranas*). If brands are to enter the mass market, they must establish a way to tackle this. Companies and brands such as Unilever have more than just heritage, they have a consumer business geared to give them access to the Indian masses.

Adapt

India is not one single market but, as Kishore Biyani, a successful retailer, says, a "mass of niches". Brands must understand this and adapt accordingly. This is important both to capture the imagination of the population and on a regional and local level. Each state in India has its own religious and cultural identity and relevant brands can create a powerful dynamic. For example, Godrej has a network of local retail branches providing products and advice to local farmers and communities. Each store is subtly adapted to meet local needs, from the product to the style of imagery used, creating a strong local bond. Many brands use celebrities to transcend these boundaries; Amitabh Bachchan is an example.

Brand Bachchan

Amitabh Bachchan is an icon of the Bollywood silver screen. Born in 1942 he is a screen actor known as the "Big B" to millions of adoring fans. He first gained popularity in the early 1970s and has since become one of the most prominent figures in the history of Indian cinema.

His appeal is more than the gravel in his voice or his movie-star looks. He has had a colourful life; early success on the screen, a stint as a politician, a 15-year ban from the press and a slump followed by a rise to the top again. He is also a proud family man, married only once, with a successful son (Abhishek) and glamorous daughter in-law (the ex Miss World Aishwarya Rai). These ups and downs, morals and integrity give him universal appeal throughout India. This makes him attractive to sponsors as he can transcend many of the age and religious barriers that pervade society. As a result he can be seen endorsing everything from soft drinks and pens to food to banks.

Blend functionality and originality

Of the international brands vying for consumers' rupees, the ones that have understood and adapted to the market are having the most success. They understand that being exotic is not enough –there must be substance beneath the style. One of Nokia's best-selling products is a simple dust-proof phone, short on functions, long on battery life. It would not make it past the playground gates in Europe, yet in India it is perfect. Its dustproof features are highly practical; its torch feature is great for power cuts; and its long battery life is even better. Supported by a great advertisement, Nokia had an instant success.

Complexity

Complexity is something Indians are used to, perhaps because of the extraordinary bureaucracy that envelops the workings of the state. This is best illustrated by the dabbawalas of Mumbai, a group of workers managed by a charitable trust. After husbands have left for work, many wives prepare a hot meal that is placed in a tiffin tin (a cylindrical metal container called a "dabba" in the local dialect). This is then picked up from the house, amalgamated with others from the neighbourhood and delivered to the correct workplace. The delivery team of 4,500 semi-literate men collect and deliver 175,000 packages a day with almost 99.99 % accuracy, and there has never been a strike in their 125-year history.

Self-expression

India is all about maximalism, volume and colour turned full on. As Diana Vreeland, editor in chief of Vogue, says: "Pink is the navy blue of India." If you are not colourful, you just won't cut it. India is too noisy and too brash for understatement to appeal. Simplicity is boring and uninteresting. Minimalism is seen as frugal and unengaging. Foreign brands have to lose their bashfulness if they are to succeed on the vibrant streets of India.

Respect the past – project the future

India may be accelerating towards the future, but there is still a strong sense of pride in its past. Himalaya is a small Indian cosmetics brand but it is growing fast. Why? Because it is grounded in the traditions of Ayurveda, an ancient system of medicine. Himalaya studied ancient texts and uses natural indigenous herbs, subjecting them to modern pharmacological and safety tests to produce new, highly differentiated products and therapies for modern times.

Be strategic, not tactical

Winning brands will be those that move from being tactical to being strategic. Too many companies focus on the consistency of image and the drive for short-term tactical sales rather than real brand-building activity that invests in the brand, connects with the consumer and increases real brand value. Businesses should take the time to:

- understand consumers – their lives, their families and their social networks;
- use these insights to invest in R&D in order to deliver brands with a real difference;
- tap into consumer confidence;
- communicate in a bold and colourful way;
- support their brands with high-quality production and delivery (traditionally an advantage held by foreign companies).

Conclusion

Charming but also chaotic and confusing, India presents a huge challenge to any western firm seeking to establish its brand in the Indian market, not least because of the growth in popularity of home-grown brands. But for those that make the effort to understand the market and adapt to it, the potential is enormous, and they will become the tigers in the new and emerging India.

Notes and references

1 www.tata.com
2 www.theubgroup.com
3 Gallup research, 2006.
4 Gopal, A. and Srinivasan, R., "The New Indian Consumer", *Harvard Business Review*, October 2006.
5 Godrej consumer research, 2007.
6 www.verdict.com

15 Branding places and nations

Simon Anholt

The reputations of countries (and, by extension, cities and regions) function rather like the brand images of companies and products, and they are equally crucial to the progress, prosperity and good management of those places. This was the observation which led the author, a decade ago, to coin the term "nation brand".

However, his preferred term, "competitive identity", better communicates the fact that managing the reputations of places has more to do with national and regional identity and the politics and economics of competitiveness than with branding as it is usually understood in the commercial sector. All places certainly have their brand images, but the extent to which they can be branded is still, quite properly, the subject of intense debate. Many governments, most consultants and even some scholars persist in a naive and superficial interpretation of "place branding" that is nothing more than standard product promotion, public relations and corporate identity, where the product just happens to be a country, a city or a region rather than a bank or a running shoe.

The need for proper understanding in this area is crucial. Today, the world is one market; the rapid advance of globalisation means that every country, every city and every region must compete with every other for its share of the world's consumers, tourists, investors, students, entrepreneurs, international sporting and cultural events, and for the attention and respect of the international media, other governments and the people of other countries.

Places get their brands from public opinion, not from marketers or governments. In a busy and crowded world, most of us do not have time to learn about what other places are really like. We navigate through the complexity of the modern world armed with a few simple clichés, which form the background of our opinions, even if we are not fully aware of this and do not always admit it to ourselves. So Paris is about style, Japan about technology, Switzerland about wealth and precision, Rio de Janeiro about carnival and football, Tuscany about the good life, and most African countries about poverty, corruption, war, famine and disease. Most of us are much too busy worrying about ourselves and our own countries to spend too long trying to form complete, balanced and informed views about 6 billion other people and nearly 200 other countries. When you haven't got time to read a book, you judge it by its cover.

These clichés and stereotypes – whether they are positive or negative, true or untrue – fundamentally affect our behaviour towards other places and their people and products. National image matters. And it matters more and more as the world becomes more connected and the globalisation of society, communications, commerce, education and politics continues to advance. Countries, cities and regions that are lucky or virtuous enough to have acquired a positive reputation find that everything they or their citizens wish to do on the global stage is easier: their nation brand goes before them like a calling card, opening doors, creating trust, generating respect and raising the expectation of quality, competence and integrity.

Places with a reputation for being poor, uncultured, backward, dangerous or corrupt will find that everything they or their citizens try to achieve outside their own neighbourhood is harder, and the burden of proof is always on them to prove that, as individuals or as organisations, they do not conform to the national stereotype. Compare the experiences of a Swedish and an Iraqi manager in the international job market, or of an exporter from Bangladesh and one from Canada. Compare the ease with which a mediocre tourist resort in a highly regarded country can gain glowing media coverage and celebrity endorsement, with the difficulties experienced by a unique, unspoiled destination in a country with a weak or poor reputation. Compare the way consumers in Europe or America will willingly pay over the odds for a product they have never heard of before just because it is "made in Japan" rather than the identical product that is "made in Vietnam". Compare how widely and positively the international media will report on an ordinary piece of policy from the government of a country that is reputed to be fair, rich and stable, with the resounding media silence or sharp criticism that greets a wise, brave and innovative policy from the government of a country that is saddled with a negative brand image.

All responsible governments and regional administrations, on behalf of their people, their institutions and their companies, need to discover what the world's perception of their place is, and to develop a strategy for managing it. An important part of their job is to try to build a reputation that is fair, true, powerful, attractive, genuinely useful to their economic, political and social aims, and honestly reflects the spirit, the genius and the will of the people. This huge task has become one of the primary skills of national and regional administrations in the 21st century.

How place image is built

Most countries and regions communicate with the outside world, and thus create their images in the minds of others, through six basic channels or areas of activity:

- Tourism promotion, as well as people's first-hand experience of visiting the country as tourists or business travellers. This is often the loudest voice in branding the nation, city or region, as tourist boards usually have the biggest budgets and the most competent marketers.
- Exports of products and services. These can act as powerful ambassadors, but only where their place of origin is explicit.
- Government policy, either foreign policy which directly affects others or domestic policy which is reported in the international media. Diplomacy is traditionally the main route by which such things are communicated to the outside world, but there is an increasing closeness between policymakers and the international media.
- How the country or region attracts inward investment and recruits foreign "talent"; the attitude towards expansion into the country or region by foreign companies.
- Cultural exchange and cultural activities and exports. A world tour by a national opera company, the works of a famous author, national sports teams.
- The country or region's inhabitants. High-profile leaders, media and sports stars, and the population in general – how they behave when abroad and how they treat visitors.

For clarity, these "natural" channels of communication can be shown as the points of a hexagon (see Figure 15.1).

The theory behind managing the identity and reputation of a country, city or region is that if you have a good, clear, believable idea of what the place really is and what it stands for, and co-ordinate the policies, investments, actions and communications of all six points of the hexagon so that they reinforce this message, you stand a good chance of building and maintaining a powerful and positive internal and external reputation. This will benefit exporters, importers, government, the culture sector, tourism, immigration and almost every aspect of international relations.

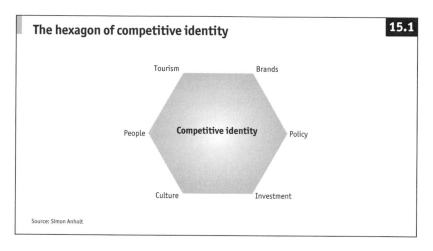

The hexagon of competitive identity **15.1**

Tourism — Brands

People — Competitive identity — Policy

Culture — Investment

Source: Simon Anholt

Implementing competitive identity

Getting everybody in the country, city or region to speak with one voice, and do it well, is just part of the solution; on its own it will not achieve a dramatic enhancement of the national or regional image as a whole. What really makes a difference is when a critical mass of the businesses and organisations in a place becomes dedicated to the development of new things: new ideas, new policies, new laws, new products and services, new businesses, new buildings, new art, new science, new intellectual property. When these innovations seem to be proving a few simple truths about the place they all come from, the reputation starts to move. A buzz is created, and people start to pay attention and change their minds.

The great thing about implementing the strategy in this way is that all these actions benefit the country independently of their effect on its reputation. They are good for the businesses and organisations and people that carry them out, so the money invested in them is also an investment in the country's economy, rather than simply being spent on marketing communications or design and gone forever.

Governments should never do things purely for brand-related reasons; no action should ever be conceived of or dedicated to image management or image change alone. Every initiative and action should be carried out for a real purpose in the real world, or else it runs the risk of being insincere, ineffective and perceived as propaganda or "spin" (not to mention a use of taxpayers' money that is extremely hard to justify). But there should be something unmistakable about the way in which these actions and initiatives are done – the style and method of their conception, selection and delivery, the context and the manner in which they are presented, the way in which they are aligned with other initiatives – that little by little will drive the country from the image it has acquired by default towards the one it needs and deserves.

Brand management for countries should be treated as a component of national policy, not a discipline in its own right, not a "campaign" and not an activity that can be practised separately from conventional planning, governance, economic development or statecraft. Just as the best-run corporations see brand strategy as virtually synonymous with their business strategy, so the best-run countries should build awareness and understanding of brand management into their policymaking.

Measuring the nation brand

In early 2005, the author launched two regular global surveys of consumer perceptions of countries and cities: the Nation Brands Index (NBI) and the City Brands Index (CBI). Together these surveys poll around 47,000 individuals in 55 countries every 3–12 months on their perceptions of each point of the "hexagon" (see Figure 15.1 on the previous page) in respect of 40 countries (NBI) and 60 cities (CBI).

Both surveys have proved that the brand images of places are remarkably stable: almost no country in the NBI has gained or lost more than one percentage point in the four years since the survey was launched. People form their opinions about other countries and cities gradually throughout their lives as a consequence of many different inputs and influences. Such opinions become deeply rooted in the cultures of populations, and seldom change very much or very quickly.

Events which may seem really significant within a country – a domestic political crisis, a crime wave, a national scandal – seldom cause so much as a ripple in the country's international reputation, even when they are reported in the international media. People may ask how badly their national reputation has been damaged in the eyes of the world by the latest political upheaval, economic crisis or natural disaster, or how much it has benefited from the latest sporting, commercial or cultural success. The answer is usually the same: the world, generally, did not notice and would not care much even if it did.

This indifference to the affairs of other nations is not surprising: we all have plenty to think about in our own countries and in the international arena without worrying too much about what goes on in a country we may never visit and that we could not reliably point to on a map. We are attached to our images of other countries because they form a reassuring, largely unchanging and simple guide to the complexities of life in a wide and complex world. As a result, most of us have a strong natural resistance to altering our views about other countries and their populations, and it takes something pretty extraordinary or personal before we are prepared to do so.

However, as the NBI and the CBI have shown, there are exceptions to this pattern. When a country's image does change, it is rarely because of something that happens to or in that country (or indeed because of anything that it says). It is usually because of something that a country has done (or is widely believed to have done) to others. The most dramatic example of this was the collapse in Denmark's image in some predominantly Muslim countries following the publication in 2005 of cartoons lampooning the Prophet Mohammed. In Egypt, for example, Denmark dropped from 14th place to 38th, the bottom of the ranking, and has still not fully recovered.

Yet even the changes in image which result from a change in behaviour on the part of a country (this usually means the government of the country) do not seem to be long-lasting, and the indications are that most people soon revert to their previous beliefs about the country and its people. This is probably because the brand images of countries are rooted in some kind of truth, and to some degree do serve to summarise the real nature of the nation. Most countries, at some level, get the brand image they deserve.

Countries that are perceived as warlike or quarrelsome will not undergo a dramatic change in reputation just because they have gone to war or quarrelled with their enemies once again; but they may have to remain blameless and peace-loving for generations before that negative image starts to fade (although it might fade rather sooner if they become cast as regular victims of others' aggression). Countries with a reputation for social justice and tolerance, forged over generations of enlightened cultural, social and political behaviour, can, it seems, rest on their laurels for centuries. They can even be embroiled in ethnic unrest and political scandal for years before people beyond their own populations and nearest neighbours start to revise their views.

National reputation evolves over time, and although it generally lags a long way behind reality, its relationship to the truth (accepting, of course, that there is never one simple, single truth about something as complex as a country, city or region) depends on the intensity and frequency of that country's dialogue with the rest of the world. Countries that are active in international politics, commerce, culture, society or a combination of all four – as business people would say, countries with more "consumer touch-points" – generally find that their image tracks their reality more closely than those that are less active, and they will have more accurate and more up-to-date images.

Countries such as the UK, France, China and the Netherlands, which have had empires in the past, may still be enjoying the benefits of decades or centuries of busy cultural, political, social and commercial transactions with far-flung countries, even if the unpleasant military and political details are long consigned to the history books. What remains is the sense of intimacy and familiarity with the other country's ways of living and the complex interweaving of national cultures and histories, which would take generations to untangle. For all these reasons, national reputation is much more of a fixed asset than a liquid currency.

Nation brands are virtually the same thing as stereotypes and clichés: they are more often based on ignorance and prejudice than on reality and experience, and they are frequently unfair. But this does not mean that reputation can be ignored or excluded from serious political or economic debate, simply because it belongs to the sphere of "perception" rather than "reality". Whatever the distinction between perception and reality, perceptions determine people's behaviour just as much, if not more, than reality does.

There is not a lot that nations and cities can do about this. National image was not created through communications and cannot be altered by slogans such as "Malaysia – Truly Asia" and "New Zealand 100% Pure", or logos such as Hong Kong's dragon and Miró's sun symbol for Spain. These are examples of marketing communications, sometimes used to market tourist attractions and sometimes used in the (usually vain) hope that applying product-style marketing techniques to the entire state or city will improve its image or profile.

Brand management in the commercial sphere only works because the company that owns the brand has a high degree of control over the product itself and over its channels of communication, so it can influence consumers' experience of the product and the way in which the product is presented to them through the media. On balance, a good company with a good product can, with sufficient skill, patience and resources, build the brand image it wants and needs and which its product deserves.

Places are different. No single body, political or otherwise, exercises this much control over the national "product" or the way it communicates with the outside world. The tiniest village is infinitely more complex, more diverse and less unified than the largest corporation, purely because of the different reasons people are there. Places have no single, unifying purpose, unlike the simple creed of shareholder value that binds corporations together (although, arguably, the United States once did have a kind of "corporate strategy" which gave rise to a kind of "brand strategy") – a contract of employment is mainly about duties, whereas a social contract is mainly about rights. Of course, there have always been heads of state who attempt to run their countries like corporations and exercise control over the "brand" by controlling the channels of information, but this kind of control through propaganda can only work within entirely closed societies. It is one of the positive side-effects of globalisation that in our media-literate and constantly communicating international arena, propaganda is not so much evil as impossible.

Nonetheless, governments can do three important things with their national reputation:

◪ They can understand and monitor their international image in the countries and sectors where it matters most in a rigorous and scientific way, and understand exactly how and where this affects their interests in those countries and sectors.

◪ If they collaborate imaginatively, effectively and openly with business and civil society, they can agree on a national strategy and narrative – where the country is going, and how it is going to get there – which honestly reflects the skills, genius and will of the people.

◪ They can ensure that their country maintains a stream of innovative and eye-catching products, services, policies and initiatives in every sector, which will keep it at the forefront of the world's attention and admiration, demonstrate the truth of that narrative and prove the country's right to the reputation its people and government desire to acquire.

More engagement, not simply more communication, with the rest of the world can enhance the profile of places, and higher visibility generally means stronger appeal. The NBI suggests that the more we know about a country, the more we are prepared to forgive its transgressions and admire its strengths and achievements.

In contrast, countries that are not well known are not usually viewed positively. Iceland, for example, may be one of the world's richest nations per head of population, have a uniquely beautiful natural landscape and a rich and ancient culture, and be successful in many other ways, but few people know enough about it to see it in positive brand terms. In the fourth quarter of 2006 it was ranked 19th in the NBI, which compares poorly with its cultural cousins, Norway, Denmark and Sweden, even though the only sense in which Iceland is objectively inferior to these countries is in the size of its population, land mass and, consequently, its global influence in economic, political and cultural terms. It will be interesting to see whether the near collapse of its economy in late 2008 will have an impact on its scores in the next NBI survey. As the financial crisis has been so widely spread, it is possible that the negative impact on Iceland's overall ranking will be moderate; however, since Iceland had a rather weak image in the first place, a "major news story" such as this might have a disproportionate effect on the country's overall reputation, since it will be one of the few facts people actually know about Iceland.

The opposite is not always true. Big, powerful nations such as the United States and China can certainly attract negative perceptions, although the more well known a country is, the more people are able to differentiate between the positive and negative aspects of its brand. On the whole, people are most attracted to countries that project clear, consistent values and behaviours on the issues that people value, such as competent government, friendly population and economic opportunities.

Perceptions of a country that is the regular focus of world attention, such as Israel, can be much more volatile than those of countries that stand outside the glare of the world's media, such as Canada or New Zealand. This volatility is increased if the country's prominence is mainly based on a single issue: in Israel's case, its role in regional conflict. In such cases, the country's image can shift as rapidly and as dramatically as people's perceptions of the issue itself, because the country becomes synonymous with the conflict. Countries with more complex, rich and diverse images have some immunity from this volatility. The United States, for example, is no better liked than Israel in many parts of the world, but because its reputation is more broadly based and extends far beyond the purely political, ideological and military sphere, its overall reputation suffers much less from the unpopularity of its government's foreign policy.

Changes in opinion and attitude that affect only a subset of the world's population will also have less of an impact on a nation's global brand. In the first quarter of 2006, the NBI showed that the brand image of Denmark and the Danish people was severely damaged in countries with predominantly Muslim populations by the cartoons controversy. The effect of the controversy on some of these countries was sustained: Denmark was still ranked overall as low as 25th by the Egypt panel a year after the events took place, and in the last quarter of 2007 the Egyptian panel still ranked the Danes last in its NBI "people" ranking. However, the negative impact of the controversy was far less noticeable among the NBI survey population as a whole and had completely disappeared a year and a half after the controversy broke. In the 2008 survey Denmark ranked 13th in the overall global ranking, compared with 14th a year earlier.

Sustained change in nation brands generally takes place slowly over a number of years. It happens in three principal ways:

◾ A country can advance or fall back in one or more brand dimensions through complex economic and social processes in that country. For example, China's economic growth is gradually leading to the country's identification with better quality and more sophisticated products, despite the setbacks caused by poor-quality products and fakes. But reduced social cohesion in a country, leading to increased anti-social behaviour, can damage the reputation of its people.

◾ Even if nations themselves do not change, the values of people observing them can and do change, and this affects the way those nations are perceived. For example, there appears to be a growing "green" consciousness among some sections of the world's population, benefiting nations such as Sweden that have a good reputation for environmental responsibility and penalising nations such as Italy that do not. Italy's brand image has declined faster between 2005 and 2008 (almost 4%) than any other country in the NBI apart from China. This has happened not because Italy's brand image has deteriorated but because its appeal is less and less in tune with people's values. Italy is, quite simply, going out of fashion.

◾ The reputations of countries, and especially of smaller countries, can be improved or damaged by the actions of their governments. Governments are more likely to do damage, but improvements can be brought about through comprehensive and co-ordinated brand strategies between different sectors, as has been shown by New Zealand and occasionally by well-marketed and well-managed global events such as the Olympic Games or the soccer World Cup.

Conclusion

Not every government, or indeed every population, treats international approval as an important goal, but when we speak of the brand images of places, we are talking about something rather more significant than mere popularity.

A country's brand is a clear and simple measure of its "licence to trade" in the global marketplace, and the acceptability of its people, hospitality, culture, policies, products and services to the rest of the world. The products of a country with a weak or negative brand will generally sell at a discount on the global market; those of a country with a middling or neutral brand will sell at their intrinsic market value; and those of a country with a powerful and positive image can sell at a premium.

The only sort of government that can afford to ignore the impact of its national reputation is one which has no interest in participating in the global community, and no desire for its economy, its culture or its citizens to benefit from the rich influences and opportunities that the rest of the world offers them.

It is the duty of every responsible government in the global age to recognise that management of the nation's international reputation, one of the most valuable assets of its people, is given to it in trust for the duration of its office. Its duty is to hand over that reputation to its successors, whatever their political persuasion, in at least as good health as it received it, and to improve it if possible for the benefit of future generations.

If the world's governments placed even half the value that most wise corporations have learned to place on their good names, the world would be a safer and quieter place than it is today.

16 Brands 2.0: brands in a digital world

Andy Hobsbawm

Ipsa Scientia Potestas Est. (Knowledge is power.)
Sir Francis Bacon, *Meditationes Sacræ. De Hæresibus*, 1597

Modern branding is a system heading for crisis. To understand why, we need to understand how profoundly networked digital information is changing everything. It is the lifeblood of the economies in which brands operate, it flows through the markets they serve, it forms and amplifies the culture they reflect, and it connects the societies in which their customers live. In other words, this digital connectivity is creating a brand new world which will need a new kind of brand.

There are five parts to this argument:

- The end of information monopolies. The shift from an industrial to a digital information age is changing the relationship between consumers and brands.
- Go with the flow. People sit at the centre of their social networks and information webs, into and around which all things swirl – including brands.
- Be a verb not a noun. Brands need to find active roles to play in this constantly agitating environment and generate a stream of innovations that connect with the passions of their communities.
- Be a guide not a gatekeeper. Brands need to interpret information when they can no longer be stand-ins for it.
- Brand new world. It's a time of accelerating and destabilising change and future consumers may choose to embrace or reject brands just as quickly.

The end of information monopolies

Modern branding came of age in an era of industrial information. At the end of the 19th century, new technologies had industrialised the economy, creating mass production and mass distribution for mass markets. Media industries like publishing and movie studios became part of this new breed of titanic corporations. They too were built on large-scale investments in modern infrastructure and the cultural goods they made (from newspapers and films to television shows) became mass manufactured, communicated and consumed much like Model T Fords.

Broadcast TV, radio and print advertising expanded with the economy and contributed to its growth by promoting new products through high-reach media channels. Populations were already moving into cities which became centres of gravity for making and selling this type of information. In urban environments it was easier to cluster around and share these universal stories and media messages made in factories of cultural meaning.

It was possible for Orson Welles's infamous CBS radio adaptation of *The War of the Worlds* in 1938 to cause widespread panic only because nearly 3m people were listening to the same broadcast and thought there was a real alien attack. In communication terms, this was an Orwellian world with big screens where central authorities told people what to think. In the case of brands, and sometimes governments, a progression of print, radio and as-seen-on-TV advertising was used to tell people that "Guinness is good for you", that "Your Country Needs You", or that Rice Krispies "Snap, crackle and pop".

Some of today's most enduring brands from Coca-Cola and Singer sewing machines to American Express were built in this way. This is how Coca-Cola could realistically claim to "teach the world to sing" in 1971 with a radio and television advertising jingle which became a top ten hit in the American and British music charts and has since spawned over 75 different cover versions (it is still one of the 100 best-selling singles of all time in the UK).

It was a society where large institutions dominated all forms of information – from news and entertainment to details about products and the companies that made them. Brands became a way of summarising this information in one place.

Some 20 years ago Apple's 1984 advertisement could sum up the signs of the times for you, Levis or Nike could let you know what was cool, and as late as 1997 IKEA could still tell you to "Chuck out your chintz", just because that was how they said the world works. The costs for consumers to find this out for themselves were high since e-mail and mobile phones were not yet part of the mainstream and Google had not been invented, so brands served as useful information surrogates. In effect, brands were built on information monopolies.

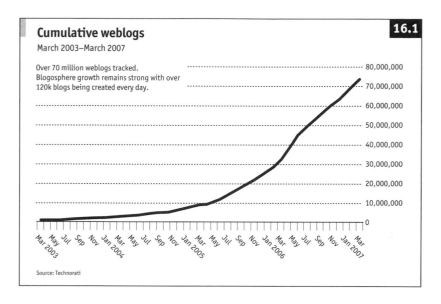

Cumulative weblogs

16.1

March 2003–March 2007

Over 70 million weblogs tracked.
Blogosphere growth remains strong with over
120k blogs being created every day.

80,000,000
70,000,000
60,000,000
50,000,000
40,000,000
30,000,000
20,000,000
10,000,000
0

Mar 2003 · May · Jul · Sep · Nov · Jan 2004 · Mar · May · Jul · Sep · Nov · Jan 2005 · Mar · May · Jul · Sep · Nov · Jan 2006 · Mar · May · Jul · Sep · Nov · Jan 2007 · Mar

Source: Technorati

The rise of digital information networks

Today, it is well understood that this mass-media world is splintering into niches. In 1965, three national TV advertisements could reach 80% of American 18–49 year-olds. Some 40 years later, you needed 117 prime-time spots to reach the same proportion of the population. TV channels in the average American household have more than tripled since 1994 and over three-quarters of Americans are now online, many in micro communities based on individual enthusiasms.

The types of digital media people can access have exploded – even software applications (Google, Facebook) have morphed into media owners with advertising inventories. Converged information and multi-media content now streams through new communications channels and technologies such as wireless broadband, smart mobile devices and search engines, low-cost content production tools (Garageband, iMovie), free collaboration and publishing software (wikis, blogs, RSS), and a free global distribution system thanks to social networks and peer-to-peer networks.

These new media are interactive, immersive and socially connected, radically different from the old media archetypes. A new culture of active consumer participation in media has arisen in which content can be created and shared across digital networks; consumers have almost total access to information and the ability to communicate it instantly.

219

Along with many industries such as health care, media or finance, the knowledge monopolies that brands enjoyed have been undermined by this online word of mouth combined with access to information sources and professional databases previously only available to specialists.

This can be seen clearly in fashion publishing. Streetwear blogs, sites such as Flickr, MySpace and YouTube, and niche social networking fashion sites such as MyStyleDiary or Stylehive have made it easy to see and connect with other people who are into the same fashions anywhere in the world, every day – not when the editorial calendars of media organisations decide something should be published.

See through brands

Modern marketing is now a global conversation between hundreds of millions of customers in blogs, social networks, discussion groups, review sites and countless other word-of-mouth forums, where they judge, reject, embrace and endorse the brands in their world. Travel recommendation site Tripadvisor.com, for example, carries 15m customer reviews and has been adding them at a rate of more than 115,000 a week since late 2007.

There are sites for brand fans and brand terrorists in equal measure. Try Googling a random brand name followed by the word "sucks" (for example, Sony, Dell, IKEA, Ford, Disney and, ironically, Google). There is now a Wikipedia for whistleblowers. On Wikileaks.org anyone can post comments and leak documents untraceably and anonymously about governments and corporations all over the world.

Brands such as Dell may spend $1.5 billion per year on marketing, but that doesn't help when consumers Google "Dell customer service" and, after some official dell.com links, find results such as the following on the first page (at the time of writing):

- "YouTube – Funny Dell Customer Service Call"
- "My unbelievable experiences with Dell"
- "Consumer complaints about Dell Computer's Customer Service"
- "Cuomo Sues Dell For False Advertising, Failure To Provide Services"
- "I tested Dell and they failed"
- "Want to complain about Dell? Forget it"
- "Growing pains hit Dell's customer service"
- "If you've exhausted the normal routes of solving your problems with Dell try sending an email to..."

These days a brand is no longer what a company claims it is, as *Wired* magazine's Chris Anderson observed, "but what Google says it is". Even if a brand manages to control the distribution of some information online, it can never control what people are saying about it. While every entry on the first page of a Google search for "BMW" is an official BMW site, apart from one Wikipedia listing, not one of the top ten links on Google Blog Search is controlled by the BMW brand.

Companies are used to not just controlling the distribution of information they want to communicate, but also giving away as little as possible about the information they don't want to release. These days you cannot control, censor or cancel out the information you don't want people to have. It is a time of total transparency, from pricing to ethical behaviour; everything that can be known about a brand will be.

Go with the flow

Brands will need to find a place in this swirling, memetic media system where all sorts of information freely flows: word of mouth, fashion, trends, imitation, flattery, truths, half-truths, rumour, panic, entertainment, news, deals, alerts, brands, friendships, passions, tastes, memories, moods – pretty much everything that makes up our personal and professional lives.

Furthermore, this information ecosystem is in a permanent state of agitation and change thanks to a torrent of new technologies. Innovations in online video or social networking or mobile applications, say, are like new chemical elements which set off chain reactions and interact violently with everything else. Eventually things settle down for a bit, until the next disruption sets it all off again.

Linear communications based on the industrial model of message, sender and receiver are becoming redundant in this world where everyone is connected and information feeds back into itself.

Harvard research into social networks shows that because every node in the network is a sentient, responsive individual, changes in mood and lifestyle can spread through the system like tastes in fashion, music, films, books and food. Observing the flow of activities through social networks such as Facebook, MySpace, Flickr and Twitter, researchers discovered that people also copy powerful behaviours like happiness, depression, altruism, a need for privacy, drinking, obesity or stopping smoking.

A 32-year study into the viral spread of obesity across a social network of 12,067 people revealed that, regardless of distance, close mutual friendship had the greatest impact on behaviour (see Figure 16.2 on the next

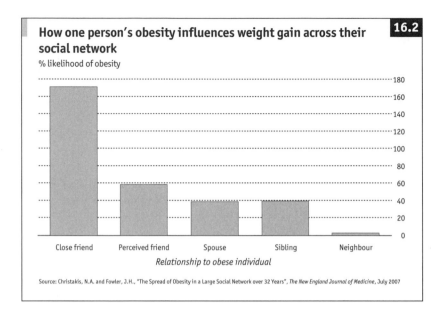

How one person's obesity influences weight gain across their social network
16.2

% likelihood of obesity

Relationship to obese individual

Source: Christakis, N.A. and Fowler, J.H., "The Spread of Obesity in a Large Social Network over 32 Years", *The New England Journal of Medicine*, July 2007

page). A forthcoming study of peer influence by Nicholas Christakis and James Fowler, authors of this study, proves how "social contagion" operates the same way across online social networks.

The identity of the modern individual is already complex, with many overlapping relationships and affiliations. Different loyalties and desires constantly compete for attention and blur together: family or friends, city or state, club versus national team, work/life balance, and so on. The fluidity of these social networks compounds this.

Online, people try out many different roles and identities, for example user names in social networks or avatars in games (there are now more avatars than people in the United States). An increasing amount of our selves already flows over digital networks along with what we say, think and do. In the future, these identities will always be in motion.

Nearly 20 years ago, a classic British Airways television advertisement hired thousands of extras to form a smiling face seen from above and told us that BA was "bringing the world together". Today the internet brings the world together and brands need to offer interactions or experiences or events that are picked up and transmitted in this flow.

They often need to behave like media companies or software applications to do so. This is why BMW makes short films, Burger King makes X-box games, Starbucks sells books and music, and American Airlines makes Facebook widgets to help brand fans share travel tips and experiences with each other.

Consumer innovation

There is no question that armed with new tools and technologies, consumers are looking for more control, filtering and choice. They are demanding the content, services, entertainment and interactions they want, on their own terms. Search engines are a powerful expression of the control over information now in the hands of individuals.

Brand managers often confuse not being in complete control of their brand with being completely out of control. It is not the same thing, although the likes of Google might argue that if you're not a bit out of control, you're not going fast enough.

Progressive companies are seeing this shift in control as an opportunity to recruit consumers to help design their next generation of products and express themselves creatively through the brand at the same time. For example, Lego gave eight competition winners a 5% royalty for products manufactured from entries created using a Lego design toolkit. Some 120,000 people joined Boeing's World Design Team to contribute to the creation of its new aircraft via an online forum. Procter & Gamble set up Vocalpoint, an innovation community of 500,000 influential mothers which uses surveys and sampling to help brands develop better offers for this audience and then spread the word to them.

Now that the media production and distribution resources you used to find in multimillion-dollar movie studios are in the average teenager's laptop, we have witnessed a Cambrian explosion of mass amateur publishing online: the millions of product reviews on Amazon, Wikipedia entries, classifieds on Craigslist or videos on YouTube, for instance, or the hundreds of millions of eBay listings and user-created profiles on Facebook, MySpace and other social networks. The most successful online consumer brands, from Google to Yahoo, are based almost entirely on these kinds of user contributions.

Be a verb not a noun

Brand owners often see their brands as suns in a solar system, centres of energy which can pull consumers into their gravitational orbit with the forces of attraction they create with their marketing. Not only do most brands not shine half as brightly as they think – consumers see just one of many distant points of light in a starry sky – but this is an outdated view based on a relatively static model.

Today's consumers do not stay in one place long enough to have brand beliefs beamed at them en masse. They exist in fluid and fragmented communities based on a range of self-selecting passions and interests. Brands should be seen as freer roving nodes in a network of individuals and their relationships.

The internet has always been about connecting people and helping them find information and community. That is what made it exciting and interesting to begin with. Brand owners should never forget how the internet was used in the first place (e-mail, forums, using free web space to post baby scans for friends and relatives). There has only ever been one magic ingredient for truly compelling net interactions: people. The more brands can help consumers share and connect with each other, the better.

As importantly, brands have to find some kind of dynamic role in this world, to behave based on a set active principles suited to a state of perpetual motion. They must act like verbs and do things in this space, rather than exist as passive, descriptive nouns. A verb expresses action, describes an active state of being. Brand as noun is; brand as verb does. Active brands are little engines of culture – creating it, transforming it and constantly working with the flow of it.

Nike, for instance, behaves like an active participant rather than a sponsor or, worse, interrupter of someone else's show. Its Run London event let runners keep track of their training runs, make public pledges to send to friends, plan routes with Google maps and share them with a community of 45,000 runners all over the capital. The follow-up event, Nike+ Supersonic, combined a race with a rap concert to promote the company's famously innovative Nike+ product, which is based on the insight that music fuels sport. A Nike+ wireless sensor connects your running shoes to your iPod Nano, displays how far and fast you've run and the calories you've burned and uploads all these details to a site where you can compete with other runners.

An active role for brands

John Grant, a marketing author and strategist, points to UK retailer Topshop as a brand which delivers a constant stream of online and offline brand innovations to bring high fashion to the high street. It does this not just with every garment in every shop but also through a range of diverse activities that connect with the tastes and desires of its audiences. From outmoded "Flopshop" in the 1990s, Topshop is now one of the UK's highest profile high-street success stories, making a profit of £100m during perhaps the worst retailing slump in two decades.

To reinvent the brand, Topshop created designer and celebrity lines with supermodel Kate Moss and is the only high-street retailer to show at London Fashion Week. It brought out a range of specialist collections targeted at certain lifestyles (Topshop Vintage, Topshop Unique, Mini Topshop, and so on). It provided an in-store style advisory service to help customers get the right look; these personal shoppers also do home and office visits armed with knowledge of the latest fashion trends and the clothes to match. In a fashion emergency you can even text the style advisers and they'll courier over their best guess at the outfit you're after the same day.

From customisable gift-wrap generators, text-message charity auctions and Valentine's Day tattoo-makers, to RSS feeds, video podcasts and desktop widgets, Topshop has found a place in this swirling system of culture and meaning. If its brand was a stick of rock you might find it in a variety of locations, packaging and flavours, but the active principle running through the centre will always be fast fashion fixes for high-street style addicts.

People have a core human need for group relationships based on what we might call the internet's geography of passion. It is not where we are or where we come from that is important, but what we care about. According to Henley Centre research, 60% of Britons have less in common with their neighbours than the folk who share their hobbies. Online, it is easy for people to track down groups across the world to which they can belong, to relate to like minds and like-minded brands on a specific dimension or passion.

The best brands can do these days is to meet customers halfway with a constant stream of connective innovations based on these shared passions and put them out there in the right places for customers to find and socialise. Brand owners must trust that customers and their communities will make this happen by word of mouth and trade these pieces of branded social currency among themselves to make relevant meaning.

What's the big idea?

This does not mean there should not still be a core point of view at the heart of all these activities. Indeed, it sharpens the need for it. More than ever brands need to have a *raison d'être*, an ideology even, that shapes and filters the things they do. There is a lot of evidence to show that the ones that do outperform the ones that do not.

The power in a strategic thought increasingly lies in its ability to serve a thousand small purposes effectively. Brands need to have the elasticity to be stretched and moulded by consumers into an infinite variety of shapes and sizes to fit their individual preferences and passions. To do this, brands need an active role through which they can generate a constant stream of small brand interactions, which exist in many different forms and places – catchy individual melodic phrases which chime when played together in different arrangements.

These days the big brand idea is to not forget about all the small ideas along the way. One recent example was Barack Obama's ground-breaking presidential campaign. His central, governing thought was simple: change, expressed in the iconic rallying cry of "Yes we can". But it was a self-organising army of individuals who spread this message far and fast in their own individual ways, using a range of campaign tools and content made available all over the net. A nation was mobilised online by making people active agents in the process of change, not witnesses to it. In a fitting campaign postscript, the bottom of every page on Barackobama.com reads: "Powered by hope and supporters like you."

Brands that think small

IKEA's role is to improve everyone's home with stylish, affordable furniture. It does this by organising furniture swaps between customers, furnishing hotel rooms with product designs customers can try out during their stay, or putting cushions on New York park benches to promote how good design improves living.

IKEA has contests to create home media storage solutions where the winning designs are made and sold as part of the IKEA range. It runs mobile loyalty clubs with special offers and games like text message trivia quizzes where the answers are in its catalogues. It creates microsites just so happy home owners can download a "Not For Sale" sign to drive away annoying estate agents.

Be a guide not a gatekeeper

People's relationships with brands change based on how much they know. AOL was a great starter brand for the internet until people got confident enough to do without the training wheels and did not need the protective wall AOL put around content. When people start buying wine they look for product brands such as Jacob's Creek or Sutter Home. But as they learn more about the subject they move to a relationship with a wine merchant such as Oddbins or Majestic, which specialises in helping them through the world of wine and editing choice on their behalf.

Individual product brands are always vulnerable to attack from fresh sources of information swirling around in this flow of media and social experiences. One year pomegranate was the superfood of the moment, but the next year the world had moved on and açai berries were the new black; tomorrow it will be something else. Expert consensus changes as fast as consumer opinion. In the future, brands offering consumers readymade solutions they don't need to think about will not be the default choice in a category if people work it out for themselves and arrive at a different conclusion.

Brands based on knowledge rather than ignorance act like guides and interpreters, not information surrogates. They may be involved in hosting places where you can find cool and interesting stuff, but they do not try to be a substitute for it. By helping consumers make sense of the world they invite them into a dialogue and a lasting relationship.

To launch the PS3, for example, Sony Playstation partnered with club promoters, artists and fashion stylists as well as magazines to create a platform for cultural content and new talent. KCTV magazine ran a fashion show, Dazed and Confused put on some live bands and Marmalade staged a multimedia show with user-generated content. All this was videoed, e-mailed, blogged about and otherwise digitally socialised by the artists and audiences.

Silicon implants

It is logical that the most successful new brands will follow the economic shift from the industrial to the information age. Billionaires such as Rockefeller and Ford, who made their fortunes from oil and engineering, are being replaced by Gates and Buffett in a world where matter matters less and chips, bits and bandwidth replace railway steel and motorway concrete as the driving force of the economy.

The future looks bright for media brands such as MTV and Disney, software brands such as Microsoft and Google, and service brands such as UPS, as well as for brands which increasingly behave like media and software and service brands such as Nike or Nokia. And for brands which carve out an active role as advisers and guides or aggregators and intermediaries in this new world – retailers such as Tesco and Amazon, branded venture capital groups such as Virgin and information intermediaries and aggregators such as Expedia.

Of course, many of these brands do many or all of these things. Google is a media aggregator with Google News and YouTube (indeed the core "Page Rank" search algorithm is based on aggregating the information about how sites link to each other created by millions of web users). It is also a media owner selling advertisements next to its own searches and other content. It provides media services such as Ad Sense syndication, Google Analytics and ad serving through the acquisition of DoubleClick. It also provides software, of course, from core search to office applications, photos, social networks, blogging, enterprise, commerce and intermediary services such as Google Product Search.

All these brands are fundamentally information-based. Even a physical retailer such as Tesco bases its competitive edge on analysing purchasing data from the hugely successful Clubcard loyalty scheme which gives it deeper customer insight than any other UK organisation.

The urge to converge: the integration of marketing and operations

We have talked about the convergence of content and culture flowing through media and information systems. Equally importantly, the lines between operations and the customer experience brands deliver are collapsing.

Spanish fashion retailer Zara – think Topshop on steroids in terms of international reach and speed of organisation – uses efficiencies to drive down costs and therefore prices, which helps generate demand. But the real story is that by focusing on real-time merchandising innovation, Zara has created a powerful marketing strategy to build the brand.

Zara staff constantly capture and profile customers' shopping behaviour on handheld devices. This information is batched and sent daily to the La Coruña design and logistics centre where a team of 300 designers modify existing patterns or create new ones based on constantly updated market activity. Designs are then transferred to computerised cutting facilities and assembled in factories via the company intranet. This flexible, network-based operation allows Zara to make and ship 10,000–12,000 new designs and over 90m articles of clothing every year, and restock 3,245 stores in 64 countries twice a week.

By using information networks to tightly integrate sales data with distribution and product development, Zara observes and responds to demand faster than anyone else, then makes and sells products faster than it can promote them through traditional campaigns. It is quicker and more efficient to put new ranges in its shops and see how they do.

Because new styles arrive twice a week in small batches and are replaced every two weeks, constant product scarcity creates a sense of urgency and desire: all stocks are effectively limited-time-only offers. Rather than talk about what it does in marketing campaigns, Zara prefers to keep doing it and invest profits in designing an irresistible retail experience and opening new stores. Most clothing retailers spend 3–4% of sales on advertising; Zara spends 0.3%.

Sometimes the lines are more blurred still. Skype, for instance, built a virtual telephony service by drawing on the computing and bandwidth resources of every user. Skype's product markets itself because people tell each other to download it (you cannot talk for free over the net unless the other person also has the software). And since every download increases the power and reach of its system, marketing and product and operations become one and the same.

Branded utility

The best strategy a brand owner can have whatever category it is in is to care about being the best in the world at what it does and actually mean it. Actions speak louder than words so brands that show they mean it in a hundred different ways, rather than just talk about it, are more likely to be believed.

It helps, of course, if you are like Apple, designing products and services like the iPod and iTunes that are special and interesting enough for people to care about, tell their friends about, create their own shared meaning around and keep coming back for more. Entertainment is traditionally the Trojan horse brands smuggle themselves inside to bypass consumer cynicism and be invited into people's lives, but so-called "branded utility" is an alternative social currency based on giving people something useful that is worth passing on. Intel, for instance, gave MySpace users an application that increased the amount of music they could store on their page.

Even if you sell something as mundane as toilet paper, you can give people something to talk about. For instance, during the 2007 Christmas holidays, 392,862 people visited Charmin's 20 hand-cleaned, high-class toilets in Times Square with the invitation: "You're in New York. Go in style."

Brand new world

A world of digital information creates relentless and accelerating change. Start-ups such as YouTube can become internationally recognised and part of global culture in a heartbeat, while 120-year-old brands such as Kodak can fall off a cliff in a few years if they do not keep up with the changing digital times. (The company that invented the consumer market for cameras and film, Kodak's shares have fallen by more than 80% in the past ten years and it has laid off 30,000 staff and lost hundreds of millions of dollars trying desperately to reinvent itself in a digital age.)

New products invented in student bedrooms quickly become a mainstream part of the global software industry, such as Linux, or evolve into global media distribution systems, such as Napster and its peer-to-peer progeny, disrupting multibillion-dollar industries along the way. Information-based sectors like the global financial markets slice up and trade packages of risk in such startlingly sophisticated ways that the banks themselves do not fully understand what they are buying and selling. Resulting crashes like the recent sub-prime mortgage meltdown bankrupted one of America's oldest and biggest investment banking brands, Lehman Brothers. Other brands such as Bear Stearns and Merrill Lynch, as well as financial giants Fannie Mae, Freddie Mac and American International Group (AIG), were saved only by being bought by other banks or bailed out directly by the government.

Everything is information and information is everything

We are living in an age when more information has been produced in the last three years than in the previous 40,000. The *New York Times* once estimated that, in the not too distant future, the "32 million books, 750 million articles and essays, 25 million songs, 500 million images, 500,000 movies, 3 million videos, TV shows and short films and 100 billion public web pages" currently stored in archives and libraries will compress onto an iPod.

Today the virtualisation of virtually everything we know is a given. If content does not already exist as ones and zeros like, say, all modern recorded music, it soon will. The world's stored knowledge and culture are being inexorably indexed, preserved and poured into an unending river of bits.

All modern commercial operations, and indeed national economies, are computerised and rely on a free and fast-flowing stream of digital information, so almost everything these days exists in a database somewhere at some point or other.

A world of new information is on the way, as more of our physical experience is measured and managed virtually with data-collecting wireless sensors. Futurist Bruce Sterling fabricated the buzzword "Spimes" to describe entities that will be so utterly smothered in traceable data, from bar-coded cradle to recycled grave, that they will exist as information all the time and objects only once in a while. There will be no need to hunt anxiously for our missing shoes in the morning, we'll just Google them.

It is unclear exactly what this means for brands in a world where everything can talk to everything else, where connected intelligence animates all inanimate objects. What happens to perfume brands, for instance, when computerised nano particles in their formulas alert us every time someone is attracted by our scent?

During this period of massive change, brands will constantly be jockeying for roles and grabbing land in an emerging, networked world. It is entirely possible that the biggest brand on the planet by the end of the next decade has not yet been invented.

Brands in the fast lane

As Alan Kay, a computer interface pioneer, once famously observed: "Technology is anything that wasn't around when you were born." For an emerging generation of consumers, "digital" is no longer a thing, it just is. The free flow of digital information is like oxygen – a natural condition of life.

The benefits of brands as handy shortcuts to help people choose how to spend their money will not hold so true for this generation. These multi-taskers, who can manage 20 simultaneous instant messaging conversations while doing their homework, won't be overloaded by choices and need brands as attention management devices. ("I've never heard a Digital Native complain about information overload," one researcher wrote, "it's a fact of life for them.") They swim in an ocean of communications and connectedness where it is more convenient to choose things recommended by people they trust. Table 16.1 on the next page shows the results of a survey of teenagers aged 12–17 in which they were asked to list what other activities they did while engaged in four main types of activity.

There will not be time to establish beliefs that organic is better or you know where you are with Persil, when choices are filtered through a constant stream of instant messages, friend feeds (which track what people you know are doing from moment to moment – for example, "Pav just became a fan of Sony"), or taste-making social networks and blogs. Not to mention Google's ultimate search ambition to bring you whatever you need of the world's information without even having to ask. There will not be ingrained cognitive biases towards certain brands when everyone in your Facebook group can tell you that it's not cool any more or that something else is much better.

Table 16.1 **How teenagers multi-task (%)**

	Went online	Watched TV	Did homework	Read
Watched TV	31	–	31	19
Listened to music	38	12	42	28
Surfed the internet	–	21	8	3
Talked on the phone	24	35	14	6
Instant messaged	22	13	6	3
E-mailed	27	12	3	2
Played video or computer games	16	18	3	2
Read	5	16	9	–
Nothing else	21	27	32	49

Sources: North American Technographics Retail and Marketing Online Youth Survey, Q4 2007; Forrester Research, 2008

People will continue to define themselves by what they buy (although because of climate change and an inevitable shift to a low-carbon economy, conspicuous non-consumption will become as important), but most of the individual product brands they choose will become much more disposable.

Modern branding was largely developed for the category of fast-moving consumer goods (FMCG), so consumers did not have to spend hours working out which grocery products to put in their shopping baskets. But branding the individual products on shelves means companies can only ever own a limited bit of our attention. In the future it will not make sense economically for the Procter & Gambles and Unilevers of the world to keep launching and maintaining thousands of brands for a slice of, say, the global polyunsaturated fats market, when they could be creating a mega-brand like Tesco instead.

There will be increasing power invested in the few higher-order mega-brands that can stay on top of this fast-moving flow and advise, guide, aggregate, consolidate, curate and innovate with a stream of products, services and brand novelties. As for the rest, when most individual product brands become as temporary and throwaway as low-cost fashion or the latest gossip, they will morph into a new category. Welcome to the world of PDCB: perpetually disposable consumer brands.

Notes and references

Anderson, C., *The Long Tail: Why the Future of Business Is Selling Less of More*, Hyperion Books, 2006.

Butler, D., "Everything, everywhere", News Feature 2020 Computing, *Nature*, March 2006.

Corcoran, C.T., "Fashion's Media Explosion", *Woman's Wear Daily*, December 2006.

Benkler, Y., *The Wealth of Networks: How Social Production Transforms Markets and Freedom*, Yale University Press, 2006.

Blakely, R., "WPP wins $1.5bn Dell advertising account", Timesonline. co.uk, December 2007

Breck, J., "More avatars now than there are people in the USA", Smartmobs.com, April 2008.

"Burger King Sells 2 Million Game Copies in 4 Weeks", Adverlab. blogspot.com, January 2007.

Carter, M., "Creating a digital echo", *Guardian*, January 2007.

"Customer-made", Trendwatching.com, 2006.

Fearis, B., "Tripadvisor reviews up to 15 million", TravelMole.com, April 2008.

"The future of fast fashion", *The Economist*, June 2005.

Grant, J., *The New Marketing Manifesto*, Texere Publishing, 2000.

Grant, J., *The Brand Innovation Manifesto*, John Wiley & Sons, 2006.

Leadbetter, C. and Miller, P., *The Pro-Am Revolution*, Demos, November 24th 2004.

McIntyre, D.A., "The Ten Worst Managed Companies In America: Kodak, H&R Block", 247wallst.com, December 2006.

Ogg, J.C., "10 CEOs Who Need to Leave: Antonio Perez of Eastman Kodak", 247wallst.com, December 2006.

Prensky, M., "The Emerging Online Life of the Digital Native", 2004.

Rheingold, H., *Smart Mobs: The Next Social Revolution*, Basic Books, 2003.

Sterling, B., *Shaping Things*, MIT Press, 2005.

Von Hippel, E., *Democratizing Innovation*, MIT Press, 2006.

"Zara profit from overseas sales", Fashionunited.co.uk, June 2007.

17 An alternative perspective on brands: markets and morals

Deborah Doane

The environment and the issue of climate change are being taken increasingly seriously. In his report released in October 2006, Sir Nicholas Stern, a leading economist, stated that "climate change was the world's greatest market failure".

The corporate sector responded, arguing that while it may have been a market failure to date, the market can find innovative solutions to the problem. Tellingly, marketing giant WPP proclaimed that green branding was no longer a marginalised issue. In its top ten green brands list in the United States and the UK, companies such as GE, Honda and IKEA appear alongside more traditional green brands, such as Wild Oats and the Body Shop.[1]

It seems miles away from where we were just a few years ago, when in her best-selling book, *No Logo*, Naomi Klein[2] argued that the big corporate brands were unaccountable bullies, who provided little benefit except to those at the top of the corporate food chain. The book was a call to arms for anti-globalisation protesters and sent a shock-wave through the corporate sector. So influential was it that *The Economist* felt the need for rebuttal and ran a "Pro Logo" special that it featured on the cover.

In the world of branding things move fast and so, too, has the debate about brands in relation to globalisation. The main issue, however, continues to be about how corporations, both big and small, behave in a global marketplace. But the question is whether or not this behaviour is a cause or a consequence of the "branding" phenomenon. Here, the answers lie in understanding the conduct of markets themselves, which, we will find, dictate the behaviour of the brand. If Stern's assessment is correct – that climate change is the world's biggest market failure – can "brands" really pull us out of the state we are in?

As a result of the No Logo phenomenon, the public has a much greater awareness of brands, holding them up to far more scrutiny than ever before. It is difficult for global corporations such as Gap, Nike, Coca-Cola or McDonald's to evade criticism on anything, from their use of water to human rights.

Consequently, the spotlight placed on them has demanded considerable action on the part of global brands, making them more accountable, in many cases, than their non-branded counterparts. In the early 1990s, Nike was a target of a massive boycott when accusations of sweatshop labour rose to prominence in the media. Nowadays, it is like a reformed sinner, having been the first in its sector (later followed by Gap) to release full details of labour audits throughout the factories in its supply chain. Meanwhile, Coca-Cola, following accusations in 2003 in India that it was draining the water that fed farmers' wells and poisoning the land with waste sludge, is now found to be engaging in everything from water-use reduction strategies to climate change policy.[3]

The Emperor's new clothes?

The anti-brand argument went like this: brands are bullies; they behave in unethical ways; they dilute culture. Big brands can threaten local competition and buy up successful smaller brands. It has long been the case that in places like India or South Africa, about the only coffee you can find is "Nescafé". Small niche local brands do not stand a chance.

But in places where ethical brands are perceived to be standing well in their own right – certainly in terms of consumer profile – the big brand bullies once again exercise their power over their smaller ethical counterparts. In 2006, both The Body Shop and Tom's of Maine, two well-known ethical brands, were bought out by large corporate conglomerations – The Body Shop by L'Oréal and Tom's of Maine by Colgate.

A brand's purchasing power extends its ability to gain access on the shelves, squeezing out and other, newer competition. Supermarkets provide better shelf space for well-known brands – probably at a price – ensuring they have a better chance of being seen and bought by consumers. At the same time, high streets around the world are looking increasingly familiar, making it difficult to distinguish between a street in Munich, Tokyo or Toronto.

One argument against the brand is that it has a tendency to dilute cultural diversity. Branding demands immediate knowledge and recognition, ideally on a global basis. You can ensure that if you walk into a Gap store in North America, Japan or Germany you will be getting the same thing. Michelle Lee, an American fashion writer, laments the "McFashion" era that the battle for the brand has created. She argues that, while the strengths of the fast-food approach to clothing give us affordability and reliability of style, "the consistency has bred a scary level of homogeneity". In the United States, 75% of men own a pair of Dockers Khakis, and 80% of Americans own at least one pair of Levi's jeans.[4] As styles from other countries become fashionable, such as the Chinese chemise or Indian-style dresses, they are also at risk of being devalued through the market. The originality that gives rise to their value as fashion items will fade and the styles will become little more than another commodity to buy, sell and replicate, eventually to their cultural detriment.

Is the brand accountable or not? Many think not, especially when it comes to social or environmental concerns. Over the past couple of decades brands have worked in chameleon-like ways. When they are challenged for poor ethical behaviour, they change names: so Altria emerged from Philip Morris, many argue as a misguided attempt to shield its non-tobacco business from the "drag" brought down by the negative reputation of tobacco and impending law claims. The *American Journal of Public Health* charged that the name change was the culmination of a long-term effort by the tobacco giant to manipulate consumers and policymakers.[5]

When you are buying a brand, whose brand are you buying? Few consumers know that Kraft Foods is owned by Altria, a tobacco company, Green & Black's by Cadbury's and Rachel's Organics by Mars. It could be argued that while consumers may choose a particular product for its ethics, if it has been subsumed by a larger brand whose other brands may be less ethical, they are in effect aiding and abetting "greenwash" without realising it.

Since 2005, oil giant BP has invested $1.5 billion in its green energy business, following its 2000 rebranding exercise "beyond petroleum".[6] Critics, however, legitimately point out that part of BP's original strategy for demonstrating its green credentials was to buy up existing producers of solar energy, rather than adding new capacity. It has now since shed those businesses in favour of the more lucrative biofuels, while continuing to invest in other carbon-intensive energy forms such as the Canadian tar sands, whose emission of greenhouse gases will far outstrip any gains to the environment made by the company's investment in renewables, which are still just a fraction of the value of the business overall.[7]

Social responsibility and brand behaviour

Corporate social responsibility (CSR) has been the business-led response to brand critics and the new notion that companies must be seen to be socially responsible. A CSR policy has become de rigueur for top companies, which make statements on everything from environmental performance to labour standards. Given the CSR hype, it would be easy to believe that things have moved much further along and that companies are taking the issue of their responsibility more seriously than they did before.

The corporate conference circuit is dotted with monthly gatherings on "social responsibility" and "reputation management". The mantra of the CSR world is that business can "do well" and "do good": the proverbial win-win. Pharmaceutical companies such as GlaxoSmithKline (GSK) point to their programmes for improved access to medicines in developing countries and partnerships with non-governmental organisations (NGOs) such as Médecins sans Frontières, and even British American Tobacco (BAT) is aiming to be the world's most socially responsible "tobacco company".

But is it really all so rosy? The "face" of a company's CSR programme is usually demonstrated through its corporate social and environmental report. Companies ranging from socially minded Traidcraft, a UK-based fair-trade organisation and development charity, to defence and aerospace manufacturer BAE Systems all now prepare such a report. In 2001 only 21 of the companies listed on the FTSE 100 index issued a separate CSR report alongside their annual report; by 2006 the figure had risen to 69.[8] However, the quantity of CSR-type reports says little about the quality of what really goes on. The Global Reporting Initiative (GRI), a framework for reporting on social and environmental matters, found that in 2007 there were little over 700 companies which were GRI-compliant reporting. Considering there are over 50,000 multinationals worldwide, this seems a drop in the ocean.

Generally companies have so far initiated a CSR programme not because of a genuine desire to "do good" but rather because it makes commercial sense. For example, GSK's programme to provide affordable access to medicines in developing countries came about because the company faced strong competition from generic manufacturers and the threat of regulation by governments. Its climb-down could cynically be seen as a defensive move against losing crucial intellectual property rights and to protect its reputation. It is unlikely to be the result of the moral imperative of tackling AIDS or malaria in sub-Saharan Africa. Many people would still argue that attempts such as GSK's are inadequate to deal with the mammoth health challenges that developing countries face.

Although there are a handful of positive outcomes of CSR, few add up to the step-change towards the kind of ethical corporation many would like to see. The UK's ethical trading initiative, for example, found that after ten years of applying the voluntary labour code to members of the retail sector, application of the code worked only in countries where labour standards (and their enforcement) were higher in the first place.

The myth of the ethical consumer

Corporate social responsibility is driven in part by the expectation that consumers will ultimately reward those companies with a better social and environmental record, and media reports on the value of green brands would have us believe that the tactic is really working. In a minority of cases there is some truth in this. A brand's espoused values can measure up to its practice. In the UK, Fairtrade coffee, with market leaders such as Café Direct well in front, now captures almost 30% of the ground coffee market; in Switzerland, Fairtrade bananas account for as much as 50% of the market.

Boycotts, for example, are a popular strategy to try to change corporate behaviour. In the UK, 28% of consumers actively boycotted a supermarket product in 2004. In a survey, more than half of all consumers agreed with the statement: "As a consumer, I can make a difference to how responsibly a company behaves."[9]

The question, though, is: does ethical consumerism really work? In spite of consumer backlash, Nestlé continues to thrive around the world, selling products such as Nescafé, Perrier and Stouffers. This has, in part, led to a Nestlé CSR-style response. Nestlé has started to market a Fairtrade coffee in response to consumer concerns about low prices paid to farmers in the developing world. Nescafé Partner's Blend was launched in 2005, complete with the international Fairtrade mark attached. But is this just window dressing? The Boycott Nestlé campaign, run by Baby Milk Action, claims that the amount of Fairtrade product Nestlé is promoting is less than 0.02% of its overall production.

If you accept that climate change is the biggest environmental threat facing modern society, you would hope that consumers would avoid behaviours that contribute to greenhouse gas emissions. Yet people have been flying more and more, and according to a report from the Environmental Change Institute, UK emissions arising from aviation are predicted to more than double between 2000 and 2030.[10]

In spite of the apparent growth of the ethical brand, truly ethical businesses continue to capture a fraction of the market overall. In the UK in 2006 the total consumer ethical market, covering everything from cosmetics to investment services, was reckoned to be worth £32.3 billion out of total spending estimated to be over £600 billion.[11] What seems to be happening to the ethical marketplace is that other less wholly ethical brands stretch their credentials to appear more ethical than they are. Advertisements from oil companies publicising their green investments ignore the sector's contribution to climate change.

Consumers, although conscious, are fairly passive. The UK's National Consumer Council notes that consumers are often unwilling to make changes in their habits. The annual ethical consumer survey, although showing a fast-growing niche ethical market, still finds that only 11% of adult consumers are regular ethical shoppers, while just 6% of adult consumers in the UK are fully committed to the cause. This is only a 1% increase over four years.[12]

Often, on the consumer side, it comes down to price over ethics.[13] According to a 2007 survey of American consumer behaviour, consumers would gladly make the greener choice if the product did not cost more. Tim Jackson, a professor at Surrey University and a member of the Sustainable Development Commission, sums up the case:[14]

This idea that you can just rely on consumers to exercise choice and become more ethical doesn't stack up. Far from placing all the responsibility on individuals to make ethical choices, you [should] systematically and progressively remove unethical choices from the market – and that, partially at least, is the role of government.

So, although there appears to be scope to encourage consumers to be more active and "ethical", the evidence strongly suggests that if we rely on them to deliver social and environmental change, we will be waiting a very long time.

Misguided intentions

CSR has ultimately failed to provide solutions to our global problems simply because it falls within a framework that provides financial rather than social incentives. Business cannot always "do well" and "do good". Put simply: business can do well, but only up to a point.

CSR strategies are part of the microcosm of the failure of markets themselves. They work only in so far as they help to protect the brand. But there is often a wide chasm between what is good for a brand and what is good for society.

Fifty or 100 years ago, when many of the big multinationals started, the aim was to provide an affordable product or service to people and make a reasonable profit at the same time. It is doubtful that the founders of any major multinationals ever set out on a path aiming to subsume other cultures, cut down forests and exploit cheap labour halfway around the world. But over the past century the role of a company has changed, and its primary function is to return capital to shareholders, not necessarily to serve the wider needs of society. In today's capital markets, companies need to grow, to find new markets in which to trade and to keep their costs down through anything from ensuring "affordable" labour to reducing tax liabilities.

When a company gives a "profits warning", the markets downgrade its share price. Consequently, investing in things like the environment or social causes, which promise longer-term and peripheral pay-offs rather than immediate pay-offs to the bottom line, becomes a luxury, and such things are often placed on the sacrificial chopping block in a crisis unless enforced through regulation.

This is no different from how markets deliver value to shareholders outside the ethics regime, even if it means sacrificing other parts of the business in the process, as in the value-destroying mergers and acquisitions frenzy of the late 1990s. In the most grotesque examples of market behaviour, the product itself becomes almost irrelevant. In the case of the now infamous Enron, the company changed from a middle-sized energy provider to a de facto Wall Street bank through its various energy trading schemes.[15] Its eventual collapse was the first in a series of corporate scandals that contributed to the worst economic downturn in over 30 years.

Business has always had to innovate and try different things and seek new sources of competitive advantage. But pretending that these business intentions will always provide the best outcomes in the interests of the greater public good is simply naive, especially when shareholders' interests are part of the equation.

There is a significant risk in business assuming the role of the social-welfare provider through misguided CSR programmes. In the United States, Cisco Systems "adopts" schools that have inadequate funding. In parts of Africa, Unilever helps to distribute condoms through its distribution network to combat the AIDS crisis. Both are probably well-intentioned programmes to deal with immediate problems. Cisco needs an educated workforce; and most companies operating in Africa are feeling the impact of the AIDS crisis. The UN Global Compact, an initiative under which companies have pledged to support and enact a set of standards on human rights, labour, the environment and anti-corruption, had more than 5,600 participants at the end of 2008. But such efforts represent a more worrying trend, about which both activists and businesses should be concerned: the increased blurring of the lines between public and private, and the abdication of state responsibility to uphold the public good.

Nike's and others' investment in labour-standards monitoring in developing-country factories is a laudable attempt to ensure at least that their workers are protected and that their brand values are upheld. But, as Daniel Litvin writes, the complexity of trying to monitor 700 factories employing 500,000 people around the world is immense.[16] It puts the brand itself at risk, as activists continue to seek out poor working conditions, whether in suppliers' factories or in their suppliers' factories. So firms such as Nike are constantly on the defensive.

Nike can tackle labour standards, up to a point. But even with the constant onslaught from protesters and continuous improvement, it actually has limited power in the wider economy in developing countries that keeps wages low and, in some countries, means that a job in a Nike factory is more desirable than being a doctor or a teacher because the wages are higher and workers' rights are protected. Part of this is simply because Nike – or Nestlé – cannot achieve improvements alone.

In this sense especially, CSR is a false economy. Would it not be better to ensure that systems in these countries – laws, regulations and so on – are developed to strengthen institutions that protect a wider portion of the population? Hannah Jones, vice-president of corporate responsibility at Nike, acknowledges what she calls "stark realisations" about the reality of the challenge:[17]

> These problems are systemic. We can't underestimate the importance of the rule of law and the role that it has in actually impacting whether or not compliance is taken seriously.

Business is, in part, to blame for contributing to the institutional vacuum in the first place. In the United States, there is no longer a school system that is adequately supported by the state because businesses, increasingly, fail to pay their share of common taxes. Corporate income taxes in the United States fell from 4.1% of GDP in 1960 to just 2.5% of GDP in 2006.[18] The OECD attributes this, in part, to countries wanting to reduce taxes in order to lure foreign investment or maintain inward investment. But this is having perverse effects, limiting governments' ability to invest in common assets, such as the environment or education. Nowhere is the issue more pressing than in developing countries, where states are already weak. The corporate sector, rather than looking for tax exemptions, should be finding ways to ensure adequate support for governments and the development of strong public services that would provide a healthy economic and social environment in which to operate.

These issues go well beyond traditional brand protection and reputation management. Brand owners should consider how best to respond to them if they want to protect their domain. Indeed, multinationals have the power, but currently lack the courage, to break ranks and call for another way forward.

Redefining brand value?

It is difficult to dispute the economic importance of brands. According to Interbrand, a brand consultancy, 80% of a major company's market value is based on "intangibles". But this heavy weighting of the brand makes many of us more vulnerable. As the values of companies on the stockmarket tumble, usually because of a lack of faith in the "brand", our savings and our pensions are at risk.

Right now, brand valuation methods focus on the economic use of the brand, with occasional considerations of things like staff training included in the equation. At least a partial way forward would be to make "brand value" less dependent on traditional economic intangibles and more dependent on genuine measures of social and environmental performance.

In this regard, arguably, something like climate change risk would be expected to be fully embedded in the valuation of a company. But this has yet to take place, either legally or in practice. In a 2007 report looking at the disclosure practices of the s&p 500 vis-à-vis climate risk, researchers found that most companies (70% of the 225 respondents) were unwilling to provide any public information on their risk exposure to climate. This is in spite of the fact that the financial risks – from regulatory risks to insurance costs – of environmental factors such as climate change are becoming increasingly obvious.[19]

Inroads are already being made in defining how to measure these things. The GRI, mentioned earlier, is something that brand valuation experts should look at and that accountants are now starting to incorporate in their narrative reporting to investors.[20] In recent years, a number of organisations have made efforts to measure "social capital", but the methodologies for doing so are not shared with the public, so it is almost impossible to tell what is being measured, let alone compare the approaches to arrive at common standards. Social capital, as a form of trust, should be able to incorporate measures of real commitment to communities, such as using local labour. There is an added business benefit to this. Shokoya-Eleshin Construction, a UK construction firm, reported that when it used local labour its buildings were not vandalised in an urban area traditionally experiencing high levels of crime.

There is a dual purpose in making the intangibles more tangible and basing them on social and environmental outcomes. Measurement will help policymakers ensure that companies pay for the real costs of their social and environmental impact (internalising externalities, in economists' terms). It will also help ensure that businesses do not make compromises in business practice that favour financial outcomes rather than non-financial ones, because all will eventually contribute to the bottom line.

A case for leadership

No corporate brand is produced with the specific intention of doing harm. But corporate leaders often avoid looking at the wider complexity of the issue. As with CSR, a business generally does what it can rather than what it should within the confines of the market. This is where corporate leaders need to confront the dilemma head-on. The challenges faced by society are not going to be addressed by a mere tampering at the margins, a small increase to a charity budget or a cause-related marketing attempt at improving brand image. There needs to be a revolution in the way that business is done.

Take, for example, companies that depend on commodities, such as Nestlé and Cadbury's. Although their work with the Biscuit, Cake, Chocolate and Confectionery Alliance in aiming to eliminate the use of child labour in cocoa plantations is crucial, they do not confront the fundamental issue of how their products perpetuate poverty in the first place. The vulnerability of people who are dependent on commodities is not something that can be brushed aside. How can commodity markets be transformed so that fair trade is no longer needed? So that a quality product is still available to consumers, but producing it does not keep people in poverty unnecessarily? It is not just a matter of protecting the corporate brand and reputation through individual defensive means: it involves the entire system. All companies will be vulnerable to criticism and consumer backlash until we recognise that fact.

The question that society should be asking is this: what businesses and institutions do we need to deliver sustainable development? And, in turn, what are the qualities of brands that will survive in a sustainable society? The Fairtrade model of business has paved a fascinating path that demonstrates how commercial success can be matched with strong socially based values. But it is a long way from where we are now for the majority of today's brands.

Big business and, by extension, big brands have been intent on responding to the concerns of activists by trying to minimise their negative impact on society and the environment and marketing these interventions as having solved the world's problems. They have not.

Ironically, at the moment, the more good a company does, the more it is open to scrutiny by global activists. Never could there be a more compelling argument than this for companies to look at their role in society, and to call for appropriate levels of regulation by governments to level the playing field. Ed Crooks, economics editor of the *Financial Times*, says:[21]

The balance between making money, protecting the environment and looking after individual rights affects all of us. We should all be able to take some responsibility for the big decisions – and that means not leaving it all to business.

Brands are unlikely to disappear any time soon; even smaller companies with an ethical aim, such as Café Direct and Innocent, eventually succumb to the temptations of "growth" and need to achieve brand recognition for long-term success. But let us hope that the smaller, up-and-coming ethical brands do not compromise their morals and their methods in the process.

The issue is not brands as such. It is how big brands, often with near-monopoly power, have behaved. Brands do have the potential to be a force for good, so long as we consider the ways in which they are valued, and couple the natural instincts of the market with appropriate regulation.

Notes and references

1 WPP Press Release, May 1st 2007.
2 Klein, N., *No Logo*, Picador, 1999.
3 www.just-drinks.com/article.aspx?ID=93336; WWF, Climate Savers Programme.
4 Lee, M., *Fashion Victim*, Broadway Books, March 2003.
5 Smith, E.A. and Malone R.E., "Altria means tobacco: Philip Morris's identity crisis", *American Journal of Public Health*, Vol. 93, No. 4, April 2003, pp. 553–6.
6 business.timesonline.co.uk/tol/business/industry_sectors/natural_resources/article3448938.ece
7 "Unconventional Oil, Scraping the Bottom of the Barrel?", WWF and Co-operative Financial Services, UK, 2008.
8 www.deloitte.com/dtt/press_release/0,1014,sid%253D2834%2526cid%253D182646,00.html
9 Co-operative Bank, *Ethical Consumer Report*, 2005

10 Environmental Change Institute, *Predict and Decide: Aviation, Climate Change and UK Policy*, Oxford University, 2005; www.eci.ox.ac.uk/research/energy/downloads/predictanddecide.pdf

11 Co-operative Bank, *Ethical Consumerism Report 2007*, UK; www.goodwithmoney.co.uk/servlet/Satellite/1200903577501,CFSweb/Page/GoodWithMoney

12 www.co-operativebank.co.uk/images/pdf/ethical_consumer_report_2007.pdf

13 www.ljs.com/fileadmin/ljs-files/studies/What_is_Green_and_Why_It_Matters.pdf

14 www.forumforthefuture.org/greenfutures/articles/602578

15 Partnoy, F., *Infectious Greed: How Deceit and Risk Corrupted the Financial Markets*, Times Books, 2003, p. 299.

16 Litvin, D., *Empires of Profit: Commerce, Conquest and Corporate Responsibility*, Texere, 2003, p. 245.

17 Statement at a conference at MIT, "Making Globalization Work for All", October 7th 2005; http://mitworld.mit.edu/video/312/

18 OECD, July 7th 2007, www.oecd.org/dataoecd/26/56/33717459.xis; KPMG, Corporate Tax Rate Survey, 2007.

19 Ceres, "Climate Risk Disclosure by the S&P 500", 2007.

20 www.GRI.org

21 Sustainable Development Commission, Business @boo.m&bust, 2001. www.sd-commission.gov.uk/pubs/ar2001/04.htm

18 The future of brands

Rita Clifton

The future of brands is inextricably linked to the future of business. In fact, the future of brands is the future of business if it is to be about sustainable wealth creation. Further, because of the interaction of brands with society, and since so many socially influential brands are in the not-for-profit sector, the future of brands is also inextricably linked to the future of society.

This chapter examines some future trends and predictions, both in business and in broader society, and looks at how brands may affect and be affected by those changes. It also explores the categories and countries that seem likely to yield some of the world's greatest brands in the future, and makes observations on what brands of all kinds will need to do to be successful.

But first, it may be useful to recap on the main themes and arguments outlined in previous chapters:

- Branding has been in existence for hundreds of years and has developed into a modern concept that can be applied to anything from products and services to companies and not-for-profit concerns and even countries.
- Well-managed brands have extraordinary economic value and are the most effective and efficient creators of sustainable wealth. Understanding the value of a brand, and how to create more value, is essential management information.
- Brands can also have a critical social importance and benefit in both developed and developing countries. This applies as much to commercial brands as not-for-profit organisations.
- Most of the world's greatest brands today are American owned, largely because of America's "free" political, commercial and social systems. But the knowledge and practice of what creates great brands can be (and is now being) applied around the world.
- Every brand, if it is to be successful, needs a clear positioning, expressed through name, identity and all aspects of products, services and behaviour. For corporate effectiveness and efficiency,

the brand and its positioning should be used as a clear managing framework for portfolio management and business unit relationships.

◪ Increasingly, brands require a distinctive customer experience in the round. Indeed, increasingly a brand is that experience, not least through the behaviour of its people. The brand should be the central organising principle for everyone and then everything.

◪ Every brand needs a strong creative idea to bring it to life through visual and verbal identity. This creative process needs not only innovation and imagination, but also the courage and conviction to carry it through.

◪ The strongest brand communications may work at the levels of information, fame creation and by creating (often unconscious) associations. Those elements which are harder to measure and justify are no less important; in fact, they are often the most important elements.

◪ Public relations for brands will succeed only if they are based on the brand promise and the internal reality of the company; people have become increasingly sceptical, and in a 24-hour news culture organisations have nowhere to hide, either inside or outside.

◪ If a company is going to invest in a brand long term, it must give its "identifiable distinctive features" adequate legal protection; and it must enforce that protection vigorously, increasingly on a global basis.

◪ Leading global brands can, and should, help the wider public understand the benefits of globalisation and free trade. But they can do this only if they open up, behave well and collectively educate about their benefits. They must also ensure they continue to innovate.

◪ Asia is showing every sign of becoming a global brand generator, although there are still challenges associated with the image of China, and it is important to understand the different consumer dynamics at work in relation to western markets.

◪ India is also a highly ambitious and dynamic market for brands, but with many social and infrastructure issues to solve. Again, understanding the blend of traditional and modern lifestyles, local culture and global aspirations, will be critical.

◪ In a "globalised" world, nations need to compete with each other for the world's attention and wealth. Active and conscious nation branding can help them do this, and at its best, it can be argued, it presents an opportunity to redistribute the world's wealth more fairly in the future.

◪ A digital world brings a profoundly and immediately connected world, where traditional models of brand control by brand owner are no longer possible. Transparency and open-minded interactivity in brands will be givens.

◪ Brands need better and socially broader measures of success. Corporate social responsibility should be about genuinely solving problems, not just about brand reputation management.

If the particular theme of increasing globalisation still makes anyone baulk, it is worth remembering the importance that China is attaching to growing its "branded commodities" as its way forward in the world and "so as to benefit the world's people".[1] While many western nations are fashionably wringing their hands about the nature of capitalism, and about brands as their highest-profile manifestation, developing nations are coming to see branded businesses, and indeed their own images, as their opportunity for development and more stable wealth and economic control. Whether it is ironic or not, western consumers' constant search for novelty and authenticity may also help ensure that the "newer" economies have an interested audience for their propositions.

But before reflecting on whether and how the main themes of this book may be carried forward in the future – and before speculating on the provenance of the world's most successful brands of the future – it is worth considering the broader future context.

The future thing

The future certainly isn't what it used to be, but nevertheless a recent book by Sir Martin Rees, the Astronomer Royal, made rather depressing reading.[2] In it he expresses the view that:

> The odds are no better than 50–50 that our present civilisation on earth will survive to the end of the century.

He puts this down to the potential for "maverick" misuse of science and/ or weapons of mass destruction. In the meantime, of course, there is always the possibility of super-volcanoes or asteroid hits.

At the other extreme, Watts Wacker, an American futurist, made it part of his working philosophy to encourage organisations to develop "500-

year" plans. This was meant to be symbolic rather than literal, but does rather stretch the point.

Steering a slightly less radical course either way, it was interesting to consider a range of predictions for the year 2025, drawn from various think tanks and futurists.[3] These included market wars over ice on the moon; widespread "designer" babies; a truly pregnant man; a derelict Silicon Valley, overtaken by technologies such as quantum, optical and DNA computers; and one which would bring Rees's doomsday scenario rather closer, widespread cyber-terrorism. These views are echoed by a recent report from the National Intelligence Agency which predicted that the next 20 years will see a world living with the daily threat of nuclear war and environmental catastrophe, as well as the decline of the United States as the dominant global power.[4]

So much, so cheerful. However, you only have to look at a random selection of quotes, sci-fi films and futurology books to understand the dangers of publishing specific predictions, and we live in hope. As far as this book is concerned, as Alvin Toffler says in his introduction to *Future Shock*, "The inability to speak with precision and certainty about the future ... is no excuse for silence."[5]

It is obviously important to try to understand general trends and possibilities in scientific, economic and social terms if we are to plan and adapt brand futures, whether for new or for existing brands. Even the strongest brands today can get stuck in a complacent time warp, overtaken by new and baggage-free competitors.

Future brand issues

From past trends, the odds might seem in favour of the top brands today still being up there in 25 years' time. As the introduction to this book pointed out, over half of the 50 most valuable brands have been around for more than 50 years. However, it is difficult to see how past performance will give quite so much reassurance in the face of the extraordinary changes we are likely to see in world power and economics in the next ten years.

The most successful technology, telecommunications and internet-based brands have already shown how quickly they can progress if they read and act on consumer and business trends in the right way – look at Microsoft, Nokia, Intel and the "new paradigm" global brands like Amazon, eBay and Google. Their challenge, and the challenge for the new social network brands, is to maintain their position and sustain their value. To do this, they will have to continue to innovate and, critically, to deepen and extend their brand relationships with customers well beyond the level of technological prowess; for long-term value, brands need emotional as well as technological appeal. Indeed, they will have to invest in their brand as their major sustainable competitive advantage.

It is not unreasonable, for instance, to imagine that a new killer application will emerge from somewhere like Bangalore in the near future. Nor is it unreasonable to suppose that the service and branding skills required to build that proposition into a sustainable brand will have developed to such a degree in India itself that global brand status is within reach. What is more, the "skill cost" difference between Asia and the United States or Europe, which has already seen global organisations such as Citibank and GE outsourcing their services to the Indian subcontinent, means that price differentials will make their brands even more attractive. In 2005, some 70% of all financial institutions used offshoring, compared with 26% in 2003, and India has an estimated 80% of global business process outsourcing. For comparison, look at the wages differential around the world in an organisation such as McDonald's: in 2003 the minimum wage per hour was \$5.15 in the United States and £4.20 in the UK, compared with 18 pence (29 cents) in China and 7 pence (11 cents) in India.[6] Established brands will indeed have to continue to leverage their trust and heritage, even while the core of their own service offering is on a passage to India to cut costs and satisfy Wall Street and the City. To take up the opportunity properly, however, India will need to work on its nation brand in terms of reliability of infrastructure and the taint of corruption.

With 1.3 billion consumers, China is the world's biggest potential consumer market. It has rapidly turned from being a hot conference topic in theory to a day-to-day working reality. The Olympic Games of 2008 provided a global platform for China to crystallise its ambitions and for its burgeoning brands, such as Lenovo, even while it struggled with the media and freedoms normally associated with capitalist markets. China has clearly recognised the importance of owning and growing brands, rather than just producing them for others, and particularly as rising costs will soon threaten its sustainable cost competitiveness with other developing markets. However, on a practical level, a study by the Engineering Employers' Federation in the UK[7] suggested that one-third of manufacturing firms were considering shifting production to China. A vivid case study of the advantages of this is illustrated by Hornby, a venerable British company, manufacturer of classic toy train sets, owner of the Scalextric brand and recently brought back to fame by the Hogwarts Express featured in the Harry Potter films and by the success of Formula One. In speaking about the advantages of moving production to China, the CEO says:

The strain on the bottom line began to ease immediately. We were able to use the savings to increase the quality and details of the models so that sales began to pick up.

Essentially, the company retained just the designers and managers at its UK head office in Margate, reducing the head count from 550 to 130, even though some observers were sceptical of the long-term viability of separating innovation and production.

One other thing Hornby's CEO outlined was his view of the fate of the company had he not moved production: "Hornby would have closed, or been taken over by a Chinese company, if we hadn't moved." This was no idle boast in the light of the case of Haier. Over 20 years ago the Qingdao Refrigerator Plant bought the production-line technology from Liberhaier, a German company, and used this as the basis for its brand name. Haier is now the world's second biggest refrigerator brand. How much of this is to do with the "borrowed" belief among some buyers that they are of German origin is debatable.

This kind of false provenance, whether real or assumed, is hardly a new idea. In the electronic goods category alone, it has been customary for UK electrical retailers to give their own-label products Japanese-sounding names, as this would give better quality associations than British-manufactured electrical goods. Think also of Häagen-Dazs, Estée Lauder, Hugo Boss and Sony as brands with a name at odds with the real country of origin and ownership. Clearly, although provenance, and authenticity in that provenance, is important in such categories as luxury and cars, so much depends on how the brands are built and managed. Many of the world's most valuable brands now transcend their country of origin. A Chinese company such as Lenovo computers will need all these world-class branding skills if its global ambitions are to be realised. Despite its acquisition of IBM's personal computing division in 2005, its ambitions to make the world's best PCs will not necessarily make it the world's most valuable PC brand. However, there is a particularly strong Asian brand case study that may serve to inspire them for the future.

Samsung, from South Korea, is one of the most spectacular global brand success stories of recent years. From a brand value of just under $2.5 billion in 1997, it grew to almost $18 billion in 2008, and seems likely to continue its success. It is the reason for its success that is of interest here. In the mid-1990s, Samsung's managers realised that they would be on the commodity and low-price road to perdition if they did not develop their own brand. They saw a real opportunity in the digital platform, invested heavily in premium quality innovation and R&D and, most telling of all, invested in their own brand rather than be condemned to the uncertainty of OEM[8] status indefinitely. They built brand awareness around the world, and resolved to use their brand value (rather than just straight financials) as a key performance measure. As the company's president and CEO said at the time:

> Competing successfully in the 21st century will require more than just outstanding product and quality functions. Intangibles such as corporate and brand image will be crucial factors for achieving a competitive edge.

This concern for other measures, and ways of measuring performance to ensure that everyone in a company continues to build brand value rather than trading on it, is perhaps something that more western companies, particularly publicly quoted companies, and the equity markets need to reflect on.

Brand America may appear to have taken a series of body blows in the early years of the 21st century. However, while it might be true to say that there are slightly fewer American-owned brands in the top 100 today compared with a few years ago, this is as much to do with market changes and self-inflicted corporate wounds as American heritage. Over half of the world's most valuable brands are still American owned. Despite opinion polls and anti-American demonstrations, consumers can be radical at the research questionnaire and reactionary at the checkout. What is more, the positive global reaction to a new president may herald a new era in American brand leadership.

However, other countries are beginning to learn the global brand game, and companies such as Coca-Cola and Nike will need to keep on reflecting their sensitivity to local cultures and habits in their management and marketing approaches. It is interesting that, whereas for the past 50 years America itself has been a strong brand, standing for freedom and lifestyle aspiration, increasing familiarity and the spread of democracy have meant that these previously "magic" qualities have lost their cachet. American-owned brands will have to work that much harder on more imaginative positionings, operations and communications for their brands if they are to withstand the challenge from all comers.

An interesting battle of retail brands and operating philosophies is potentially emerging between the mighty Wal-Mart and Tesco, a UK-based retailer. In many ways, Wal-Mart is the archetypical American business success story. It has in Sam Walton a founder with a distinctive home-cooked philosophy, with a strong service and moral ethic, and a zealous evangelism for giving people American-style life opportunities. Wal-Mart's expansion internationally has been cautious so far, as has its behaviour around its purchase and management of the Asda brand in the UK. While the retail giant has made a simple philosophy of low prices and genuine customer service work well in the United States, and has made much of its respect for employees and recent "conversion" to sustainability and environmental responsibility, there are perhaps lessons to be learned from the innovation, own-brand building and customer relationship management of the best UK grocery retailers. There are several margin-point differences between the average grocery retail businesses in the UK and those in America. While some of this difference is because of the dominant position of major retail chains in the UK, it is also because of their success in building their own brand values, and using their own-brand products and services to sustain their quality image, rather than just being price fighters against manufacturer brands. Tesco is now not only the UK's number one retailer and one of its most respected companies; it is also the world's largest online grocer. Out of the thirteen countries in which it operates, Tesco is currently market leader in six. Its stated core purpose, to "create value for customers to earn their lifetime loyalty", has driven its ability to extend its brand well beyond grocery into areas such as personal finance, health care and legal services as well as a full range of non-food items including electricals and mobile telephony. It is a brand that is trusted by people in whatever area it is operating.

This ability of a strong brand to transcend categories, and to be trusted by consumers in whichever category it chooses to involve itself, would seem to be an important property of the world's greatest brands in the future. In a hyper-competitive, over-communicated and complicated world, people will increasingly want and need to simplify their purchases and time management. What is more, in a blurring physical and virtual world, any brand will have the ability to be a powerful medium and a power retailer – if only in virtual space. Trusted brands provide ideal navigation for consumers across sectors, and as the strongest will be able to leap into categories without having a previous product or service track record, no brand will be sacred in its marketplace any more. Although it has had its financial challenges, the Virgin brand is another good example of this "leaping" ability. It has a strong vision and values around being "people's champion", innovative and irreverent, and through popular support has managed to transcend markets from airlines to cosmetics, from financial services to mobile telephony and media, from soft to hard drinks and many more. It is even expanding beyond the Earth with Virgin Galactic, the world's first "spaceline", aiming to bring "affordable ... space tourism" to non-professional astronauts.

The issue of category-defying life brands is also relevant when looking at those new or growth categories that would seem most likely to produce strong brand growth in the future. These include:

- health and well-being, including more holistic and organic lifestyles;
- leisure, entertainment and "new adventure" experiences;
- physical and emotional security;
- services for a new generation of the "new old" (a critical trend in industrialised countries);
- lifelong education;
- information and lifestyle management;
- biotechnology and genetics.

These areas could yield entirely new global brands in the future; it may well be that the most valuable brand in the next 25 years has not been invented yet. After all, Google has progressed to a top ten global brand within ten years of its invention. However, it is equally possible that an existing, trusted brand may extend or cross into these new areas.

Current product-based brands will find it harder than service or retail brands to deepen and broaden their relationships with their audiences. This is not just because they are having to invest so much of their marketing support in retail distribution, rather than spending it on consumer communication. It is also because in their current form, they lack the ability to control the total customer experience, and so engage their audiences as fully as they would like. Chapter 7 of this book highlights the increasing importance of the broader customer experience in building brands, and we should expect to see in the future many more "manuretailers": product-based brand companies developing their own retail experiences and direct relationships with their consumers, both offline and online. Unilever's experiment with "myhome", a home cleaning and laundry service, was interesting in its extension of Persil and Cif as service brands. Although it did not progress beyond its test market, it nevertheless demonstrated the company's interest in developing core brands beyond the product form – Dove Spa is the most recent example. To facilitate this process of concentration on resources, innovation and investment behind its most successful brands, Unilever has also been investing in its corporate brand and culling its smaller and weaker brands in recent years, either selling them or dropping them. As other conglomerates have been doing the same, an interesting possibility is on the cards. Not only will we continue to see further brand consolidation and corporate "musical chairs", but some of the brands that are being sold off could end up in the newer economies, fired up by entrepreneurial spirit and a new angle for selling. Think of Haier many times over.

Other areas of brand activity that are likely to increase in the future are co-branding (for example, Sony Ericsson) and celebrity branding (as in recent examples such as David Beckham and Kylie Minogue). The challenge for the former is to generate clarity about the joint brand proposition (never easy in partnership), and for the latter, to identify how to generate long-term sustainable value after the flush of celebrity fades. Interesting too are new media examples where trusted sources which started as personal blogs have grown into media brands to challenge conventional media companies; examples include the Huffington Post, which came into its own during the 2008 American elections and now has some 2.5m contributing bloggers. From the age of deference to the age of reference indeed.

It is also interesting as a trend that major corporations such as Mars and Estée Lauder have either launched or acquired brands which feel like explicit "social enterprises", and have allowed them to operate with no obvious brand connection with the corporate owner. In 1997 Mars acquired Seeds of Change, which had been launched in 1989 with a stated purpose of preserving biodiversity and sustainable development. Estée Lauder later acquired Aveda, a brand connecting "beauty, environment and wellbeing". At a conference shortly afterwards, Leonard Lauder said that Estée Lauder itself was committed to phasing out synthetics entirely, following the lead of Aveda. Using new ventures of this kind as operating test-beds for new business principles indicates that major corporations recognise that business may have to be conceived and conducted in rather different ways in the future.

Another area to mention for brand growth is the NGO (non-governmental organisation) sector. When national governments, for whatever reasons, cannot or choose not to act, non-governmental and not-for-profit organisations can play the role of "guardian brands". An example is the role Oxfam has played in the developing-world coffee crisis, where coffee farmers in the poorest countries have faced falling prices and new levels of poverty. In a 2002 report, Oxfam demanded that the multinational companies involved in coffee purchasing and marketing demonstrate a "long-term commitment to ethical purchasing".[9] In the future, raising funds will be as much of a challenge for such organisations as it has always been. To avoid the danger of appearing compromised by expedient corporate partnerships, they should perhaps think more about "selling" or licensing their intellectual property about best practices in ethical processes and measurement.

Further brand management considerations

In maximising and sustaining the value of brands in the future there needs to be more focus on:

- **Understanding the value and value drivers of a brand.** As can be seen from the Samsung case, a focus on brand value and measuring performance on the basis of the brand value added can build momentum and create sustainable growth. It is also crucial management information for mergers, acquisitions and divestments, which will continue in the future as markets shake out and consolidate. Few mergers currently deliver long-term shareholder value, largely because of overemphasis on financials and practical operations. Greater focus on brand value would help mergers succeed – as well as generating real organic growth.
- **Clarity of brand positioning.** Clarity of vision, values and positioning overall are often given insufficient attention in practice. The majority of corporate and brand visions are interchangeable, bland and viewed with cynicism. In an over-communicated world, lack of clarity will substantially reduce effectiveness and efficiency; and complex brand and sub-brand structures without a real audience rationale will reduce this still further. Clarity of strategy is also one of the leading criteria by which companies are judged.
- **Brands as total experiences, and as central organising principles, rather than just products and logos.** The success of experience-based brands at building deeper customer relationships at the expense of solely product-based brands argues strongly for every brand to think about its total "chain of experience" and customer touch points – from every personal contact to visual identity and communications, from product to packaging, PR, in-store environment – and increasingly round-the-clock presence and availability online. Technology will provide the opportunity

to build an even greater sensory experience into brands through touch, smell and sound. Whatever emerges, distinctive value can and will need to be added at every stage of the experience, or at the very least, not lost.

◪ **More compelling and more imaginative expressions of a brand's identity and brand communications.** Senior executives may not feel entirely comfortable in this area, but the ability to break through brand proliferation and communications clutter depends on imaginative and innovative creative expression. In the developed world, audiences are knowledgeable and savvy about marketing, and will increasingly "edit out" communications that they find boring or irritating. Imagination will need to be applied not just to the creative message, but also to the medium. Product placements in editorial and appropriate sponsorship of events, programmes and computer games will become more important. In particular, young people around the world have high expectations from brands, and are increasingly difficult to reach and satisfy.

◪ **The need for internal and external operations to be aligned – and transparent.** In an all-seeing digital world, and in a sharper business environment where employees at all levels can be ambassadors for or saboteurs of the company's reputation, there really will be no hiding places any more. Organisations will have no choice but to be transparent in their dealings and fulfil their promises, or to have transparency forced on them. On a more positive note, numerous studies have confirmed that investment in a company's employees, and their good treatment, translates into significantly better customer satisfaction. Customer satisfaction and loyalty are, and will be, the drivers of long-term sustainable brand value.

◪ **Rigorous legal protection around the world.** It is estimated that 7–10% of world trade is counterfeited.[10] Although international law is increasingly being upheld, even in the previous counterfeiting capitals of the world, it is likely that while there are still brands to copy, there will be willing makers and buyers of copies. Brand owners must use the full weight of the law, quickly and publicly, to prevent value loss and degradation. Brand valuation, which can demonstrate how much economic loss might be attributed to passing off, is an effective way of supporting cases such as these.

◪ **Corporate social responsibility as a core corporate responsibility.** Corporate social responsibility (CSR) has been an overused buzz term in too many organisations, and a whole new industry has grown up around it. Although good intentions may be there, organisations still often look at CSR as an insurance policy, or a more sophisticated form of cause-related marketing, rather than as core to their operations. Many responsible companies produce elaborate CSR reports, including social and environmental performance. However, it is necessary to ask whether the basic principle of separate reports is the right one, or whether there should be a more integrated and central way of dealing with these issues in the future if we are going to have the kind of world we would all want. Or at least to mitigate the pessimistic scenarios of environmental destruction and terrorism breeding in areas of poverty and exclusion that we might all fear.

◼ **Creating sustainable value more sustainably.** Sustainability is the greatest challenge of our age and brands can and should be central to accelerating it. They already generate sustainable wealth and need to be explicit about how they deliver broader social benefits, doing all this in a way that minimises impact on the environment. From a business perspective this will deliver risk and waste minimisation, in parallel with the opportunity to lead markets and use sustainability to create more value. Examples like GE's Ecoimagination and Marks & Spencer's Plan A have shown the benefit of presenting sustainability in an attractive "branded" fashion, which in turn helps consumer acceptance of and desire for sustainable lifestyles.

For those who would say "but what has this to do with business and brands", the fact that brands have the power to change people's lives and indeed shape the world we live in is not a fanciful notion, but a demonstrable fact. Brands have extraordinary economic power, often transcending national governments, and are able to connect with people's lives, behaviour and purchases across borders. Those who say that business's only concern should be to make a profit are not only missing the point about CSR at its basic level – that CSR by definition demands more than the profit motive – but also missing out on opportunities for brand leadership in the future. From more than 5,000 studies of brands around the world, leadership is the characteristic most closely correlated with the strongest long-term value.

Any brand seeking to succeed and to be most valuable in the future will need to think and behave like a leader – at the basic levels of product and service distinction, and at the more emotional levels of creativity, values and core social contribution.

The future of brand leadership

It is appropriate from time to time for governments, businesses and indeed any organisation to ask themselves what they are there for. Procter & Gamble recently restated its core purpose of improving the lives of its consumers; Samsung talks about creating superior products and services and "contributing to a better global society ... to the prosperity of people all over the world – a single human society"; and the UK government started publishing its "quality of life" indicators in 1999 in answer to challenges on how to create a more sustainable society.

It is easy, but probably not helpful, to be cynical about these kinds of statements. Ironically, one of the brakes to progress on environmental and social issues for companies has been a fear that their actions will be interpreted cynically. Although the stick is an important incentive for companies not to misbehave, opinion-forming media might think sometimes about the carrot of encouragement for corporations trying to do the right thing and struggling to balance the interests of shareholders, consumers and the public at large.

This balancing act also leads on to discussions about how businesses (and indeed governments) are measured and rewarded, as well as how to truly measure the wealth and well-being of society in general. Several academic and public studies have concluded that increases in material wealth and possessions are poorly correlated with happiness, and the UK government's Sustainable Development Commission found the same in its study of prosperity.[11] While it is easy to sit in the wealthy West and philosophise about these things when people in developing countries are dying through lack of basic services, it does nevertheless raise questions about the goal of development. The traditional prioritisation of economic success in preference to any other cannot be appropriate in the future, in either developed or developing countries. There are several references to alternative, more broad-based and sustainable measurement systems for business and society in this book. These would give a broader base to the priorities of CEOs and governments.

It would of course be better for organisations to take an active lead in setting standards in different markets. What can be termed a "leader brand" is not a brand leader in the old-fashioned sense, reflecting scale and muscle alone; rather it reflects a newer, restless and agenda-setting leadership across all areas of philosophy and operations, inside and out. Leader brands also need to take it upon themselves to explain the wider benefits of branding, and increasingly show sensitivity to local cultures, so that they continue to have licence to operate (and hopefully be welcomed) in even the most difficult parts of the world. As discussed throughout, brands can be uniting influences, and powerful social and economic developers. It is important for all brand owners and influencers to manage their brands well, and as a discernible force for good, and to ensure that they help people understand the benefits in a more informed way.

The balance of this book has been quite unashamedly "Pro Logo", but there is a conditional "Pro" here. Brands will continue to succeed if they deserve it, and, since the future of brands is the future of sustainable business and fundamental to developments in society, it is important to us all to see that they do.

Notes and references

1 Chinese Vice-Premier Wu Bangguo, reported in the *China People's Daily*, April 28th, 2000.
2 Rees, M., *Our Final Hour: A Scientist's Warning*, Basic Books, 2003.
3 "Chronicle of the Future", *Sunday Times*.
4 *Global Trends 2025: A Transformed World*, Report of the National Intelligence Council, November 2008.
5 Alvin Toffler, *Future Shock*, Bantam Books, 1971.
6 Quoted in "The great Indian takeaway", *Sunday Times*, June 8th 2003.
7 Ibid.
8 Original equipment manufacturer.
9 "Mugged: poverty in your coffee cup", Oxfam, 2002.
10 World Customs Organisation and Organisation for Economic Co-operation and Development.
11 Porritt, J., *Redefining prosperity*, Sustainable Development Commission, June 2003.

Index

Bush, George W. 121
business performance 83
business process re-engineering
  (BPR) 103
business strategy 11, 51, 117
business-to-business sector 20
BusinessWeek 27

C
Cadbury Schweppes 31
Cadbury's 236, 243
Café Coffee Day bars 201
Café Direct 55, 238, 244
Camel 16
Canada 214
capitalism 3, 181, 182, 248
  free-market 171, 176, 177, 180
  worst excesses of global 171
carbon emissions 54
carbon footprint 50, 54
Carlson Marketing Group 98
Carphone Warehouse 86, 99,
  101–2
Carrefour 174
cash flows, forecasting 18
category identity 119
cattle brands 13–14, 115
cause-related marketing (CRM)
  57–8
CBS 218
celebrity branding 255
CEO
  need for CEO attention to
    brands 11
  reputation 155
  role of 107, 149
charities 10, 53, 55, 57, 177
Charmin's Times Square toilets,
  New York 229
child labour 54

China 8, 178, 212, 247
  challenges in going overseas
    194–5
  competition 181
  economy 125, 171, 185, 187, 188,
    189, 194, 215
  going global 193–4, **194**
  the latest hurdle: Made in
    China 195–6, **196**
  Leo Burnett in 105
  local brands 189, 190, 191–2, 191
  local challenges 192–3
  luxury market 188
  manufacturers 184
  negative perceptions of 214
  potential of Chinese brands
    197, 248
  and poverty 185
  social role of brands 188
  and television 129
  values 188
  wages 250
  and western brands 177
  world's biggest potential
    consumer market 250
China Life 191
China Mobile 191, 194
choice
  diversity of 17–18, 149, 174
  ethical 239
  influence of brands 27
  and price 10
Christakis, Nicholas 222
Church of England 20
Cif 254
cinema 127, 128
Cisco Systems 94, 198, 240
Citibank 250
Citigroup 22
citizenship 148, 149, 150, 155

Stig Dagerman

Twayne's World Authors Series

Leif Sjoberg, Editor of Swedish Literature
State University of New York at Stony Brook

TWAS 676

STIG DAGERMAN
(1923–1954)
Reproduced by kind permission of P.A.
Norstedt & Söners förlag, Stockholm.

Stig Dagerman

By Laurie Thompson

The University College of Wales, Aberystwyth

Twayne Publishers · Boston

Stig Dagerman

Laurie Thompson

Copyright © 1983 by G. K. Hall & Company
All Rights Reserved
Published by Twayne Publishers
A Division of G. K. Hall & Company
70 Lincoln Street
Boston, Massachusetts 02111

Book Production by Marne B. Sultz
Book Design by Barbara Anderson

Printed on permanent/durable acid-free
paper and bound in The United States of
America.

Library of Congress Cataloging in Publication Data

Thompson, Laurie, 1938–
  Stig Dagerman.

  (Twayne's world authors series; TWAS 676)
  Bibliography: p. 159
  Includes index.
  1. Dagerman, Stig, 1923–1954—Criticism and
interpretation.   I. Title.   II. Series.
PT9875.D12Z9 1983   839.7'374   82-12084
ISBN 0-8057-6523-9

Contents

About the Author

Laurie Thompson was born in 1938 in York, England, and studied German at the University of Manchester. He lived in Umeå, Sweden, from 1963 to 1967 and taught English language and literature at the new university there, besides publishing a number of books for the teaching of English in Swedish schools. He was appointed to his present post as Lecturer in German and Swedish at the University College of Wales, Aberystwyth, in 1967. His doctoral dissertation (1979) was on Stig Dagerman, and he has published articles on modern Swedish literature (especially literature of the 1940s) as well as material for the teaching of Swedish to English speakers. Dr. Thompson has also published *Stig Dagerman: Nattens lekar* (University of Hull: *Studies in Swedish Literature*) and discusses Dagerman's *Ormen* in *Essays on Swedish Literature. From 1880 to the Present Day* (edited by Irene Scobbie [Aberdeen: University of Aberdeen, 1979]).

Preface

Stig Dagerman is not well known outside Scandinavia, and yet he was regarded there in the 1940s as the most naturally talented of the younger generation of authors who began to write as the Second World War drew to a close. Aged only twenty-two when his first novel appeared in 1945 Dagerman proceeded to astonish Swedish critics by publishing over the following four years an amount of work which would have done credit to a more ordinary writer who had been toiling away for three times as long. Although primarily a prose writer Dagerman also established himself as one of the leading dramatists of his day and gave notice that he had the potential to develop into a poet of rank, besides contributing a considerable volume of journalism to the radical press. Even those who were skeptical about his ideas acknowledged Dagerman's apparently effortless mastery over an astoundingly wide range of styles. There seemed to be no end to what he might achieve; the reading public classified him as a genius and his name was being whispered in the same breath as that of August Strindberg. Then, Dagerman fell silent and published little of note before committing suicide in 1954.

Understandably there was widespread speculation regarding the circumstances surrounding Dagerman's life and death, and the reasons for his apparently sudden silence. He was branded as one of "the young dead" who died tragically early before they could fulfill their enormous promise and was categorized in Swedish literary histories as the most typical writer of the 1940s. While there is justification for such views, there is more to Stig Dagerman than this. Popular editions of his works have remained in print and been reissued at regular intervals, and successive generations of readers have been delighted to discover in Dagerman such things as an enthralling exploration of moral problems and matters of conscience, a ruthlessly honest analysis of love and the nature of sexuality, a probing into ultimate questions concerning the meaning—or meaninglessness—of human existence, and intelligent radical social criticism which, being strongly influenced by the Anarcho-Syndicalists, is socialistic in nature and yet places individual freedom above all else. Despite the fact that Dagerman's novels are novels of ideas, his characters and settings are vividly and convincingly portrayed with an impressive sureness of touch. In recent years he has begun to attract the attention of scholars at home and abroad; the time seems ripe to bring him to the attention of the English-speaking world and to assess his achievement both as a product of his age and as a writer of extraordinary gifts with a timeless message to impart.

A book of this nature presents considerable problems. It is the first attempt to discuss Dagerman's works as a whole in some detail, and I hope it contains comments and analyses which will be of some interest to readers with a knowledge of Swedish, even to those who are acquainted with Dagerman's works. It is aimed primarily, however, at English-speaking people with little or no knowledge of Swedish. Since few of Dagerman's works have as yet been translated into English, I have included a certain amount of plot summary so that analyses of particular works might more easily be followed; in most cases these are contained in clearly subheaded sections and can be omitted by those who do not need to be informed, or reminded, of what happens in a given novel. All the quotations are in English and, unless the contrary is specifically stated, the translations are my own; references to a Swedish edition are given for the benefit of readers who prefer to consider Dagerman's own words.

In view of Dagerman's representative status and since very little has been written in English either on Dagerman or the literary background of his times, I have prefaced the discussion of his works with a brief account of main trends in Swedish literature of the 1940s and a survey of Dagerman's life and works. Subsequent chapters then consider in detail the four novels and the collection of short stories published between November 1945 and November 1949, taken in chronological order. More than most authors, Dagerman tended to write about himself and his own problems in his works, and although it is not necessary to know the biographical background such a knowledge sometimes helps in understanding a work. While the introductory chapter concentrates on aspects of Dagerman's life prior to the publication of his first novel, some relevant background data are included as a preamble to the analyses of individual books.

Stig Dagerman's main achievement lies in the realm of his prose fiction, and it is here that developments in his ideas and style can most clearly be seen. I have therefore discussed his plays and his poetry separately in chapters which follow the examination of his prose works up to the end of 1949. From 1950 to his death in 1954 Dagerman published little of substance: in view of the speculation surrounding the reasons for this silence I have added a chapter which looks at the events of his life during those years. Dagerman started and then abandoned many projects and I have selected for comment the ones which seem to me the most significant, bearing in mind his progression toward the ultimate silence of suicide. I have not attempted to discuss as a whole the volume *Vårt behov av tröst* [Our Need of Consolation], which contains some of the few stories Dagerman wrote during his last years, and also stories, poems, and articles from other periods in his life: this book was not published during Dagerman's lifetime but was compiled after his death by Olof Lagercrantz.

Finally, in the Epilogue, I have attempted to survey briefly the most important publications on Dagerman's life and works since 1954, and to summarize conclusions reached in the body of the book regarding his achievement.

Stig Dagerman is a fascinating author whose works deserve to be better known. If this monograph stimulates wider interest in Dagerman, and persuades British and American publishers that more of his works are worth translating, it will have achieved two of its major aims.

Laurie Thompson

The University College of Wales

Acknowledgments

My grateful thanks are due to Annemarie Dagerman, who not only supplied me with valuable information but also made available a number of original documents and typescripts; I am indebted also to Anita Björk for the insight she gave me into the last years of Stig Dagerman's life. Dr. Ragnar Svanström patiently answered my questions and, as Dagerman's friend and publisher, was able to throw light on a number of dark places; I am especially grateful to Dr. Svanström and to his successor as head of P. A. Norstedt & Söner, Lasse Bergström, for permission to peruse and quote from the Dagerman file in Norstedts archives and to quote from all Dagerman's works. Everyone at Norstedts was extremely helpful during my researches in Stockholm—especially Agneta Markås. Dr. Harry Järv of the Royal Library, Stockholm, has been a constant source of assistance, not only on the KB premises, and has sent me a seemingly never-ending stream of books, newspapers, clippings, photocopies, and other Dagermania. I should like to thank also Dr. Olof Lagercrantz and Red. Evert Arvidsson for helpful advice.

I am happy to acknowledge with gratitude the invaluable help and encouragement given me over the years by Hans Sandberg. Not only have his research and publications made many things clearer and easier, but he has also supplied me with extra information and read through the manuscript of this book, making many pertinent suggestions for improvements and correcting a number of errors. Emeritus Professor C. P. Magill also read the manuscript and made a large number of very useful and constructive comments, as did Professor Carl Lofmark and Professor W. Glyn Jones: I am most grateful to all of them. A special word of thanks is due to Professor Leif Sjöberg, Scandinavian editor of TWAS, who made some very helpful suggestions, and to Dr. Karin Petherick, who proposed this book in the first place. I would also like to take this opportunity to thank Mrs. G. Suff and Mrs. J. Cock, who typed the manuscript, and my wife, Birgitta, who has helped in innumerable ways.

Acknowledgments

The Swedish Institute and the University College of Wales, Aberystwyth, provided generous financial assistance to make my research in Sweden possible, and permission was kindly given by the editors of *Scandinavica*, the Hull Series of Studies in Swedish Literature, the Festschrift for C. P. Magill and *Swedish Books*, enabling me to use material—usually in adapted form—originally published by them. Parts of this book are an adaptation of my doctoral thesis on Stig Dagerman, presented at the University College of Wales, Aberystwyth, in 1979.

Chronology

1923　Stig Halvard Andersson born 5 October on grandparents' farm in Älvkarleby (ca. forty miles north of Uppsala).

1927　Adopted by father 5 February and acquired father's surname, Jansson.

1929　Moved to Stockholm (December) to live with father.

1930　Started school (Katarina norra folkskola), August.

1931　Returned to Älvkarleby, December.

1934　Moved back to Stockholm, January; started Katarina realskola, August.

1938　Started high school (Södra Latin), August.

1940　Grandfather murdered by lunatic, September; grandmother died, October.

1941　Joined Stockholm Syndicalist Youth Club, January; club secretary, April; vacation job as journalist on Syndicalist newspaper *Arbetaren*, June-August; published first article in Syndicalist Youth journal *Storm*, July.

1942　Took new surname, Dagerman, February; regular articles in *Arbetaren* from February; editor of *Storm*, spring; graduated from high school, April; won trip to Riksgränsen (northern Sweden), May, as prize in literary competition; friend killed in avalanche; enrolled at Stockholm University (fall), but studied only sporadically.

1943　Drafted into army, May; transferred to office duties due to weak heart, August: billeted at Göta Livgarde barracks, Stockholm, background for first novel; married Annemarie Götze, August; started as writer of *dagsverser* ("daily verses") on *Arbetaren* under pseudonym Qroll, August.

1945　Cultural editor on *Arbetaren* from 1 January; *Ormen* [The Snake] published by Steinsviks, November.

1946   Resigned *Arbetaren* post, January; coeditor of *40-tal*, February; taken up by Norstedts publishing house, April; summer on Kymmendö (lived in "Strindberg Cottage"); visited Germany October-November, writing articles for *Expressen; De dömdas ö* [Island of the Doomed] published, October.

1947   Premiere of play *Den dödsdömde* [The Man Condemned to Death], Stockholm, 19 April; moved to house at Vendelsö on outskirts of Stockholm, April: *Tysk höst* [German Autumn] published, May; first prize in literary competition for story "Bon soir," October; *Upptäcktsresanden* [The Explorer], a "miniature drama," published in *40-tal*, October; *Nattens lekar* [The Games of Night] published, October; left for France, November.

1948   Crisis in the Swedish Writers' Union, February-March; premiere of play *Streber* [The Go-Getter], Malmö, 30 May; premiere of play *Skuggan av Mart* [The Shadow of Mart], Stockholm, 10 September; *Dramer om dömda* [Dramas of the Condemned] published, September (contains *Den dödsdömde* and *Skuggan av Mart*); returned from France, October; *Bränt barn* [A Burnt Child] published, October; visit to Tarjei Vesaas in Norway, November-December.

1949   Short visit to France, February; premiere of play *Ingen går fri* [No One Goes Free], Malmö, 9 April, with Dagerman directing; *Judasdramer* [Judas Dramas] published, April (contains *Streber* and *Ingen går fri*); periods of severe depression, April-May; voyage to Australia from Italy with party of refugees, May-July; premiere of play *Upptäcktsresanden*, Hälsingborg, 15 October; *Bröllopsbesvär* [Wedding Worries] published, November.

1950   Cultural editor on *Arbetaren*, February-March; nervous breakdown, March; convalescence in Austrian Tyrol, May-October: translated Vesaas's novel *Bleikeplassen* [The Bleaching Place] into Swedish; work abandoned on *En hund begraven* [A Dog Buried], September; met Anita Björk, November.

1951   Left home to live with Anita Björk, January; visit to France, September-December; daughter Lo born to Anita Björk, December.

1952 Visit to Tarjei Vesaas in Norway, January-March; desperate article "Vårt behov av tröst" [Our Need of Consolation] published, March; radio play *Den yttersta dagen* [The Day of Judgment] first broadcast, 7 May (stage premiere Gothenburg, 11 October); visit to United States, July-August.

1953 Divorce agreed, March.

1954 Work abandoned on Almqvist novel, August; suicide, 4 November.

Chapter One

Introduction

Swedish Literature in the 1940s

The 1940s were dominated by the Second World War. Being neutral, Sweden was spared the ravages of war but her armed forces were in a state of constant readiness to resist invasion—both Denmark and Norway had been occupied by the Germans in 1940, and the rich deposits of iron ore in Sweden made her an obvious target. The Swedish government was forced to make concessions, and citizens were not allowed to criticize Nazi Germany and her allies in case Hitler seized upon such criticism as an excuse to invade Sweden. Swedish writers of the 1940s thus found themselves standing helplessly on the sidelines, unable to do anything but look on while civilization seemed intent on destroying itself. Most Swedes were delighted when it became clear that Hitler would lose the war, but their relief at an Allied victory was tempered by horror at such brutal events as the saturation bombing of Dresden and the dropping of atomic bombs on Japan. They received news of the extermination camps where Hitler had tried to wipe out all Jews with shocked incredulity, but were disturbed to find that the Western powers seemed to be more concerned with beating back the Soviet Union than with hunting down and punishing Nazis in Germany who had committed such terrible crimes, and at the same time reeducating ordinary Germans in the ways of genuine democracy.

The horrors and the brutality of war had deeply shocked most Swedes and they were worried about the state of Cold War which followed the cessation of hostilities in 1945; fears that the Cold War might become a hot one at any time were made worse by the knowledge that atomic bombs, and later hydrogen bombs, could easily complete the destruction of civilization in a very short space of time. Not unnaturally, literature of the 1940s was imbued with *Angst* and pessimism.

In 1944 a new literary journal was launched in Stockholm and entitled *40-tal* [The 40s]: it soon became a forum for the younger generation of Swedish writers, and although they never actually formed a school they found themselves in general agreement over attitudes and opinions. The political tendency was left-wing; contemporary events, they felt, dictated that a modern writer had to be politically and socially committed—by which they meant in fact committed to a Socialist view of society, although they usually avoided allegiance with a particular party. There is a tradition in Sweden of debating questions of current interest, be they political, social, or cultural, in the national press and appropriate journals: the small population of Sweden—still only a little over 8 million—means that such debates are truly national, and all interested parties can follow developments without difficulty and join in at will. The journal *40-tal* carried a number of articles which initiated such debates, and during the four years of its existence (1944—47) it was a reliable guide to trends in contemporary Swedish literature.

One of the most influential of such articles was by Karl Vennberg (b. 1910) and it appeared in January 1946 under the title: "Modern Pessimism and Its Opponents." Vennberg maintained that in the light of twentieth-century experience it was no longer possible to believe in any "-ism" as a panacea for all problems: "Behind us, either unsolved or only half dealt with, lie all the big crises of ideas: the crisis of Socialism, the crisis of Christianity, the crisis of humanism, the crisis of psychology, the crisis of politics."[1] No creed had been adequate to deal with the situation in which modern man found himself and one had to be pessimistic about their chances of doing so in the future. Characteristic of writing in the 1940s was a fierce individualism: Vennberg argued that the task of the modern intellectual was to analyze man's feeling of cowardice, fear, and despair rather that attempt to channel him into some optimistic and collective creed which claimed it could bring him happiness and security.

Excessive pessimism was one of the complaints leveled at the new generation of writers by critics of both the far left and the right, and the resultant debate was lively. Another was that their works were too crude, apparently wallowing in sex and violence, and couched all too often in the language of the gutter. Defenders of the new literary style, however, drew the critics' attention to events actually taking place in the world: how could anyone exceed in print the violence of the battlefield or of the concentration camps at Auschwitz or Buchenwald? Moreover, times of war are invariably times of licentiousness in private life—the alleged debauchery and moral abandonment were merely naturalistic descriptions of what was actually happening. The new wave of writers claimed they were being honest and describing life as it is, instead of suppressing uncomfortable facts and describing life as some people felt it ought to be.

Advocates of this point of view looked to America for their models. The current craze in the cinema was "tough" movies featuring Humphrey Bogart, and the literary fashion from the United States was the so-called "hard-boiled" approach of such writers as Hemingway, Caldwell, and Faulkner. In 1943 a group of Swedish writers actually founded a school which followed the example of the American hardboiled authors: they called themselves the New Vitalists, and the leaders were Sven Forssell (b. 1914), Bertil Lagerström (b. 1916), Mårten Edlund (b. 1913), and Gustaf Rune Eriks (b. 1919). The new generation of Swedish writers which emerged soon afterwards applauded the outspoken, realistic treatment of sex and violence in works by the New Vitalists, but objected to their basic philosophy, which seemed to suggest that sensual excess was a legitimate "escape route" from the troubles of everyday life. For politically committed authors there was no escape route, and they objected to the antiintellectual approach of the New Vitalists. Critics who condemned writers like Lars Ahlin (b. 1915) and Stig Dagerman for excessive concentration on sex and violence were misguided: such elements were not included for their own sake, but to illustrate a point, and in the scheme of their novels they were always subordinate to the intellectual analysis of the situation under discussion.

While the hard-boiled approach to literature was the main transatlantic influence, Swedish literature in the mid-1940s was much affected by current European trends. French existentialism was widely discussed and many intellectuals found it a philosophy ideally suited to the time, with its pessimistic emphasis on the meaningless nature of life and the isolation of the individual possessed by *Angst*. Plays by Sartre and Camus were frequently performed on the Swedish stage, their novels discussed on the literary pages of newspapers and journals, and a number of translations made into Swedish. In 1946, the year in which Sartre published his famous essay *Existentialism and Humanism*, the journal *40-tal* carried a Swedish translation of the central essay of Camus's *The Myth of Sisyphus* with its theory of the absurd, which was received with great interest and fascination.[2]

The dreamlike novels and stories of Franz Kafka, with their guilt-ridden heroes, were admired and imitated in Sweden. Karl Vennberg was largely responsible for introducing the works of this German-speaking Jew from Prague to the Swedish reading public; he published two introductory essays on Kafka in 1944 and 1945 (the latter in *40-tal*), and was involved in the first Kafka translations in book form to be published in Sweden: *The Trial*, *Reflections of a Dog*, and *Metamorphosis* (all 1945).[3]

The older generation of Swedish writers naturally continued to write during the 1940s, but their styles and literary philosophies were already established and the influences discussed above are less marked in their works. They were outraged by the war, of course, and depressed by the future prospects. Although muzzled by the strict censorship laws during the war, several of them published thinly disguised historical works attacking Nazi Germany and the whole idea of war, Vilhelm Moberg's *Rid i natt!* [1941; Eng. tr. H. Alexander, Ride This Night!, 1943] being the most famous example. Eyvind Johnson's *Krilon* series (1941—43) was a masterly account of political reactions to Nazism while Pär Lagerkvist's novel *Dvärgen*, [1944; Eng. tr. The Dwarf, 1945] dealt with the evil that is always present in mankind and leads him into violence and conflict.[4]

The younger generation was bursting with pent-up energy and enthusiasm for literature and debate. Confined by the war within the boundaries of Sweden, yet deeply affected by the momentous and shattering events taking place in the outside world, they were eager to express their radical zeal in literary form as soon as restrictions were lifted. It was in poetry that the new style of writing first manifested itself. Prewar Swedish poets were impressed by such Anglo-Saxon pioneers as T. S. Eliot and Ezra Pound, and came increasingly under the influence of Fenno-Swedish poets like Elmer Diktonius (1896—1961), Gunnar Björling (1887—1960), and Rabbe Enckell (1903—

1974). A key figure in mainland Swedish modernism is Gunnar Ekelöf (1907–1968), whose innovations were recognized in the 1930s; but it was Erik Lindegren (1910–1968) and Karl Vennberg who led the way to a widespread acceptance of the modernistic style in the following decade. Probably the most influential work was Lindegren's *mannen utan väg* [1942; Eng. tr. the man without a way, 1969], a series of forty poems based on what the poet called "the exploded sonnet": the verse form is that of an unrhymed sonnet, but the imagery relies heavily on the apparently paradoxical association of ideas and sensations rather than logical progression. As the title implies, the cycle deals with the insecure position of mankind in the modern world. Lindegren uses a series of striking and frequently sensuous images together with carefully chosen musical rhythms—he acknowledged the influence of Stravinsky as Ekelöf had done before him—to convey his message that even in a period like the 1940s when the future looked bleak, man must not give up but must continue to search for some way of asserting the superiority of life over death. Lindegren was accused in some quarters of incomprehensibility, and the whole modernistic movement of the 1940s was labeled "obscure." There is no doubt that *the man without a way* is a challenging work, but although difficult it is by no means incomprehensible. The younger generation of Swedish intellectuals welcomed Lindegren's masterpiece as an expression of their own feelings in a poetic form which seemed eminently suitable to the content. Nevertheless it is understandable that, at first, the general reader was bewildered by parts of *the man without a way* and the subsequent flood of modernistic poetry in similar style, just as it was predictable that there would be an outcry from conservative critics concerning its alleged obscurity.

Karl Vennberg is, after Lindegren, the most influential of Swedish postwar poets. His style is elusive: dry, ironic, and in comparison with Lindegren's sparse in imagery, Vennberg's poetry is intellectual, analytical and frequently marked by the juxtaposition of traditional poetic language with officialese or colloquialisms. His two important collections of poetry published in the 1940s were *Halmfackla* [Straw Torch, 1944] and *Tideräkning* [Reckoning Time, 1945], the former of which contains one of the most typical and most often quoted poems of the period, "Om det fanns telefon" [If there were a telephone]. In stark language, unrhymed and unpunctuated, the poet lists the various ways he and his friends—representing neutral Sweden, perhaps—would help a mortally wounded soldier, presumably fighting in the Second World War. Unfortunately, however, none of them is possible since no equipment is available, and in any case the dying man is beyond aid. The final four lines reveal the key to the poem: "However we shall fight over the body / for the right to bury / the stunted limbs / of Western culture." Vennberg's approach, featuring dry intellectual analysis tinged with pessimism, was widely emulated and, together with Lindegren's sumptuous imagery, it set the tone for the modernistic poetry of the 1940s.

Looking back at the 1940s many years later, Vennberg referred to an "inner group" of young writers who would meet fairly regularly for discussions and readings. Besides himself and Lindegren, the group included Axel Liffner (b. 1919) and Sonja Bergwall (b. 1907) (in whose home they frequently met), Lars Ahlin, Werner Aspenström (b. 1918), Olov Jonason (b. 1919), Lennart Göthberg (1920–1946), Ragnar Thoursie (b. 1919), Sven Alfons (b. 1918), and occasionally Stig Dagerman. The only important name missing from the list of those now recognized as leading *fyrtiotalister* is that of novelist Sivar Arnér (b. 1909).

Lennart Göthberg and Werner Aspenström, together with Claes Hoogland (b. 1916), were the founding editors of *40-tal*. Göthberg quickly established himself as one of the most perceptive critics of his generation and seemed destined to become a highly influential figure in modern Swedish literature when he was killed tragically in a road accident in 1946. Aspenström has grown steadily in stature and is becoming recognized as one of Sweden's finest postwar poets besides being a notable dramatist. His collection of poetry published in 1946 had a title typical of the period, *Skriket och tystnaden* [The Shriek and the Silence] and, in a style reminiscent of Vennberg's commented ironically on the confused atmosphere of the 1940s. Aspenström's breakthrough came in 1949 with his *Snölegend* [Snow Legend], an anthology remarkable for its highly effective nature imagery although the social comment characteristic of the 1940s is a constant background presence. The same year marked a significant change in the poetry of Sven Alfons with his *Backspegel mot gryningen* [Rear View

Mirror toward Dawn]; the sensuous warmth of his fairly conventional early love poetry was replaced by an ironic style reminiscent of Vennberg and other poets of the 1940s, rich in allusion and quotation and imbued with a deep sense of unease which seemed to reflect the spirit of the age. The feeling of desperation and impotence created by the war and its aftermath was also at the heart of Ragnar Thoursie's poetry collection *Emaljögat* [The Glass Eye, 1945]. The socialism which endows Thoursie's later work with optimism is no more than a background presence in *The Glass Eye*, in which the imagery shows clearly the influence of Lindegren.

Swedish prose in the 1940s was rarely as apparently obscure as the poetry, although it frequently seemed "difficult" in comparison with the large-scale and technically unadventurous novels, largely autobiographical and written by auto-didacts, which had been characteristic of the 1930s. The important criterion from the point of view of those sympathetic to the aims of the younger generation was that the works embodied a genuine attempt at intellectual analysis of contemporary problems, and the authors did not shrink from expressing difficult concepts in complicated form when the need arose. All traditions were challenged by the writers of the 1940s, and conventional literary forms were no exception. The three leading novelists of the younger generation were Ahlin, Arnér, and Dagerman.

Lars Ahlin is a lifelong Socialist and an intellectual who contributed important theoretical articles to literary discussions in the 1940s besides writing some of the period's outstanding novels. Most characteristic of the "forties style" are *Min död är min* [My Death Is Mine, 1945] and *Om* [If, 1946], which are saturated in *Angst* as the guilt-ridden characters wend their tortuous way through situations requiring them to face up to facts and make moral decisions, aspects of life which the writers of the 1940s considered were typical and essential, yet so difficult to carry out in practice. Most untypical of the general trends, however, is Ahlin's Lutheran Christianity, which is central to all his works. Like Vennberg, Ahlin seems constantly to be attempting to reconcile his socialism with his religion, while most writers in the 1940s were either atheistic or agnostic. Ahlin is a challenging and intellectually stimulating author to read and he goes further than most in his technical experiments, notably in *If*.[5]

Sivar Arnér's works most typical of the 1940s style are more conventional in form than Ahlin's, but like his they bear witness to a formidable intellect and illustrate the urge to analyze contemporary events and situations. *Plånbok borttappad* [Wallet Lost, 1943] is ostensibly about a hot-dog salesman attempting to obtain justice for a friend who has been insulted by a coarse but better-class customer. In fact the novel is concerned mainly with the so-called Winter War between Finland and Russia in 1940 and turns into a plea for pacifism, as did the title story of Arnér's collection *Skon som krigaren bar* [The Shoe the Warrior Wore, 1943]. In the 1950s Arnér was to become a leading apologist for "Tredje ståndpunkten" ("The Third Point of View"), arguing for Swedish neutrality independent of the two main power blocs but based on socialism; always a moralist, Arnér's pacifist views are based on the argument that morality is invariably overcome by brute force in a war, irrespective of the rights and wrongs of the combatants.

Stig Dagerman is usually thought of as being the epitome of Swedish literature in the 1940s, and contemporary critics referred to him as a barometer of his times. All the typical traits discussed above are present in Dagerman's works. He shared the Socialist philosophy common to most of his generation, albeit in a refined form, and he acknowledged influence from Kafka and Faulkner. He had some reservations about Sartre but was enthusiastic about Camus. *Angst* permeates all Dagerman's writings, which are characterized by technical subtlety and high intelligence—when his characters do attempt to retreat from the problems of the world into unthinking sensuality they invariably discover that the compensations of antiintellectual bliss are inadequate.

Dagerman was remarkably receptive, and although he was not scholarly or even very widely read, he was abreast of all intellectual and cultural developments in the 1940s and incorporated them into his writings. He was quite capable of absorbing the characteristics of a given writer's views, style, and attitudes on the basis of a few extracts and articles in current magazines coupled with attentive listening to discussions carried on by his friends—Dagerman very rarely spoke on such occasions, but appeared to have almost total recall of what had been said. It is therefore hardly surprising that he seemed to reflect all the current trends in his works. Reviewers maintained they could find traces of a very large number of writers in Dagerman's style, many of whom Dagerman had never read: they were not necessarily entirely wrong, however, thanks to his astonishing receptivity.

Stig Dagerman: The Man and His Works

Stig Halvard Jansson—he did not take the name Dagerman until late in his high-school career—was born in 1923, the son of a rock-blaster who became a municipal laborer in Stockholm.[6] His parents were not married and his mother, a telephone operator from northern Sweden, disappeared out of her son's life some six weeks after his birth. Helmer Jansson, his father, was by the nature of his work almost always away from home during the early years of his son's childhood and Stig grew up on his grandparents' farm at Älvkarleby, a village some forty miles north of Uppsala. Stig Dagerman's subsequent life and writings show clearly that the absence of a mother was a great handicap deeply felt by the young boy. In an autobiographical sketch dating from 1948 Dagerman wrote how he would stand for hours by the farmyard gate, watching ladies ride by on their bicycles: "Cycle past. . . . But I know that one day one of them will slow down, jump off by the gate, run forward and lift me up in her arms. It will be my Mummy, whom I have never seen."[7] Stig Dagerman did not meet his mother until he was a grown man—she felt, reasonably enough, that it would be better for her son to have no contact at all with her than for him to see her only fleetingly on rare occasions.

The section of the autobiographical sketch quoted from ends: "Everyone else in the world has parents. I have only grandparents." Helmer Jansson rarely visited his son, but when Stig was six years old he moved to a working-class district of Stockholm to share a cramped apartment with his father, who was now married. Relations between father and son were cordial but not very deep, and Stig seems not to have gotten on well with his stepmother. Apart from a two-year period back at his grandparents' farm in the early 1930s Stig Dagerman lived in Stockholm for the rest of his life; however, he was never entirely happy there and regarded himself always as a country boy from Älvkarleby.

The love which a child can normally be expected to give to its
parents was transferred in this case to the grandparents, who were
simple, hard-working, and pious souls famed locally for their gener-
osity. In the 1920s and 1930s, Sweden had many thousands of
unemployed men who tramped around the countryside looking for
work and charity: the Janssons invariably gave such men food and
allowed them to sleep in the hayloft. In later life Stig Dagerman
always referred to his grandparents with great affection, praising their
industry and kindness; they figure in several of his works, as do the
farm and the tramps. He had insight from an early age into the
hardships faced by the poor and unemployed, and the class solidarity
displayed by his far-from-rich grandparents helped to instill socialist
ideals into the young Dagerman.

In 1940 Stig Dagerman's grandfather was brutally murdered by a
lunatic who attacked the old man in his fields and stabbed him
repeatedly. Stig, heartbroken, was moved to write his first poem.
Shortly afterwards his grandmother died: she never recovered from
the shock of her husband's murder. Two years later, Stig Dagerman
was on a skiing holiday in northern Sweden, a prize given by a
newspaper for a short story; he grew very friendly with another boy at
the same hotel. One morning when Dagerman was indisposed, the
friend went out skiing alone and was killed in an avalanche.[8] "When I
came back," Dagerman wrote in the autobiographical sketch, "I
knew irrevocably what I must do. I had to become a writer. And I
knew what I had to write: the book of my dead friends." In his darker
moments he believed that he and all who came into close contact with
him were marked men (or women), threatened by the shadow of
death.

As a schoolboy in Stockholm Stig Dagerman became very interested in politics, and more especially in anarcho-syndicalism, a
development of Anarchist theories stemming from the Russians
Michael Bakunin (1814–76) and Peter Kropotkin (1842–1921),
later refined by the French Syndicalist Georges Sorel (1847–1922).
This is a branch of socialism which disapproves strongly of authoritarian organizations with a central directorate remote from the rank
and file; instead, it maintains that power should be devolved to local
groups where individuals cooperate willingly for their own and the

common good. Anarcho-syndicalism is also known as "free social-ism,"since it attempts to combine socialistic philosophy with max-imum freedom of the individual, the latter being a crucial aspect which its advocates believe is missing in more conventional socialism such as communism, or the dominant political creed in Sweden, So-cial Democracy.[9] Anarcho-syndicalism was surprisingly strong in Swe-den in the mid-1940s and Stig Dagerman joined its junior branch, becoming editor of its monthly journal, *Storm*. His first wife, Anne-marie, was the daughter of active Anarcho-Syndicalists who had fled Nazi Germany, and they met at local branch meetings. The move-ment had its own daily newspaper, *Arbetaren* [The Worker], and Dagerman became a regular contributor, even managing to write large numbers of articles during his military service in 1943-44. Dagerman remained faithful to anarcho-syndicalism and *Arbetaren* all his life, even if the ties became less strong in his last years. At the height of the Cold War a number of left-wing intellectuals deserted anarcho-syndicalism and joined the Social Democrats or Commu-nists, accusing *Arbetaren* of being too pro-American. Swedish Anar-cho-Syndicalists felt that, despite everything, America was still a country which upheld freedom of speech and thought: Free Socialists could not condone the suppression of freedom in the Soviet Union even if there were aspects of society in that country which they considered to be preferable to Western capitalism. In his journalism Dagerman criticized American policy but also remained a constant opponent of communism in all its forms. His political views were passionately held and frequently come to the fore in his novels, especially the earlier ones.

Dagerman's first novel, *Ormen* [The Snake], appeared in 1945 and was followed in 1946 by *De dömdas ö* [Island of the Doomed]. Both novels were highly praised by the literary cognoscenti and the author was almost immediately recognized as a representative figure of his generation. Neither novel is easy to read, and they were hardly best-sellers. Besides displaying a degree of mastery over narrative tech-nique astonishing in so young and inexperienced an author, both novels are characterized by an atomosphere of intense *Angst*.

The Swedish word is *ångest*, and there is no exact English equiva-lent. Psychologists usually use the German word *Angst*, which will be used in this book in preference to the nearest English terms, "anxiety" and "dread." Dagerman is not always consistent in his use of the word and sometimes uses such terms as "fear," "horror," and "terror" without distinguishing shades of meaning. What is meant is the existential *Angst* felt by many people in the modern era when traditionally accepted codes of belief and behavior no longer seem meaningful, and man seems adrift in a world indifferent to his presence. At times—and this was especially true of the 1940s, when the world was torn apart by a horrific war which seemed to betoken the madness of man and the imminent destruction of civilization—one is possessed by an overwhelming sensation of inability to cope with life, severe guilt feelings, and a fear of some mysterious force which seems about to wreak destruction. This is the *Angst* central to Dagerman's life and thought, and to those of his characters, who sometimes seem to seek out deliberately situations bound to fill them with terror, as if they were searching for some definable cause which could explain their elusive feelings of *Angst*. It was a characteristic of the age, but no Swedish writer of the 1940s produced works as consistently and totally imbued with an atomosphere of *Angst* as Stig Dagerman.

Dagerman's first great popular success was his play *Den dödsdömde* [The Man Condemned to Death], which was first performed in the spring of 1947. He, his German-born wife, and their two small sons moved from a little apartment in working-class Stockholm to a rambling villa in an outer suburb, and their way of life changed almost overnight. Hailed as a young genius and the bright new hope of Swedish literature, Dagerman was constantly pestered by journalists and photographers requesting interviews, editors requiring stories or articles, and endless streams of people demanding his valuable time. Despite their attentions, Dagerman continued to produce a succession of works with apparently effortless ease and rapidity; increasingly the word "genius" was being used both by serious critics and the general public.

Dagerman had spent the fall of 1946 in Germany and written a series of articles for a Stockholm newspaper, *Expressen*, on what he had seen there. They were made into a book, *Tysk höst* [German Autumn, 1947], which was regarded by some as the finest and most perceptive writing on contemporary Germany in Swedish and served further to establish the author's reputation. A book of short stories appeared in the fall of 1947, *Nattens lekar* [The Games of Night]; by then Dagerman and his wife had left Sweden for a prolonged stay in France, punctuated by frequent visits home to attend first nights of his plays. Two new plays, *Streber* [The Go-Getter] and *Skuggan av Mart* [The Shadow of Mart], were completed by the end of 1947 and performed in the spring and early fall of 1948, respectively.

By the time the Dagermans returned to Sweden in October 1948, the manuscript of another novel was complete: *Bränt barn* [A Burnt Child] was published in time for the Christmas rush and proved to be the author's greatest success. It was a new tour de force of technique and more accessible to the ordinary reader than his previous novel, dealing as it does with the love problems of a young man in contemporary Stockholm in a basically realistic fashion. *A Burnt Child* was soon translated into several major languages, and it seemed as though Dagerman was on the brink of world success. By the beginning of 1949 a dramatized version of the novel was ready, entitled *Ingen går fri* [No One Goes Free].

Everything seemed to be going well, but there were rumors that Dagerman was having problems in his private life. As if to show that any such problems were irrelevant to his writing, Dagerman completed yet another novel in the fall of 1949, *Bröllopsbesvär* [Wedding Worries]. Although critics were not unanimous in greeting the new novel as an unqualified success, a substantial body of opinion rated it as at least the equal of anything he had written to date, and it was noted that once more the style was quite different from that employed in its predecessor; critics were generally agreed that Dagerman's talents were prodigious and his potential seemingly boundless.

What was not realized was that *Wedding Worries* was destined to be Stig Dagerman's last major work. His private problems had been of greater significance than most people had suspected, and he suffered a nervous breakdown in the spring of 1950 which led to hospital treatment in Stockholm followed by a period of convalescence abroad. Dagerman's marriage had been under severe strain for some time, and early in 1951 he left home to live with the famous Swedish actress Anita Björk, who was then at the peak of her career. The couple married in 1953 after a divorce which Annemarie Dagerman had long resisted on the grounds that the affair would pass over eventually as so many had done before. Anita Björk was able to bring to Stig Dagerman an adoring and inspiring love and access to the glittering, glamorous life of the theater and films.

Although Dagerman embarked on a series of new projects after the success of *Wedding Worries* , he was unable to complete anything except a few stories, poems, and articles and a radio play, *Den yttersta dagen* [The Day of Judgment], which was performed by Swedish Radio in May 1952. On 5 November 1954, Swedish newspaper readers were stunned to discover that late the previous night, Stig Dagerman had been found dead in his car: he had blocked the door and windows of his garage and started the engine.

Controversy was rife. To be sure, Dagerman had written little of note for about five years, but his earlier achievements had placed him in the front rank of young Swedish writers and various fragments had suggested that he was far from being a spent force. The circumstances of the author's death and the mystery surrounding the years of silence after such a remarkably productive spell led to prolonged speculation on these and related matters.

Since Dagerman's suicide it has become generally realized that many of his problems were psychological and can be traced back to his childhood; due to an unfortunate combination of circumstances they were made worse in later life, and he began to have difficulty in writing as early as 1948. Relevant aspects of what is now known about Dagerman's life and problems will be referred to in connection with subsequent discussions of his works, since such details occasionally help to explain parts of a novel or play. Knowledge of them is not essential, however, for contemporary readers find with pleasure that Dagerman's works deal with universal problems of morality and conscience, of sexuality and social philosophy, of love, compassion, and justice.

Chapter Two

In Fear and Trembling:
The Snake

Background

Stig Dagerman was appointed to the permanent staff of the Anarcho-Syndicalist newspaper *Arbetaren* in 1943 and was a regular contributor to the cultural pages despite his conscription for military service between the spring of 1943 and the fall of 1944. His army duties were as a clerk and he was billeted at the Göta Livgarde barracks in Stockholm. One day, while out on a training exercise, a fellow conscript captured a snake, put it into his haversack, and took it back to the barracks, where it unaccountably escaped and caused panic among the soldiers, who feared they might find it in their beds at night or among their clothing when they awoke next morning.[1] The incident made a big impression on Dagerman and he used it as the basis of his first novel, *Ormen* [The Snake], written mainly in 1945 and published in November of that year. The parts of the book dealing with army life reflect accurately the frustration felt by many an intelligent conscript; however, in making the snake, a standard symbol for the causes of fear, the central symbol of the book, Dagerman was doing more than merely illustrating the half-suppressed *Angst* at the back of the minds of soldiers in a neutral country who were watching the horrors of the Second World War raging all about them, wondering if and when their turn might come, too.

The snake symbol runs through all Dagerman's works, and the intensity of terror which it invoked for the author can be traced back to an incident when he was three years old and out for a walk in the woods with his uncle. The impressionable young boy was terror-stricken when he almost stepped upon a snake coiled on the path in front of him.[2] This encounter triggered one of Dagerman's many phobias, and for him the very word "snake" was synonymous with fear for the rest of his life.

In April 1945, when *The Snake* was already quite far advanced, Dagerman had a poem published in the literary journal *40-tal* entitled "Snake in the Grass."[3] It typifies the author's use of the snake as the symbol of insidious fear which lurks in the subconscious mind of modern man—and more especially man in the 1940s, aware of the horrific ravages of war and the seemingly inevitable destruction of civilization. The atmosphere is well established in the first three stanzas:

> Naked feet, the dew, a cliff path winding.
> A spider's probing thread, a thistle's blue patrol.
> Silent I lie, a snake in hiding,
> with fangs that foster terror in man's soul.
>
> The grass awaits its dew's evaporation.
> A hungry flower awaits a pollen-laden bee.
> The money-lender waits for compensation.
> I wait to strike at feet that stray near me.
>
> Now flow concentric rings of nervous laughter
> and startled screams betray the wagtail's nest.
> I'm here: no creature's safe from me hereafter,
> There's no safe spot where naked feet can rest.

It is a universally applicable symbol, but Dagerman's own snake phobia accounts for the intensity of terror with which any mention of a snake in his writings is always associated.

The Snake has a motto, preceding the text, which relates the central symbol of existential *Angst* to the author's theoretical writings and his view of the role of the author: "If poetry is a drawing-room entertainment, I will go out into the twilight with darkened foot and make friends with the snakes and the little gray desert rat. If poetry is an essential element of life for someone, don't forget your sandals, watch out for piles of stones! Now the snakes are hunting after my heel, now

I am disgusted by the desert rat." If this statement seems a little obscure at first sight, the novel makes it clear that Dagerman is maintaining that while one may not be able completely to overcome one's *Angst*, one should not attempt to ignore or suppress it: one is less vulnerable if one accepts its existence and is prepared for its manifestations. The words are ascribed to "My friend Scriver," who is a character in the novel and, like his creator, an army clerk who is also a writer. The status of Scriver as an alter ego of the author becomes more obvious when one realizes that the motto is in fact a quotation from Dagerman's article "Diktaren och samvetet" [The Poet and His Conscience], published in the summer issue of *40-tal*, 1945.[4] In this article Dagerman argues that a modern writer must be politically committed and, writing with deep inner conviction, must point out tirelessly the ills of contemporary society.

Like Dagerman, Scriver argues in accordance with the tenets of anarcho-syndicalism. Scriver's symbolic enactment of what he claims is an honest intellectual approach to literature and politics at the end of *The Snake* illustrates Dagerman's reaction to criticisms that anarcho-syndicalism is impractical. He had become cultural editor of *Arbetaren* in January 1945 and had made use of the newspaper to attack not only Capitalists and reactionaries, but also conventional Socialists and Communists. In an article on anarchism published in 1946 he admitted he was aware of the fact that, as an Anarchist and pessimist, his contribution toward changing the world could only have symbolic significance: "Being a politician of the impossible in a world where all too many are politicians of the possible is, in spite of everything, a role which can satisfy me personally both as a social being, an individual and the author of *The Snake*."[5]

In *The Snake* Dagerman created a plot out of events and situations he had experienced personally, and used it to express his views on contemporary Swedish politics and culture. In keeping with the mood of the times, the novel is an expression of *Angst* and explores the existential dilemma of modern man, highlighting the necessity of making a morally right decision in an apparrently meaningless, even absurd world.

Plot

The structure of *The Snake* is unconventional in that it falls into two distinct halves, each with a completely different set of characters. The first part, entitled "Irène," concerns a young woman of that name and her activites over an approximate twenty-four-hour period at some unspecified date in the early 1940s in Sweden. Having had serious disagreements with her parents, Irène now works and lives at an army camp in Stockholm. She is basically what is known conventionally as "a good girl," but she has strong, passionate yearnings and at times longs to cut loose from her inhibitions and be morally abandoned like so many of her contemporaries. She is sexually attracted to Bill, a tough private soldier at the camp, and although her better instincts warn her that he is a ruthless adventurer whose life-style is remote from her own rather prim background, she agrees to accompany him to an orgiastic party in an unoccupied summer cottage outside Stockholm. The arrangement is made one hot, sultry morning, and since it is her free day, she agrees to travel ahead of the soldiers and their girlfriends who will be attending the party, and to make the appropriate preparations. Irène is aware that while Bill is protesting his interest in her, he is simultaneously conducting an affair with Wera, a waitress with far fewer moral inhibitions than Irène has: but she determines to suppress this knowledge and to be as loose as her rival in an attempt to win Bill for herself. While traveling to the cottage by train, she meets her mother and becomes involved in a heated argument. Her mother accuses Irène of an immoral life-style, an accusation which cuts Irène to the quick since, although she knows that such a way of life is foreign to her, the determination to be morally abandoned is her main aim on this particular day: after a brief altercation, Irène throws her mother off the train, presumably to her death. Meanwhile, Bill has been involved in a training exercise during the course of which he captures a snake and places it in his haversack. He uses the fact that his sergeant is terrified of snakes to acquire a late pass for the evening. He pauses en route to dally with Wera and becomes involved in a fight over the girl, as a result of which he is placed under arrest: but he escapes and proceeds to the party, taking with him the snake in his haversack. During the afternoon, Irène has survived an attempted rape by a bloodstained butcher's boy, but she has suppressed her qualms concerning the fate of her mother and is determined to abandon herself to the activities of the evening despite the fact that Bill has also invited Wera to the party. The evening progresses in an orgy of drunkenness, violence, sexual license, and attempted murder. Although there have been moments when Irène has almost been forced to admit to herself once and for all that she is unsuited to this way of life, she persists in her determined efforts to be abandoned until Bill releases the snake on to a table around which the assembled revelers are crowded: the snake slithers straight toward Irène, who interprets it as an accusation. She screams in terror and admits her guilt with regard to her mother's death—and, by implication, accepts her unfittedness for the way of life she is trying to adopt. In a brief epilogue, she tries desperately to find evidence proving that the events of the day were in fact just a horrible dream. Her hopes are raised when she and Bill search the railway track and fail to find her mother's body. But then they realize that they are searching the wrong stretch of track: Bill abandons her, roaring with cruel laughter, while Irène is finally forced to accept the reality of her situation.

The second part of the novel is called "We Cannot Sleep" and concerns the thoughts and experiences of a group of army conscripts—two of them clerks, the rest General Duties men. They are all restless and afraid; although the cause of their anxiety is not made known until quite late in the book, it is eventually revealed that it is due to the presence of a snake which has escaped in their section of the barracks. The origins of the snake are never made unequivocally clear, but the assumption is that it is the same one that Bill captured in the first half of the novel. The men are tainted by the all-pervading fear which seems to fill the barracks; they cannot sleep and instead they lie awake telling and listening to tales of violence and terror. After an uncomfortable day's work, they all leave camp on a late pass and go their various ways: subsections of "We Cannot Sleep" follow each of the men in turn in a series of apparently independent stories, the main connection being their shared anxiety.

Two men attempt to seduce two girls and end by disrupting a private party; one fails to intervene although he knows that a homosexual sailor is seducing a young boy; a group of soldiers sit in a café and discuss politics; a loner is teased by his colleagues and a summary of his life history is presented; one soldier, also a writer, becomes involved in literary and cultural arguments and eventually falls to his death while attempting to walk along a high ledge from one house to another. It soon becomes apparent that through these stories the author is conducting an analysis of the political, social, and cultural situation in contemporary Sweden. In the stories "The Iron Band" and "The Flight That Didn't Come Off," and to a lesser extent in "The Snake," very little actually happens and much of the space is taken up by theoretical discussion. In "The Mirror" and "The Rag Doll," characters experience situations in which they either fail too late to realize the facts or they fail to react in a responsible manner to the facts which are known but unacknowledged. The individual adventures in these two chapters portray characters faced with dilemmas on a personal level which reflect the more general dilemmas in the other stories, the implication being that citizens should accept the realities of political, social, and cultural life and act accordingly. Failure to do so can only result in widespread *Angst* and instability.

Several reviewers commented upon the apparently tenuous connections among the various sections of the novel, and one or two even suggested that *The Snake* was a collection of short stories rather than a novel.[6] Most people would agree that it is a novel, however, the unifying links being the theme of facing facts which runs through all sections, the all-pervading atmosphere of *Angst*, and, most tellingly, the snake symbol. It is a remarkable first novel, distinguished by an atmosphere of intense *Angst* which occasionally explodes into an outburst of terror, and by striking intellectual analysis of the contemporary situation. Moreover, Dagerman displayed an astonishing mastery of narrative technique which made discerning critics acclaim the arrival of a potentially great writer, a view shared even by many of the reviewers who did not care for the content of *The Snake* and who disagreed with his analyses.

"Irène"

The summary of the plot in the "Irène" section of *The Snake*, with its harping on sex and violence, will have been sufficient explanation for why some contemporary readers were shocked and repelled by the novel. Superficially it might seem that Dagerman was gathering together as many examples as he could fit into the plot of extreme behavior in the image of the American "hard-boiled" school, and couching the excesses in tough, slangy, and at times coarse language, merely for sensational effect. A careful reading shows that this is not the case. Sensual excess as a refuge from and consolation for the unbearable *Angst* of modern life is explored by Dagerman as a possible solution, but rejected. This is clear from "Irène" alone, and confirmed by Scriver in the final chapter of the novel when he condemns the "hard-boiled mystics" for an antiintellectual approach to life which seeks to reduce all problems to matters governed by glands and intestines (269).[7]

Irène's main problem is her inability to accept facts. She continually represses what she knows to be true with the result that she is constantly plagued by *Angst*, which builds up inside her until it can no longer be contained, whereupon it bursts out like floodwater through a ruptured dam, leaving her drained and devastated. Irène refuses to acknowledge a number of things of which she is well aware, such as the true character of Bill, the false nature of his "love" for her, the killing of her mother. All these, however, can be traced back to a more fundamental failure to accept reality, namely her insistence on trying to go against her nature, to be a morally abandoned type of person, which she clearly is not. "Irène" is basically a psychological study of the heroine, but her individual problems reflect the more general ones which Dagerman saw as being central to the 1940s: a tendency to adopt wishful solutions which ignore the conclusions suggested by intellectual analysis.

One of Dagerman's most impressive skills as an author is his ability to create striking images. The high density of imagery in the first part of *The Snake* is obvious from even a cursory glance at the opening chapter:

It was so hot that one could almost have roasted coffee on the rails. The gravel between the sleepers glittered sharply while on the other side of the railroad track lolled a field of half-ripe oats. Beyond the field a cluster of the red wooden houses of the village clung together in a clump and from the center of the clump a flag-pole stuck up like a sharp toothpick. The station-house colossus lay pressing down on to the flat stretch of land and small pillars of dust stood on the gravel yard in front. Far away in the distance a train was approaching out of the green infinity. Smoke floated out of the funnel and lay along the track like little mushrooms. It was nearly one o'clock, and the train arrived to give the dozing village a dig in the ribs. (9)

The sheer mass of imagery soon induces in the reader a slightly bemused reaction which tends to reflect the minds of the characters on this hot, sultry day. Although the action is naturalistic and the language of the original abounds in colloquialisms and slang couched in words spelled unconventionally so as to echo the sound, the inventive images add a veneer of surrealism to the story.

As frequently happens in Dagerman's works, a number of striking images emerges from the mass of imagery; three significant ones in the "Irène" section of *The Snake* are the snake itself, rats, and knives. While each of these is a fairly common and conventional symbol, they all represent phobias from which the author suffered; this may well be an important reason why Dagerman is able to create such an intense atmosphere, since the terror associated with the symbols has such personal origins.

The author's first confrontation with a snake has been discussed. Rats and mice, too, had horrific associations for Dagerman, originating in a childhood trauma when he had watched workmen teasing a rat trapped in a deep hole and eventually impaling the terrified animal with a sharp-pointed paling. He always had vivid memories of the rat scurrying around the hole in a vain attempt to escape the paling, and of its scream as the point pierced its brain and the blood spurted forth. When he used a rat as a symbol, it invoked for Dagerman not only the usual disgust most people feel for these verminous killers with the twitching tail and gnawing teeth, but also the look of terror in a bloodstained animal's eye and its blood-curdling death-scream.[8]

Although Dagerman was well aware of the Freudian significance of knives and similar sharp-pointed instruments, he saw them primarily as potential weapons. As a child he had acquired the disturbing habit of taking a carving knife to bed with him—in an autobiographical story written when he was about twenty-four his alter ego explains that the *Angst* in the room where he slept was so great that it would be unbearable without a weapon with which to defend himself.[9] Annemarie Dagerman tells how, when her husband felt a fit of depression approaching, he would remove every knife in the house—presumably as a protective measure to avoid triggering off his thoughts in the direction of a potential suicide weapon;[10] perhaps also the sight of knives reminded him of the stabbing of his grandfather.[11]

In "Irène" the knife symbol appears in a number of guises linked by the basic knife characteristics of a sharp point and a cutting edge. In Chapter 5 Irène repeatedly attempts to suppress thoughts concerning Bill's flirtations with Wera and her own position as a rival of Wera's: Dagerman describes the situation in terms of Irène's holding a knife to her own throat in order to prevent herself from uttering unwanted thoughts. By this stage the knife has already acquired symbolic significance by dint of its appearance, in the form of a bayonet, in Chapter 2. It is a hot morning following an unusually warm night, and Irène has been sleeping naked. She walks over to the window of her room in order to converse with Bill, whom she hears passing, having first wrapped herself up in a sheet from the bed. Bill invites Irène to a party that evening; Irène is very tempted, but hesitates on account of Bill's rough manner and his presumption that he has only to suggest something for her to obey him. "What if I don't want to?" she asks. "What if I tell you to go to hell?" Bill responds by drawing his bayonet and sticking it into the window ledge between them. "You will," he says.

She watched the bayonet tremble like a javelin that has just landed, she saw the sharp blade and the yellow oil gliding down towards the tip. And she looked past the bayonet and saw the man standing there behind the blade, and suddenly everything was as it had been a few moments before. So hot, so bewildering, so much blood in one place. And without a word she let the sheet drop and stood there naked in the window. And she leant her giddy head forward past the bayonet toward the man and he bit her mouth in a frenzy and as they kissed the bayonet fell over on the window-ledge and she cut her wrist on the sharp edge and it was like two bites. One in the mouth and one there. (16)

The bayonet represents Bill's superior strength and his potential violence which force Irène into submission; equally obviously it has a sexual significance, suggesting that the submission of the weaker to the stronger is paralleled by the girl's surrender to her sexual urges. Immediately after Bill's departure, Irène feels once more that she hates him; but she represses such thoughts, determined to give herself up completely to her emotions. Hence the reappearance of the symbol as a knife when she wishes to suppress her rational doubts about Bill's behavior and to think only about the sexual goals which lurk behind her decision to prepare for the party that evening (39). Later in the "Irène" section while the orgy is in progress, the knife becomes a sharp-pointed fishing hook: every time Irène sees Bill and Wera together, it is as if the hook is being turned inside her breast (104 ff.).

The snake first appears in Chapter 3 when a group of soldiers including Bill and led by a Sergeant Bohman lie in hiding on a slope prior to "attacking" a rival group as part of a training exercise. Bohman is suddenly transfixed by the sight of a snake coiled in front of him, its head swaying from side to side and its forked tongue darting in and out with an ominous hissing noise. "The whole of his body contracted to form one enormous muscle of terror" (20); his fear results in a failure to give the appropriate orders and his group is attacked by their opponents—in more realistic circumstances, they would have been annihilated. The more general inference regarding the effect of fear on troops in wartime is easy to draw. Bill is unabashed, however, and he captures the snake. Toward the end of the chapter, he uses the snake and his knowledge of Bohman's terror to persuade the sergeant to authorize special leave that night, thus enabling him to attend the planned party. Shortly afterwards, Bill dozes for a while in his barrack room and has a mysterious dream in which he sees Irène and Sergeant Bohman kissing on a bench by the golf course: Bill is carrying a grenade, and is about to throw it at the couple when it explodes and turns into a clutch of small snakes (29).

In this way, Dagerman suggests that Bill's power over Bohman thanks to the snake is paralleled by his power over Irène, which was previously symbolized by the bayonet, and a link between the two symbols is forged.

In the later part of the section named after her, Irène's latent *Angst* is represented by a little animal with sharp teeth gnawing away at her inside; no specific animal is named, but the gnawing and general description suggest a rat. Irène attempts to contain the animal by placing make-believe cartons over it, but the animal soon gnaws its way through and she has to place another, larger, carton over it, and so on in a continuous process (65 ff.). The obvious implication is that Irène is attempting to repress her subconscious thoughts, in which she knows the truth about Bill's interest in her, and about her own nature which is unsuited to the project on which she has embarked, thus preventing them from rising into her conscious mind—a clear reference to Freudian psychology. As the symbol develops, the animal acquires a twitching tail, reinforcing the comparison with a rat; at times, the tail seems to sway rather like the snake that had previously terrified Sergeant Bohman, and then it acquires sharp, thornlike projections which are associated with the fishing hooks referred to above as part of the knife theme. Clearly this ratlike creature represents a combination of the sexual and violent influence exerted on Irène by Bill.

The climax of the "Irène" section comes at the end of Chapter 8. All those present at the party crowd around a table laden with bottles and empty glasses, and Bill unexpectedly releases the snake. Everyone is terrified, but no one more so than Irène for she sees with horror that the angry reptile, after a brief hesitation, is sliding ominously toward her: the *Angst* which underlay Irène's relationship with Bill is exposed. If the snake has been the symbol of *Angst* attacking Irène, as it were, from an external source, the ratlike animal inside her has symbolized the *Angst* inside her. The accusing approach of the snake evokes a response from the rat which can no longer be contained by the cartons and it rises up inside Irène to burst forth in the form of a scream. Her repressed thoughts rise into her conscious mind and she is forced to face facts:

And she knows that it has been true all the time and that everything she has done and everything she has said has had no other purpose than to shut out her terror. And her terror is the little animal which nothing can check any more. And suddenly she screams, or rather it is the little animal that screams, for she herself is devoid of will and the scream bubbles out of her like the carbon dioxide in a lemonade bottle. And then the scream turns into words and she is afraid of them and starts to run: "It's true," she hears herself scream, "it's true. She's dead." (115)

She must first acknowledge the worst of her crimes, namely that she has killed her mother by throwing her off a train. The real source of her *Angst* goes deeper than that, however, a fact that she will eventually have to face as she examines her own personality. The real theme of "Irène" is the conflict between rational thought and instinctive emotion, a conflict which was to recur frequently in Dagerman's subsequent works, no doubt connected with the fact that it was a problem which constantly created havoc in his private life.

"We Cannot Sleep"

The style in the second half of *The Snake* is more subdued; the imagery is less dense, although here too striking symbols emerge, and in several cases there is a reference to them in the chapter headings. The military background is authentic, and the susceptibility of the soldiers to the all-pervading fear is made more credible by the poor morale which so often dominates inactive military camps: many an ex-conscript will recognize the malingering, the conspiracy to avoid work or any kind of responsibility, the antagonism toward authority, the pointless chores. Behind this depiction of a particular group of soldiers lurks the situation in which all the Swedish armed forces found themselves in the Second World War—the need constantly to be standing by without ever being called to active service.

Beyond the military context, however, the conscripts in "We Cannot Sleep" stand as representatives of society as a whole. The picture of the army as an organization in which ordinary individuals are without responsibility or significant employment, but are directed, frequently in meaningless fashion, by some remote central organization whose representatives are completely out of touch with the masses—all this corresponds closely to Dagerman's criticism of contemporary society from his Anarcho-Syndicalist standpoint.

The chapter which rehearses the author's political views most clearly is entitled "The Iron Band." Virtually nothing actually happens in the chapter: a group of soldiers sit around a table in a café and discuss politics. Edmund attacks the role of the centralized, authoritarian state, claiming that although the modern welfare state provides its citizens with security, it robs them of individual freedom. There is a danger, he feels, that the ordinary citizen will be seduced by a comfortable and superficially happy existence and hence will overlook the fact that the price to be paid is that he is placing himself entirely in the hands of some remote authority. In fact, claims Edmund, the man in the street accepts a few insignificant benefits of security on a small scale in exchange for what is really enormous insecurity; there can be no real security when one's whole existence is at the mercy of faceless authorities beyond one's control. How many conscripts would be in the army were it not for the fact that they are forced to enlist in accordance with laws brought in by the state which is supposedly providing the individual with security?

"I feel oppressed," said Edmund, "it's as if an iron band were pressing in on my skull when I think that there are laws which no-one has asked me if I'll accept but which make me more or less defenseless. . . . I feel threatened, I feel damned well threatened by whoever it is that provides me with this security." (212)

Edmund's views are very similar to those expressed by Dagerman in an article, "My Views on Anarchism," published early in 1946.[12] In it Dagerman suggests that whereas in earlier times oppressive governments instilled *Angst* in their subjects by such means as starvation or the Inquisition, the modern welfare state instills *Angst* "by means of uncertainty, the essential inability of the individual to control his own fate."

Here, then, is the political argument put forward by Dagerman to explain the *Angst* felt by most people in the modern era. In "Irène" many of the heroine's problems were caused by her failure to acknowledge what she knew subconsciously to be true; in "The Iron Band"

Edmund argues that a parallel action in a political context is immoral. Having once felt the iron band and realized that the prevailing social and political system constricts the individual, any attempt to repress that knowledge would merely compound the *Angst*.

The chapter entitled "The Snake" concentrates on Gideon and his gradual awakening to the facts of his situation. He is a loner who is teased by his comrades, but as the survey of his life shows he is also typical of the petty bourgeoisie. Dagerman devotes several pages to a detailed account of Gideon's background. He seems to stand for an old order which has been shaken by the Second World War and his standards, inculcated into him by his life-style, are those of order, cleanliness, duty, and tradition. His career seems safe and his promotion assured, but like his father before him Gideon gradually realizes that this apparent security is an illusion. Nevertheless, his instinct to conform makes him easy to manipulate; he believes in the importance of his country, and although he tries to be nonpolitical, he soon finds himself following the line laid down by the propaganda-makers. In other words he is conditioned and manipulated by the state, an example of the way in which an individual loses his freedom as described by Edmund. Gideon's self-discipline, referred to as "his ability to deceive himself" (256), seemed at first to be a praiseworthy virtue but is gradually revealed as part of the process causing him to lead an existence based on illusions rather than reality. It is suggested that to lead an ordered and well-disciplined life, conforming to conventional rules and standards, is a way of concealing one's *Angst*.

Having become increasingly aware of the falseness of his position, Gideon feels more acutely his isolation from his fellow soldiers. Like Irène, Gideon tries to go against his nature and to behave more like the people around him. His attempts to find comradeship among his fellow conscripts are clumsy and poorly understood; moreover, their forced and unnatural qualities betray the fact that he is deluding himself even now. Gideon must face up to his *Angst* in his own way, and not seek comfort and solace through forced companionship.

The similarities between Gideon's position and that of Irène are no doubt an important reason why the chapter is entitled "The Snake." It is the penultimate chapter of the novel, but only here is it revealed that the cause of the soldiers' panic is their fear of the released snake.

Most of Gideon's comrades are able to forget their terror quite quickly as life reverts to normal after the snake is found dead, but for him it is a turning point. He recognizes the symbolic nature of the snake, as the author states quite explicitly: "But when he eventually discovered that his fear did not go away, he finally realized—although it cost him a large part of what he had always believed in hitherto—that the snake had simply been a symbol or an excuse; sooner or later it would have had to happen anyway" (256).

Two of the chapters in "We Cannot Sleep" do not contain theoretical discussion. The central symbol in each is contained in the title— "The Mirror" and "The Rag Doll"—and their significance relates to Dagerman's insistence that one must be honest with oneself, analyze a situation, and take what ever action is required without hesitation or excuse.

In "The Mirror" two soldiers pick up two girls and attempt to seduce them but are interrupted and invited to attend a mysterious gathering at which one of the men, Laxen, converses with a pretty but rather pathetic young lady who turns out to be blind. He has a guilty conscience about his earlier seduction attempt and drunkenness, the excess to which his *Angst* has driven him; at first he tries to be cruel to the young lady but then he repents and writes "I love you" on a magazine he places in front of her—failing to notice that she is blind. When Laxen does realize, he is disgusted with himself and his self-revulsion is depicted symbolically when he stares at his own image in a mirror in the hall, dislikes what he sees, and smashes the glass.

Laxen's *Angst* made him very afraid of being isolated, but he eventually understands that his attempts to seek companionship were selfish and contained as much of a desire to be cruel as to be loving. When he repents and tries to tell the blind girl he loves her, he is still too self-centered and fails to take account of the fact that she cannot read his message. The chapter seems to suggest that people should be frank and honest in their dealings with others, and indeed with themselves. They should not wallow in self-pity but should face up to the facts of their situation and help others to do the same. A genuine expression of love might be the answer, but in Laxen's case it is too puny and comes too late: for him there is nothing but oblivion and self-hatred. In a wider context the message seems to be that people should be less self-centered but should foster a genuine concern for others and create a community spirit, thus satisfactorily breaking their own isolation.

In "The Rag Doll" Sörenson looks on while an eight-year-old boy is picked up by a homosexual sailor, taken back to the man's ship, and seduced. Once more the theme is that of illusion versus reality. The young boy's grandmother persists in believing that her grandson is the pure and innocent child he had been years ago, although it is made clear to the reader that he is in fact a young ruffian. He needs a different kind of care now than he did then. Purity and innocence are soon ruined in the squalid world of today—and this is symbolized by the rag doll. The old woman remembers giving the doll as a present to the boy when he was four, and stresses that "he takes it to bed with him every night and cannot go to sleep until he's given it a good-night kiss" (241). In fact, the young lad treats it very roughly and has cut open the doll's head with his knife. "Where has all the innocence gone to?" asks Sörenson as he contemplates the shabby doll (241). Sörenson himself bears a considerable burden of guilt for he has watched the seduction of the boy and knows full well he could have intervened to prevent it from happening. He finds the boy's doll in his pocket at the end of the chapter and drops it into the dirty water on the Stockholm waterfront. Sörenson knows he will bear the guilt of his failure to intervene for the rest of his life, and guilt is linked with *Angst*. He "had thought that it was possible to run away from the *Angst* aroused by what happens to others as one can run away from a bar without paying for the drinks" (243). In reality, of course, no one can escape from facts by repressing knowledge of them.

The final chapter in *The Snake* is intriguing, not least because the snake was found dead in the previous chapter and life has returned to normal in the barracks. In "The Flight That Didn't Come Off" Scriver, Dagerman's alter ego, never actually returns to camp but instead dies a symbolic death while trying to prove a point. It is a chapter full of theoretical discussions, this time mainly in the literary and cultural field although there are clear political implications. There are distinct links between Scriver and Edmund, the Anarcho-Syndicalist who felt the oppressive power of the state like an iron band around his head. Both men claim that their *Angst* is the greatest in the world, and both argue for "Free Socialism." Scriver attacks what he calls the "philosophy of harmony" of conventional socialism: it is soon clear that he is attacking the same aspects of the modern welfare state as had annoyed Edmund so much. Scriver concentrates on the cultural parallels, however, and stresses that the "philosophy of harmony" is an antiintellectual creed which involves individuals in renouncing the right to think independently. "The tragedy of modern man," says Scriver, "is that he has ceased to be afraid. That is unfortunate since the consequence is that he is gradually forced to cease thinking" (269). Existential *Angst* must be accepted—one must not run for shelter under the wing of the paternal state but must somehow learn to cope with it.

The equivalent of running away from the reality of life in a literary context, according to Scriver, is New Vitalism. Dagerman frequently attacked the antiintellectual approach of this school and had suggested in a review of Faulkner's *Light in August* that Swedish epigones seized on the trappings of the hard-boiled style of a master like Faulkner but lacked the subtlety of the originals—it was like using a craftsman's fine drill to bore holes in an oak tree, he wrote.[13] The New Vitalists sought blissful peace of mind in sensual intoxication by the simple means of neglecting intellectual analysis and ignoring uncomfortable facts. Scriver maintains that what is needed is "a new epoch of intellectualism which can give people at least some courage to look *Angst* in the eye instead of creeping away to the grottoes and bedrooms of infantile mysticism. It may be necessary to run away, but in that case not in the naive way advocated by the hard-boiled school" (273).

Scriver claims that what they are doing is like climbing out of a window, but climbing back into the same room through a different window—in other words they are not facing up to the basic problem at all. An intellectual analysis of the situation would lead to the enlightened author to climb into a different room: and Scriver, full of beer after a long discussion, attempts to demonstrate his point by climbing out of a window several floors above ground level, making his way along a narrow ledge to the neighboring house, and climbing through a window there into a new room. Inevitably he loses his footing on the ledge and the novel ends as he falls to his death in the street below.

"The Flight That Didn't Come Off' can be seen as a sort of epilogue to the whole novel in which all the themes are summarized. *The Snake* ends on a question mark, however: if the analysis of the contemporary situation was correct, why does the author's alter ego die, having failed to prove his point by means of the symbolic climb? To draw the apparently obvious conclusion that Scriver's analysis must have been wrong would be to negate at a stroke the argument developed over the book as a whole. The answer must presumably be that Scriver's death illustrates the point that awareness of one's *Angst* and its causes does not put the individual in a comfortable and secure position—that is the realm of the "philosophy of harmony," which is based on illusions. It is an ironical and pessimistic ending.

A Disciple of Faulkner and Kafka?

The Snake did not become a bestseller, but it was widely recognized among the author's generation as an eloquent statement of what most of them felt about culture, politics, society—life in general. Thinking young Swedes in the 1940s were in sympathy with Dagerman's ideas, while the fiction in which he had dressed his thoughts seemed ideally suited to the age in its bold use of language, its outspoken treatment of sex, drunkenness and violence, its brilliant depiction of military life in a neutral country. The reviews which annoyed Dagerman more than any others were those which branded him as an "Angst-Romantic": he saw himself as an "Angst-Analyst."[14] The misunderstanding was due to a failure on the part of some critics to realize that in much of *The Snake* the author was parodying the hard-boiled style in the sense that those of his characters who sought antiintellectual solutions failed to find them.

Thirty-five years later *The Snake* still seems a remarkable first novel, less dated in its appeal than one might expect. It has its faults, of course. There is a tendency to repeat the same message too often and some of the theorizing sits rather awkwardly in context. The whole novel gives a somewhat episodic impression—apart from the division into two parts, the sections in the second part seem to be arranged in an arbitrary order; moreover, the fact that the snake is found dead in the penultimate chapter emphasizes the fact that the final chapter is linked with the rest of the book on a theoretical level but hardly at all in terms of a narrative link. This stresses the intellectual and analytical aspects of the work but adds fuel to the fire of those who feel that *The Snake* is a collection of stories rather than a novel. The unifying factors are surely sufficient to qualify it as a novel, but it was certainly a bold experiment for a young author in his first book.

Dagerman acknowledged that while there were distinct echoes of French existentialism in *The Snake*, his chief influences came from Kafka and Faulkner.[15] The sultry, oppressive atmosphere of the American's novels, the violence and the hard drinking, and stylistic devices such as variations on stream-of-consciousness techniques—all these aspects can best be seen in the "Irène" section of the novel. The most obvious influence of Kafka is the overwhelming sense of guilt which affects all the characters, and descriptions of the barracks in "We Cannot Sleep" remind the reader of how buildings seem to share and indeed accentuate the guilt borne by Kafka's characters. Parts of "The Rag Doll" are also reminiscent of the restrained style of Kafka, when the whole environment seems to conspire threateningly against the guilt-ridden Sörenson. Although the influence of Faulkner and Kafka was easily detected, it was not, however, a question of aping other writers' styles so much as the acknowledging of kindred spirits.

Chapter Three

Doomsday:
The Island of the Doomed

Background

Nineteen forty-six was a local election year in Sweden, and political debates were prominent in all the media. It was in the February edition of *40-tal* that Dagerman published his significant article "My Views on Anarchism," and he joined the editorial board of that journal in the same month. He was one of the chief instigators of the "Open Letter to Our Government" published in the April issue of *40-tal* in which a number of writers protested about a subject which had long been a favorite area for agitation among Anarcho-Syndicalists, namely, the trade links between Sweden and the Fascist Spain of General Franco; the shortlived Syndicalist regime in Catalonia in the 1930s made the Fascist dictatorship in Spain particularly abhorrent to Anarcho-Syndicalists and Dagerman. He was also a leading speaker at the "Spain Meeting" organized in March 1946 by the left-wing organization Clarté. In 1946, Dagerman published 206 satirical poems in *Arbetaren*, his so-called "Daily Verses," most of them commenting scathingly on current events from an Anarcho-Syndicalist point of view; several of them attacked Spanish fascism and the apparently tolerant attitude of the West toward Franco, in spite of recent experiences of Nazism.[1]

Another favorite object of attack were the Nazi war criminals and the Nuremberg Trials, which were approaching their peak in the summer of 1946 before the sentences were passed in October.[2] Many Swedes believed that the high-ranking personalities at Nuremberg, while deserving nothing but the harshest possible treatment, were being made scapegoats while millions of lesser offenders were escaping almost unscathed throughout Germany. They suspected the motives of the Western powers, feeling that the stamping out of Nazism was taking second place to a desire for German support in the imminent battle with the Soviet Union,[3] and many Swedes were horrified by American atom bomb tests at Bikini in June and July 1946. The Cold War was developing, and political trends seemed to confirm that the *Angst* central to Existentialist philosophy was a central aspect of life in the late 1940s.

Stig Dagerman was busy with his second novel in the early part of 1946, and according to an interview given the following year it was intended—on one level, at least—as a political novel and an apologia for anarcho-syndicalism.[4] Dagerman claimed that it was "a defense of individualism. It is also meant to be an attack on the tendency to use ideas as means of instilling terror, as political truncheons. Ideas should be used as toys—as Socrates did in his lectures!" True to his instinct for expressing key ideas in striking symbolism, Dagerman made the climactic section of his novel a struggle between a Fascist and an Anarcho-Syndicalist over the details of a picture featuring a lion to be scratched into a rock: indeed, the title of the new work was to be *Kampen om lejonet* [The Fight over the Lion].[5]

In April, Dagerman was taken up by Sweden's second-largest publisher, Norstedts. This firm was looking for an outstanding young author to "adopt" in their ceaseless battle with mighty Bonniers and had been advised that Stig Dagerman had a great future: the considerable financial security and publicity which only a large publishing house could provide was now Dagerman's for the asking, and his private future must have seemed rosy despite the worrying state of public affairs. In June, Dagerman and his family—they had one small boy and his wife was in an advanced state of pregnancy with the next—moved to the Stockholm archipelago for the summer. Mindful of the implications, Stig Dagerman selected Kymmendö, the island featured by Strindberg in his novel *Hemsöborna* [Eng. tr., The People of Hemsö, London, 1959], and he even went so far as to rent the cottage in which his august predecessor used to stay. Dagerman's novel would never achieve the popularity of *The People of Hemsö*, but here was an ambitious young man staking a claim to a place among the great.

The summer was hot and Kymmendö attracted a stream of writers and artists keen to make merry with the Dagermans and the Aspenströms—like Stig Dagerman, Werner Aspenström was at the beginning of an illustrious career: besides being a coeditor of *40-tal* he was to become one of the outstanding poets of the period, and fru Aspenström was a talented artist.[6] Despite the apparently idyllic seclusion of Kymmendö, there were endless distractions. The deadline drew near, and Stig Dagerman in fact wrote the last nine chapters (some 60 to 65 pages) in a single all-night session at the phenomenal rate of about fifteen minutes per page.[7] This part of the novel is complicated, but the intellectual control and the consistency of the symbolism never falter: it was a remarkable achievement and illustrates the extreme facility Dagerman seemed to enjoy as a writer. Such hectic periods of creativity were to become a hallmark of Stig Dagerman; with hindsight it seems clear that what appeared to be impressive displays of outstanding talent were perhaps ominous indications that a light which burned so brightly and furiously might soon burn itself out.

At the last moment, Dagerman informed his publishers that he had changed the title: the new novel was to be called *The Island of the Doomed*.[8] It appeared in the autumn of 1946.

Plot

The Island of the Doomed is a complicated novel of ideas in which situations and actions symbolize states of mind and possible solutions. The basic plot is comparatively simple but hardly begins to indicate the subtleties and richness of this novel. As was the case with parts of *The Snake*, it seems to be made up of an incredible series of disasters and instances of warped behavior; however, there is a surrealistic atmosphere in the novel which makes the exaggerations as acceptable as they would be in a dream.

Following a shipwreck, seven people—five men and two women—are cast away on an island. It is a small island inhabited only by a flock of blind seagulls and innumerable lizards—the word "lizard" will be used here, as in the original Swedish, although the creatures seem to be the grotesque iguanas, which can grow to a length of several feet and look like prehistoric monsters with their armorlike scales and spikes. The only provisions the castaways have managed to salvage from the ship is a single water tank, and one of their number purposely empties this under cover of darkness. Since it is a tropical island with no source of fresh water, the relentless, scorching sun makes survival impossible.

The novel is divided into two parts: the first part, "The Castaways," which occupies some three-fifths of the total number of pages, takes each of the seven characters in turn and, in subtitled chapters, presents their past lives in a series of flashbacks. All of them bear heavy burdens of guilt and are trying to run away from reality—they are doomed long before the shipwreck takes place. The second part of the book is entitled "The Fight over the Lion" and is subdivided into seventeen numbered chapters. The reactions of the castaways to their plight are recorded, as are ways in which they meet their deaths.

One man, a boxer, is badly injured and dies almost as the novel begins: he is the only one who sees the water tank being emptied, but is unable to reveal the culprit. The others are understandably angry but blame the wrong man. While burying the dead boxer, the castaways uncover a white rock under the sand and decide to engrave upon it some symbolic messsage—a gesture aimed ostensibly at an eventual search party but in fact a statement of their own philosophy of life. The two dominant characters and the ones who survive longest are Lucas Egmont, in many ways a spokesman for the author, and Captain Wilson. The latter wishes to scratch into the rock a picture of a lion with its dead prey while Lucas insists on the lion's being alone. Both images are meant to symbolize isolation, but while Captain Wilson's lion suggests loneliness based on brutality and oppression, Lucas Egmont's lion is more pathetic and lacks the cruel streak—indeed, Lucas claims that his lion is seeking solidarity with all other sufferers.

Lucas Egmont wins the battle, but *The Island of the Doomed* ends as the victor, the sole survivor, wades into the lagoon in full knowledge of the fact that a killer fish is lurking just below the surface. It is an ending full of evocative references to Existentialist theories of the absurd, meaningless actions, and suicide.

Seven Lives

As usual Dagerman provided his novel with a meaningful motto; printed on the title page of "The Castaways" is the sentence: "Two things fill me with terror: the executioner inside me and the axe over my head."[9] In the case of the seven castaways the external source of terror—the axe—is obviously the perils of the tropical island following the shipwreck. All of them have an internal source—the executioner—in the form of heavily guilt-laden consciences. (Lucas Egmont claims near the end of the novel that conscience is "merely an idyllic euphemism for our terror" [301].)[10] In order to clarify their *Angst* the author presents crucial incidents in the past life of each character in turn.

Lucas Egmont's guilt seems to be irrational in origin: indeed he spends much of his life searching for some specific "crime" which can justify or at least rationalize his guilt feelings. To this end he steals money from the bank in which he works, but the crime seems petty compared with the enormity of his guilt. It is Lucas who empties the water tank at the end of the opening chapter in the novel, and this terrible deed seems as though it might be sufficient, although the satisfaction which it gives him is illusory and shortlived.

Lucas Egmont suffered a childhood trauma which haunts him continually. He came from a privileged background and one day was out riding, immaculately dressed, when his horse died under him. A group of urchins gathered in silence to stare at Egmont's discomfiture, and for some inexplicable reason this increased greatly his feelings of guilt at what had happened. His guilt appears to be linked with his realization of the artificial gap that separates himself from the urchins, caused by the class difference between them. Egmont's father is an eccentric aristocrat of the old school who beats his son unmercifully with a whip after the incident, telling Lucas that brooding does not become a person of higher rank and adding that "guilt is only felt by the weak, that's what they're there for" (18). Lucas had felt sorry for the dead horse, but is commanded by his father: "Never feel pity, it only makes you look ridiculous and takes up valuable time" (17).

In later life when guilt feelings beset Lucas Egmont, the scars caused by his father's beating grow tender—and the description of them as thin strips of red crisscrossing his back becomes a part of the pattern of imagery in the novel. Egmont cannot accept the aristocratic creed of his father and the rest of his class but is always haunted by pity and empathy for the oppressed. This is why he is adamantly opposed to the image of the lion with its freshly killed prey at the end of the novel: Lucas Egmont's sympathies are with the victim.

The second castaway is Jimmy Baaz, a boxer. He, too, suffered a childhood trauma in that he and his friends discovered a mysterious large parcel by the pier near his home, wrapped up in sailcloth and tied with red cord. They used it for all kinds of games and were horrified when they eventually discovered the parcel contained a dead body. Jimmy's horror was compounded when shortly afterwards he found a shirt belonging to his father, a local smuggler, hanging in the kitchen by a piece of red cord identical to that used to tie up the corpse. Jimmy's flight from reality began at that moment, a flight from the horror of the dead body and, more especially, the presumed guilt of his father and his own unsuspected discovery of this secret he could never share.

As a boxer, Jimmy Baaz became a folk hero but, despite his universal acclaim, he was always afraid of meeting people, afraid that someone might discover his guilty secret. His voyage on the doomed ship was an attempt to run away from people who knew him, but even there he was thwarted and recognized by one of the passengers. The moral is obvious: one cannot escape from one's guilt. Jimmy's *Angst* is symbolized by the red cord which secured the fateful parcel he had found as a child, and his obsessive memory of that occasion is stirred repeatedly as death approaches on the island—the red light of dawn sends lines across the sky reminding him of the cord, for instance, and a spider's web over his head seems to be made of red cord. The link with the long, thin scars on Lucas Egmont's back needs no elaboration.

Tim Solider is the only member of the crew of the ship to survive the wreck. He is a giant of a man with great physical strength, but he is inhibited by a slave mentality. He can never rid himself of a feeling of inferiority and gauche behavior as befits a member of his lowly class. The name "Solider" suggests, paradoxically, solidarity: Tim cannot even claim this as a virtue and he is frequently reminded by guilt feelings of an occasion when he was a strike-breaker and, more-over, failed to assist a comrade who had been mishandled by police. Tim longs to do some act which will assert him as a useful member of society and atone for his selfishness. He eventually overcomes almost irresistible urges to keep for himself a box of provisions he has discovered, and donates it for the good of all the castaways—only to find that the box in fact contains nothing but glass beads. It seems that fate as well as his own character is conspiring against Tim Solider to keep him in his place as a witless, weak-willed manual worker, exploited continually by his "betters" and denied credit for his useful and considerable efforts. He is the epitome of the exploited worker in a capitalist society.

Madame, the elder of the two women on the island, is associated primarily with the motif of numbness. She had a large sexual appetite as a young woman, and was quite incapable of being satisfied by her crippled husband. Consequently, she took a series of lovers—weak men with powerful cars who tried to make up for their lack of potency with impressive horsepower. Madame's emotions remain unstirred, even when she becomes pregnant by one of her lovers. Her son is mentally defective; his appearance and movements are subhuman, and after a vision in which she sees him in the form of a lizard, she becomes obsessed with the idea that he actually *is* a lizard rather than a boy. His lack of human feelings and understanding is clearly a reflection of her own benumbed senses. When the accident occurs at sea, she flings her son down a staircase and into the water which is surging into the crippled ship; her guilt, which she tries to resolve on the island, revolves around the question of whether she has actually murdered a human being, or merely killed an animal—and hence whether she herself is fully worthy of the designation "human."

Madame is both terrified and morbidly fascinated by the lizard population on the island, and eventually kills one by crushing it with a stone; she needs to do this in order to decide whether the creature she killed on the ship was really human. It is never stated what conclusion she reaches, although she obviously *wants* to believe she is not guilty of murder. The chapter ends as she "throws herself down onto her knees and kisses the slowly softening scales of the lizard with her bleeding lips; the old hypocrite" (112). Like many a Dagerman character before and after her, Madame is refusing to face facts and hiding from the enormity of her deeds behind excuses. She is unfeeling, insensitive, but refuses to admit it and grasps at any excuse to avoid doing so.

Boy Larus is an airman whose problem is that he is far too willing to accept discipline imposed upon him by a higher authority. He becomes incapable of independent action, a situation highlighted when a comrade is accidentally shot by a hail of bullets during target practice. Insead of going to his aid and calling for help, Boy Larus weakly obeys the order of his superiors who, ignorant of the tragedy, want him to continue raising the targets at which they are shooting. Boy's ideal is the Spartan boy—the legendary figure who concealed fox cubs inside his clothing and refused to acknowledge their presence or even to react to the excruciating pain as they ate into his flesh. This is the positive image of self-control and discipline beloved of the military minded, but Dagerman shows in Boy the negative side of his "ideal." Boy Larus is constantly plagued by two symbolic wounds (from the mythical fox cubs of the Spartan boy) every time he is subjected to pressure to obey commands. Like the other characters on the island, Boy has attempted to flee—in his case by deserting from the air force—but his desertion is discovered by Captain Wilson, who uses his knowledge and superior rank to cow Boy Larus into terrified passivity while he submits him to a homosexual assault. The wounds throb as never before. The degradation and horror into which Boy Larus's compulsive submission to orders leads him is a telling satirical comment on the ideal of duty and authoritarian discipline.

Draga, frequently referred to as "the English girl," has sexual problems. She is linked with a number of Freudian symbols which seem to recur whenever she is mentioned—snakes, flagpoles, elephants' trunks, crawling insects, shrinking rooms, and so on. Draga had an unhappy childhood in which she was constantly persecuted by a cruel father; at a time when she was sexually curious she was led to associate all contact with males with pain and terror. She longs for warmth and security, but fails repeatedly to find it: a boyfriend who threatens to kill himself for her sake in fact attempts to rape her.

It is Draga who recognizes Jimmy Baaz, having heard the ship's captain telling someone who he is. When Jimmy is dying, and indeed, after he is dead, Draga finds in him an ideal recipient for her abundant love. He is a person toward whom she can direct all her sexual desires and her longings for love without any fear of his reacting in any way which will disturb the fantasy. From the beginning Draga's sexual fears have driven her into a world of fantasy remote from harsh reality, but she sees in Jimmy an opportunity of combining dream and fact. It is a perverse hope, of course, and she seems mad to the other castaways. Yet again Dagerman presents his readers with a character who persistently refuses to accept reality but instead retreats into illusion after illusion.

The last of the castaways to be examined is the complicated figure of Captain Wilson. As his military rank implies, he is used to commanding and controlling, and he believes in Nietzschean principles of power. Wilson is a cold and remote figure, professedly incapable of normal love and tenderness. He is an ascetic whose ideal existence involves the avoidance of all companionship in favor of complete submersion in his own ego. This inevitably leads Captain Wilson into elitism; if there is to be any contact with others at all, they must be conquered and subdued. Any human relationship must be either a failure—Captain Wilson's marriage collapses—or a degrading experience: he becomes a homosexual and transvestite. He believes that such isolation confers absolute freedom—"freedom from the need to seek companionship, the need to open doors when no doors exist, the need to smile when one wants to cry, the need to caress when one wants to scratch, the need to look for friends when one has just learnt that the world is full of enemies" (171). Captain Wilson has tried his hand at writing, claiming that to do so is "to condense my isolation," but he rejects it as a flight from reality: "What is the whole of literature compared with a single successful suicide?" he asks rhetorically (183–84). His arguments are formidable, but he fails to realize that his retreat into isolation and the ultimate extension of this, suicide, is itself a flight from reality.

It will be clear from this account that all seven of the castaways are subjected to an enormous burden of *Angst*. They have failed to come to terms with it and are fleeing from the real world in a vain attempt to escape it. Part II of the novel, "The Fight over the Lion," depicts the climax of the flight from reality and the opportunities the characters have to overcome their *Angst*.

The Struggle

The struggle over the symbol to be carved into the rock is obviously central to any interpretation of *The Island of the Doomed* and in the course of it the full significance of the past lives of the castaways becomes clear. As is frequently the case with a good novel of ideas, there is scope for a considerable range of interpretations, depending on which aspects of the general trends the reader wishes to stress. There is little doubt that there is something of the author himself in each of the characters, appropriately embellished to suit his fictional purposes. At the other end of the scale, as it were, one can also see the seven castaways as representatives of the *Angst* felt by a cross-section of mankind in the early stages of the postwar nuclear age, with the shipwreck standing for the climax of the Second World War.

Two main themes will be examined here since they cannot be ignored in any detailed interpretation. It has already been mentioned that the author himself was keen to stress the political origins of *The Island of the Doomed*, and the political and social implications of the struggle over the lion symbol must be taken into account. At least as important are the continual references to existential philosophy, which are interwoven with the familiar Dagerman themes of illusion, guilt, and *Angst*. The two main themes frequently overlap, but the aspects relating to Existentialist theories are most crucial to the struggle over the symbolic lion and will be treated first.

Moral Choice in an Absurd World

In interviews Dagerman acknowledged being influenced by French Existentialist thought—he could hardly have avoided it since it was a main topic of discussion in Sweden in the immediate postwar years; nevertheless, he intimated that the direct debt had been exaggerated by critics. [11] No attempt will be made here to analyze "The Struggle over the Lion" exhaustively from an Existentialist point of view, but a discussion of Dagerman's treatment of the theme should enable readers familiar with Existentialist philosophy to judge the extent of the influence.

When the castaways discover the white rock while burying Jimmy Baaz, they reject the idea of making a statue out of it and decide instead to carve into it a symbol which will represent their agreed view of the meaning of life. It is clearly an absurd situation—common sense would suggest they should attempt to catch fish or dig for a fresh-water well;   instead they are in effect volunteering to commit suicide in order to create a symbol which will probably never be seen by another human being. It seems to be the ultimate in meaningless acts.

The definition of what is meaningless is central to existentialism. Heidegger, following the lead given by Kierkegaard, states that *Angst* is a result of man's intense longing to know that he exists. As man proceeds through life he becomes increasingly aware of the fact that he cannot know and understand the world about him, nor can he fully know and understand himself: the only sure guide to the fact of his existence is his death. A corollary of this is the realization that all life is meaningless. Man's only hope is to accept this fully. Philip Mairet puts the next stage of the Existentialist argument clearly and concisely:

. . . although his personal fate is simply to perish, he can triumph over it by inventing "purposes," "projects," which will themselves confer meaning both upon himself and upon the world of objects—all meaningless otherwise and in themselves. There is indeed no reason why a man should do this, and he gets nothing by it except the authentic knowledge that he exists; but that precisely is his great, his transcendent need and desire. Not many are capable thus of authenticating their existence: the great majority reassure themselves by thinking as little as possible of their approaching deaths. . . .[12]

In *The Island of the Doomed* Dagerman does not follow these arguments exactly, but there are some close parallels.

The two main protagonists in the struggle over the symbol to be carved into the rock are Lucas Egmont and Captain Wilson, and both claim to have realized that life is meaningless. Besides being an act which might justify his guilt feelings, Egmont's deliberate emptying of the water tank could be seen as a demonstration of the meaningless nature of any attempt by the castaways to survive. He has just had an experience, however, which has made him fully aware of his *Angst*, as a result of which he concludes: "I believe in the meaningless nature of the whole, but the unintentional meaningfulness of the part" (226). Although life is meaningless, there are certain acts or principles which can be made meaningful: and Egmont's traumatic experience has convinced him of the evil nature of Captain Wilson's search for absolute loneliness.

The incident which brings Lucas Egmont face to face with his guilty conscience concerns Tim Solider. Because of Tim's lower-class submissiveness, Captain Wilson assumes he was guilty of emptying the water tank and attacks the crew member with his fists. Unfortunately Tim falls onto a lizard and squashes it. The blood excites two other lizards which attack Tim in turn, biting deeply into his chest. While the other castaways feel the "criminal" is receiving his just deserts, Lucas Egmont leaps to Tim's aid, removes the lizards, and dresses the stricken man's wounds with pieces of his shirt. It is a significant intervention which seems imprudent and also meaningless—imprudent because Egmont is likely to betray his own guilt to the other castaways and thus invite attacks upon himself, and meaningless because everyone on the island is doomed to die anyway. Lucas Egmont's action stems, however, from recognition of the fact that his guilty conscience is due to his own upper class origins as a result of which he went on to lead a life which ignored the sufferings and hardships of the poor and needy. The aid he gives to Tim Solider—a representative of the working class about which he has had a bad conscience—is a positive act which shows he has recognized the cause of his *Angst* and, in his new state of awareness, is able to counter it. Of course Lucas Egmont is unable to put right the wrongs of the world and his action is meaningless compared with the vastness of injustice in general; but it has symbolic value and is thus meaningful for Egmont himself. Provided he can be consistent and carry through to their logical conclusion the consequences of this new awareness, Lucas Egmont is no longer running away from his *Angst*.

It is thus essential for Lucas Egmont to oppose Captain Wilson's ideas about loneliness—a state of isolation which depends on exploitation of one's fellow men. More important than survival—life is meaningless, after all—is what Sartre calls "a free commitment" to an ideal which is meaningful as far as Egmont's existence is concerned. He cannot allow Captain Wilson to dictate that a symbol should be carved into the rock which expresses the ideal of isolation. Wilson suggests as a model for the carving a picture of a lion embossed on his jackboot as a trademark. The lion is sitting on a freshly killed human being and Wilson argues for it because, he says, it symbolizes "isolation, the triumphant isolation of a lion which has just disposed of its last enemy, the only one which still barred its way to isolation" (229). Lucas Egmont insists that if the symbol is to be a lion, then it must be a solitary lion, thus eliminating the cruel brutality of Wilson's lion with its prey. "I won't go as far as to say that it represents fellowship," explains Egmont, "but it demonstrates calm strength, a complete personality, harmony which at any moment can be shattered by the roar of a wild animal. Terror and harmony in the same figure, that's my lion" (284). The castaways agree to go for a walk and think things over, then to reassemble by the rock at sundown in order to decide between the alternative symbols.

Only Lucas Egmont and Captain Wilson survive as long as that. The other four were not really interested in the struggle over the lion symbol: each of them was obsessed by his or her individual *Angst*, but none could face up to the problem and accept the guilt that weighed down on their consciences. As Lucas Egmont puts it, they had not understood "the essential task of mankind: to tell at least half the truth about the whole lie which is the world" (282). During the course of the afternoon the extreme heat and their desperate thirst combined with their obsessions bring them to an early death.

Madame's original problem was her lack of feelings and her eventual obsession became the question of whether she had murdered a human being or killed an animal when she threw her son down the staircase on the sinking ship. She was perversely delighted when Tim Solider was attacked and, as she thought, killed by the lizards. She thought she had "found her Jesus" in that Tim was suffering in her stead and thus purging her of her sin. In fact, of course, she is merely running away from the truth; she cannot continue to do so and survive. She stands on a cliff top and, in a feverish vision, imagines that she is being pursued by thousands of lizards seeking revenge—and she falls to her death on the rocks below.

Boy Larus is obsessed by his compulsion to obey orders. He does make an attempt to overcome Captain Wilson's influence before the white rock is discovered: he is possessed by desire for Draga and rapes her on the beach, ignoring orders from Captain Wilson to leave her alone. He is delighted, but fails completely to realize that in submitting to the forces of his own desires he is merely emulating the acts of the Captain by brutally exploiting a person weaker than himself and using her for his own ends. It is the same kind of exploitation as is depicted in Captain Wilson's symbolic lion and does not begin to penetrate beneath the surface of his own problem. Boy Larus does not even realize the effect his attack had on Draga, mistaking her struggles for passionate pleasure. When Draga lures him into another attempt to make love to her on the cliff top, she orders him to turn his back on her at the last second, and he of course obeys: and she thrusts him to his death over the edge. Boy Larus's fatal weakness remains with him to the very end.

Draga's disgust with sex thus leads her ultimately into murder, although one cannot but sympathize with her treatment of Boy Larus. Her perverted insistence on lavishing all her love and care on the dead Jimmy Baaz is in stark contrast to her rape by Boy Larus: she longs to give but cannot bear to receive, and Jimmy cannot respond whereas Boy forces his attentions on to her. After killing Boy Larus she runs down to the beach, digs up the body of Jimmy Baaz, wraps her skirt round his rotting corpse, then runs madly into the sea and commits suicide. Love clearly involves both giving and taking, and Draga never begins to achieve a balanced attitude toward it. She runs away from reality all her life and is still running away as she dies.

Tim Solider almost survives long enough to support Lucas Egmont in the struggle over the lion, but his fatal incapacity for solidarity with his fellows lets him down; Tim appreciates Egmont's act of compassion in rescuing him from the lizards and is determined to respond by backing his new friend, only to be thwarted by an act of self-interest. While preparing to rescue the box of beads which he thought contained food, Tim had killed a seagull and sent it tumbling into the waves. As he waits for the others to return to the white rock Tim sees the body of the dead bird floating near the shore and is overcome by irresistible pangs of hunger which are stronger than his good intentions: he catches the floating corpse, and runs off to devour it but traps his foot in a rocky crevice and is drowned. The man's determination to eat the seagull himself seems to be a petulant reaction to the failure of his genuinely noble gesture in donating what he thought was a box of provisions to the whole party instead of keeping the contents for himself. The tragicomedy of his flight across the beach with the dead bird in his arms, looking stealthily to left and right lest he is observed and has to share his booty, confirms that Tim Solider is too much of the cunningly selfish working man with a chip on his shoulder for him to display genuine solidarity with his comrades. His constant fear of exploitation and lack of confidence in his ability to make a contribution toward the common good is not overcome; Tim Solider, too, fails to come to terms with his *Angst*.

The scene is thus set for the final stages of the struggle over the lion; the secondary figures are out of the way and the two chief protagonists confront each other. Captain Wilson claims to have come to terms with his *Angst* by embracing loneliness willingly; Lucas Egmont has faced up to his guilt feelings and found a meaningful attitude to life in compassion with fellow sufferers. The scene where Egmont intervenes to save Tim Solider is paralleled by an incident in which Captain Wilson intervenes to save Lucas Egmont, preventing him from drinking liquid from a fruit which the Captain knows is poisonous. Both men were placed in situations in which they had to make a moral choice, and both men acted to save the lives of fellow humans in grave danger. Whereas this action led Lucas Egmont into a new state of awareness and gave him a new strength, enabling him to transcend the merely physical perils of the island, Wilson's action serves to demonstrate the falseness of his position. Had he allowed Egmont to die, Captain Wilson would have survived as the strongest of the castaways and achieved his professed aim of complete isolation. He does not do so because, in spite of his claims to the contrary, Captain Wilson is afraid of isolation and needs human fellowship: he refuses to acknowledge this and continues to flee from the source of his *Angst*. In true Existentialist spirit (and in a way reminiscent of Hemingway), Dagerman suggests that moments of terror can have positive results provided one is prepared to accept the full implications. Typically, he implies that man is a social being who cannot survive in isolation based on contempt for his fellows.

Not surprisingly after this episode, Lucas Egmont wins the final struggle with Captain Wilson, tricking him into swimming across the lagoon as part of a contest. A symbol of the terror which lurks everywhere in wait for those who have failed to come to terms with their *Angst* is a deadly swordfish which suddenly rises from the still waters to devour anything which enters the lagoon. Egmont is aware of its presence and knows the Captain will die: Wilson, having failed to face up to his *Angst*, is surprised and killed instantly. Lucas Egmont is thus the sole survivor on the island, and the author is clearly suggesting that Egmont's version of the lion symbol and his view of life are superior.

Life itself may be meaningless, but once a person has accepted that fact, specific actions can be meaningful in that they are symbolic of what an individual would like life to be like: it is therefore important that such actions are morally praiseworthy. Dagerman frequently places in Egmont's mouth the phrase "the right action," a term widely used in Swedish cultural circles in the latter part of the 1940s, especially after Vennberg's famous essay on pessimism. [13]

There is a farcical twist to Lucas Egmont's desire to perform "the right action," however: he cannot remember what a lion looks like and is thus unable to carve into the rock the symbol he has fought for! His plight leads him to a new moral problem: should one condemn a man who intends to do the right action but is prevented through no fault of his own? Surely not! He therefore considers good intentions as the guideline and coins the phrase "the right direction" instead of "the right action." The goal for which one is aiming may be an illusion (and can in any case be no more than symbolic), but the important thing is the direction, for one has control over that but not over the goal. Lucas Egmont concludes that conscious control is the key concept and decides that he cannot distinguish between right and wrong actions "but only between controlled and uncontrolled actions, between conscious and unconscious ones" (300).

There remains a final problem: how is one to be aware of the right direction in which to point one's conscious or controlled action?

According to Lucas Egmont's musing this depends on the position in time and space allotted to the individual by a combination of pure luck and the world order (that is, the social and political context in which one finds oneself). To establish the right direction one has to analyze meticulously the situation in which one exists and combine one's conclusions with the dictates of one's conscience:

Our awareness is affected by our conscience, which is merely an idyllic euphemism for our *Angst*, for *Angst* reminds us continually of the right direction and if we suffocate our *Angst* we also lose the possibility of pointing ourselves in a definite direction and we surrender ourselves to a series of stupid private explosions, now here and now there, which create the greatest possible damage and the least possible results. Therefore we must keep our *Angst* alive in us, like a permanent ice-free harbor which helps us to get through the winter, the bubbling undercurrent beneath the ice-covered rivers of the winter. (301)

Having discovered the right direction for him, Lucas Egmont has fulfilled himself and justified his existence. In a euphoric state he wades out into the lagoon and surrenders himself to the deadly fish, which kills him in an instant.

Politics and Morals

The important characters in the novel from a political point of view are Captain Wilson, the harsh elitist and authoritarian; Lucas Egmont, the man who feels guilty about his supposed social superiority and craves to align himself with the underdog; Tim Solider, the worker with the slave mentality and inadequate feelings of solidarity; and Boy Larus, who seems to be the epitome of a man who has lost his individual freedom thanks to the authoritarian regime under which he has been living. The latter two tend to be the foils of the former, whose opposing political philosophies are represented in detail.

The Fascist tendencies of Captain Wilson are fairly obvious—one notices immediately his aloof arrogance, his assumption of superiority reminiscent of a Nietzschean superman, his insistence on discipline as a way of life, his sadistic cruelty, as well as such unmistakable symbols as his highly polished jackboot. Dagerman originally intended to make the link with Nazism even more obvious by giving the man a German name, Besserwiss (roughly translatable as "Knowall"). In his valuable essay "De dömdas ö—en politisk idéroman" [The Island of the Doomed—A Political Novel of Ideas], Hans Sandberg has shown how the character of Captain Wilson was based to a large extent on the theories of National Socialism contained in the book *Psykopaternes diktatur* [Dictatorship of the Psychopaths] by Ingjald Nissen; originally written in Norwegian, this book appeared in Swedish in 1945 and Dagerman was evidently acquainted with its contents.[14] Nissen picks out various characteristics of Nazi philosophy and ideals which seem to be reflected in Captain Wilson: an important one is the promasculine bias and the tendency to form men-only groups and power structures, held together by strict discipline, in the form of concentric circles around a dominant leader. This leads in the direction of homosexuality, a characteristic of Captain Wilson, who displays both the dominant masculine tendencies and the passive female tendencies—he is also a transvestite—which are associated with homosexuality. Another aspect of National Socialism, according to Nissen, is the treatment of women as prostitutes: and Wilson displays this trait as well. Nissen also picks out the mediaeval courtly ideal, so strong in German Romanticism, as something taken up by the Nazis—Nissen linked its artificial conventionality and lack of actual physical contact with the homosexual aspects of Nazism. Captain Wilson is frequently depicted as a Knight in armor; in fact, Lucas Egmont describes him as an empty suit of armor (221).

Taken together with the more obvious Fascist tendencies, Sandberg's depiction of Captain Wilson as archetypal National Socialist is convincing, particularly when one remembers that *The Island of the Doomed* was written at the time of the Nuremberg trials. Nevertheless, as Sandberg is well aware, to link Captain Wilson too much with specific political creeds would be mistaken and tie the novel too closely to a particular period of history. The links with the 1940s are obvious and important, but the symbolic significance of *The Island of the Doomed* is surely broader than this. It will be recalled that in *The Snake*, Scriver explained that a writer always takes an extreme case to represent a concept he wishes to symbolize: Captain Wilson is clearly steeped in National Socialism and Fascist ideology, but Dagerman is

193512

using him to represent all political philosophies that depend on a centralized system of authority involving the exploitation of some individuals by others. Boy Larus's compulsive submission to the commands of those in authority over him certainly echoes the standard excuse of the SS members accused of war crimes after World War II, "We were only obeying orders"; the link with the Spartan boy surely extends the reference, however—Sparta was the authoritarian Greek state in contrast with democratic Athens—and there are suggestions of Nietzschean master-slave relationships. In *The Snake* and in his theoretical writings such as "My Views on Anarchism" Dagerman criticized authoritarian tendencies even in professedly democratic states. Any hint of central authority is anathema to an Anarcho-Syndicalist.

Lucas Egmont clearly has a social conscience. In his early life it manifests itself as irrational guilt feelings, but his awareness of its true character is made quite specific in his arguments with Captain Wilson about the lion symbol. Egmont is not so obviously an Anarcho-Syndicalist as were Scriver and Edmund in *The Snake*, but there are details which indicate that he believes in "free socialism" rather than conventional socialism, quite apart from knowledge of Dagerman's well-known sympathies. In his summary of the development of his social conscience in Chapter 14, Lucas Egmont attacks all political parties for their preoccupation with peripheral questions which results in perpetual postponement of effective measures to put right social injustice. "For those of us who were weighed down with guilt," he says, "there was no organization. The needy were championed by people who had ceased to feel guilt, if indeed they had ever done so, because they lived under the illusion that they were doing such a tremendous amont to ameliorate it" (289). Anarcho-Syndicalists feel that this is an inevitable development in centrally organized movements (such as Social Democracy, which dominated Swedish politics from 1932 to 1976); they themselves have no organization beyond the minimum necessary to set up local groups cooperating willingly among and within themselves. They believe in ideals rather than ideas—another point taken up by Lucas Egmont. Moreover, when Egmont champions his lion because it symbolizes "terror and harmony in the same figure," the use of the word "harmony" is rather surprising until one remembers Scriver's scathing criticism of "the philosophy of harmony" in *The Snake*. [15] Egmont's lion symbolizes only modified harmony, that is, material well-being and happiness but also an awareness of the problems, hardships and potential tragedies of life—an awareness which equips the individual to deal with them.

Tim Solider is an example of the typical working man created by an authoritarian social system. He lacks dignity, he is treated with contempt, and he has an inferiority complex; although his wish is to contribute to the general good, he has little idea of how to do so, the odds are stacked against him and he is hampered by the streak of selfishness which is inevitable in a system which does not encourage the ideal of brotherhood and genuine solidarity with the oppressed (even though it may pay lip-service to it).

A number of Swedish critics have questioned the depth of Stig Dagerman's commitment to anarcho-syndicalism, maintaining that it does not figure prominently enough in his creative works. [16] It seems an unfair claim to make when one examines Dagerman's first two novels in detail. To be sure, the specifically Anarcho-Syndicalist nature of the socialism advocated in *The Island of the Doomed* is less obvious than in *The Snake*. On the other hand, one can hardly be very specific about the dogma of a political creed which intentionally avoids dogma. It is true that the political content of Dagerman's later completed works dwindled, but the Anarcho-Syndicalist elements are strong in his first two novels.

Style and Technique

The Island of the Doomed has been criticized for being tuned to too consistently high a pitch of tension. It is true that there are few moments of relief in the novel, but it is after all about a group of people in extremis. The intensity of their physical suffering reflects the turmoil in their minds, and their feverish fantasies are conveyed by Dagerman in frequent passages of image-laden prose which give the novel a distinct surrealistic flavor. In the opening chapter, for instance, Lucas Egmont wakes up gradually after a restless night on the beach and sees his own hand on the sand beside him:

With his gaze hunched up in fear behind trembling membranes, he saw his own hand come creeping toward him over the sand. A bloated, toad-like animal with bleeding limbs. Go away, he wanted to shriek, leave me alone—but the animal only dug holes in the sand from which dazzling white columns of smoke, thin as copper wire, rose skywards.

Notice his predicament: he wanted to shriek but that was impossible for him as his swollen tongue was like a large, trembling fist in his mouth. (8)

All the characters have fantasies in which they see their *Angst* projected in the form of some rather disgusting or frightening animal—Jimmy Baaz sees a spider, for instance; Draga sees swarms of small beetles; Captain Wilson sees a snake; Madame sees lizards.[17] Generally speaking the animals are figments of the characters' imagination, usually associated with some early trauma which has linked the animal with terror in the mind of that particular individual.

Three animals actually exist on the island and assume symbolic significance. The blind seagulls have a mysteriously ominous air and seem constantly to threaten the castaways. They are vulturelike, and as Captain Wilson points out to Lucas Egmont they are waiting for the survivors to die so that they can eat them as carrion. They seem like harbingers of death, constantly reminding the castaways of their approaching doom. The lizards are just as mysteriously ominous as the seagulls, and they emit an unpleasant smell when injured which reminds the castaways of decay and death. Their potential dangerousness is highlighted when they attack Tim Solider. They seem to be close to the ultimate in nonhuman qualities, and are linked with the theme of numbness by Madame. When the pair of lizards attack Tim Solider, this seems to confirm that numbness and passivity are not just regrettable foibles but potentially deadly dangers to be avoided at all costs. Lucas Egmont, being aware in the existential sense, is alert to the possible danger and can overcome the lizards but the other castaways are always liable to be surprised. The swordfish in the lagoon, the third of the animals, is the most deadly of all. It lurks constantly under the calm surface of the water, but strikes with devastating effect whenever anyone or anything trespasses on its territory. The castaways are thus threatened on land, in the air and in the water: there is no escape for them, they are well and truly doomed.

The actual length of time the castaways are on the island is never made clear. Most of the action takes place on a single day, however, but the time progression is by no means straightforwardly linear. The flashbacks covering the previous lives of the seven castaways confuse the time scale, and individual chapters concentrate on different characters, narrating the same events from different points of view. This confusion of the time scale adds to the surrealistic qualities of the novel, and it is intensified rather than resolved by the fact that the chapter headings in the first part follow the passage of time from morning till night: "The Thirst of Dawn," "The Paralysis of Morning," "The Hunger of Day," "Worry at Sundown," "The Obedience of Dusk," "The Longing of Evening," "The Fires of Night." The sun rises and sets with relentless regularity, in contrast with the turbulent confusion in the minds of the castaways.

Most of *The Island of the Doomed* is narrated by a third-person narrator, but there is occasionally a lapse into *erlebte Rede* and sometimes inner monologue. Such aspects of the narration are not obtrusive, however, and do not disturb the reader. If the novel is difficult to read it is because of the high degree of *Angst*-ridden tension and the density of imagery which forms a network of associations and cross-references which is far from easy to keep track of, especially at a first reading. It was this relentless consistency in the imagery and the complete intellectual control over the various complicated strands of *The Island of the Doomed* which particularly impressed Dagerman's biographer, Olof Lagercrantz, and led him to declare that of all Dagerman's works, this is the greatest and the one which will live longest.[18]

The Island of the Doomed deserves to be much better known. Had it been written in a major language, it would surely have been recognized as one of the outstanding novels of the mid-twentieth century.

Chapter Four

Playing Games:
The Games of Night

Background

Stig Dagerman had made plans with his publishers for a collection of short stories in the spring of 1946, although no contract was signed until March 1947.[1] The book was completed by the end of July 1947,[2] and on sale in the autumn. Most of the stories were written in 1947, but Dagerman composed four or five while holidaying on Kymmendö the previous summer.

In October 1946, Stig Dagerman embarked on a memorable journey to Germany; like all his generation in Sweden, he had been prevented by the Second World War from making the foreign excursions which are part of the highly desirable background experience for young writers and journalists. Dagerman's reputation as a journalist and up-and-coming author was such that the Stockholm daily newspaper *Expressen* had commissioned him to travel around war-ravaged Germany and report on what he found in a series of articles: he knew the language and had a number of contacts there through connections of his wife's family.

Dagerman's widely praised book *German Autumn* was published in May 1947. After the fantastic "landscape of terror" he had conjured up in *The Island of the Doomed*, he had now become acquainted with a reality of devastation and ruin which was in many ways more horrific than anything his imagination could produce. He depicted the nightmarish landscape with more insight than any ordinary reporter and displayed sympathetic understanding for the state of the bombed-out Germans living in damp cellars and crumbling ruins. He was sarcastic about the ex-Nazis who continued to prosper, and highly critical of the allied approach which seemed indifferent to justice. Most telling, however, was Dagerman's sympathy with the ordinary Germans. Their diet and living conditions had been called "indescribable": Dagerman disagreed and proceeded to describe them in squalid, disgusting but heartbreaking detail. Less perceptive reports tended to suggest that the Germans deserved no better, claiming that "Nazism is still alive in Germany." Certainly some people who ought to have been punished were escaping punishment; but to tar all Germans with the same brush was stupid, maintained Dagerman. Here were millions of ordinary people who had been subjected to years of skillful propaganda and who were now struggling in unheard-of misery. What they needed was sympathy and rehabilitation, understanding and assistance. Many reports about Nazism still flourishing were grossly misleading: "People asked the Germans living in squalid cellars if they were better off under Hitler and these Germans answered: 'yes.' If one asks a drowning man if he was better off when he was standing on the quay, the drowning man will answer: 'yes.' "[3]

An inevitable result of the success of *German Autumn* was that pressure was put on Dagerman to use his more realistic style in his creative works. When his short-story collection, *The Games of Night*, appeared, some reviewers claimed that it was possible to detect which of the stories had been written before the German journey, and which ones afterwards, on the basis that the latter were more realistic in style.[4] It is a fact that Dagerman did move toward a realistic style and *The Games of Night* contains a wide range of variations across the spectrum from realism to expressionism and surrealism—indeed, the author's mastery of such varied styles is one of the chief merits of the book. The specific claim that a watershed can be detected in *The Games of Night* is not accurate, however. An examination of some of the original typescripts together with a series of draft contents lists drawn up by Dagerman in the spring and summer of 1947[5] suggests the following order of composition (nine of the seventeen stories were published independently before the book appeared, and the bibliographical references are given in parentheses):

1945
   "The Hanging Tree" (*Vi*, December)

1946, late summer and autumn prior to the German journey

"The Man Condemned to Death" (*40-tal*, November)
"The Unmerciful" (*Idun*, November)
"My Son Smokes a Meerschaum Pipe" (*All världens
berättare*, December)
"Salted Meat and Cucumber" (*Julkvällen*, December)
"Our Nocturnal Resort" (*Vintergatan*, December)

1947, January-May (after the German journey)
"When It Gets Really Dark" (*Vi*, April)
"Bon Soir" (*Vårt hem*, October)
"The Man from Milesia"

    May-June
"Open the Door, Richard!" (*BLM*, July)
"The Games of Night"
"Where Is My Iceland Jumper?"

    June-July
"Sleet"
"The Stranger"
"Men of Character"
"The Man Who Wouldn't Cry"
"The Tower and the Well"

It will be clear from this list that realistic stories like "The Unmerciful" and "Salted Meat and Cucumber" were written before Dagerman
went to Germany, while expressionistic or surrealistic stories such as
"The Man from Milesia" and "The Man Who Wouldn't Cry" were
written after his return.

    One of the most interesting facts to emerge from the draft list of
contents which seems to have been compiled in the spring of 1947 is
that Dagerman evidently planned *The Games of Night* as a coherent
whole, rather than a random collection of short stories. The eighteen
stories are divided into four sections, each of which has a motto
characterizing the group of stories it contains:

I (40 pages): But what has old age done other than grow old?
    What has old age done to deserve greater reverence?

    *"Bon Soir"
    "The Stockholm Car"

*"Salted Meat and Cucumber"
"Where Is My Iceland Jumper?"

II (95 pages): Don't let your opportunity slip, for you will never
be condemned to death again.

*"The Red Wagons"
*"Our Nocturnal Resort"
*"The Man Condemned to Death"
*"My Son Smokes a Meerschaum Pipe"
"The Alley of Respect"

III (90 pages): Be grateful for the heat of a fever, for if there
were no such thing as fever we would be immured
in ice.

"Fever"
*"The Hanging Tree"
"The Railroad Crossing"
*"The Unmerciful"

IV (55 pages): The darkest darkness is best, for it will rarely
grow darker.

*"The Man from Milesia"
*"When It Gets Really Dark"
"Big Silent Houses"
"The Well"
"This Naked Day"

Comparison with the published version of *The Games of Night* shows
that eleven of these eighteen stories number among the final seventeen ("The Well" was retitled "The Tower and the Well"); two
("The Stockholm Car" and "The Red Wagons") were withdrawn and
published elsewhere, while the rest seem never to have been written.
An asterisk appears to indicate that the story had already been
completed, which shows that "Where Is My Iceland Jumper?" and
"The Tower and the Well" were evidently planned but not actually
written at this stage.

In the final version, the grouping is abandoned but traces of it remain. The title story is added to Group I, and these five stories come first. The original Group III comes next, and the following five stories seem to fit into it. "Fever" and "The Railroad Crossing" disappear, but three new ones are added: "Open the Door, Richard!", "The Stranger," and "Men of Character." Dagerman seems to have had trouble keeping Groups II and IV apart: they merge in the published book and follow after Group III. Besides "The Red Wagons," the three unwritten stories are withdrawn ("The Alley of Respect," "Big Silent Houses," and "This Naked Day") and one new one is added, "The Man Who Wouldn't Cry." Even though Dagerman dropped the idea of dividing his short-story collection into sections, the careful planning and the grouping by theme is significant and suggests that the work is a more coherent whole than is usual with books of its type. Knowledge of the planned divisions helps in the formation of a satisfactory interpretation of some of the stories, and it will be helpful to discuss them in turn.

Autobiographical Stories of Childhood

The motto for Group I seems to be a typically rueful comment by Dagerman on the fact that many of the problems he faced in childhood were still with him as an adult. Seen in a broader context, the implication is that growing old is nothing especially praiseworthy in itself: the vital point is what one learns as one grows older, and how one improves as a result. Autobiographical elements are prominent in all the first five stories of the book.[6]

The title story, "The Games of Night," is based on the author's life as a young boy in the cramped flat (one room and kitchen) he shared with his father, stepmother, and her son in a working-class district of Stockholm. Like Åke in the story he slept in the kitchen and was often kept awake at night by apprehension concerning the inevitable noisy argument between his parents that would ensue when his father returned home after an evening's heavy drinking.

"The Games of Night" is a characteristic Dagerman story about a small boy's experiences of *Angst* and his efforts to cope with it. He lacks the security and comfort which parental love can bestow—indeed, unobtrusive references in the story indicate that he hates his parents for the terror he feels when they argue, but he attempts to sublimate his hatred (and his fear) by indulging in fantasies in which he makes his father a well-meaning man whom he can help to return home early in a loving mood by all kinds of supernatural means. Åke uses his "night games" as a desperate means of keeping his *Angst* at bay; when reality returns with his drunken father's arrival he needs a weapon as a childish means of protecting himself from personified terror and—another authentic autobiographical touch—he takes into bed with him a carving knife from a kitchen drawer: "The *Angst* in the kitchen is so great that it couldn't be endured without a weapon" (12).[7] Only when the dreadful screaming and arguing have subsided and he hears the familiar and comforting sound of love-making from his parents' room can Åke relax and go to sleep. The story ends with Åke running away from his mother when, the following afternoon, he is sent to the bar in order to extract the housekeeping money from his father, but he fails. In his nighttime fantasies he could have succeeded—"the games of night are much better than those of the day" (13). As Åke's symbolic flight indicates, many a problem can be solved in one's imagination whereas harsh reality exposes the inadequacy of the individual in his efforts to cope with situations beyond his comprehension. Clearly, the strong autobiographical element in the story suggests that Dagerman's lack of a loving relationship with his parents played a significant part in his own obsession with *Angst*.

A similar implication can be discerned in "Sleet," in which a visit from young Arne Berg's great aunt from America highlights the difficulty members of the family have in showing affection for one another. Arne contrasts this coolness with the obvious sexually based affection between his uncle and one of the farm girls, and he feels very lonely and not a little afraid when he contemplates his lack of a father and the absence of security and tenderness between himself and the rest of the family. In later life Dagerman referred to his "twisted sex-life as a child,"[8] and while "Sleet," set on a farm based on that owned by the author's grandparents, can be read as a partial explanation of the young Dagerman's exaggerated interest in sex, the mixture of fascination and revulsion which characterized his attitude toward it is illustrated further in "Bon Soir." It is a study of puberty in which young Sune is obsessed by sex and arranges to meet a young waitress for his sexual initiation. At the last moment, however, she is arrested for spreading venereal disease; Sune vomits, gasping: "Is there no limit to how dirty all this can be?" (34).[9] Besides illustrating Dagerman's ambivalent attitude toward sex it can be interpreted as suggesting that an inability to cope with the complicated nature of sex is a fundamental cause of *Angst* in any individual.

"Salted Meat and Cucumber," which is based on Dagerman's experiences at the Älvkarleby village school in 1932, implies that the criteria which form the basis of most moral judgments are unreliable, and that one should perhaps refrain from making any: it may well be better to think instead in terms of compassion with those who need sympathy. A similar message emerges from "Where Is My Iceland Jumper?", one of Dagerman's finest stories. In brilliantly handled interior monologue style it gradually reveals the pitiful inadequacy of the Stockholm dustman, Knut, who originates from a farm in Uppland and is almost certainly a portrait of the author's father.[10] Already in disgrace for getting drunk at his mother's funeral, he returns to the farm for the burial of his father and, despite all his good intentions, disgraces himself once again. Being a citizen of Sweden's capital and claiming therefore to be superior to his country cousins, Knut swaggers and exaggerates his past exploits and tries to be the dashing playboy he obviously is not: as he grows more drunk, the squalid truth of his degradation emerges, and his family is horrified at the disgrace he has brought on them yet again. Despite his silliness and his posing, Knut has irresistible appeal and the reader cannot help but feel sorry for this helpless man who, in his awkward way, perhaps loved his father more than anyone. Knut's days of innocence and youth are now gone forever, and his father's death means the severing of the last links with that happy time, symbolized by the Iceland jumper he used to wear as a child. Isolated and spurned by all those around him, Knut has no ideas about how to survive the problems ahead and can merely ask pitifully: "Where is my Iceland Jumper?" His *Angst* has reached terrifying proportions.

The reader is torn between disgust and contempt for Knut's activities, and sympathy with his plight; yet the story is extremely funny, one of the most amusing things Dagerman ever wrote. In later life when he felt unable to write at all, Dagerman would often look back nostalgically at "Where Is My Iceland Jumper?", commenting that he had never been able to recapture the pleasure he obtained from writing it.[11]

The heading planned for the section of autobiographical stories was: "But what has old age done other than grow old? What has old age done to deserve greater reverence?" As far as the author is concerned, the answer seems to be: "Not very much!" He himself was still beset with *Angst* at the time of writing *The Games of Night* and he had not come to terms with the kind of problems which so disturbed the young boys at the center of the first four stories—Dagerman's two novels had been full of characters with similar problems, as was his private life. The author seems to be reminding his readers that *Angst* is not something which suddenly affects the middle-aged, or even young adults. It may be that people grow aware of different aspects of *Angst* later in life, but its seeds are sown much earlier: "The child is father of the man."

Love and Hate

The planned heading for Group III implies that passionate emotions are to be welcomed—they may lead to discomfort and unhappiness, but one should at least be pleased that one can feel emotions of any sort: this was one of the themes in *The Island of the Doomed* and recurs in several of Dagerman's later works. Two of the next five stories in *The Games of Night* were in the original Group III, "The Hanging Tree" and "The Unmerciful"; they suggest that the "fever" is usually associated with love, jealousy, and even hatred. A similar message is contained in "Men of Character," while emotional numbness is a key element in "Open the Door, Richard!" and "The Stranger."

The links in this group of stories are less strong than in Group I, and in view of the fact that Dagerman abandoned his classifications, it would be unwise to overstress their interrelationships. "The Hanging Tree" is the story which is most closely connected with the imagery of the group heading; it concerns the passionate jealousy of a man, Karl, who suspects his wife of being unfaithful with a handsome friend of the family. Karl's rage is such that he almost strangles his wife but restrains himself just in time (118) and goes skiing through a snowbound forest as a means of cooling his passions. He passes a tree where that very afternoon the body of a dead man had been found hanging and in a frenzied surrealistic vision he imagines that all the trees in which anyone has ever committed suicide are piled high up on his head (120); he almost breaks under the strain. The symbolic fantasy reflects the turmoil in his mind: as a consequence of his jealousy and humiliation Karl had been tempted to commit suicide himself, but the memory of the dead man's body being carried away brings him back to his senses. Having been on the brink of the ultimate excess, he withdraws and is able to see things in a more sensible perspective. If his emotions have driven him to such extremes, they must be exceptionally strong and hence the great love he must have for his wife is worth cherishing and fighting for. Karl has reached a new stage of awareness and is now able to cope with his *Angst*: 'The hard knot of *Angst* loosened, the terror was banished. Oh, now he knew how layers of ice should be melted, how even pain itself can produce warmth. Oh, to seek one's tree. To dare to seek one's tree. To find the hanging tree, the tree in the forest of *Angst* which alone radiates *Angst*. How friendly all forests seem after that!' (120). The tree imagery is rather forced but no doubt derives from the fact that the story is based on yet another autobiographical incident. [12]

In one sense, "Men of Character" is a reversal of "The Hanging Tree." Karl felt unloved, but comes to appreciate the strength of his own love; Alice starts by believing she is loved by two men but ends with realization of the fact that she is loved by neither, nor does she love them. At the conclusion of "Men of Character" Alice voices her desperation in a spine-chilling outburst of hysterical laughter which is more disturbing in context than a scream would have been (195). Her isolation is matched by that of the pathetic woman in "Open the Door, Richard!", [13] but characteristic of the latter is her inability to communicate any emotion at all—she merely shuts herself away in a room and refuses to come out in spite of the cajoling and bullying of her husband. She knows she is unwanted and responds by cutting herself off from all contact. "How lonely must I make myself before someone finally discovers my loneliness and rescues me? Beats down my door?" (132) she asks. Dagerman's implied answer is that she must first take positive action herself and stop running away from the problem.

"The Stranger" is a Kafkaesque tale—it was originally entitled "The Metamorphosis."[14] A husband becomes increasingly disturbed when he realizes that he has absolutely no recollection of his past; not only does he fail to remember the context of some old snapshots of himself and various companions, he cannot even recognize himself in his photographs. He is shattered by his loss of identity and his wife is horrified when she discovers that he is no longer the person she loved and married, but that he has in fact changed—literally—into a completely new person: she smashes his skull with a hammer (165).

The stories in this group suggest that love is an insecure, unreliable emotion and to place too much faith in its lasting qualities would be to invite an excess of *Angst* when things go wrong (as they surely will). If it is, or appears to be, lost, the sensible reaction would nevertheless be to accept the jealousy or hatred into which it turns as a sign that one is still emotionally alive in spite of everything: to succumb to unthinking numbness would be fatal.

Gloomy Prospects

It is in the remaining seven stories that Dagerman's original intention of dividing the book into related groups breaks down almost completely. Groups II and IV become intermingled and examination shows that the dividing line between them was indeed too vague for the author to persist in trying to enforce it. Most of the stories have distinctly surrealistic or absurd elements, and the general trend is for an individual to be faced with a disintegrating world which drives him to despair. Several of the stories—most of them from the original Group IV, which was to be headed "The darkest darkness is best, for it will rarely grow darker"—deal with people who are so incapable of coping with life that their minds become deranged: "When It Gets Really Dark" and "The Man from Milesia" come into this category. Others feature hypocrisy and deception, such as "The Man Who Wouldn't Cry" and "The Tower and the Well."

Some of the stories in this group are the weakest in the book and it is by no means clear just what the author is trying to express in them.

It is extremely difficult to distinguish dream from reality in "When It Gets Really Dark," which seems to describe the disintegration of a mind into madness. More satisfactory is the surrealistic dream sequence which forms "The Man from Milesia," in which characters appear and disappear mysteriously, and women move in unison as if choreographed and point accusing fingers at the central character (262), while beams of light shine out from two eyes in a painted portrait (268) and, when the picture is moved, the nail holes continue to radiate "naked horror" (271). It eventually transpires that the accusing fingers and staring eyes are manifestations of guilt in Ralph Singerton's deranged mind following his murder of a girl in his bed: the whole story has been a nightmare and lasted only a few hours instead of the several days and nights described in the dream. Both these stories show how *Angst* and guilt can easily drive a man insane, and the same fate seems to befall the father in "My Son Smokes a Meerschaum Pipe" as he becomes obsessed by his son's smoking habits and mysteriously blames them for his own inability to communicate with people.

"The Man Who Wouldn't Cry" is an amusing comment on hypocrisy and the absurd nature of social conventions; it reminds the reader of stories by Kafka in which an absurd premise is taken for granted, after which they proceed in realistic fashion to a logical conclusion. A man is ostracized, persecuted, and threatened with dismissal from his work because he is unable and unwilling to weep when the whole country is ordered to mourn the death of a famous actress. He refuses to be hypocritical, but the guide in charge of an old nunnery in "The Tower and the Well" sets out to dissemble and deceive while pretending to be the only honorable and authoritative person in the story. He is eventually exposed by two old ladies who demonstrate the falsity of almost all his statements about the history of the building. Feeling suddenly very tired and old, and locked in his tower by the two old ladies, the guide concludes that: "Weariness is very good, weariness is always good and particularly good when one practises the difficult art of being one's own prisoner. Great calm and a certain capacity for avoiding excitement are also very good, for in order to endure himself a man must have pretty good nerves" (232). These two stories illustrate two sides of Dagerman's own character, his impatience with the hypocrisy of conventional society, and his own infinite capacity for deception and hypocrisy. He was well aware of the latter aspect, which was to be at the center of his next novel, and the gloomy context of the group in which these stories occur indicates his impatience with his own inadequacies.

Hope for the Condemned?

The two remaining stories in *The Games of Night*, "The Man Condemned to Death" and "Our Nocturnal Resort," were originally destined for Group II: it seems likely that Dagerman moved them to the end of his collection of stories since, whereas most of the others deal with individuals who undergo *Angst* associated with some specific aspect of their existence, these put the *Angst* in a broader context. This would be in accordance with his evident desire to link his stories in a meaningful way rather than at random.

When the book was published in the fall of 1947, the content of "The Man Condemned to Death" was already well known as a result of the enormous success accorded to the dramatized version which had been first performed in Stockholm the previous spring and widely publicized. [15] A man condemned to death for murdering his wife is reprieved when the executioner is indisposed and, during the resultant delay, someone else confesses to being the real murderer. A group of curious journalists take him off for a magnificent meal and provide him with a beautiful girl; instead of making love to her he kills her and is returned to prison—and this time he is definitely guilty. Although one can interpret the story in several ways, most people saw it as a symbolic depiction of the state of the world after the Second World War. Generations of soldiers, even nations, had been "condemned to death" during the war, but after 1945 they seemed unable to adjust to the "reprieve" and, in a state of *Angst* caused by the threat of nuclear war and the intensifying Cold War, appeared set to bring upon themselves the death they had previously escaped. "One cannot be condemned to death in the morning and condemned to life in the evening," claims the condemned man (294). Whether Dagerman was depicting the mood of what Auden called "The Age of Anxiety" [16] or, on an even larger scale, was referring to Original Sin, it is tempting to believe that he was trying to suggest that the individual cases of *Angst* in the first fifteen stories were part of a universal pattern.

"Our Nocturnal Resort" is placed last of all in the collection and its final position is justified on two main grounds. The nocturnal games and visions at the end of the story complete a circle by returning to the theme of "The Games of Night" with which the collection opened. Moreover, the story ends on a positive note, suggesting that the pessimistic picture drawn in "The Man Condemned to Death" and, indeed, in the earlier part of "Our Nocturnal Resort" need not necessarily imply that the future is hopeless. A popular interpretation of the story is that it depicts the situation of the artist in society,[17] a person who searches for beauty and meaning in a depressing world and whose task it is to make his fellow men aware of his discoveries. There is much to be said for this reading. Although it is not the only possibility, however, the most satisfying interpretation is that "Our Nocturnal Resort" is a symbolic depiction of life from a social and political point of view. Such a reading explains a lot of details that would otherwise be difficult to understand, and is in line with the trend of Dagerman's previous works.

The seaside resort represents society, which seems at first glance to be well organized and flourishing. Just as the apparently clean, beautiful, and cheerful resort is flanked by a pebbly cove full of rubbish where the main sewer flows out into the sea (296, 308), society has many aspects which are squalid and unjust. A man called Sisyphus has the self-appointed task of pointing out the imperfections of the resort from the top of a disused lighthouse, and tells anyone who cares to listen that what might at first seem comparable with a beautiful, smiling lady is in fact more like a brashly made-up whore who can only disguise superficially her basic ugliness and degenerate state (300). Sisyphus represents writers; in his article "The Writer and His Conscience," published two years previously,[18] Dagerman had maintained that one of the chief functions of a writer is to point out the imperfections of society. The unusual name must be a reference to Camus's essay "The Myth of Sisyphus," a Swedish translation of which had appeared in *40-tal* at about the time when "Our Nocturnal Resort" was being written;[19] it implies that his task is endless and unrewarding besides relating the ideas behind the story to theories of the absurd and French existentialism—ideas concerning awareness and pessimism also central to the mood of 1940s literature in Sweden and discussed in connection with *The Island of the Doomed*.

Not all the holidaymakers are grateful for having the seamy side of the resort pointed out to them, just as many citizens prefer to be coddled by a paternal state and to ignore the disadvantages. An ironic comment on the overzealous nature of the "harmonious" state is the permanent presence of a lifeboat patrolling the bay: should an adventurous and independent bather venture out beyond the permitted area, he is immediately picked up and returned, protesting, to the beach (298). There is an exaggerated and faintly ridiculous air to the whole, which is given a grotesque touch by the fat and flabby ladies splashing away astride inflatable rubber swans in pastel colours: "How I love swans!" they cry, suggesting a sarcastic comparison with the legend of Leda and the swan (308). Everything in the resort seems to be a distorted reflection of the ideal it is claimed to be.

Should there be any doubt that criticism of the centrally organized welfare state is coming from the political left rather than the right, Dagerman inserts a symbolic depiction of workers being exploited by capitalists. Young boys dive from a cliff top after coins thrown into the water by rich guests at a superior holiday hotel (302 ff.). Sometimes there are nasty accidents, but these are regarded as being unfortunate disturbances in the smooth running of things, almost deliberate attempts by the boys to affront their "employers" rather than tragedies for the divers.

"Is there no forgivness for us?" comes the question in the concluding section of the story (309). Man seems to have organized his society extremely badly, and Sisyphus's attempts to draw attention to the failings have not had much success: as emerged from similar discussions in earlier works, an individual can only have a symbolic effect on the course of events, according to Dagerman. But Sisyphus and his special friends have the night, when they can row out to a rock in the bay and survey the resort from a distance when, in spite of all the mistakes and drawbacks, it seems a marvelous place to be (310 ff.). Bearing in mind the Existentialist connotations of Sisyphus, this must mean a rejection of suicide as a way of escape. The implications

seem to be that at night one can contemplate the resort objectively
without being distracted by the petty imperfections and insanities of
society, and can dream about its ideal (and idealistic) possibilities—
just as one can have highly desirable political and social ideals which
may be very difficult to bring about in practice. In Dagerman's view
the ideal social system would be based on anarcho-syndicalism, and he
acknowledged that he was "the politician of the impossible."[20]

The stories in *The Games of Night* are saturated in *Angst*. Repeatedly
individuals suffer because they try to avoid recognizing its existence
and retreat into comfortable illusions. Unlike the nocturnal fantasies
of Åke in the title story, the night games played by Sisyphus and his
friends in "Our Nocturnal Resort" are not aspects of escapism: "They
live with open eyes, and they don't turn a blind eye to either the dirt
or the beauty" (312). Having achieved a state of awareness based on
reality and not illusion, they can accommodate their *Angst*.

Stylistic Games

A criticism frequently leveled at Dagerman is that there is little
variation in the themes he writes about: one becomes tired of hearing
so much about *Angst*. This is an objection which could be raised in
connection with *The Games of Night*. The impression of monotony is
avoided, however, thanks to the remarkable stylistic virtuosity displayed by the author, who demonstrates his mastery over an astonishing variety of narrative styles and techniques.

The autobiographical stories of childhood are, perhaps naturally
enough, the most realistic of the groups. Dagerman is rarely completely realistic, however. The reader is constantly aware of concealed
threats which tend to disturb the comfortable tenor of the story—in
keeping with the author's conviction that *Angst* is rarely far below the
surface of anyone's consciousness. In the title story, subtle touches of
style introduce a dimension which transcends realism, quite apart
from the fantastic nature of Åke's dreams. When the drunken father
returns home, for instance, there are aspects of surrealism in the
description: "And then the thing the silence has been waiting for
happens. The mother twists violently on the bed and a scream pours
out of her mouth like blood" (12). The passage is concise but

concentrated, and contains associations with several motifs in the story. The personification of silence relates to Åke's need for a knife to defend himself from the *Angst* in the kitchen, and the apartment seems full of intangibles which have been made solid and ominously real by personification. The violent movement and scream of the · mother represent the culmination of all the waiting for this moment and can be seen as an attack on the silence which conceals her *Angst*, hence a parallel with Åke's fanciful knife attack on his *Angst*. It thus seems natural that the scream is described in terms of blood welling forth.

There are several touches of surrealism in "Men of Character," such as the amusing description of Alice as she lies to her husband: ". . . she climbs out of herself and stands by her side, adjusting every movement before she makes it so that she manages to do nothing but credible things" (185). Dagerman interpolates the image to distinguish between conscious and subconscious thought, and frequently refers to the way in which subconscious awareness is repressed so as to avoid a confrontation with one's *Angst*. The most extreme example of this is the nightmarish "The Man from Milesia"—". . . I fell and fell and fell through a hubbub of cruel dream worlds," says the main character (277).

Some aspects of the man's dream worlds are not supernatural, however, but reminiscent of the tough world of American B-movies, populated by elusive salesmen, seedy Negroes, and gangsters' molls. There is a similar atmosphere in "When It Gets Really Dark," reminding the reader that Dagerman was a compulsive moviegoer; in later years he was to become actively involved in writing film scripts. He uses film techniques as a stylistic device in "The Man Who Wouldn't Cry," the story being punctuated by miniature synopses or scenes which read like extracts from movie scripts from the 1940s. A good example is when the rows of filing cabinets in an office remind the hero of a morgue: "The policeman pulls out a drawer. . . . The fiancée shakes her head. The policeman shrugs. Wrong drawer. Only at the fifth attempt does the fiancée step aside to let the viewer see. There is a dead man in the drawer. White, grinning face. Gunshot wounds in the forehead. The fiancée nods her confirmation. The policeman shrugs apologetically. Change of scene" (197). The story is an absurd one, and obtrusive stylistic devices such as this alienate the reader, encouraging him to think more about the "meaning" of the story.

The autobiographical stories of childhood at the beginning of the collection illustrate interesting variations in narrative perspective in spite of obvious similarities. In "Sleet" the story is told in the first-person form in the present tense by a nine-year-old boy: as a result, the reader is left to draw conclusions about the boy's family and the events of the story since the narrator sees everything through juvenile eyes and does not completely understand all that happens. In "Salted Meat and Cucumber," although the central character is also a nine-year-old boy and the story is in the I-form, the narration is in the past tense and the narrator is clearly an older man looking back on his childhood. He can thus comment on events with the insight of an adult.

A further variation on the first-person narrative is "Open the Door, Richard!" which is an exercise in stream-of-consciousness techniques (and also notable because it is the only story in the collection narrated wholly by a woman). It is a skillfully narrated story which stands comparison with most of its type; but it pales into insignificance beside "Where Is My Iceland Jumper?", a prolonged and cleverly sustained inner monologue which is generally agreed to be one of Dagerman's most brilliant pieces of writing. The woman in the former story is confused and psychologically disturbed, yet she seems to think quite clearly and logically and expresses herself in rather sophisticated images which can only come from a narrator striving to do her thinking for her in language he imposes onto her speech. Knut in "Where Is My Iceland Jumper?", on the other hand, talks and thinks in a mixture of Stockholm slang and Uppland dialect, liberally sprinkled with exclamations and colorful curses. His train of thought is confused and the narrative staggers along beneath a burden of asides, accusations, protests, excuses, and self-deceptions. When Knut describes his moment of humiliation on returning home from Lapland to find his wife with a lover, the description springs from *his* mouth, not that of a knowing narrator; he lies, exaggerates, curses, and portrays the scene in strikingly vivid fashion:

So, yours truly comes straight back from this Lapp shit-heap, I says. . . . By God, but she'll be glad to see me, I thinks to miself as I unlock t'door. Damn me, there sits t'little bugger necking with this bloke in t'kitchen. Half naked 'e is, so it's not 'ard to guess what they've been up to, I says. Now I's allus been nice to t'old lady, you know that, Baker, you know me: so I just lifts 'er out of t'road. But as for t'fancy-man, well, I drags 'im up off t'sofa. Get dressed, you're in for a punch-up, I yells at 'im, an' I tecks off mi BD. (92)

The truth of the matter is revealed bit by bit, and the reader eventually discovers that in fact Knut was spurned by his wife, beaten up by her lover, and thrown out unceremoniously. Knut is a preposterous character, but his weaknesses are so transparent and he is so vividly and entertainingly alive that the reader cannot help but be drawn to him—thanks largely to the tour de force of stream-of-consciousness technique achieved by Dagerman in this story.

An effective shift in the point of view of the narrator comes in "The Stranger." In the early part of the story the narrator views events through the man's eyes; but the point is that the man loses his identity. He is disturbed by his inability to remember the past and is afraid to look into a mirror: ". . . not even being able to recognize oneself, that's so disastrous that every mirror becomes a traitor. Who knows in advance what face it's going to reflect?" (158). At this point in the story the man actually becomes a different person, and appropriately enough the point of view is that of his wife for the rest of the narration.

Similar but more subtle is the shift in "The Tower and the Well," which begins by being narrated from the guide's point of view; the reader is encouraged to support his efforts to outwit the aggressive and badly behaved young people who vandalize his beloved nunnery. By the end of the story the guide has been exposed as a fraud, and the point of view changes: instead of seeing events through the eyes of the guide the reader finds that he is observing the old man objectively with the narrator. The linguistic device of referring to the visitors to the nunnery as 'The General Public," with capital letters, involved a judgment of them and suggested that they should be dismissed as unworthy intruders; when the point of view changes at the end, it is the guide who must be judged unworthy—which is not necessarily the same as saying that he loses the reader's sympathy,.

A similar linguistic device is employed in "Men of Character." The point of view changes frequently, but the presence of an objective third-person narrator making his own subjective comments on the story is announced by the sarcastic use of phrases given initial capital letters. Sometimes the narrator gives the point of view of Alice, sometimes the forester, sometimes the schoolmaster, sometimes a neutral observer: but the narrator's own judgments are made clear when first the forester and later the schoolmaster claim: "I have Character." The fraudulent nature of the forester is exposed by his search for "The Irresistible Reply," his welcoming of "The Scene, the Big Scene," and his belief that "Justice" is on his side. Used thus, capitalization is the author's equivalent of an actor's exploitation of tones of voice.

In his review of *The Games of Night*, Staffan Björck commented that Dagerman's astonishing mastery over such a range of styles made the book seem more like an anthology by several hands—strangely enough, he almost wished it were, for so much talent in a single writer was frightening.[21] Be that as it may, *The Games of Night* was widely praised. Seen in perspective from the 1980s, the more realistic stories seem to have lasted better than the expressionistic ones, but the virtuosity of the author is still one of the most impressive features of the collection. Dagerman was doubtless right to abandon the proposed division into groups, which would have imposed too rigid restrictions; however, knowledge of his original intentions gives insight into the coherent form of *The Games of Night* as a whole and makes the achievement all the more impressive.

Chapter Five
Soiled Purity: *A Burnt Child*
Background

Shortly after *The Games of Night* was published, Stig Dagerman and his wife set off on a journey to France via Holland and Germany. Ivar Harrie, then cultural editor of *Expressen*, had been pleased with the success of Dagerman's German articles (later published as *German Autumn*) and hoped to see it repeated with a series of twenty-seven articles on France during the coming nine months. Dagerman was quite well advanced with his play *The Go-Getter* and finished it by mid-December. He followed it immediately with another play, *The Shadow of Mart*, which appears to have been completed or almost completed in January 1948.[1] Despite this apparent flurry of productivity, Dagerman's letters to his friend and publisher Dr. Ragnar Svanström reveal that he was having great difficulty in settling down in Paris, and he commented that ". . . as long as my environment doesn't sit down and be quiet in the way that I'm used to I can only write drama, and more particularly drama with short speeches."[2]

France was in a state of economic and political chaos. Winter was setting in, fuel was scarce, food short, and the home comforts that Swedes had been used to despite the war were sadly lacking. Dr. Svanström arranged for food parcels to be sent to the Dagermans, who were in financial difficulties—especially after the devaluation of the franc at the end of January. Dagerman wrote that he found the French people "sour, impolite and egotistical," and the best he could do to counter the chill of winter, made worse by strikes and shortages, was to go to the post office and read the Tunisian section of the telephone directory![3]

Understandably, Dagerman had trouble in writing the articles for *Expressen*. His state of mind was not improved by the disputes in the Swedish Writers' Association, which were intensified after the Soviet annexation of Czechoslovakia in February 1947. Most of his friends among the writers of his generation supported what was called the crypto-Communist line, while he followed his fellow Anarcho-Syndicalists in condemning the Soviet Union, finding himself aligned somewhat surprisingly with right-wing opinion in Sweden. Whatever the rights and wrongs of the affair, Dagerman was upset by it.[4]

Only five of the articles on France were written, and the project had to be abandoned.[5] Stig Dagerman's pride suffered a severe jolt, and he also suffered financially since he had to repay the expenses advanced by the newspaper to help cover the costs of the stay in France. The money was paid by Norstedts and added to the debt Dagerman had already incurred when his publishers paid most of the purchase price of his new house the previous year; the slide into debt on a serious scale had begun. A new book—preferably a bestseller—was needed to restore Dagerman's confidence and help to ease his debts. The public was hoping for a novel in the new realistic style they had discerned and appreciated in *German Autumn* and parts of *The Games of Night*, and Norstedts naturally hoped their protégé could produce one. Dagerman embarked on two projects: a novel based on his play *The Go-Getter* and another based on his experiences in France, to be called *Desert Memories*.[6] Neither came to anything, and the future looked bleak.

Stig Dagerman had been toying with another idea for a novel, however, and had discussed it with Ragnar Svanström while he was in Sweden for the opening of his play *The Go-Getter* in Malmö in May. The Dagermans spent July and August in a primitive cottage on an islandlike peninsula in Brittany, and during this time Stig turned his idea into the novel which was to be his most popular work, *A Burnt Child*.

Part of the novel takes place on an island which the author was able to base on his environment in Brittany; most of it is enacted in a small apartment on Södermalm, the working-class area of Stockholm. Bengt's home in the novel is a realistic reproduction of the apartment where Stig Dagerman lived with his father and stepmother in the 1930s and early 1940s, and the funeral described in the opening chapter is based on that of the author's stepmother. The two aunts in the novel are based on Dagerman's aunts, and a number of incidents are projections of his own experiences. He too attended classes at the university in Stockholm when the same age as Bengt in the autumn of 1942 and depended on his father for financial assistance, and he too completed military service thereafter. The suicide attempt at the end of *A Burnt Child* is based on a similar attempt by the author himself, and Bengt's reactions, his euphoria after the deed, are an accurate reflection of Dagerman's own feelings after he had cut his wrists.[7] One could go on, but it is clear that *A Burnt Child* has a considerable autobiographical element and that the main character, Bengt, is in many ways a projection of the author. The problems faced by Bengt reflect those with which Stig Dagerman himself had been struggling: deception and self-deception—facing facts and being honest about one's own nature; also the uncomfortable nature of love, the thin dividing lines between love and hate and love and violence, the gap between rational actions and uncontrollable passions, and the guilt associated with it all. Bengt longs for purity, but is not quite sure what the concept involves. Eventually, he has to settle for acceptance of what cannot be controlled.

Plot

Bengt's mother has just died, and the opening chapter depicts the circumstances surrounding the funeral and the ensuing meal at a nearby restaurant. Bengt seems to be very upset by his mother's death and disturbed by the hypocrisy of most mourners. He is particularly worried about the evident dissimulation of his father's grief and bemused when Knut (the father) gives him a handkerchief to dry his tears which smells strongly of perfume. At the reception, Bengt receives a telephone call intended for Knut, and realizes that Gun, the woman making the call, is his father's lover. Bengt's reaction seems to be shock, increased distrust of his father, exaggerated love for his dead mother, and hatred of Gun. He becomes obsessed by Gun, neglecting his fiancée, Berit, and trailing his father until he tracks Gun down to her work as a cashier at a cinema. When Knut brings Gun home, Bengt makes an exaggerated point of reminding all present of his dead mother and being excessively unfriendly toward his father's lover. While protesting disgust, Bengt goes out of his way to find Knut and

Gun in compromising circumstances; he neglects his studies, insults his fiancée, and argues with his father, telling himself that he is the only one who really loved his mother and honors her memory.

Gradually, Bengt is forced to admit that the real reason for his strange behavior is that in fact he is in love with Gun himself. He has been caught in a web of deception and has to try to accept that he has deceived himself most of all. When Gun and Knut, Bengt and Berit spend a few days together at a summer cottage on an island owned by Gun, Bengt is torn by passion and frustration and vents his spleen on everyone, including himself. He still maintains that he hates Gun, although it is by now obvious to even the most casual of readers that he is motivated by jealousy when his father and Gun are together. Shortly after their return to Stockholm, Gun calls on Knut one evening and finds only Bengt at home. She admits later that she knew his father would be out. Bengt and Gun make love.

Bengt is called up for military service but manages to arrange some days alone on the island with Gun, deceiving everyone else into believing he is away on a course. The early part of the holiday is idyllic, but Bengt is still not able to reconcile his guilt at what he tells himself is his betrayal of his mother's memory and the fact that he ought to hate Gun. He is insanely jealous of Gun's lovers—not only Knut, but also earlier lovers such as Erik, who gave Gun both the island and her black dog. Bengt beats the dog ruthlessly with a stone and then drowns it in a most unpleasant scene where he vents all his pent-up frustrations and guilt on the animal.

Knut and Gun marry just a fortnight short of the anniversary of Bengt's mother's death. Bengt moves in with Berit, but they are far from happy even though Bengt still protests that in fact he hates Gun. They all go to the island for the anniversary of the funeral: it is very cold, the snow lies deep and they travel out to the island on kick-sledges over the ice. The conflict inside Bengt reaches a new peak and he cuts one of his wrists in a suicide attempt. It is not successful, but he seems to reach a new state of awareness as a result of the feeling of serenity and calm he experienced when on the brink of death.

Afterwards, he and Gun make love with new intensity. Despite the fact that she is now his legal mother, Bengt has come to terms with his guilt in that he can accept the exaggerated nature of his defense of his mother's memory, and ignore Gun's relationship with anyone else. They cannot deny the validity of their passion irrespective of any moral considerations or guilt feelings about other relationships, and Bengt can accept the situation with open eyes.

Bengt's Deception

Of all Dagerman's novels, *A Burnt Child* is the most obviously controlled and tightly constructed. It develops in linear fashion over a period of a year and is not split into two distinct halves like his previous novels. The preponderance of short sentences is immediately noticeable and the style is measured, lacking in the mass of imagery which had characterized its predecessors and in what Dagerman's detractors sometimes called his hysteria. Alternate chapters are narrated by a third-person narrator, usually from Bengt's point of view, and these are interspersed with letters, usually written by Bengt to himself. It is frequently obvious to the reader that in the conventional narrative certain facts are being suppressed—as when Bengt finds almost all his walks taking him past the cinema where Gun works, for instance. The reader then expects the whole truth to be revealed in the letters which he takes to be Bengt's soul-searching: he soon realizes that this is not the case, however. He is thus presented with two versions of an event or situation, both inadequate, and must deduce the truth for himself. Only then can he appreciate the extent of Bengt's self-deception, which is one of the main points of the novel.

Bengt is justifiably horrified by the extent of the hypocrisy he notices in the opening scenes—the number of funeral cars is far in excess of what is needed, people seem to be more interested in the outward show of the funeral and reception than its actual significance, the guests are not particularly fond of the dead Alma and can barely refrain from making critical comments; worst of all, Bengt notices that his father's sorrow is simulated. The perfumed handkerchief borrowed from Knut and the mysterious telephone call from Gun make it clear to Bengt that his father has a lover, and this of course casts further doubt on the genuineness of Knut's mourning. The reader naturally sympathizes with Bengt and feels that he is the only sincere person present.

It is much later in the novel that Bengt admits that his feelings for his mother are not as pure and loving as he pretends in the opening scene. After acknowledging to himself that his mother's ugliness and fear of water were embarrassing (163) and her constant complaining annoying (163), Bengt eventually reveals in a letter to Knut that he found his mother "quite unbearable" (239). Despite appearances, therefore, Bengt's hypocrisy was as great as anyone's in the opening chapter, and his claim to be "pure" in comparison with his father was a false one. This realization puts Bengt's actions and statements into a new light. Bengt is fascinated by the perfume on the handkerchief lent him by his father and later has dreams concerning Gun; he wakes up chewing the handkerchief. In view of events and claims, and the assumption then that Bengt's sorrow is genuine, the reader concludes that Bengt was dreaming about his father's relationship with his lover, and his own anger at the situation. Later, one wonders if this is entirely true. In his letter to himself about the same incident, Bengt omits all reference to the erotic elements of the dream and the fact that he woke up chewing the handkerchief. Perhaps Bengt's erotic instincts were stirred from the very start and he uses his exaggerated claims to be seeking purity and respect for his mother's memory as a form of defense against the erotic lure of Gun and an illicit relationship. It is after all at the end of the first chapter, as the mourners are leaving the funeral reception, that Bengt burns his hand on the candle that had been burning at the table in the place laid for the dead woman. The heat of the candle flame, later developed into the flames from a volcano, becomes a symbol in the book, denoting passion. The motto printed on the title-page of the novel reads: "It is not true that a burnt child fears fire. It is attracted to fire like a moth to a candle flame. It knows that when it comes too close, it will burn itself once more. Even so, it comes too close."

It is difficult to elicit the exact point at which Bengt falls in love with Gun, although it is clearly much earlier than he is willing to admit. In Chapter 11, "Meeting at Dusk,"[8] when the pair make love for the first time, Bengt admits that he has loved Gun since before their joint midsummer celebrations on the island; he refers to his evening walks which always seemed to lead him past the cinema where Gun works, also to his dreams, and he admits that when he kissed Berit, his fiancée, he would close his eyes and imagine he was kissing Gun (197). This is a startling admission, for if one delves into the details of the novel and sorts out the time sequence, the inevitable conclusion is that Bengt must have been in love with Gun, or at the very least fascinated by her and ready to fall in love with her, even before he had met her. Alma's funeral took place in January. Bengt's "evening walks" begin at the end of March, in Chapter 5 (71); but it is over a month earlier, toward the end of Chapter 3 (58), that he first goes out of his way to walk past the cinema where Gun works and sees the black dog his father soon afterwards brings home. His ill treatment of Berit is referred to as early as Chapter 2, "Letter in February" (38).

The apparently outrageous suggestion, therefore, that at his mother's funeral, Bengt is erotically stimulated by the discovery that his father is having a passionate affair with another woman is by no means far-fetched.

Should the reader hesitate to doubt Bengt's protestations of honor and righteousness, his maneuverings and deceptions in connection with his university studies should be proof enough. Bengt does not hesitate to lie about his attendance and his failure to take examinations, nor does he scruple to accept money from his father for expenses that have not been incurred, or to forge entries in his study-book in order to cover up his deceptions. Bengt's account of these incidents in the letters to himself is transparently hypocritical, and his sophistical reasoning in an attempt to justify his deeds can satisfy no one. Bengt is obviously an outrageous liar, but the most disturbing aspect of his lies is the craving to accept his hypocritical explanations as satisfactory. He is determined not to recognize the truth about himself despite the fact that the explanations he accepts are so far out of step with his actions.

The Dog

Before Bengt actually meets Gun, he comes across her dog. The dog figures prominently throughout the novel and clearly has symbolic significance concerning the relationship between Gun and Bengt, and Gun and Knut. When Bengt tries to commit suicide, there are various references to the dog he has killed, and the suicide note he leaves describes the world and his reasons for wanting to die in terms of dogs.

The dog first appears in Chapter 3, when Bengt sees it in the vestibule of the cinema where Gun works (58). Shortly afterwards Knut brings it home, claiming to have bought it cheaply. That night Bengt has a dream involving the dog; he himself is referred to as Gun and is wearing a red dress bought by Knut—supposedly for Alma but in fact for Gun—and the big black dog comes toward him and embraces him (60 ff.). The extent to which Bengt is already jealous of his father's physical contact with Gun is debatable, but the dog is clearly associated with Gun and Knut in a sexual context.

In Chapter 7, "Tea for Four or Five," Knut brings Gun home for the first time. Later in the evening Bengt surprises his father and Gun making love on the ottoman at home (134); Bengt pretends to find the incident unexpected and shocking despite the fact that he has gone to elaborate lengths to ensure that he would catch them in just those circumstances. Immediately, Bengt takes the dog down to the courtyard and beats it unmercifully with the dogleash. The dog struggles, but cannot escape. The description of the beating is extraordinary: "Every blow hurts him, for it is himself he is beating and he has to clamp his mouth closed so as not to scream with pain. So as not to scream in triumph as well, for it is also her he's beating. He has suddenly realized it is her dog" (136). The final sentence is misleading, for Bengt has clearly known for a long time that the dog belongs to Gun: it seems to be another example of his determination to suppress his awareness of certain facts. When Bengt claims to be beating Gun, it is more than simply beating her vicariously in the form of one of her possessions; the dream in the third chapter showed that the dog was associated with Gun's sexual relationship with Knut. Since Bengt has just seen Gun and Knut making love, he is beating her as a form of punishment, but, as Bengt has an erotic interest in his father's mistress, and has intentionally sought out the sight he claims is so disturbing, any vicarious beating of Gun must be a masochistic attack on himself. The dog seems to be associated with Gun's eroticism, and it is precisely this which attracts Bengt, although he refuses to acknowledge the fact.

When Bengt and Gun are together on the island, Bengt becomes afraid of the dog because it has seen forbidden sights. It has been a witness to their illicit lovemaking (214). But there is more to it than that. Bengt is still trying to convince himself, in the face of all evidence, that he is a pure soul who is better than those around him since he alone has not betrayed the memory of his mother. He has done so, in fact, of course, and his lovemaking with Gun is proof. He does not, however, want to admit consciously what he knows is really the truth, and hence he has considerable guilt feelings about his love for Gun. The dog represents Gun's sexuality, and so he can focus his need for revenge on the dog. Moreover, Bengt has a further excuse for attacking it when he establishes that it was given her by one of her former lovers—especially in view of the fact that his name was Erik, the same name as the man Bengt had recently realized was his mother's lover several years previously. The dog thus has three levels of symbolic meaning: Bengt sees it as a symbol of Gun's guilty past which must be wiped out before he can love her properly himself; the reader also sees the dog as a symbol of Gun's erotic appeal which affects Bengt so deeply and yet which he fights to avoid admitting; in addition Bengt is attacking something which threatens to arouse from his subconscious the as yet unacknowledged fact that Gun is a mother-substitute in the Freudian sense.

Bengt kills the dog (234); but the dog was only a representative, and his action does not begin to reach the real root of the matter.

Following Bengt and Gun's fortnight on the island, their affair appears to be over and, although it is not explicitly stated one concludes that they do not meet thereafter except formally. Not, that is, until after the wedding between Gun and Knut, and the visit of all four main characters to the island in January, exactly one year after Alma's death (243 ff.). Because of the occasion, Bengt's urge to claim that he is steadfast with regard to his mother's memory is particularly strong: however, the presence of Gun and the sight of her fondling and being fondled by Knut makes Bengt's erotic attraction to her unbearable. The killing of the dog was supposed to have signified the end of this, but of course it did not. Bengt's passions are so strong that they are at last overcoming his hypocritical claim to love his mother's memory above all else: his guilt and *Angst* are building up inside him and an explosion seems imminent. He seems to have only one defense left open to him, the ultimate one of suicide. Since it is the fact of his love for Gun which is driving him to this extreme, even though he will not admit it, it seems eminently appropriate that he should choose to hang himself, using the dogleash which still remains in the cottage. He fails when the branch he has chosen breaks (255).

Shortly before his first suicide attempt, Bengt watches his father and his stepmother fondling each other, and contemptuously compares them with dogs (254). Their lovemaking is purely animal passion, and he feels superior since he claims that his own driving force is on a much higher plane, namely his memory of his mother and the ideal of purity and moral rectitude he associates with it. When, after the failed attempt to hang himself, Berit tells Bengt he looks like a dog, that is the last straw (258). Bengt is now compelled to recognize the fact that his moral stance is a fake and that he is driven by animal passions himself. He cuts his wrist with his father's cut-throat razor (259). Even though he is rescued, his suicide attempt is not a failure from Bengt's point of view. He is driven to it because he has been forced to accept the truth about himself and his passions. He has become aware in the existential sense. As a result, he can make love to Gun afterwards without the inhibitions and self-deceptions he had to cope with previously. He has realized that normal considerations and conventions are unimportant compared with the acceptance of the truth about oneself, one's emotions, and one's existence.

Earlier in the same chapter, Bengt had written his suicide note which forms the penultimate chapter. In view of subsequent events and realizations, Bengt is able to instruct Berit to tear it to pieces—its attitude and underlying philosophy are now recognized as false. Nevertheless, it is presented to the reader and is comprehensible in view of the significance which is acquired by the dog in the course of the novel.

In his letter Bengt imagines the world populated entirely by dogs—suggesting that people are ruled by their passions in everything they do. Most people are little dogs, which implies that their passions, their thoughts, their very existences are routine and ordinary. Bengt claims, however, that he is a large dog, because he has been aware of the ideal of purity beyond the petty world of passions. He is a large dog because he had the courage to attempt to achieve that purity by honoring the memory of his mother and renouncing the others for their pettiness and betrayal, also because he deceived the others into thinking he was genuine about it; but he is a small dog because he also deceived himself into believing the same thing. Bengt has recognized the squalor of a world ruled by petty passions and conventions, even if he was unable to live in any other way himself. "The only advantage of being a large dog in the land of little dogs is that in that case one isn't ashamed of dying. But even a large dog cannot avoid being ashamed of living, least of all a large dog. That's why I'm doing what I'm doing" (268). The dilemma seems typical of Dagerman's usual ambivalent attitude toward sex—a mixture of fascination and disgust.

Having actually cut his wrists, Bengt has committed himself completely to the view of life expressed in the letter. Having then been restored to life, having paid the price, as it were, he is able to accept the squalid nature of life ruled by passion for what it is and to transcend it. In his new state of awareness, Bengt realizes that the conventional moralities which persuade us to censure the passionate realities of life and the "weakness" of character which prevent us from overcoming them are meaningless. "In order to begin living, one must have begun dying," he concludes; and he feels a deep-seated sense of peace (269).

Reason and Passion

In his letters from France, Dagerman frequently compared the country to a desert. On one occasion he gave his implied isolation and desolation a biblical twist, referring to himself as "The voice of one crying in the Paris wilderness";[9] when his financial problems were particularly acute and Norstedts sent him an extra check to help out, his telegram acknowledging receipt read: "Thank you. The desert is blooming once more."[10]

The desert image occurs in the closing sections of *A Burnt Child* and, indeed, the final chapter is entitled "When the Desert Blooms."

The atmosphere in this chapter is sublime, for Bengt has achieved a state of awareness and can indulge his passions without guilt or remorse. Before this happy state was reached, when life seemed formidable and hostile, Bengt's existence was like a desert—an inhospitable landscape offering little but loneliness and suffering. The isolation was occasionally punctuated by outbursts of passionate emotion, be it love or hate: the dividing line is thin, as Dagerman frequently suggests in all his works; these outbursts are compared to volcanoes erupting (an image with obvious Freudian overtones). The relationship between Bengt and Gun after their stay on the island is described in terms of a frozen desert and the imagery is thus tied in with the motifs of "hot" and "cold" which have figured more or less unobtrusively throughout the book.

Alma died in January. The coldness associated with death was reflected in the cold weather and snow of the January day when the funeral took place. A candle was lit and positioned in Alma's vacant place at the table during the funeral reception; after becoming aware of Gun's relationship with his father and possibly feeling the first stirrings of erotic stimulation within himself, Bengt burned his hands on the candle at the end of the chapter (33). In retrospect it seems that Dagerman arranged this contrast between heat and coldness so as to link the cold with Alma's death and hence with Bengt's assumed moral scruples associated with his yearning for purity; heat on the other hand was connected with passion.

The affair between Bengt and Gun proceeds to the accompaniment of appropriate changes in the weather as the year goes by. They first meet in May; the first visit to the island is at midsummer and the second in September. In addition, Bengt is hot when he abandons himself to passion but cold when his reason takes over, reminds him of his supposed duty to his mother and censures him for his "impure" tendencies. When Bengt makes his suicide attempt it is January once more, exactly one year after his mother's death, and minus 36°C. He has just been forced to acknowledge that almost all his actions over the previous year have been governed by his passionate love for Gun: suicide is the ultimate response of his reason, the last logical defense open to him in his attempt to assert his moral scruples associated with his mother's death.

When Bengt is rescued and can accept his passion in full awarenesss of all the circumstances, the cold begins to disperse. Having accepted his own personality and the situation in which he finds himself, Bengt no longer needs to deceive Berit or his father; when they visit his sick-bed, the new warmth that radiates between them grows greater and greater, despite the severe frost outside (270 ff.). When Gun visits him, she climbs into his bed and they make love. The relationship between them has been described as a frozen desert, but now the snow melts because they can at last accept the reality of their relationship: "Their white desert melts. And look, the desert is blooming. They love the desert. They love each other in great measure, but they love their desert most of all—not happier than before, not better either, but much less foolishly. . . . They are wise, because wisdom is being in love with life. But foolishness is being ashamed of love" (272).

Bengt's new awareness is not a romantic escape from reality. The symbol for his life is still a desert, and he knows there will be hardships and problems, but his recognition of the reality of his own makeup and that of existence enables him to cope without panic. He now knows the desert is much larger than he had ever imagined (that is, life's difficulties are even worse than he had thought). Bengt can console himself, though, with the thought that the larger the desert, the greater the number of oases! "Before we realize that, we must pay dearly. A volcanic eruption is the price. That is dear, but there are no cut prices. Therefore we must bless our volcanoes, thank them for dazzling us, for only when we are dazzled can we see properly. And thank them for burning us, for only as burnt children can we warm others" (273). The tiny flame of the candle at the beginning of the novel has now grown into the enormous fire of the volcano, suggesting that the small stirrings of eroticism in Bengt grew to gigantic proportions as his affair with Gun developed.

The superior power of passion compared with the controlling force of reason was depicted in the chapter describing Bengt's and Gun's fortnight together on the island in terms of "A Tiger and a Gazelle," to quote the chapter heading. The narrator compares Bengt's reason with a young gazelle at a water-hole: it can be overcome in a flash by a tiger (219). Clearly, the tiger stands for Bengt's emotions, which are irresistible when aroused. The imagery is rather more complicated than it might seem at first sight because in this chapter Bengt has still not acknowledged the facts of his situation. He is still trying to convince himself that he is morally superior because of his loyalty to his mother; when he succumbs to passion, it is complicated by his various attempts to diguise its real cause—anger with Gun for having tempted his father into an affair which seems to besmirch Alma's memory, for instance, and hatred for Gun, who seems able to enjoy animal pleasures and not to distinguish her relationship with Bengt from her numerous affairs with other people in the past. Bengt feels she should be crippled with guilt because of such circumstances. Or rather, the hypocritical code of morality he is claiming to adhere to makes him think so, and turns his love for Gun into emotions which vary between animal passions and intense hatred.

"Be grateful for the heat of a fever, for if there were no such thing as a fever we would be immured in ice." This, it will be recalled, was the planned heading, eventually abandoned, for one of the groups of stories in The Games of Night. [11] The imagery is conventional, but the continuity from Dagerman's previous work to A Burnt Child is obvious. Indeed, the thread can be traced back to The Island of the Doomed, where frigidity and numbness were depicted in terms of coldness, particularly in connection with Captain Wilson. The animal imagery of the lizards and the lion is clearly not a parallel to that of the gazelle and the tiger, but the general trend of this aspect of The Island of the Doomed is similar to the implications of A Burnt Child. The problem of numbness, the inability to experience emotion to the full, was one which constantly taxed Dagerman both in his works and in his private life. The constant fear was that guilt feelings and suppressed Angst would so confine the senses that eventually one was no longer capable of genuine emotions. That occasionally there should be "volcanic eruptions" of passion was a comforting fact: at least it showed one was emotionally alive.

There is a lot of autobiography in A Burnt Child, suitably embellished for fictional purposes. Of considerable interest in view of the mounting psychological problems which were already troubling Stig Dagerman is the maternal theme. A psychologist would no doubt trace many of Dagerman's problems to his lack of a mother, a lack which he obviously felt deeply. Part of the attraction Gun has for Bengt is as a mother substitute, and a repressed realization of this is no doubt one of the factors which increases Bengt's guilt at being erotically attracted by her. At the end of the novel, both Bengt and Gun accept this aspect of their roles with open eyes: for Bengt in his new state of awareness, Gun is both mistress and mother, and both of them find the situation eminently satisfying.

Interesting though the autobiographical aspects may be, the more universal significance of *A Burnt Child* must be the reader's primary concern. The reader is invited to question the conventional meaning of concepts such as purity and morality, right and wrong. Perhaps the biggest outrage in the novel to a conventional moralist is the incest theme, the idea of Bengt making love to his mother—his mother in law (i.e., stepmother) rather than his natural mother, but shocking even so. The message seems to be that such facile and conventional ideas of right and wrong are misguided. Being true to oneself, accepting facts irrespective of artificial conventions, seems to be held up by Dagerman as "the right direction," to use a phrase from *The Island of the Doomed*. The concluding sentences of *A Burnt Child* preach an Existentialist message: "But moments of peace are short. All other moments are much longer. Knowing this is also wisdom. But since they are so short we must live in those moments as if it were only then we were alive. They know this, too" (273).

The critics generally greeted *A Burnt Child* with enthusiasm and the Swedish reading public was delighted to find that the trend toward a more realistic style had been continued. The book appeared at the end of October 1948 and was reprinted twice before Christmas. It is the most accessible of Dagerman's novels and is still the most widely read of all his works.

Chapter Six

Increasing Chaos: *Wedding Worries*

Background

Having returned to Sweden from France in time for the opening of his play *The Shadow of Mart* at the Dramatic Theater, Stockholm, in September 1948, Stig Dagerman found himself preoccupied with drama and the theater for the rest of the year. He was feeling more acutely now the effects of his being estranged from most other writers of his generation as a result of the split in the Swedish Writers' Association. The years of his great friendship with Bengt Ekerot were beginning; Ekerot was one of Sweden's leading actor-directors whose home was in Malmö in the far south of Sweden, and Dagerman was to spend a lot of time there in the next few years. He tried hard to make himself at home in the bohemian theatrical circles which now more than ever were his haunts.

In February Dagerman had written an article for the new literary journal *Prisma* on his dramatic theories, and brought into circulation the term "the de-dramatized drama," arguing for a reduction in importance of theatrical effects and the restoration of primary importance to the words of a play.[1] Besides being a leading young novelist Stig Dagerman was establishing himself as one of Sweden's leading contemporary dramatists. In November he took part in a much-publicized debate on the theater in Uppsala, an event which proved to be rather less significant than had been expected, and then spent much of December in an isolated cabin near Oslo working on a stage version of *A Burnt Child* . He planned to direct the first production himself, with assistance from Bengt Ekerot (who was to play the leading role), the opening being scheduled for the following March.

Stig Dagerman was extremely busy in late 1948 and the first half of

1949, but his state of mind was far from settled. His marriage had been under strain for some time and things were deteriorating; moreover his failure to complete the articles on France for *Expressen* weighed heavily on his mind, and he was determined to return to France to finish the task in 1949. He was awarded a travel scholarship by Norstedts in celebration of their 125th anniversary and spent it on a journey to Paris, planned to take place in January and February 1949. The bad fortune which seemed to attend all Stig Dagerman's contacts with France continued to afflict him, however, and he had a bad attack of influenza which resulted in curtailment of the trip, and no sooner had he arrived in France than he was robbed, being left helpless until his publishers could have extra money transferred to Paris for him.[2] Needlesss to say, no article for *Expressen* was written.

Dagerman was able to find some relief from his worries and depression by throwing himself wholeheartedly into his work with the production of his dramatized version of *A Burnt Child*. Eventually entitled *No One Goes Free*, it finally took place in April and received quite good notices (cf. p. 120). The author's depression grew worse, however, and he became involved in emotional entanglements, which did not improve matters. He decided to commit suicide and even went so far as to send a letter to Bengt Ekerot, designed to be opened after his death. In it he wrote: ". . . don't think I am doing this willingly. I am incurably ill, suffering from a devilish illness which manifests itself in a constant hatred of myself and an endless capacity for hurting others. For their sakes I can't hold out any longer. Perhaps not for my sake either."[3] The suicide did not actually take place, but Dagerman was obviously in a serious condition.

An opportunity to get away from the most immediate worries came with an offer from the Swedish film company, Sandrews. They wanted Stig Dagerman to accompany some 15,000 persons of mixed nationality who were leaving Europe and emigrating to Australia; the ship would leave from Italy and the journey would take about one month. On the basis of his experiences Dagerman was to produce a film script: the completed film would be in English and have a famous but unspecified Holywood director.[4] Ragnar Svanström was not too happy about the project since Dagerman had signed contracts with Norstedts for a book of poems to be called *Resebrev* [Travel Letters] and a novel, *Pingvinerna* [The Penguins], and had already received advances on royalties;[5] he relented, however, and Dagerman left in May for Naples. The sailing had been delayed and he was in a very depressed state of mind, having once more contemplated suicide.[6]

The voyage was not a success for Stig Dagerman, who was again faced with failure to complete a project—the film script was never written, nor was the travelogue which he had hoped to write as a side product. Moreover, he disembarked at Sydney in the middle of a bitterly cold Australian winter; the town was torn by strikes, and thanks to industrial action by miners, candles and lanterns were the only source of heat. To make things still worse, Dagerman had progressed no further with his planned book of poems and had no ideas for *The Penguins*. Things looked bleak indeed—but salvation came out of the blue with sudden inspiration for a new novel dealing with life on his grandparents' farm in Älvkarleby. The ideas for *Wedding Worries*, as the novel was finally called, took shape in the author's mind, but Dagerman had considerable troubles in writing them down.

Stig Dagerman was by now a national celebrity and was constantly being bombarded with requests for interviews, photographs, articles, stories, poems, guest appearances, and so on. Getting down to serious work needed considerable willpower, and his state of mind was far from good. Dagerman's emotional problems and marriage difficulties were still present, and a farcical turn of events had suddenly magnified the author's financial problems to a size which could no longer be ignored. Before leaving for Australia Dagerman had arranged for some repairs to be made to his house and received an estimate for 8,000 crowns. Norstedts, who had advanced the money for the villa, contacted builders of their choice to do the work and the costs escalated with frightening rapidity, the eventual charge being over 50,000 crowns, considerably more than the house had cost only three years previously.[7] When these debts were added to the money advanced by the publishers to repay the costs of the year in France to *Expressen*, and the advances on royalties for books never written, the amount of money Stig Dagerman owed began to take on ominous proportions. He badly needed a series of bestsellers to put things right.

The house business had its amusing side and it became a minor theme in *Wedding Worries*. Dagerman, however, was under considerable pressure to write the novel quickly in spite of all the difficulties he was undergoing, and he found it almost impossible to respond. The repairs had produced chaos in his house, where there was only one inhabitable room and insufferable noise. He spent several weeks running away from the chaos, the domestic problems, the constant interruptions; he stayed with friends, spent periods in cottages rented or borrowed from acquaintances, and tried to write *Wedding Worries* in time for what the Swedish publishing world calls "The fall book flood." He delved into experiences from his childhood, and worked into the novel all kinds of things that happened to him during these months. As he explained in an autobiographical sketch, "everything had to go into it that happened while the book was being written: the elks outside the cabin, the chaotic firework display at a neighbor's crayfish party and the people I love or hate just now. And above all the fear that streams forth from the telephones that ring all day long and the feeling of security which only the night can bring."[8]

Whereas *A Burnt Child* had been an austere and disciplined book, carefully planned and tightly constructed, *Wedding Worries* was superficially chaotic. Of course, it has a plan and the chaos is much more meaningful than is immediately apparent, but the novel is intentionally confusing, reflecting the circumstances in which it was written.

Plot

The plot of *Wedding Worries* is extremely difficult to summarize. There are a number of subplots and themes which intertwine to give the book its special character and a bald statement of the main action is grossly inadequate to convey the contents of the book, but an attempt will be made here to cover the main points.

The action covers a single day on a farm in rural Uppland, references to towns suggesting that it is situated about a hundred miles north of Stockholm (it is obviously based on the farm where Stig Dagerman spent his childhood at Älvkarleby). The farm is owned by Viktor Palm, and on the day in question his daughter Hildur marries a butcher, Westlund, from a nearby village. The morning is devoted to preparations, the afternoon is when the ceremony takes place at the local vicarage, and the evening and night are spent celebrating, an occasion which deteriorates into a drunken orgy and ends with the sun rising on a new day with almost everyone sleeping off the effects, many of them in places where they ought not to be, such as under hedges, on floors, or in someone else's bed. It is an amusing novel but with tragic undertones, written in Uppland dialect.

Hildur, the bride, has been in love with a young man, Martin, who, some months earlier, left the area in an attempt to get work and earn enough money to come back and marry Hildur. Meanwhile, Hildur discovers she is pregnant; she can wait for Martin no longer and agrees to marry the hard-drinking, pompous butcher Westlund, whose first wife had died sometime previously. Hildur is kind, sweet, and gentle, universally liked and worthy of a better fate: but as she says, in a phrase which becomes a motif in the book, "you have to make the most of what you've got."

Victor Palm, her father, has become old and strange. He built an extra storey onto his farmhouse and then retired to this upper floor, whence he refuses ever to come down (although Hildur discovers he sometimes creeps down at night and sits in the old farm machinery in an attempt to relive his lost youth). He is afraid of being old and unwanted, and hence put into the local Old Folks' Home; and so he lives in self-enforced isolation in his attic room. Hildur, however, shows Viktor the love he thought he would never receive and induces him down to her wedding, hence also back into society.

Hildur's mother, Hilma, is also very old, but is full of love and keen, as she puts it, to do at least one good deed before she dies. She persuades her old admirer, the singer, to come from his room at the Old Folks' Home and sing at Hildur's wedding. The old man is living on past glories, the highlight of his life being his application to become an opera singer. His attempt to sing at the wedding reception is catastrophic, no sound coming forth. He returns in deep sorrow to the Old Folks' Home, where he manages to sing and bring joy to a mad inmate, but instead of the glorious notes the singer thinks he hears, all that flows from his mouth in fact is a stream of blood, and the old man dies—but dies happy because *he* thought that he was singing again as well as ever.

Hildur's brother and sister play minor roles. Rudolf is in charge of the farm, but still hesitates to take any major decision without consulting his father despite the fact that the latter has shut himself away. Irma is approaching middle age and embittered, her future prospects limited by the fact that she has an illegitimate son. She seems to have loved Martin in the past, the missing father of Hildur's child; the reader eventually discovers that it is Irma who has informed Martin of Hildur's imminent marriage to Westlund, no doubt done in the hope that Martin would transfer his affections to her. The farm laborer Sören is also involved in a minor way. He is conducting an affair with Svea, who is Westlund's housekeeper, and eventually agrees to marry her, although he had hoped to avoid doing so.

Westlund considers himself superior to his circle of acquaintances, largely because he has spent some time in America and thus—hilariously—considers himself a sophisticated cosmopolitan. He has had a comfortable sexual relationship with Svea, which he must now renounce when he marries Hildur, and he has also been intimate with Rudolf's girl friend, Rullan. Westlund competes in the district with fellow butcher Simon, much of their time being spent in petty attempts to score off the other. On the wedding day they agree to become partners.

Westlund's daughter Siri is an idealistic young girl who hates her father's philandering and objects to his apparent indifference to her mother's memory. She has visions of a pure and handsome lover who will appear like a knight in shining armor to rescue her from her squalid environment, but during the wedding celebrations she loses her virginity to a young tramp, Ivar, who is rather less than pure.

Three tramps figure in the story.[9] Filip writes poems and tries to sell them on his wanderings; Ivar is a former streetcar driver who accidentally killed a drunk; the third, Sixten, is a mystery figure. He proves eventually to be Martin, who has returned to the farm in time for Hildur's wedding, apparently hoping he might somehow be able to prevent it and win back Hildur.

There are numerous other minor characters and incidents, notably the young man Ville, who is tired of his roguish parents and the lack of prospects or love for himself and attempts to commit suicide—but he is rescued by the wedding guests and returned to his parents, who begin to realize at last that a loving relationship with their son is something worthwhile. The various subplots interact, similar or contrasting situations occurring in rapid succession. Although there is no single, clear story line, the multitude of incidents combine to create a comprehensive picture of events on this country wedding day which proves to be so significant in the lives of so many of them. When the merrymaking is at its height, Martin confronts Hildur alone and attempts to ravish her. She repulses him and shortly afterwards his body is found hanging in an outbuilding. Tragedy has undermined the celebrations and reminded those of the guests who needed reminding of the true nature of life. Some ideals are shattered during the course of the novel, but several people mature to a new awareness: they confront their *Angst* and take the first step toward learning to live with it.

Swan Song

In his autobiographical sketch "Wedding Worries and Others,"[10] Dagerman reveals that the first working title he thought of for his new novel was "Three Tramps," and he recalls an incident in 1931 when, as a small boy, he thought he had seen carved into a beam in an outhouse the initials of a young man who had courted one of the girls on the farm. The girl was due to marry someone else the next day: what would happen if the former suitor had returned as a tramp and asked to be present at the wedding celebrations? Young Stig soon realized the initials were old ones, but pretended they were new and informed the family. "Tension, worry and fear took possession of us all and did not disperse until the final candle had burnt itself out on the wedding night." On his way home from Australia, via the United States, Dagerman began to develop the old idea into a novel with the key theme the relationship of the tramps to the wedding celebrations, a study of the various ways in which they were excluded from normal life.

As he meditated on the idea Dagerman gradually became dissatisfied with the limitations imposed by the title. On a walk through San Francisco he saw the name "Swan Song" and decided that this would be a preferable title. "The tramps faded into the background and I prepared the way for me to enter into the celebrations myself. The failed old singer, who had been only a vague background figure thus far, stepped forward into the limelight and embodied the idea contained in the title: the wedding would be many people's swan song." Dagerman announced this title to journalists who were waiting to greet his return home at the airport in Stockholm, but he had to change it once more when he discovered that a Swedish book had already been advertised for the coming fall entitled *Swan Song*. "I was helped to find the freedom implied by the title *Wedding Worries*, which meant that the celebrations themselves with all the sensual possibilities they contained became the main character."[11]

The autobiographical sketch was written in 1950, and Dagerman could not have known that *Wedding Worries* was in fact his own swan song in the sense that he would never manage to complete another novel. His comment does suggest, however, that he may have had premonitions of this—a frequent theme from this time on was his fear that the words which previously had flowed so fluently and easily from his pen would no longer come forth when bidden, and his recurrent thoughts of suicide may also have influenced him. In any case, the comparison between himself and the old singer is quite explicit, the worn-out artist living on past glories but now incapable of performing. It is a highly pessimistic view of his own powers as a writer and bodes ill for his future as a private individual.

The singer is marked by death from the beginning of *Wedding Worries*, for the pastor informs the reader on his first appearance that he has not long to live (76).[12] Like Hilma, the singer has an ambition to do something good and useful before he dies, but he will not realize that he is a shadow of his former self, living on dreams and memories. He is lonely and rejected, a useless failure: and he knows this. He will not admit it, however, and hence his *Angst* is great. Kind-hearted Hildur and loyal Hilma nourish the singer's illusions by assuring him of how beautifully he sang at the wedding reception (165 ff.) but other guests reveal the harsh truth to him. The singer is able to triumph over death nevertheless, despite the fact that his illusions are shattered even more comprehensively when he discovers that the warden of the Old Folks' Home has never posted to the opera house the letters in which the singer placed so much foolish hope (237). He seems to have reached the rock bottom of degradation, but he triumphs even so because his final action is to communicate through song with a poor lunatic and fellow resident in the home (or he thinks he does): the lunatic's eyes light up in joy and understanding as the singer produces wondrous sounds, "And he notices immediately and with boundless joy: Tokanders hears him singing, Tokanders's eyes are chained fast, not to him but to the song. . . . And now his song is heard over all the earth, the hedgehogs hear him and awaken, the plants of the sea sway in time with his song, he climbs over mountains, he is a hurricane which lashes the wilderness until it bleeds. He stands alone in the night with his straw hat pressed against his chest, the straw hat belongs to the greatest of giants, he will fill it with song. He raises it to his mouth and lets the song pour into it like the driving rain, will it never be filled?" (239).

The singer's death is clearly symbolic and is universalized by the series of images which give a lyrical atmosphere tinged with expressionism to the scene. It is a tragic death since his "song" was really his life-blood bursting out of his mouth and into his handkerchief. There has been no *real* communication through art, not even with the lunatic, for the reader realizes that what has inspired Tokanders is not the song but the bundle of unposted letters. Ironically the act of human kindness performed by the singer toward Tokanders is shown to be more powerful than art. This is a key theme in the novel, namely that the only way in which life can be made bearable and meaningful is by showing kindness and love to our fellows, a theme reflected in the last of the four chapter headings: "Where is the friend whom everywhere I seek?" (which is in fact the first line of a well-known Swedish hymn). [13] Insofar as the singer is an alter ego of the author, it is a bitterly pessimistic comment on his art, and shows how Dagerman craved meaningful human contact as a means of helping him to survive his psychological difficulties.

The singer, then, dies in a moment of tragicomic triumph; Martin commits suicide; Ville is saved from suicide. Some characters are waiting for death as a release, others fear it, and some of them long to do something good in their lives before it arrives. Some personages in the novel are wholly or partially responsible for committing, or almost committing, murder; others are almost murdered. The final chapter of *Wedding Worries* ends with almost everyone asleep or dead, and the lyrical introductory section to the chapter sets the tone with a series of death images: "Some come floating downstream, their hair always spreads out in the opposite direction. Many lie out in the meadows, some meadows look like battlefields of a morning, but without blood. Some lie in holes. This little black hole—is that supposed to be my home? . . . We find many on glaciers, their arms melting, and some hang in the trees in the mornings, hang straight down as if they were standing still in the air" (283). It is a lyrical hymn to the peace and comfort of death, as if the characters in the novel as well as its author were resigned to death and ready to bid it welcome. The wedding celebrations and the events leading up to them have acted as a catalyst for many of the people concerned and led them to make decisions which involve coming to terms with their *Angst*, as a result of which they can face up to both life and death with equanimity.

Love and Isolation

What enables characters who had feared death (and life) to change in such a way that they can accept it is the realization that they are loved by another human being—love in the widest sense, not merely passionate love between two individuals.

In an interview published a little over a month after *Wedding Worries* first appeared, Dagerman claimed that the most important part of the book was the section concerning Ville, the poacher's son who is so disgusted with his parents and the way of life they are leading him into that he makes several attempts to commit suicide. Dagerman seems to be overstating his case somewhat since Ville and his story are incidental to the main story line centered upon the marriage of Hildur and Westlund and the subsequent festivities. Nevertheless, his situation exemplifies the clearest example of the importance of love, of human contact in a life which seems dominated by gloom and isolation. Dagerman commented: "It seems to me that life can be so hard that it appears to be completely meaningless, but so long as there are other people who help us and whom we ourselves can help, there is a meaning after all. Solidarity is the most beautiful quality I know. Soidarity not just with a class or a party—although that's where it starts, of course—but with the whole of humanity, even with the whole of Nature."[14]

Ville is about to commit suicide when his attention is distracted by a spider spinning its web between two fir trees: the sun is shining on the web and the whole scene is so beautiful that Ville extinguishes the fuse on the stick of dynamite that should have blown him up in order to watch the spider complete its task (205). He is about to make another attempt when he is foiled by a little boy, lost in the woods who prevails on Ville to take him home (206). After Ville's kindness to the boy, he too is treated with kindness and understanding by the wedding guests, and eventually realizes that his father and family, despite all their faults, love and need him (210). Having sought in vain for his father's love in the past, but desperately needing it, Ville is lucky enough to find that details of morality are irrelevant and that love between father and son can be enjoyed by both of them at last. Both have escaped from their isolation.

Viktor is lured down from his attic room and out of his self-imposed isolation because his daughter Hildur not only goes upstairs to plead with him—he is usually ignored and never visited except on business—she actually weeps a little when she thinks how badly she has treated her father in the past by not showing more love and understanding (80). What Viktor finds when he rejoins the world by coming downstairs is not ideal from his point of view—just as Ville could not change the criminal tendencies of his father, for instance, Viktor cannot alter the fact that he is too old to run the farm as he used to do. Love of one's fellow men is centrally important, but it must be combined with an acceptance of the limitations imposed by oneself and by the circumstances of one's life.

Making the Best of Things

Alongside love and death, the third main theme in *Wedding Worries* is resignation. It is central to an understanding of the main character in the book, Hildur, and is acted out in miniature, as it were, by Siri, Westlund's daughter from his first marriage.

Siri expresses most clearly the romantic search for an ideal lover. Her disapproval of her father's philandering and his betrayal of her mother (demonstrated by Westlund's marrying Hildur and symbolized by his determination to remove the picture of his former wife from its place on the wall) shows that Siri is attached to the *idea* of an ideal marriage. She clings to the ideal regardless of the facts which show clearly that her faith in it is misplaced. The ritual she goes through when carefully washing and tending her body in order that she might be ready when her Fairy Prince comes along confirms that she is living in an unreal world (135). There is an undertone of cynicism in the description of her dream which is overloaded with blatant sexual symbolism, the implication being that she is idealizing emotions which have a rather more base and mundane foundation: "He leans down over the meadow, she is a meadow. She is a large sheath, she is a scabbard for a saber. One day the shining knight appears, he has walked gently over the meadow, there is no rust on his blade. Nothing exists save the star gleaming and the shining knight approaching, the shining saber coming to rest in its scabbard after the battle. It is red with blood, the scabbard is filled to the brim, it causes no pain" (134).

Siri's ideal of love contrasts startlingly with the way in which she actually loses her virginity, going off during the wedding celebrations into a damp oat field with Ivar, the tramp (266). Nevertheless, Siri is not ashamed of her action and defends herself with the statement that she felt sorry for the tramp. Hildur supports her, asking rhetorically what more one can do than feel sorry for someone. Compassion—the key to an awareness of the meaning of life in *The Island of the Doomed*.

The whole of Hildur's character and her fate in *Wedding Worries* is governed by resignation. It is implied though not precisely stated that she had idealistic dreams of love in connection with Martin, the father of her child. When he goes away and Hildur discovers she is pregnant, she is placed in an awkward predicament: she has before her in her sister Irma an example of the fate which awaits her if she remains faithful to her ideal of love and hopes that Martin will eventually return. Irma has been deserted and has grown embittered as a result of the isolation she is forced into through being an unmarried mother who has kept her child. Hildur makes the best of things and decides to marry Westlund: she certainly does not love him, but her action shows compassion for the butcher and is doubtless in the best interests of her child. It is an unselfish act and one which Hildur carries out in full awareness of the implications and consequences.

Like Siri, Hildur is placing herself in a position which involves apparent degradation. It is degrading for a beautiful, gentle, and generous girl like Hildur to sacrifice herself for a poseur like the drunken, womanizing butcher Westlund. Her position is made somewhat more acceptable to her when Martin traps her in the farmyard and attempts to ravish her on the ice-pile (261): it seems that his motive in returning for the wedding was not so much love for Hildur as a decisive triumph over Westlund on his wedding night. It is a discovery which further degrades Hildur, but it has the consolation of removing her guilt at not having waited for Martin.

Should there be any doubt that Westlund is unworthy of his bride, it is dispelled when he drinks himself senseless before joining her in the bridal bed. Hildur is not looking forward to Westlund's embrace and closes her eyes: when she opens them and finds she is making love not with Westlund but with Simon, however, she does not protest. Having decided to "make the best of things" Hildur has abandoned her impossible ideals and thus exposes herself to degradation; and having once embarked on such a course, she feels a compulsion to punish herself to the limit. "Something makes us choose the most humiliating form of degradation in preference to a lesser one," comments the narrator (292). But what?

Instead of describing what happens between Hildur and Simon, Dagerman uses the highly effective device of inserting an anonymous letter to the correspondence columns of a newspaper on the subject of degradation and redemption, thus neatly universalizing Hildur's situation and thoughts. The letter points out the tendency to seek degradation, then asks: "Have we perhaps experienced all too thoroughly the misery of victory, success and exaltation to enable us to believe any longer that we should attain redemption by that route?

What then, is redemption? I believe that redemption is the process by which we are suddenly able to accept that this life is meaningless, empty, cold and indifferent, in itself a void" (293). The train of thought continues in Hildur's mind as she lies awake, and now alone, in her marriage bed. She has attained a state of awareness in the existential sense by experiencing extreme humiliation and realizing that it does not matter; to use the terminology of *The Island of the Doomed*, she has realized the meaninglessness of the whole, but she finds meaning in the part by moving in "the right direction." By acknowledging the meaningless nature of life she asserts her own existence and thus achieves a form of peace. In an image which represents the culmination of the house imagery that has recurred throughout the novel, Hildur sees herself and her circle of friends and relations as component parts of a house. Everyone has a role to play and all are important and necessary—"even a dirty stone under the foot scraper" (295). Given this new awareness, the conventional ideas regarding the rights and wrongs of Hildur's behavior pale into insignificance; much more important is the understanding and compassion she has displayed toward her father, her new step-daughter, and even Westlund.

Themes comprising compassion, love, understanding, tolerance, and a desire to do good deeds invite speculation as to whether Dagerman was trying to pass on a Christian message in *Wedding Worries*. Lars Ahlin, the other outstanding novelist of Dagerman's generation, was a convinced Lutheran as well as a Socialist, and it does seem as if Dagerman were moving toward a similar view of life—moreover his grandparents and their family, who provided the factual basis for the novel, were motivated by low-church Christianity. Dagerman was certainly searching desperately for some creed which could convince him that life was worth living, but the fact remains that he never embraced Christianity. A confessional article written in 1952 begins: "I lack a faith and can therefore never become a happy man, for a happy man ought never fear that his life is a meaningless drift toward certain death. I have inherited neither a god nor a firm base in life from which I could call upon a god to pay me any attention. . . ."[15]

Confusion and Serenity

Stig Dagerman claimed that whereas *A Burnt Child* had been a controlled and carefully measured novel, *Wedding Worries* was "an uncontrolled, indulgent and brash book containing lots of people."[16] It depicts characterful peasant folk in the unsophisticated hurly-burly surrounding a country wedding, its preparations and its aftermath. Although some critics thought the folksiness was overdone, the majority of reviewers felt that Dagerman had been very successful in capturing the spirit of rolicking bucolicism. Comparisons were drawn with the folksy writings of Tage Aurell, and with Strindberg's novel *The People of Hemsö*; one critic found the amiable rogues of *Wedding Worries*, indeed, the whole range of rough-hewn but generally well-meaning characters, reminiscent of Bellman's collection of Stockholm originals in his Fredman cycles.[17] To a present-day reader familiar with Dagerman's works, *Wedding Worries* seems unmistakably characteristic of the author; but reviewers—possibly reluctant to admit the full extent of Dagerman's versatility—claimed to find the influence of an impressive list of writers, including in addition to the three mentioned, Ahlin, Almqvist, Caldwell, Chekhov, Faulkner, Hamsun, Höijer, Eyvind Johnson, Lagerkvist, Lo-Johansson, Martinson, Sartre, Shakespeare, and Tolstoy.

Unusually for Dagerman, the novel is divided into only four chapters, although each of those is subdivided further by means of an asterisk between sections. The four chapter headings are couched in old-fashioned language smacking of the Bible: "Who is knocking at the bride's window?," "Who can tell where my torment is seated?," "Take what thou hast and be thankful,"[18] and "Where is the friend whom everywhere I seek?" The effect of the headings is not merely to evoke rather old-fashioned rustic simplicity, but also to suggest that beneath the bucolic veneer are happenings of timeless significance.

Subdividing the chapters enables Dagerman constantly to vary the narrative perspective and to flit from one subplot to another in a fashion which is sometimes, intentionally, slightly bewildering. The story does not unfold in linear fashion, but the same event is recounted from different points of view in successive sections of the novel. In the opening chapter, for instance, the most significant event is that very early in the morning of Hildur's wedding day, someone knocks on the window of her room but has disappeared by the time Hildur is able to investigate. Each of the five subsections covers more or less the same period of time and all hear the knocking (or see a shadowy figure running away) from their own location. In this first chapter there is no doubt about who is conducting the inner monologue since the author is introducing some of the main characters. As the novel proceeds, however, there are occasions following an asterisk in the text when it is by no means clear which characters are concerned until several pages have elapsed.

There is no doubt that this is intentional on Dagerman's part. The confused state of mind of most of the characters grows more marked as the day progresses, the worries and problems intensify and the alcohol flows in ever-increasing amounts; this is reflected in the somewhat bewildering intertwining of subplots, many of them dealing with unanswered questions. The uniform dialect spoken by all the characters, and also by the third-person narrator who sometimes makes his presence felt among the mass of inner monologue and *erlebte Rede*, helps to create in the mind of the reader a state of less-than-complete clarity appropriate to the general blurring of dividing lines and overlapping of stories. Distinguishing features of individual characters are very rarely linguistic. Westlund has some favorite phrases, such as "This is something that'll have to change," and the "In America . . ." with which he commences so many of his boasts. On the whole, however, individual characteristics are not linguistic— Irma cannot resist pinching people, Mary loves everything plastic, Rudolf is obsessed by his handmade wooden rake and his ambition gradually to make a rough stone smooth by urinating on it. Spoken style alone does not allow the reader to differentiate between individuals, and this sometimes helps to increase the confusion.

Even in passages which are narrated by an apparently objective third-person narrator, his distinctive identity is frequently blurred and he tends to be affected by the character he is describing. As Hildur approaches the vicarage where she is to be married in preference to the church, a fairly common Swedish custom, the scene is described by a third-person narrator: but he is strongly influenced by Hildur's thoughts (150). The recurrent phrase "Take what thou hast and be thankful" is passing through her mind as she steels herself to make the best of her situation and marry a man she does not love. The phrase originates with Svea, who uses it in an anonymous note to Hildur, commenting nastily on the mysterious knocking at the bride's window (145). Now, every time the narrator uses the word "take" the leitmotif interposes itself in his narrative, usually italicized:

The vicarage has a short concrete stairway, six steps and an iron rail, it takes an eternity to get up it. She takes one step at a time *take what thou hast and be thankful* smoke is coming from the minister's brewing shed, a mowing machine is clattering from the meadow down by the lake. The vicarage has a wide, yellow door with a glass pane in, and a chain on the inside since the Tillberga murder, she takes hold of the handle, *take what thou hast and be thankful*. She takes her handkerchief, a little wet ball, take the handkerchief thou hast and be thankful. . . . The door has a handle of cool brass, Hildur takes hold of it, *take what thou hast and be thankful*. (150–51)

The proverblike phrase is associated with Hildur but is taken up by the narrator and repeated in succeeding sections of the novel in connection with other characters, such as the singer.

The wedding day is a time of busy activity and bustle, but there are times when the author relaxes the pace of the epic narrative and introduces passages of considerable lyrical beauty, as if the characters badly needed to rest after all their lively activity. In such passages, the people in the novel seem to merge with nature—reminding the reader of Dagerman's comment that he was advocating not only solidarity between men, but between men and nature. At the end of the novel, following the chaos of the festivities and the upheaval of Hildur's realization of the facts of her situation after her degradation, the narrator contemplates all the characters asleep as the sun rises. The petty affairs of the Uppland peasants have been given universal significance, and the description suggests the broader implications and timelessness by referring to "mornings" in the plural and extending the place from a farm at Älvkarleby to "all over the earth": "In the mornings we find them sleeping, on their side, on their back, or hanging, they have such sweet faces. They didn't mean any harm.

They are sleeping all over the earth and no one has the heart to wake them. They are sleeping so soundly, but what happened happened, they didn't mean any harm" (296). The repeated phrase "they didn't mean any harm," reminding the reader of the narrator's elevation of good intentions and "the right direction" over normal ideas of good and evil in *The Island of the Doomed*, stands as a sympathetic and affectionate epitaph for the rough but likable characters who have been featured in *Wedding Worries*.

The individuals are listed and their resting place described (even the dead are said to be "sleeping"). And then the description is extended to include representatives of the whole of nature, and universal concepts, before coming back to the individual on the farm to conclude the novel: ". . . With her key under her pillow, old mother Bjuhr is sleeping in the bedroom and Karlsson is sleeping at Hagström's table and Hagström at his own. The pike is sleeping in the reeds and the hedgehog in the hedgerow. The toad is sleeping in the well and the rain in the clouds. Death is sleeping in life, and life in death. Lorelei is sleeping on her rock, she has gray hair. But the bride lies awake. And the wedding night passes" (297). The Lorelei reference is problematical but presumably refers to Heine's famous poem, which begins: "I don't know what it can mean, but I'm so sad. A fairy-tale from long ago, I can't get it out of my head."[19] In the poem, stress is placed on the gold color of her hair; the change to gray suggests that the siren who has lured so many love-stricken sailors to their deaths is herself old and tired, and needful of rest.

In *Wedding Worries* Dagerman manages to capture a subtle quality which invests simple folk in what are often squalid circumstances with a certain nobility which elevates their fate to one of timeless significance; the comparison with Bellman's Fredman and his circle was a perceptive one. Characters are steeped in *Angst*, but there is a new air of resignation and a desire for love and tenderness which sometimes seems to be a longing for love in the Christian sense. Apart from the style, a notable difference between *A Burnt Child* and *Wedding Worries*, and Dagerman's previous works, is that the political element has virtually disappeared. In *The Snake* and *The Island of the Doomed* the autobiographical elements were balanced by the author's missionary zeal as a politically committed writer keen to present a case for anarcho-syndicalism. As his private problems increased and the apparently effortless ease with which he had been able to write in 1945−47 began to desert him, it seems that Dagerman concentrated on autobiographical situations and Existentialist messages at the expense of his political enthusiasms. The technical virtuosity is still there in his later novels; indeed, his touch seems more sure than ever. The average reader at the end of the 1940s must have wondered what style Dagerman would next show himself to be master of, and his fifth novel was awaited with great expectations.

It never came.

Chapter Seven

Dramatist of Promise

The De-Dramatized Drama

Sweden has not been blessed with outstanding playwrights since the death of Strindberg. Few twentieth-century Swedish plays are known outside Scandinavia, and of dramatists who have achieved success inside Sweden the best have frequently been better known in the field of prose or poetry—Pär Lagerkvist (1891–1974), for example, and Hjalmar Bergman (1883–1931), Werner Aspenström (b. 1918), and Lars Forssell (b. 1928). Stig Dagerman was probably Sweden's outstanding dramatist in the late 1940s and early 1950s, and his plays were performed throughout Europe and elsewhere, albeit with only moderate success.[1]

Dagerman is associated particularly with a dramatic theory set out in a well-known article, "Entrérepliker" [Entrance Lines], published in the journal *Prisma* in 1948. His ideas do not seem especially revolutionary when read today but they clearly struck a raw nerve, as it were, in cultural critics and practitioners of the time, for the article led to a lively debate.

Dagerman's main point was that the spoken word was undervalued in contemporary drama. In poetry, and to a lesser extent in prose, Swedish writers were rebelling against conventions and creating a new type of modernistic literature; but these young rebels were ignoring the drama. According to Dagerman the fundamental reason for this was that the drama was traditionally the best equipped branch of literature for reproducing reality, but in the contemporary Swedish theater it was not properly appreciated that a mere aping of real life was a superficial form of realism. Techniques associated with lighting, stage sets, sound effects, and not least acting had now reached such a high level of achievement that the central figures in a theatrical production were frequently the director, his technicians, and the

actors. Their dominance had led to too much emphasis being placed
on dramatic effects, which could often be best achieved without
words; the playwright was being forced into a peripheral position.
Dagerman argued that the production of a play was necessarily a
collective operation and that the dramatist should be restored to his
rightful place as a full and equal member of the collective: this meant
the avoidance of dramatic effects for their own sake and the use of
words to produce other effects—lyrical atmosphere, for instance.
"To promote the whole truth at the expense of dramatic truth is just
now a necessary task for the dramatist. . . . The drama, this art in
which everything seems to have the effortless ability to be *plus grand
que soi*, should at last grant the Word an opportunity to show that it is
plus grand que soi, and thus to demonstrate that the truth about life is
very much greater than itself—which is when all is said and done
what all great art tries to prove." This attack on dramatic effects led
Dagerman to coin the phrase "the de-dramatized drama," which
became a key phrase in dramatic criticism of the late 1940s and early
1950s.

The cynical evaluation of the theory is that it is a rationalization of
Dagerman's shortcomings as a dramatist. Many of the best-known
Swedish plays this century have been adaptations of novels and short
stories, and two of Dagerman's plays were dramatizations of his own
prose works: *The Man Condemned to Death* is based on the short story of
the same name, and *No One Goes Free* is a reworking of his novel *A
Burnt Child*. A close comparison between the two versions of these
works suggests that while Dagerman was potentially an extremely
good dramatist with an instinctive feel for dramatic effects and
dialog, many of the techniques he used so successfully in prose did not
transfer satisfactorily into the theater without considerable modifica-
tion, and the result was a marked reduction in tension.

Too often, slack or slow-moving sections of Dagerman's dramas fail
to hold the attention of the audience consistently or completely. His
characters sometimes indulge in overlong monologues, in the course
of which any antics of the actors run the risk of distracting from the
point of the speech rather than adding to it. The obvious example of
this is Gabriel's monologue at the end of *The Shadow of Mart*, which
lasted twenty-eight minutes on the occasion of the play's first produc-

tion.[2] Gabriel's mother sits in a chair, dead, while Gabriel himself talks. Almost all reviewers commented on the scene's excessive length and mentioned restlessness in the audience—one critic even remarked that as the scene wore on, the primary interest of the audience was to concentrate on the actress playing the part of the dead mother in the chair: how could she remain immobile for such a long time?[3] If one contrasts this with sections of *The Snake*, for instance, where many pages are devoted to the actions and thoughts of Irène alone, it becomes clear that one's attention is retained by aspects of narrative technique which could not possibly have been employed in *The Shadow of Mart*.

Dagerman's most consistently "de-dramatized" play is *The Explorer*. It is significant that this is also an extremely short play: its static nature would probably be intolerable to an audience if stretched out over an hour and a half or more. It should be noticed that Dagerman maintained in "Entrance Lines" that the "de-dramatization" of the drama should only be a temporary phenomenon, a consciously exaggerated reaction to the excessive stress placed on dramatic effects; he did not rule them out, but asked that their importance should be reduced. Dagerman's more successful plays have sections in which there is considerable dramatic tension, and it is such sections which critics doubtless had in mind when they pointed to Dagerman's potential as a dramatist but claimed that he had not completely fulfilled his promise. This is a fair assessment.

The Man Condemned to Death

The first play by Stig Dagerman to be performed in public was a one-act sketch, *På tåget* [On the Train], which he had written in a couple of hours in 1942 and given to a friend as a Christmas box, being short of cash as usual and unable to afford a "real" present.[4] It was performed in 1943 by an experimental theater group and was sufficiently successful to attract a short notice in the literary journal *Bonniers Litterära Magasin*, where Holger Ahlenius referred to it as "the droll little sketch."[5] The author had forgotten about it and was unaware of the planned production until he was invited to attend rehearsals.

With this "involuntary debut" in mind, Dagerman referred to *The*

Man Condemned to Death as "my first real play." It was performed in April 1947 at the Dramatic Theater, Stockholm in a widely praised production directed by Alf Sjöberg. The short story on which it is based was written the previous summer and published in the November/December issue of *40-tal* in 1946, prior to its inclusion in *The Games of Night*. In the fashion typical of Dagerman in the hectic early years of his career, he turned the story into a play in three late-night sessions "to the constant accompaniment of strong, bitter Chinese tea, English cigarettes and American jazz records."[6]

The plot of the play is basically the same as that of the short story with the same name. A man found guilty of murdering his wife is reprieved when the executioner is indisposed and at the same time news arrives of a confession by someone else. The man is taken out for a celebratory meal and provided with a whore, but he kills her and is returned to prison, this time unmistakably guilty.

Dagerman was lucky in that Alf Sjöberg's production of *The Man Condemned to Death* was brilliant, creating a mysterious, dreamlike atmosphere appropriate to the Kafkaesque happenings in the play. Later productions elsewhere were generally not nearly so successful, the London production being particularly disastrous.[7] Sjöberg managed to conceal the fact that large portions of the play are static with a strong emphasis on words and ideas rather than on dramatic conflict. The play was awaited with considerable interest by the theatergoing public since Dagerman's reputation, based on *The Snake* and *The Island of the Doomed*, was as a leading "1940s writer" and as such, a radical young man highly critical of establishment values in Sweden and regarded with suspicion by critics and readers of "the old school"; and yet his "first real play" was being performed by the most prestigious Stockholm theater—the Dramatic Theater is in all but name the Swedish National Theater. It was an enormous success and made its author a public figure overnight.

Dagerman suggested in the theater program that the main character could be interpreted as a representative of a whole wartime generation: "And who are the condemned men? They could be soldiers returning home at the end of the war, these men are condemned to death a thousand times who come home from the front with their bodies covered in invisible fatal wounds. The fatal shots were never actually fired, it is true, but the air is thick with the spent lead that is the fear of death. The man condemned to death could be one of these soldiers who have returned home, and he is so surprised to be alive that he is incapable of living. He dies because he is already dead ('a man condemned to death does not die when the axe falls but when the sentence is passed,' a soldier does not survive battles, it just looks as though he does)."[8]

This was the popular interpretation of the play taken up by critics, but there are other possibilities, as the author pointed out. "When I wrote the play I was the man condemned to death myself, of course, that is why I wrote it." In a prologue added to the play but not in the story, however, a man recounts some strange happenings in a nearby park leading to his finding a book entitled: *What Is the Meaning of Death, or Why Do We Live?* This and biblical references in the prologue suggest that the guilt borne by the man condemned to death is Original Sin, so that he can be interpreted as standing for the whole of mankind.

The Man Condemned to Death is an expressionistic play reminiscent of Lagerkvist's dramas, and its logic is that of a symbolic dream rather than of real life as the condemned man seeks a crime which will provide him with something definite to which he can attach the guilt he bears. He cannot understand why the public should fete him after his release when only a few hours before they were convinced of his guilt and the suitability of his punishment: he has not changed at all, so why should their attitude to him change? His emergence through the prison door is a unique happening, since it is unheard of for a condemned man to do anything but enter the prison through that door, never to return; and the door acquires symbolic value. It is echoed in the door to the cell-like room in which Louise, the whore, tries to persuade the condemned man to make love to her before he kills her—an effective scene in which the dramatic tension rises to a climax.

To a reader of the play, the suspense in that scene makes it even more obvious that two earlier scenes were sadly lacking in that quality, and it is evidently thanks to Sjöberg that this was camouflaged in the Stockholm production. One is the prologue, where the first twenty minutes of the play are characterized by a complete lack of action as Petrus merely relates to the warder what strange events had taken place in a nearby park shortly beforehand. The other is the dinner, when the man condemned to death is entertained by the peculiar men who form the Reprieved Club. All of them have narrowly escaped death on some previous occasion and, like the "hero" of the play, all of them are unnamed (in accordance with expressionist conventions). Instead they have titles such as The Explorer, The Almost Crucified, The Duelist, The Rapids Shooter; most of the meal—which is a device to gather characters together and let them talk, an old novelist's trick—is taken up by retelling of the stories surrounding their lucky escapes.

Despite the weaknesses of the play, the subject matter caught the imagination of the theatergoing public—at a time when the Cold War was intensifying and the world was living in constant fear of the atomic bomb, the *Angst* of the man condemned to death found an echo in many people's souls.

The Explorer

The Explorer was published in *40-tal* in the fall of 1947, subtitled "Miniature Drama in Four Acts," and was not actually performed until October 1949, when it was produced in Hälsingborg with moderate success. It appears to be an offshoot of *The Man Condemned to Death*, in which play an Explorer is chairman of the Reprieved Club. There is an element of social criticism in the play—the Explorer does very little himself, is carried everywhere by native bearers, and has a guide who knows "undiscovered" territory well, indeed, has even lived there: nevertheless, the Explorer receives all the credit and the contribution of the servants is unrecognized. More important, however, are the doubts the Explorer has about his calling, first hinted at in the earlier play but expanded here, which create in him strong feelings of *Angst*. He has a great desire to discover new territory, but although he will not acknowledge it, he is aware of the bogus nature of his discoveries: the territories are there in any case, people have visited them before, and there is even a native population. His "discovery" of a territory has no effect on the existence of the area, the only change takes place in the attitude of people toward it—another echo from *The Man Condemned to Death*. In addition to his insecurity based on doubts about the validity of his discoveries, the Explorer is deeply worried about the goal he is ultimately seeking. Having traversed a desert, penetrated a jungle and traveled down a tropical river, the party is now floating out to sea. The Explorer is terrified and has a nightmare during which he emits a shriek. He explains himself afterwards: "I dreamt that we had arrived. I dreamt that we had reached the sea. And that it felt just the same as now"(p. 148).

It is possible to see the Explorer as a representative figure standing for modern man, eager for new experiences but conscious of the fact that they are only "new" from his own point of view. Perhaps most appropriate is an interpretation which sees the Explorer as representing a writer, and more particularly as a projection of Dagerman himself. In "Entrance Lines," Dagerman wrote that "a writer is naturally exposed to constant doubts, as is any traveler (doubts not only about his "calling" but about poetry in general); he is constantly assailed by recriminations which strike at the very core of his existence." The word "traveler" is an odd one to use in the context unless Dagerman was referring particularly to *The Explorer*. When the play was written in 1947, Dagerman's way of life was undergoing great changes following the success of *The Man Condemned to Death*. He was naturally apprehensive about his new life as a successful author in the public eye (although he was equally naturally attracted by some of the trappings of success) and worried about the demands and expectations of his publishers and the reading public: the bestsellers demanded of him need not correspond to what he really wanted to say and the way in which he felt best able to say it.[9] These considerations made the already questionable profession of a writer even more ambivalent. To proceed through life seeking ever new experiences to use as material in one's works, continuing the search for some ultimate meaning, may seem to be an activity of doubtful value when it entices one away from the secure and familiar surroundings of one's origins. On the other hand, failing to respond to the urge to have new experiences, to attempt to fulfill one's potential and to live up to the demands made upon one by circumstances, is also a betrayal.

As a play, *The Explorer* is not particularly outstanding: its main interest lies in the fact that it is the most consistently "de-dramatized" of Dagerman's dramas. It is clearly a difficult play to produce satisfactorily: very little actually happens, the title character spends the first two acts asleep and is dead by the time the fourth act begins—his murder having taken place off-stage. The four acts consist of characters talking to each other, discussing ideas and doing very little. The stage settings are expressionistic "landscapes of the soul" rather than realistic places—the directions describe the desert, the jungle and the tropical river as "every member of the audience's idea of (such a place)" and are clearly not meant to be represented realistically. The Gothenburg production used slides and back projection techniques, a potentially satisfactory solution although the audiences were evidently not very impressed. [10] The play was first broadcast on the radio in 1952, and it may well be that *The Explorer* is best suited to that medium: a stage production needs action and dramatic tension, features which are sadly lacking in this "miniature drama." An outstanding production and a highly effective climax made the first performance of *The Man Condemned to Death* a success and seemed to suggest that Dagerman's theory of the de-dramatized drama might have much to recommend it; *The Explorer* shows that even a short play constructed consistently and exclusively in accordance with the theory has serious defects when it comes to a stage performance.

The Go-Getter

Dagerman's next play, *The Go-Getter*, was in his mind even before the first performance of *The Man Condemned to Death* in April 1947, but it was not completed until the middle of December. The author claimed in an article that he dictated most of the second half of the play to his wife as he drove his car southwards to Paris in November. [11] It is a straightforward propaganda play based on Socialist principles, and was first performed at the Folk Park (i.e., amusement park with open-air stage) in Malmö in May 1948. The production was by Bengt Ekerot and during the summer the company toured Sweden with the play, performing in "folk parks" throughout the land.

The plot is based on the circumstances surrounding a firm in which the author's father worked as a codirector in the 1920s and 1930s. It was run as a workers' cooperative on Syndicalist lines, and Dagerman no doubt heard colorful stories from his father about how one of the group—Blom in the play—was gradually corrupted, betrayed his colleagues, and sold out to capitalist interests, thus securing his advancement. *The Go-Getter* makes the firm an automobile workshop run by four worker-directors; Blom is the go-getter who negotiates with a rich Director behind the back of his colleagues and tricks them into selling the firm to the Director—whereupon he is promoted to manager at an increased salary, overseeing his former friends.

As is usual with propaganda plays of this sort, one's reactions are tempered by one's politics: on the whole, Conservative critics tended to criticize the play, Socialist ones to praise it. Considered as a play, it is competently fashioned but suffers from the faults characteristic of propaganda plays, where everything seems to be colored black or white and people caricatured as The Good Man or The Evil Villain.

Blom is a melodramatic villain, who betrays Socialist principles and becomes a caricatured manipulator-cum-bore-cum-ass—an archetypal rogue, in fact, with a sadistic streak. When he and the Director appear on stage together, one actually has sympathy for the latter, despite the fact that the Director is the caricatured epitome of capitalist villainy. One is clearly meant to sympathize with John Nilsson, the Syndicalist and genuine idealist: however, Nilsson is a wooden figure who does not come to life satisfactorily, a criticism that can fairly be made of all the characters. Parts of the plot seem contrived, and some aspects of the action are imposed without sufficient justification in the body of the play. Åke Lundgren's peculiar hobby of swinging about his working-class flat on a trapeze suspended from the ceiling seems somewhat unorthodox, to say the least, and quite out of keeping with the realism of the rest of the play. One can only assume that it is intended to be a Freudian reference, but neither that nor the opportunity it affords of allowing the author to explain Lundgren's death in terms of picturesque suicide are sufficient grounds.

The Go-Getter is Dagerman's most overtly political work, written at a time when political divisions were appearing among writers of his generation. The journal *40-tal* had ceased to exist; trouble was brewing in the Writers' Union in connection with attitudes to the Soviet Union and the imminent annexation of Czechoslovakia; anarcho-syndicalism and its organ, *Arbetaren*, were being exposed to severe criticism from more conventional Socialists. It is understandable that at this time Dagerman should be keen to write a play so obviously sympathetic to Socialist ideals, and in particular Syndicalist ones. Nevertheless, judged from an artistic point of view, *The Go-Getter* is one of Dagerman's weaker works.

The Shadow of Mart

The Shadow of Mart was written soon after *The Go-Getter* and completed by January 1948,[12] although it was not performed until September of that year when Göran Gentele's production was mounted at the Dramatic Theater, Stockholm—an occasion memorable for the breakthrough as an actor of Per Oscarsson in the leading role of Gabriel.

The play is rather short on action. As the title implies, the martyred hero Mart dominates proceedings although he is already dead. His mother, Mme Angelica, reveres his memory and constantly upbraids Gabriel for failing to measure up to the standards set by his elder brother. Gabriel is shortsighted and shy, not to say cowardly. Eventually he can endure no longer the humiliation heaped upon him by his mother and shoots her. The play ends with a long monologue, the closing minutes of which are enlivened by the appearance of Mart's shadow which grows larger and larger until it dominates the whole stage.

On the page Mme Angelica appears to be a villainous witch hopelessly biased against her younger son, melodramatic in her attempts to belittle him and to glorify the memory of his elder brother—references to people who glorify the exploits and memory of the Second World War are clear. Gabriel gives an actor plenty of opportunity for a virtuoso performance, but there must be a constant danger of overacting since Gabriel's weaknesses are so exaggerated and so stressed, with barely a saving grace on the positive side. The audience is bound to feel sympathy for the wretched man, but their sympathy is in constant danger of becoming mere sentimentality as Gabriel's humiliations multiply. The constant presence of the dead Mart in the background, weighing heavily on Gabriel's shoulders, is skillfully contrived by Dagerman, although the repeated praise of his prowess grows almost as tiring as the unrelieved disasters that combine to form Gabriel's character. The revelation that Mart was not nearly as much of a paragon as was made out does not come as a surprise, although it is undoubtedly a relief.

Too often and for too long, the characters merely talk and not enough happens in the play: the climactic monologue at the end might work well if it were drastically shortened—as it is, the dramatic tension disperses about halfway through and the attention of the audience is inevitably lost. Dagerman falls into the trap primed for any author who tries to write a play strong on ideas and tends to create caricatures rather than rounded characters: the secondary figures of Thérèse and Viktor illustrate the point, but the two major persons are caricatures, too, although the actors have the opportunity to conceal the fact. On the occasion of the first performance they did just that, and Tora Teje as Mme Angelica and Per Oscarsson as Gabriel were generously praised by the critics. *The Shadow of Mart* was by no means a failure, but it was probably made to look better than it actually is by outstanding acting performances.

The Man Condemned to Death and *The Shadow of Mart* were eventually printed together in a volume entitled *Dramas of the Doomed*. By design, the book appeared in the bookshops the week after the first performance of *The Shadow of Mart*—that is, in September 1949. The coupling together of the two plays emphasized the links between them. Just as the earlier play was—on one level—the portrayal of a generation doomed (according to Dagerman) by circumstances and the judgments of others, so the latter play illustrated the unfittedness for life of those who did not die in the war. They may be technically alive, but the sentence of death still hangs over their heads and they are incapable of a normal life. This may seem an unnecessarily gloomy attitude to some observers—but in view of Dagerman's subsequent development and fate, who can say that he did not believe it himself?

No One Goes Free

The novel *A Burnt Child* was Dagerman's most successful work
from the point of view of sales, and a dramatized version of it was
completed early in 1949. Originally entitled *Year of Mourning,* it was
scheduled to be performed for the first time at Malmö in March, in a
production directed by Dagerman himself. In fact the opening was
postponed until April, by which time the title had been changed to
No One Goes Free, a quotation from an exchange between Bengt and his
father in Act II. [13] The part of Bengt was played by Bengt Ekerot, and
it was an open secret that Ekerot, an experienced director, assisted his
friend considerably during rehearsals.

In adapting his novel for the stage Dagerman was naturally forced
to make changes and simplifications which resulted in significant
alterations in character and in the central conflict. The device of
interposing letters written by Bengt, usually to himself, between the
conventionally narrated chapters, so successful in the novel, was
clearly impossible in the theater. Symbols imposed by the narrator in
A Burnt Child had to be abandoned in the play—the tiger and the
gazelle, for instance, and the imagery in the final chapter when the
frozen wilderness melts, the desert blooms and Bengt's emotional
outbursts are compared to volcanoes. The motifs of heat and coldness
were retained, but in simplified form; similarly the subtlety of the
dog symbol had to be made more straightforward—being a present
from a former lover, it simply represents Gun's loose morals and erotic
appeal. These and other enforced changes dictated that Bengt's character should become less complicated, and the maternal theme is
greatly reduced in significance. The search for a mother-substitute is
much less prominent in the play than in the novel and greater stress is
placed on a more rational reason for Bengt's guilt: he refused to go
shopping for his mother on the fatal day, despite the fact that she was
unwell, claiming to be studying although he was actually playing
cards. *No One Goes Free* is thus a comparatively straightforward account of a confused young man with high standards of "purity" who
nevertheless finds that he loves his father's mistress and thus has to
compromise, reluctantly accepting the debased moral standards of his
elders.

Being to a considerable extent relieved of her significance as a mother-figure, Gun is a rather ordinary (if quite sensible) "man-eater." Her erotic desire for Bengt in *No One Goes Free* seems to be on a fairly uncomplicated physical level, and the rumblings of Freudian psychology are little more than a distant echo. As a corollary, Berit's situation as a rival for Bengt's affections is clearer: the Berit of *No One Goes Free* is a stronger, more likable and admirable character than the Berit of *A Burnt Child*. Similarly Knut is more sympathetic in the play than in the novel; he does not need to be so hypocritical about his attitude to his dead wife and his own infidelity is more evenly balanced by the greater stress placed on Alma's adultery. The shift in emphasis makes the insincerity and self-seeking of Knut's sisters of more relevance to the central theme, which is no longer Bengt's inability to distinguish between Gun as a mother and Gun as a mistress but rather the extent to which one's actions after a bereavement are a betrayal of a dead person's memory and that to which they are governed by illusion and hypocrisy. More prominent treatment of the sisters in the novel would have detracted from the core of its meaning; in the play it is appropriate.

No One Goes Free was received warmly but not enthusiastically. It has obvious faults—the staccato dialogue seems terse in the extreme, the verbal repetition is frequently tiresome and some of the symbolic action (such as Bengt's staring out of the window at the butcher's shop and refusing to close the blind) is labored. The first two acts tend to drag, but there is dramatic tension and developing interest as more of the extent of the depression and illusion in the play is revealed: the pace quickens after Gun's appearance in Act III and the progress of the relationship between her and Bengt holds the attention of the audience. Despite its faults, however, *No One Goes Free* is one of the more satisfying of Dagerman's plays. While the novel probed more deeply into the psychology of the main characters and provided Dagerman with a vehicle to display his technical virtuosity, the stage version sensibly simplifies the problems and presents them in a way immediately comprehensible to a live audience. Dagerman's ability to do this confirms that he was already a competent dramatist.

No One Goes Free and *The Go-Getter* were combined in a volume entitled *Judasdramer* [Judas Dramas] and published in April 1949, to coincide with the opening of the former in Malmö.

The Day of Judgment

The Day of Judgment was the last work of creative literature that Stig Dagerman managed to complete. It was commissioned by Herbert Grevenius for the Swedish Radio series of "Peasant Dramas" and first broadcast in May 1952, having been completed during a winter holiday in Norway while Dagerman, Anita Björk, and their newly born daughter were staying with Tarjei Vesaas, the Norwegian novelist, at Ytre Vinje, Norway. It was generally well received, and was produced on stage at the Gothenburg City Theater in October of the same year, without any significant alterations to the text.

In an interview given in connection with the Gothenburg production Dagerman commented on the origins of his plot: "I regard peasant society as my home environment. What happens in *The Day of Judgment* goes back to impressions of my youth on Grandfather's farm—he was a father to me in every way. When he was murdered by a lunatic during my formative years, this was far and away the most important incident of my youth."[14]

Despite the happiness connected with the birth of his daughter and his love for Anita Björk, the time when *The Day of Judgment* was written was a period of distress for Stig Dagerman. He had just informed Ragnar Svanström of his inability to complete a planned novel, and a visit to Paris had failed to produce any more articles for *Expressen.* His negotiations with his wife in his efforts to obtain a divorce were entering a critical stage, and his financial affairs were in chaos. The play thus seems to be yet another of Dagerman's highly personal works, set against an autobiographical background and reflecting the author's own mood at the time of writing.

Every character in *The Day of Judgment* bears a heavy burden of guilt. All have failed to offer support and help, and this failure or betrayal gives them extremely guilty consciences. The question is asked: if this were your last day on earth, what would you do? Each character would like to do some good deed, but in fact they fail in their good intentions.

The Day of Judgment is an odd play. The background is an authentic Uppland farming situation, with realistically convincing characters—rough, brusque, even crude at times yet with a countryman's stubborn superstition and a warm-hearted streak. But Dagerman introduces a strong element of mystery, even mysticism. Someone is hovering outside near the farm—stealing tools, eating eggs, opening doors, knocking on windows. Different people give widely varying descriptions of what must presumably be the same intruder, but although it is fairly obvious from the start that he must be a former lover of Tora's (the daughter of the family), the issue is confused by references by the servant girl to Siv's peculiar father, who is a drunken tinker. To complicate things still further, Magnus, the old farmer, is haunted by Matte, a drunkard for whose death over twenty years previously he feels responsible. Each character sees the ghost created by his or her own particular guilt embodied in the mysterious stranger. There are far too many omens, too much heavy-handed mystery, and the ponderous pace of the play is exaggerated by the static nature of the scenes. *The Day of Judgment* has its effective parts but it would have benefited by being reduced ruthlessly in length and by the removal of excessive omens.

Dagerman himself seemed to be aware of the unsatisfactory nature of the play and called it "a preliminary rehearsal" for what he called "the real peasant play" he planned to write later. It was never written, although a synopsis exists and was published in *Bonniers Litterära Magasin* in 1954 under the title "Snöresan" [The Snow Journey].[15]

There is no doubt that Dagerman had considerable potential as a dramatist—indeed, his achievements make him worthy of mention among the leading half-dozen or so Swedish playwrights this century. His instinctive mastery of language enabled him to create remarkable verbal effects, and while his theories of a "de-dramatized drama" tended to work against him, the discipline of writing a play and taking into account all the time what is practicable in the theater was undoubtedly useful in restraining Dagerman from some of the excesses which are sometimes apparent in his novels. It is doubtful, however, whether he would have developed into a dramatist rather than a novelist first and foremost. His plays have distinct weaknesses and his virtuosity as a master of narrative styles was ideally suited to the prose genres: his plays tend to lack the subtlety of his novels.

Chapter Eight
Marginal Poet

For several years, Dagerman toyed with the idea of publishing a collection of lyric poetry. He never achieved this ambition although two books published after his death contain a representative selection of his achievements in verse. The volume *Vårt behov av tröst* [Our Need of Consolation] has a section containing sixteen poems, almost all of them published previously in various journals and newspapers; the selection includes almost all the best of Dagerman's genuinely lyric poems. The other volume, *Dagsedlar* [Calendar Pages], was edited by Lasse Bergström and Örjan Wallqvist and appeared on the last day of 1954: it contains 152 of the 1,350 or so "daily verses" published during the years 1943–54 in *Arbetaren*.[1]

The daily verses are a good example of occasional poetry and are often of a high standard. Some were written at home and telephoned in to the editor, but many were written amidst the noise and bustle of a crowded newspaper office: even when he was struggling with the tragic inability to write during the last years of his life, Dagerman was still able to produce his daily verses. He would pick an item of current news, which was printed in brief at the head of the poem, then write three or four verses of simple comment—usually ironic but sometimes very moving. The standard varies, of course, but Dagerman's facility with rhyme and rhythm, his instinctive feeling for the *mot juste* and the striking image shows that he had the potential to develop into a poet of rank.

Most of the daily verses are ephemeral, making a political point with wit and, occasionally, venom on such topics as capitalistic excesses, Communist suppression, bureaucracy, the monarchy, nuclear bombs, anti-Semitism, Franco's Spain. The satire is sometimes crude, but usually to the point and thought-provoking. The better poems are not merely witty and sarcastic but show compassion with the wronged, the oppressed, with ordinary people who have suffered in some way at the hands of Authority.

Occasionally a genuine lyric appeared in the familiar spot on page 5 in *Arbetaren* usually reserved for Dagerman's regular verses, such as the beautiful and melancholy "Fall." It was printed only a week before Dagerman died, and seemed to foreshadow his imminent death as it created the autumnal atmosphere in Stockholm, with leaves falling from the trees and dusk gathering: "To die is to go on a journey/ From a branch to the firm ground beneath."[2]

It is obviously impossible to recapture the quality of a poem in translation, but the following versions of typical daily verses—by no means the best or the most lyrical—might serve as examples:[3]

The Holy City

On Christmas Eve two small children
froze to death in a Rome slum

The Holy City was frozen,
The holy night chilly as sin.
Two children froze stiff in a hovel:
They couldn't find room at the inn.

But the stars kept on shining so brightly;
No shepherds came seeking a stall,
There were no three kings: no one noticed
An occurrence of interest at all.

It happens quite rarely that angels
Come singing their songs at your door.
—The Holy City was frozen,
But Holy, the same as before.

                                        28 December 1950

Beware of the Dog!

"It is really scandalous that people
living on National Assistance should
be allowed to keep dogs." —Remark
made by Poor Law official

We all know the law isn't perfect:
The poor are allowed to keep dogs.
Now, the spider's a nice tax-free insect:
They could keep such a pet in their clogs.

Why should people without any money
have big dogs that eat like a horse?
They could play with the flies when it's sunny,
and with rats in the winter, of course.

It's the State that finances this folly,
which means that the tax-payer pays.
Act now or they'll all have, by golly,
an elephant one of these days.

We could clear up the problem quite quickly.
Shoot the dogs! That's what I say!
Then shoot the poor and the sickly:
we'd all save on taxes that way.

5 November 1954

The poems in *Our Need of Consolation* vary from a short, simple lyric like "Bäst är . . ." [It's best . . .] through prose poems reminiscent of Lagerkvist, such as "Människan som älskar" [The Man Who Loves] to the cycle of love poems in free verse entitled "Birgitta Suite." In the later poems, Dagerman is obsessed with death, and the self-reproach so typical of his articles and letters in the 1950s, alternating with enthusiastic outpourings of love, seems a constant background presence. Familiar themes recur, such as this version of "Judge not lest ye be judged" in "Bäst är . . ."

It's best . . .

It's best in good time
To learn to forgive
First the others
Then oneself

It's best to wait too long
To learn to condemn
But if
But when:
Last the others
First oneself

It is a slight poem, but simple and effective.

It is noticeable that while the daily verses are usually rhymed, most of Dagerman's lyrical poems are unrhymed. The rhymes in the former frequently contained a hard-hitting point, rounding off a witty or satirical turn of phrase with a flourish. Dagerman was good at this but seems to have had trouble in using rhyme in other contexts: even when his lyrical poems have a regular meter and orthodox stanza divisions, rhymes are generally absent. When he does rhyme a poem it frequently tends to create embarrassing problems for the poet which are not solved satisfactorily. "Snake in the Grass" (1945) is an effective poem, creating an atmosphere of expectancy and foreboding, while *Angst*, embodied in the snake, lurks in wait for us all over the countryside. Its weakness, however, is most noticeable in the fourth stanza where the rhyme for *tornister* ("haversack") seems very forced: *botanister* ("botanists"). Much better is the powerful poem "The Rat in the Hole," written at the same time, which is unrhymed:[4]

The Rat in the Hole

A memory

The telephone laborers' spades
the newly tarred telegraph poles
the tangles of copper wire
the thermos flasks with too much cream in the coffee
the caps with the badges on the gate post
the dry summer
but all the soggy earth from the freshly dug holes
big white worms so far down

and then one morning a rat at the bottom
and then the sharp axe
the newly sharpened wooden stake

and then the flight of the rat
this threshing circle of rat and stake
and then the bloody end of the stake
and then the rat digging
and the scabby fur wet with clay and blood
and then the reflection in your eye
red blood, yellow clay and this gray circle
and then the surprise of the stake point
        at its contact with the rat's head
and then the green cat
and the stake point's liberation
but not from the blood

and finally
this mistrust of the hole
this mistrust of the pole in the hole
this mistrust of the insulators on the pole in the hole
this mistrust of the cables through the insulators
                on the pole in the hole
this mistrust of the hay wisps on the cables through
                the insulators on the pole in the hole
this mistrust of the rustling of the hay wisps on the
                cables through the insulators on the
                pole in the hole
this mistrust of the humming over the rustling of the
                hay wisps on the cables through the
                insulators on the pole in the hole
this mistrust of the memory of the reflection in an eye
                of the bloody stake end
                and then the stake end's suprise
                at its contact with the rat's head
and then the mistrust of the hole
                which bears the pole
                which holds the insulators
                which breathe the cables
                which lift the hay wisps
                which house the rustling
                which is drowned by the humming
                which is drowned by the little blood-covered
                rat's scream
                and then the reflection in an eye

The opening secton sets a scene in impressionistic fashion, picking out details which stimulate all the senses. The second section is also impressionistic but much more horrific: the hopeless flight of the terrified animal, the deadly weapon in the shape of a sharp-pointed stake, the understated death of the rat as the stake penetrates its brain. The vocabulary in the second section is more emotionally charged than in the previous one: the black and white of the opening becomes blood-red, clay-yellow, fur-gray; the recurring "and then" tends to echo the rat's desperate rushes round and round the bottom of the hole and, in the original Swedish, *s* sounds aid the impression of sharpness in connection with the axe and the stake. The use of "your" in the phrase "and then the reflection in your eye" is subtly effective, suggesting sympathy with the rat as the approaching stake point is reflected in its eye. In the third section the list of associations illustrate Dagerman's hypersensitivity: things apparently remote from the incident are connected with it in the poet's mind by means of a series of associations, suggesting that his whole future life will be affected by memories of the rat's terror as its death approached. Then, finally, the almost startling appearance of verbs for the first time: it is as if the flood-gates of memory have opened and associations come surging out in a fast flow culminating in the first mention of the rat's screams, which is emphasized by virtue of the shortness of the line following after the longest line in the sequence of associations. The last line takes the reader back to the fourteenth line from the end, suggesting that the final sequence is about to begin again—and so on ad infinitum. "The Rat in the Hole" is a disturbing and highly effective poem; the emotion is intense and sincerely felt, the details vivid, the use of the rhythm and sound extremely skillful.

Dagerman's seemingly infinite capacity for finding striking and appropriate images reminds the reader of his Welsh contemporary Dylan Thomas (1914—53). Like Thomas, Dagerman could write superb snatches of poetry when he was able to discipline his talents sufficiently; like Thomas, Dagerman could also ruin a stanza with a striking but inappropriate image. "Birgitta Suite" is a cycle of six poems, full of wistful self-criticism and longing for love, full of effective images—such as this one describing the poet's own weary and frustrated state in 1950, and his longing for love in the period before he met Anita Björk:[5]

> There is a sea where fallen stars can sleep
> When their pain is extinguished for ever.
> I am a fallen star myself, Birgitta.
> I fell wrongly. I fell to earth.
> I am a part of the earth's pain.

In section five, however, some of the imagery jars hopelessly. It starts by describing the beloved as an open book in the poet's hands—a conventional but acceptable image which is soon reversed when he maintains he is an open book in her hands. But then the atmosphere is ruined by the ridiculous image: "I am a serial in the weekly magazine of life./ All we have is the October issue." The idea is appropriate enough, but the Swedish words *föjletong* ("serial"), *veckotidning* ("weekly magazine") and *oktober månads nummer* ("October issue") sound far too mundane in the idyllic context in which they are placed.

Olof Lagercrantz, the editor of *Our Need of Consolation*, is himself a poet and his estimate of Dagerman as a lyricist in his preface to the book is accurate and worth repeating: "In his best moments he was an excellent lyric poet . . . but sometimes his artistic tools, so reliable in fashioning prose, failed him when it came to sculpting poetry."[6] The potential was undoubtedly there: whether Dagerman would eventually have fulfilled it if he had lived is a moot point.

Chapter Nine
The Need for Consolation

The last five years of Stig Dagerman's life were characterized by intensified domestic problems, more frequent periods of depression leading to several suicide attempts, increasing debts, and a whole series of new ideas for books, for many of which he received an advance on royalties although they never progressed far beyond the planning stage.[1]

Feeling tired and depressed after the completion of *Wedding Worries*, Dagerman returned to *Arbetaren* as cultural editor in the beginning of 1950 in the hope that a journalistic routine would help to restore his zest for writing.[2] Edvard Ramström, editor-in-chief of the newspaper at the time, maintains that while Dagerman remained the same likable, shy, and modest person who had become cultural editor in 1945, the old fluency had gone. What he wrote was excellent journalism, but an enormous effort was now needed to produce even a short book review. The big crisis came when Dagerman was required to write an article commemorating the death in February 1925 of Hjalmar Branting, the former Social Democratic Prime Minister of Sweden. Dagerman struggled with the article for days but failed to produce anything satisfactory; his despair led to a nervous breakdown and he received hospital treatment in Stockholm.[3]

At the end of May the Dagerman family traveled to the Austrian Tyrol. The relaxation seemed to have the desired effect, and Dagerman was soon working on a translation into Swedish of the Norwegian novelist Tarjei Vesaas's work *Bleikeplassen* [The Bleaching Place]; by the end of June he felt well enough to embark upon a new novel of his own which had been in his mind for some time. Dr. Svanström was delighted but solicitous, wondering whether his protégé's health was really up to the strain; but he was justifiably enthusiastic about the planned novel, which was to be called *En hund begraven* [A Dog Buried].[4] Dagerman's letters reveal his own excitement about a book that was to be a political satire set in the future, in the spirit of such works as Huxley's *Brave New World*, Orwell's *1984*, and Karin Boye's *Kallocain*. By the beginning of September Dagerman was able to send his publisher the typescript of the opening chapter, which describes an interview by "teliviphone"—a cross between a television and a telephone—between the author, Corporal Dagerman of the Writers' Corps, and the censor, a General Pompell, of the "Language Defense Force." The latter tries to compel Corporal Dagerman to make preposterously silly changes in a text he has written, which the corporal naturally refuses to do. As a result, he explains at the end of the chapter, "Darkness and silence settled over the room. I was alone. I was alone and a nine-year career as an author was over." (The book is set in 1955, and the details of Corporal Dagerman's life and career correspond with those of the real Stig Dagerman.)

The novel was planned to become an attack on Soviet satellites and what Dagerman called "semi-democracies," and to include some satirical comments on contemporary Swedish politics. In subsequent chapters it was to deal with a thesis submitted at the University of Leningrad entitled "Are Dachsunds Necessary?"; since the answer was negative, it became necessary to examine the position of dachsunds throughout the civilized world. The plot was to concentrate on matters affecting a dog cemetery in Sundbyberg, a district of Stockholm which had become "a restricted area with compulsory visas, flying morality police, Freedom Comissioners and Boards for the Distribution of Citizens' Happiness, full of experts, expertists and expertitists as well as geniuses of the 1st, 2nd and 3rd salary grades." An official of the cemetery was to become, inadvertently, leader of a resistance group and his home would develop into a haven for the free dachsunds of Sundbyberg until his treachery was discovered. After being chased and drowned in a nearby river, his death would become "a triumph for freedom" when a saboteur released all dachsunds on the day of the funeral and they proceeded to follow him to his grave.

The completed section is witty and amusing, the frequently absurd humor reminiscent of the tone adopted so successfully in the author's "daily verses" and characterized by subtle linguistic inventiveness. Its topicality and playful tone seemed to indicate that *A Dog Buried* was destined to be a bestseller—just the thing needed to restore Dagerman's confidence. Hardly had the first chapter been received by Norstedts, however, when Dagerman wrote to inform them he was incapable of writing any more of the book and was abandoning the project.[5] Ragnar Svanström arranged to have the completed chapter printed in the final issue of the journal *Prisma*, and it was eventually included in the posthumous collection of Dagerman's writings edited by Olof Lagercrantz, *Our Need of Consolation*.[6] Lagercrantz places it in the short-story section, and it is not clear to the reader that "A Dog Buried" is in fact the first chapter of a planned novel—although its incomplete nature is obvious.

The following year, 1951, was critical. Dagerman had left his wife and family, a situation which troubled his conscience deeply, and the inevitable arguments over a protracted divorce settlement left him in a depressed state. The family home was sold, resulting in a loss of some 50,000 crowns, and the total amount Dagerman owed his publishers seems to have been approaching six figures by now, and rising.[7] Although Norstedts realized that they could recoup the debts in the long term through profits on the sales of Dagerman's books, they badly needed action in the short term—and understandably, pressure was put on the author to complete one of the various projects he claimed to have in hand. Unfortunately for them, Dagerman was now living with Anita Björk and finding in their mutual happiness a shelter from more worrying aspects of his life. Although his inability to concentrate on completing a book nagged his conscience, Dagerman was cushioned from the financial implications of his failure by the fact that Anita Björk's career was at its peak and her income was more than adequate for them both. The pattern of his life seemed now to be established as a series of happy moments alternating with periods of deep despair.

In an effort to regain his self-respect as a writer and ease the pressure being placed on him by his publishers, Dagerman made an attempt to write a book based on his voyage to Australia in 1949, to be called *Full orkester* [Full Orchestra] and due for publication in October.[8] Assurances made to Norstedts that Dagerman was "writing at full steam" contrasted strangely with rumors in the press suggesting that he was spending all his time at bohemian parties in theatrical circles in southern Sweden. In mid-September Dagerman informed Norstedts that he was unable to finish the novel. He was fully aware of the desperate situation he was creating for himself, but felt helpless to do anything about it; comments made by people who knew him at this time confirm that he seemed desperate, and frequently refer to his being at times in an almost trancelike state as if his worldly affairs could no longer touch him. "I feel like the worst kind of confidence trickster," Dagerman wrote to Ragnar Svanström. "If I didn't have Anita by my side I wouldn't know which way to turn."[9]

Only one page of this projected novel exists, a typewritten sheet in Norstedts archives:

The Traveler

I am leaving behind solid dreams and loose connections. I am leaving a promising career which promised me self-respect and general acclaim. I am leaving a bad reputation and the promise of an even worse one. I am leaving a few hundred thousand words, some written in moments of happiness, most in misery and for money. I am leaving a chaotic financial situation, a vacillating stand on the important questions of the day, some second-hand skepticism in good condition, and a hope of liberation.

I am taking with me on the journey some useless knowledge about the globe, some superficial reading in philosophy and the Third Point of View [i.e., Swedish neutrality], a longing for annihilation and a hope of liberation. I am also taking a pack of cards, a typewriter and an unhappy love of European youth. And finally, I am taking with me the vision of a tombstone, raised in the desert or on the bed of the ocean, and bearing the following inscription:

HERE LIES

A SWEDISH AUTHOR

HE DIED IN VAIN

THE CRIME WAS INNOCENCE

FORGET HIM OFTEN

THE WORLD SITUATION RAISED THIS MEMORIAL.

The inscription is of course a parody on the famous poem by Erik Blomberg on the Ådalen riots of 1931, when troops opened fire on demonstrators and killed five people, after which the Social Democrats came to power in Sweden and ruled virtually without interruption until 1976.[10]

But 1952 started more hopefully, with the completion of the radio play *Den yttersta dagen* [The Day of Judgment]. Any euphoria produced by this achievement appears to have been shortlived, however, for March saw the publication of Dagerman's moving article "Our Need of Consolation Is Boundless."[11] It is a beautifully written essay, but ominous and frightening, full of self-condemnation and thoughts of suicide:

I can sit in front of a fire in the most secure of rooms and suddenly sense how death is surrounding me on all sides. It is in the fire, in all the sharp objects around me, in the weight of the roof and the mass of the walls, it is in the water, in the snow, in the heat and in my blood. What is human security if not a consolation for the fact that death is so close to life—and what a poor consolation which only reminds us of the thing it is trying to make us forget!"

What seemed to hurt the author most was his conviction that he had failed to live up to his talent, and by doing so had failed himself and all those who believed in him. "I am such a slave to my talent," he wrote, "that I dare not use it for fear of having lost it." This causes depression, but he becomes a slave to depression since he hopes to make artistic use of it: it is a vicious circle and he seems unable to break out. His conclusion is ominous: "I seem to realize that suicide is the only proof of human freedom."

The general air of depression lingered until the spring of 1954, when prospects suddenly became hopeful once more. After a series of projects that came to nothing, Dagerman began to plan an ambitious novel on a large scale, based on the tragic life of the Swedish Romanticist turned Realist C. J. L. Almqvist (1793 – 1866), and he actually managed to complete the prologue.[12] Anita Björk recalls[13] how her husband was so delighted at concluding a whole chapter successfully that he woke her up in the middle of the night, eyes sparkling with joy and relief, carrying into their bedroom a tray containing coffee, cakes, and a burning candle—the last word had just been typed, and such an achievement called for celebrations! Unfortunately, Dagerman was unable to progress any further with the planned novel, and all that remained among his papers when he died were a few sketches for later chapters, notably a few pages about the American Civil War.

The prologue, which does not refer directly to Almqvist at all, was published posthumously under the title *Tusen år hos Gud* [A Thousand Years with God], and was lavishly praised—excessively so for a fragment which is undoubtedly clever and witty but rather contrived. Be that as it may, the potential for it to develop into a successful novel of high quality is undoubtedly there.[14]

There is a directness and precise simplicity of language in the fragment which suggests a development of the style the author adopted in *A Burnt Child*; however, whereas the earlier novel is predominantly realistic, *A Thousand Years with God* is decidedly surrealistic. The prologue describes a meeting between Sir Isaac Newton and God, who comes to earth in the guise of Claes Jensen, a sailmaker, and has to endure a series of tribulations as an introduction to the human condition. The nature of these representative human experiences show how pessimistic Dagerman's view of life had become. Jensen is first beaten and spat upon by a servant, the suggestion being that man must learn to endure the most absurdly unjust punishment and humiliation without retaliating. He is then terrified by being placed in a room with a snake, his introduction to the fear and *Angst* which are inseparable from human existence. When he attempts to secure justice for a black convict who has been wrongly imprisoned, the only gratitude he receives is to have his hand bitten by the victim. He finds that love is illusory when, in a scene reminiscent of Almqvist's novel *Drottningens juvelsmycke* [The Queen's Necklace, 1834], the girl to whom he has sworn lasting love proves to be a lay figure. Finally, the food he eats to satisfy his hunger is disgustingly filthy and served in the most humiliating circumstances. Newton emphasizes the moral: "Do not put thy trust in the goodness of man but learn to love a beggar's food."

Humiliation, terror, betrayal, degradation: such is the lot of the mere human. Repeatedly Jensen is given cause to hope—but always his optimism is dashed. The themes are familiar ones in Dagerman's works, the surprise being what Newton calls the "impossibility of Love." The author's love for Anita Björk was well known; however, by 1954 Stig Dagerman's depressions and periods of mental instability were getting worse and he acquired an obsessive jealousy of his wife, being convinced that she was having an affair with almost every leading man she played against, on stage or screen.[15] It seems that he was beginning to doubt whether even his wife's love could save him.

Stig Dagerman could not believe in a god, but the vain search for consolation in religion, noticeable in *Wedding Worries*, is continued with the Almqvist fragment. *A Thousand Years with God* can be read as the desperate assertion of a tortured soul that even if God exists, he is helpless to assist humans in distress. God's powers are severely limited, according to Dagerman, by the fact that his creation of the world automatically places him outside it. The tragic circumstance at the heart of the prologue is God's inability qua creator to be a part of creation. When he takes on the identity of the sailmaker Claes Jensen he is tortured and humiliated as may perhaps fit a human but as cannot befit a god: the only weapon with which God can assert his true superiority is the miracle—but for a god to bring about miracles is merely to underline the fact that he is remote from humanity, and that the gap can never be bridged.

A Thousand Years with God is a deeply pessimistic fragment, but the mood is not all gloom. There is considerable humor in the basic symbol, which is the reversal of Newton's law of gravitation. Newton's servant enters his master's room and is perturbed to find himself floating up to the ceiling; all dropped objects join the servant up aloft instead of falling to the ground, with amusing consequences. When Newton dies, the English establishment—especially the church—is horrified to discover that although normal gravitation has been restored in general, his body and the coffin in which it is placed rise to a height of about three feet and can only be made to sink to the ground when they are draped with coils of enormously heavy chain. The absurdity and irony of the scene are most appealing.

Ragnar Svanström tried to persuade Dagerman to persevere with the Almqvist novel, but it was finally shelved in August 1954.[16] Dagerman seems to have decided that he was now beyond redemption. In the last weeks of his life he made several suicide attempts in his garage, blocking doors and windows and starting the engine of his car. Usually he switched off the engine before being affected too seriously by the fumes, but on the night of 4 November 1954, he left the switching off of the engine too late and was discovered the next day by his son, lying dead over the front seat. He had tried to scramble out of the car but was overcome by monoxide fumes. He was buried in Stockholm on 12 November. The funeral was an elaborate affair, with funeral orations by Ragnar Svanström, Evert Arvidsson, Lars Ahlin, Bengt Ekerot, Tore Zetterholm, and Bo Setterlind; the list of those present reads like a catalog of leading Swedish cultural figures of the time.

In November 1964, the author's remains were transferred from Danderyd cemetery and reburied in his home village of Älvkarleby. Stig Dagerman would certainly have approved of this action, initiated by relatives: he was never completely at home in Stockholm, and an essential part of his character remained unchanged as the simple country boy from a small Upland community, bewildered and un-comfortable in the sophisticated bustle of life in the capital.

Chapter Ten
Epilogue

Very occasionally a writer emerges and, seemingly over-night, captures the attention and imagination of a nation or a generation; his works strike a chord in the collective consciousness of his contemporaries, who can identify and sympathize with his characters. Stig Dagerman was such a writer in the Sweden of the late 1940s, and the main theme of his works which aroused such sympathetic reaction was *Angst*. The possessor of outstanding natural talents as a narrator, Dagerman was able to exploit his own psychological handicap and place it in the context of the deep-seated unrest and anxiety that followed in the wake of the Second World War, producing novels and stories widely considered to be among the finest of their period in Swedish.

In the years that have passed since Dagerman was most active as a writer, *Angst* has not receded as a characteristic of modern life—rather has it become more marked, more extreme. The world totters from one crisis to another as the weapons of destruction become potentially more devastating, the environment more threatened, and the pressures of day-to-day life more intolerable. On 17 July 1980, an editorial in the *New York Times* commented on the anxieties of contemporary existence and the increasingly widespread use of drugs to enable individuals to cope with the stress of everyday living, stating: "Incredibly, more than 20 million Americans are expected to take a single tranquilizer— Valium—during the year." This would seem to suggest that the subject matter of Stig Dagerman's books is at least as relevant today as it was in the 1940s.

As is frequently the case with highly praised writers, however, Dagerman's stature suffered somewhat in the years following his death. In view of the much-publicized nature of his life and his sensational suicide it is understandable that many people were preoccupied with such aspects rather than with his works.

In December 1954 Dr. Ragnar Svanström, Dagerman's friend and publisher, collected three of his own newspaper articles and published them in the form of a booklet, which was distributed as a "Christmas gift" by Norstedts. The title, *Stig Dagerman. Några minnesbilder* [Stig Dagerman. Some Memories], gives an indication of the contents: in some twenty pages of text Svanström provides interesting snippets of biographical detail but makes no attempt to discuss Dagerman's works. In 1958 Olof Lagercrantz published his eagerly awaited biography, entitled simply *Stig Dagerman*. Lagercrantz was given access to Norstedts archives and to various letters and papers possessed by Dagerman's family and friends; his conclusion was that Dagerman's problems were mainly psychological and that his debts, pressure from publishers, expectations of readers and critics, and his marital difficulties were all of minor importance. This view naturally did not satisfy everyone, and indeed it does seem that Lagercrantz may have underestimated some or all of the secondary factors; nevertheless, there is little doubt that the main trend of his conclusions is correct.

It is tempting to dwell on this aspect of Stig Dagerman, but his chief significance for posterity depends upon his literary achievements. Apart from a brief discussion of the fragment *A Thousand Years with God* Lagercrantz makes no attempt in his biography to analyze any of the works save the novel he considers to be Dagerman's finest achievement, *The Island of the Doomed*. Many serious students of literature would agree with this judgment, but the novel happens also to be the most difficult of Dagerman's works to read and understand: there was very little reaction to Lagercrantz's comments on *The Island of the Doomed*, and no book devoted to Dagerman was published for another seventeen years.

In Swedish literary histories stress is generally placed on two aspects of Dagerman's works: the extent to which they are typical of 1940s writing and the suggestion that they indicate an enormous natural talent which was not always sufficiently disciplined and, in view of the author's early death, did not live up to its full potential. [1]

Until the late 1950s the only criticism of Dagerman's works apart from that included in literary histories appeared in newspaper and magazine articles. What was needed was serious and rigorous study in depth to demonstrate the subtlety and the wide-ranging variations on

the theme of *Angst*, which, together with an extraordinary command
of narrative techniques, made Dagerman one of the foremost Swedish
writers of this century with a timeless appeal over and above his
representative status as a man of the 1940s. Such studies began to be
made in the 1960s,[2] and in 1969 Hans Sandberg completed the first
postgraduate thesis on Dagerman. This concentrated on political
aspects of the works and included penetrating analyses of *The Snake*
and *The Island of the Doomed*. Especially in the case of the latter novel
Sandberg was able to demonstrate that the political and social arguments were more solidly based in Anarcho-Syndicalist theory and
more consistently developed than had previously been properly realized. The publication of Sandberg's book *Den politiske Stig Dagerman*
[The Political Stig Dagerman] in 1979, based on his thesis, has made
this material more readily accessible. In 1970 Ola Løsløkk's study of
The Island of the Doomed [3] tended to confirm Lagercrantz's judgment
that the imagery was more controlled than had widely been assumed,
and the depth and richness of this novel began to be clearer. Shortly
beforehand, in 1969, Egil Törnqvist had published a study of *A Burnt
Child* and concluded:

Stig Dagerman is usually reckoned among the natural talents in Swedish
literature. There is no doubt a certain amount of truth in this: we know that
he often wrote his books at express speed. But it would be of course naive to
believe that creating a book is synonymous with writing it down. *A Burnt
Child* is, as we have seen, composed in very calculated fashion, even in
details. The novel hardly gives the impression of having been conceived in a
state of inspired trance. Perhaps there are grounds for revising our view of
Dagerman as the Umballa of the 1940s.[4]

In the 1970s a few scholars outside Scandinavia began to take a
serious interest in the works of Stig Dagerman. Notable among them
was the Belgian Georges Périlleux, whose doctoral dissertation (presented in 1975) placed Dagerman in the context of French Existentialism and illuminated the philosophical side of Dagerman's writings.[5]
Interest was shown also in England, France, Czechoslovakia, and
Italy. What was most significant about work done on Dagerman in
the 1970s was that scholars were finding sufficient material to justify

serious investigation of Dagerman's works per se, not merely as examples of the 1940s style.

Meanwhile Dagerman's prose works had remained in print more or less constantly in Sweden and had continued to sell.[6] Significantly, perhaps, the least-read novel is *The Island of the Doomed*—the one which has attracted most attention from scholars, but all four novels and the short-story collection *The Games of Night* were published in cheap, popular editions in the 1960s and 1970s, film versions were made of *The Snake* and *Wedding Worries*, and television dramatizations of some of the short stories proved popular in the late 1970s. Impressed by the continuing and widespread interest shown in Dagerman, Norstedts embarked in 1981 on the publication of a critical edition of his collected works in eleven volumes, edited by Hans Sandberg.

While Dagerman's verse is often competent and at times effective, and while his potential as a playwright was considerable, it is on his prose works that his ultimate reputation must depend. It is not difficult to find aspects of these which invite criticism. It is impossible completely and convincingly to defend his tendency to wallow in sex, violence, and death, a habit which sometimes results in aspects of his plo.; becoming overloaded with perversions and bizarre behavior—a friend unacquainted with Dagerman reading the manuscript of this book was baffled by a typing error in the plot section of *The Island of the Doomed* and commented that he would not be surprised to learn that the hero had been raped by a tadpole. It should not be overlooked that the "hard-boiled" nature of the action is sometimes exaggerated on purpose in the interests of parody, and frequently a surrealistic impression is part of the aim. Nevertheless, even allowing for the philistinism which occasionally lies behind criticism of this nature, there is no doubt that Dagerman is sometimes overindulgent. At times, too, Dagerman is carried away by his fondness for striking images which evidently came so readily to his mind, and the result borders on the grotesque.

It is to be hoped, however, that the scholarly criticism of Stig Dagerman's works will have persuaded potential readers that he wrote exciting and stimulating books worthy of much greater attention than has been devoted to them so far. The only prose works by Dagerman published in book form in Britain and the United States are the novel *A Burnt Child* (1950) and a selection of stories and essays entitled *The Games of Night* (1959), while *The Condemned*, a version of Dagerman's play *Den dödsdömde*, was included in an American volume of Scandinavian plays (1951). Dagerman has fared better in Germany and, more particularly, in France, where most of his prose writings are available in translation[7] and he has acquired the enthusiastic support of the vociferous novelist J. M. G. le Clézio.[8]

Even in translation the positive attributes of Dagerman's stylistic facility are striking. He seems to have an effortless command of the whole range of styles from naturalism to surrealism and expressionism, from dialect and slang to the lyrical and the rhapsodic. Despite the impression of spontaneous outpourings which is sometimes given by his very fluency, research has shown that there is consistent intellectual control over the imagery and ideas in the best of Dagerman's works—a feature clearest perhaps in *The Island of the Doomed* and *A Burnt Child* but by no means absent from other novels. Even in *Wedding Worries*, where Dagerman admitted he was intentionally creating an atmosphere of confusion, the control over symbolism and motifs is much tighter than appears to be the case at first: here as elsewhere the lack of strict discipline is at the comparatively superficial level of incidental detail. Dagerman claimed more than once that he generally preferred to write quickly, with a minimum of linguistic revision, since he wanted to create an impression of lively and fresh spontaneity rather than of carefully polished but relatively lifeless prose. As Törnqvist pointed out, actually writing down a novel is not the same thing as creating it.

While few of Dagerman's works end happily, there is more humor in his style than he is generally given credit for, and all his novels abound in irony. Although the satire in his "daily verses" is sometimes crude, it is frequently apposite and effective—and ought to warn the readers of his novels and stories that there is often much more in an apparently straightforward statement or incident than meets the eye. The narrative technique is seldom uncomplicated in a work of Dagerman's and is used to comment or enlarge upon the story being told in such a way that the form becomes inseparable from the content.

Dagerman's novels and the best of his stories can be read on a number of levels. He is always enquiring about the meaning of life; in concluding that there is none he is clearly much influenced by contemporary Existentialist philosophy and the mood of the 1940s, but who can claim that the intervening years have produced evidence to refute such pessimism? True to his Anarcho-Syndicalist politics, Dagerman never falters in his consistent and fierce defense of individual freedom. Like his mentors in both these movements Dagerman concludes paradoxically that there can nevertheless be a meaning in life for an individual in a social context. Life itself may be meaningless just as conventional values are pointless if based on ideas or systems which have failed to take account of their fundamental lack of meaning: but there *is* meaning in compassion, in love, in solidarity with the lonely and oppressed. Dagerman's works always advocate such virtues. He deals with fundamental questions of morality, but always places such problems in a social context and always expresses his ideas fervently and passionately in a fashion which convinces.

Dagerman's mastery of narrative technique and his advocacy of ideas worth considering seriously constitute an important part of his status as a writer; however, he would not be as outstanding as he is were it not for his ability to create convincing, living characters and authentic environments. Dagerman possesses to an unusual degree the natural storyteller's eye for pertinent detail. Anita Björk maintains that to visit a place or to go for a walk with Stig Dagerman and to experience it through his eyes (and ears!) was a revelation: he would pick unerringly on characteristics which immediately encapsulated the spirit of a scene as well as its appearance.[9] The technique is apparent in innumerable places in his works—the barrack room and mess in the second part of *The Snake*, for instance, which not only looks authentic but somehow exudes also the atmosphere created as a result of its being used by generations of bored and frustrated conscripts; or the funeral at the beginning of *A Burnt Child*, where the atmosphere of the apartment before the guests proceed to the black cars against the snowy white background is imbued with suggestions of excessive ceremony, hypocrisy, feigned emotion, and restless boredom as well as genuine grief. Even when a scene is surrealistic Dagerman highlights details which linger in the mind, such as the hideously ugly and repulsive (and potentially dangerous) iguanalike lizards and the ominous blind seagulls which inhabit *The Island of the Doomed*. In these environments Dagerman places rounded characters splendidly memorable in their apparently contradictory strengths and weaknesses—the marvelously outrageous yet pathetic Knut in "Where Is My Iceland Jumper?", for instance, or Hildur in *Wedding Worries*, an intriguingly human mixture of resoluteness, compassion, love, fear, and resignation.

It has long been recognized in Scandinavia that Stig Dagerman was a writer of outstanding natural talents, although acknowledgment of the true stature of his actual achievements has been slower in coming. In an age dominated by existential *Angst*, Dagerman's works have a relevance which suggests they are worthy of much wider recognition. The time is ripe to acclaim Stig Dagerman as one of Sweden's most important twentieth-century novelists.

Notes and References

Chapter One

1. Karl Vennberg, "Den moderna pessimismen och dess vedersakare," *40-tal* 1 (1946):5.
2. Albert Camus, "Sisyfosmyten," *40-tal* 8 (1946):304—6.
3. Karl Vennberg, "Franz Kafka," *Horisont* 5 (1944):39—55; "Inledning till Kafka," *40-tal* 2 (1945):1—13; *Den sanningssökande hunden och Förvandlingen* (Stockholm: Forum, 1945; (with Caleb J. Anderson) *Processen* (Stockholm: Wahlström & Widstrand, 1945).
4. For further information about the three writers mentioned see the following volumes in the Twayne World Authors Series: *Vilhelm Moberg* (by Philip Holmes, TWAS 584, 1980), *Eyvind Johnson* (by Gavin Orton, TWAS 150, 1972), *Pär Lagerkvist* (by Robert Spector, TWAS 267, 1973).
5. For further information about Ahlin see the *Lars Ahlin* volume in the Twayne World Authors Series (by Torborg Lundell, TWAS 430, 1977).
6. Unless otherwise stated the biographical material in this section is based on (1) accounts in Olof Lagercrantz, *Stig Dagerman* (Stockholm, 1958); Hans Sandberg, "Det frihetliga alternativet," (Ph.D. dissertation, University of Uppsala, 1969); (2) correspondence and memoranda in Norstedts archives, Stockholm; (3) information supplied to me by Annemarie Dagerman. See Chronology for details about Dagerman's changes in his surname.
7. Stig Dagerman, "Ett barns memoarer," *All Världens Berättare* 3 (1948); reprinted in *Vårt behov av tröst* (Stockholm, 1955), pp. 11—21.
8. This incident is treated in considerable detail in Jonas Sima, "Första akten i författardramat Stig Dagerman," *Arbetaren* 21 (1962).
9. Dagerman's links with anarcho-syndicalism are discussed in detail by Hans Sandberg in his dissertation (see note 6) and his book *Den politiske Stig Dagerman* (Stockholm, 1979). An account in English of this and similar movements is to be found in George Woodcock, *Anarchism* (Cleveland: Meridean Books, 1962).

Chapter Two

1. See Bengt Bernholm, "Vår yngste dramatiker," *Veckojournalen* 2 (1947):26, 44, 45.
2. Ibid.

3. Stig Dagerman, "Orm i gräset," *40-tal* 4 (1945):15. Reprinted in *Vårt behov av tröst,* p. 187.

4. Stig Dagerman, "Diktaren och samvetet," *40-tal* 6 (1945):1–7. Reprinted in *Vårt behov av tröst,* pp. 217–26.

5. Stig Dagerman, "Min synpunkt på anarkismen," *40-tal* 2 (1946): 56–59. Reprinted in *Vårt behov av tröst,* pp. 227–32. Gunnar Ekelöf (1907–1968) was also a passionate believer in individual freedom and independence of thought, and frequently made statements in his poems of which Dagerman and other Anarcho-Syndicalists would have approved. "De folkhemske" in *Non serviam* (1945) criticizes the paternal state, for instance, while a poem of particular interest in the present context is "Till det omöjligas konst" [To the Art of the Impossible] in *En natt i Otočac* (1961).

6. E.g., hb (= Hugo Bergh), "Ett överflödigt bokalster," *Sydsvenska Dagbladet Snällposten* 6 December 1945; Michel Mohrt, "La difficulté d'être Suédois," *Le figaro littéraire,* 1 September 1966.

7. In this and subsequent quotations from and references to *Ormen* the figures in parentheses refer to the page number in the 1955 edition, published by Norstedts.

8. Dagerman wrote a poem about the incident, "Råttan i gropen. Ett minne," *40-tal* 4 (1945):14–15. Reprinted in *Vårt behov av tröst,* pp. 185–86. The poem is translated on p. 128–29 of this book.

9. "Nattens lekar" in *Nattens lekar,* Stockholm, 1947, p. 12.

10. Unless otherwise stated all comments attributed to Annemarie Dagerman were made in conversation with Laurie Thompson in January 1975.

11. See p. 10 above.

12. See note 5.

13. Stig Dagerman, "De tidigt dödsdömda," *Arbetaren,* 10 March 1945.

14. "Min synpunkt på anarkismen"; see note 5.

15. E.g., anon., "40-talist läser klassiskt, Goethe blir ofta utsliten," *Dagens Nyheter,* 6 September 1946.

Chapter Three

1. Not many "daily verses" from 1946 are accessible now to anyone unable to peruse the files of *Arbetaren.* Olof Lagercrantz quotes two on Franco on pp. 227–28 of his biography (30 January 1946, 28 March 1946), and Sandberg also prints the former on p. 120 of his bibliography.

2. Of the three poems from 1946 in *Dagsedlar* (Stockholm, 1954), two refer to the Nuremberg trials—'Samvetet i Nürnberg" (5 June 1946) and "Ångestens demokrati" (4 October 1946).

3. In *Den politiske Stig Dagerman* Hans Sandberg explains that while Dagerman's fellow Anarcho-Syndicalists deplored the barbarity of the Nazis, they felt that the new system of government imposed by the victorious Allies was not a satisfactory replacement insofar as the individual was still dominated and manipulated by a central authority. Punishing Germans who had been conditioned to obey orders was not tackling the root cause of the problem: to do that would need a revolutionary reform of the social and governmental systems even in parliamentary democracies.

4. Sune Stigsjöö, "Jag mötte den dödsdömde på Drottninggatan," *Husmodern* 35 (1947).

5. Dagerman's original contract for the novel was with Steinsviks and refers to a work entitled *Kampen om lejonet*. The title is retained in correspondence throughout the summer between Dagerman and Knut Korfitsen, the publisher's reader assigned to the task by Norstedts. This information is taken from material in Norstedts Archives, which will be referred to in subsequent notes as (NA).

6. An account of the summer on Kymmendö is given by Werner Aspenström in his book *Sommar* (Stockholm: Bonniers, 1968), pp. 57−71.

7. Ibid., p. 65; see also Urban Stenström, "Nattforcering med radiomusik för Dagermans 'Bröllopsbesvär,' " *Svenska Dagbladet*, 6 December 1949.

8. "Jag har bytt namn på härligheten—De dömdas ö, tycker du det är bättre eller sämre eller lika likgiltigt som det gamla, Kampen om lejonet?" The letter, which accompanied the completed manuscript, is not dated, nor is it addressed to a particular person. It is, however, almost certainly to Knut Korfitsen and probably dates from late July (NA).

9. In her article "Djuret och skräcken. En studie i Stig Dagermans författarskap," *Samlaren* 1965, pp. 96−114, Agneta Pleijel suggests that the motto is reminiscent of a statement by Kant: "Two things fill my soul with ever new and ever increasing admiration and awe the more often and the more assiduously I reflect upon them: the starry heavens above me and the moral law inside me." There may be an intentional reference, but it would be unlike Dagerman to refer to German philosophers in detail and there is no evidence to support the suggestion.

10. Here and in connection with all subsequent quotations from and references to *De dömdas ö*, the figure in parenthesis refers to the page number in the 1946 edition published by Norstedts.

11. Dagerman told several interviewers in 1947 that he felt he had little in common with Sartre (e.g., Stigsjöö—see note 4). In 1975 Georges Périlleux presented his doctoral thesis in Belgium on the relationship

between Dagerman and the French Existentialists and concluded that although there are similarities between Dagerman's work and the thought of Sartre and Camus, their influence is limited. "It is most often a case of assimilating impulses which the man's temperament made him predisposed to absorb, and reproducing them in a personal synthesis," Périlleux maintains.

12. The extract is taken from p. 14 of Mairet's introduction to his own translation of Sartre's *L'Existentialisme est un humanisme*: J. P. Sartre, *Existentialism and Humanism* (London: Methuen, 1948).

13. Karl Vennberg, "Den moderna pessimismen och dess vedersakare," *40-tal* 1 (1946):1−11.

14. Hans Sandberg, "De dömdas ö—en politisk idéroman," *Samlaren* 1972, pp. 62−90. A slightly modified form of the essay is incorporated in Sandberg's book *Den politiske Stig Dagerman*, pp. 61−107.

15. See p. 31 above.

16. E.g., Staffan Björck, "Den dödsdömde," *Dagens Nyheter*, 26 September 1958.

17. For a detailed discussion of the animal imagery in *The Island of the Doomed* see the article by Agneta Pleijel referred to in note 9.

18. Olof Lagercrantz, "Drama om skuld och gemenskap," *Dagens Nyheter*, 18 June 1956; cf. also p. 148 of Lagercrantz's biography.

Chapter Four

1. Memorandum by Ragnar Svanström, 11 March 1947 (NA).

2. Letter from Dagerman to Herr Selander, 22 July 1947 (NA).

3. Stig Dagerman, *Tysk höst* (Stockholm, 1947), p. 15.

4. E.g., Kai Henmark, "Dagerman och religionen," *Dagstidningen* 8 July 1957; reprinted in Henmark's *En fågel av eld* (Stockholm, 1962), pp. 122−27.

5. The typescripts and draft contents lists were kindly made available to me by Annemarie Dagerman.

6. Unless otherwise acknowledged statements here and on subsequent pages about autobiographical content are based on information in Lagercrantz's biography, Sandberg's dissertation, and on my conversations with Annemarie Dagerman.

7. Here and in connection with all subsequent quotations from and reference to *Nattens lekar*, the figure in parentheses refers to the page number in the 1947 edition published by Norstedts.

8. The phrase is used in an autobiographical sketch quoted by Lagercrantz on p. 236 of his biography.

9. Besides Lagercrantz's book, the autobiographical background to "Bon soir" is referred to in Dagerman's own article "När jag var båtbud," *Pressbyrån* 6 (1952). Dagerman mentions the incident with the waitress in "Entrérepliker," *Prisma* 2 (1948). "Bon soir" won first prize in a literary competition held in the spring of 1947 (the prize was awarded in the fall).

10. Dagerman's father used to go out of his way to deny that he was the model for Knut, but while friends and relatives refuse to confirm the connection, their knowing smiles tell their own story.

11. A letter containing this claim is quoted by Ragnar Svanström on p. 23 of his booklet *Stig Dagerman. Några minnesbilder* (Stockholm, 1954).

12. Hans Sandberg told me that Annemarie Dagerman informed him of the factual background.

13. The title is taken from a song popular in the 1940s. Annemarie Dagerman says her husband played the record nonstop while composing the story.

14. In Kafka's *Metamorphosis* (*Die Verwandlung*, 1912) a man awakes one morning to find he has changed into a beetle.

15. The dramatized version of "Den dödsdömde" is discussed on pp. 111–114.

16. W. H. Auden, *The Age of Anxiety: A Baroque Eclogue* (London: Faber & Faber, 1948).

17. E.g., Staffan Björck, "Ensamhetens sagor," *Ord och Bild* 1948, p. 321.

18. Stig Dagerman, "Diktaren och samvetet," *40-tal* 6 (1945).

19. Albert Camus, "Sisyfosmyten," *40-tal* 8 (1946).

20. Stig Dagerman, "Min synpunkt på anarkismen," *40-tal* (1946).

21. See note 17.

Chapter Five

1. The dates are based on correspondence between Dagerman and Ragnar Svanström, 14 December 1947, 15 January 1948, 9 February 1948 (NA).

2. Letter from Dagerman to Svanström 5 November 1947 (NA). This letter was actually written in Amsterdam, but the sentiments reflect the mood of Dagerman's letters from Paris.

3. Letter from Dagerman to Svanström 14 December 1947 (NA).

4. A full account of the affair and its effect on Dagerman is given in *Den politiske Stig Dagerman*, p. 126 ff. A discussion of it in English is to be found in Laurie Thompson, "Prose in the 1940s," in *Essays on Swedish Literature*.

From 1880 to the Present Day (Aberdeen: University of Aberdeen, 1979), ed. Irene Scobbie. The relevant pages are 223—24.

5. Dagerman did not abandon the project altogether until July (letter to Svanström 4 July 1948, NA), although he had informed *Expressen* by mid-May that he was finding it impossible to write the articles (memorandum by Svanström, 25 May 1948, NA). The ones published as planned are listed by Sandberg in his bibliography, items 638—42.

6. Letters from Dagerman to Svanström 14 December 1947 and 18 March 1948 (NA).

7. These assertions are based on information in Lagercrantz's biography and Sandberg's dissertation, and comments made to me by Annemarie Dagerman (who confirmed the accuracy of Lagercrantz's and Sandberg's data).

8. The original edition of *Bränt barn*, published by Norstedts in 1948, does not number the chapters; some subsequent editions do so, however. Page numbers in parentheses here and in subsequent quotations from or references to *Bränt barn* refer to the original edition.

9. Letter from Dagerman to Svanström, 14 December 1947.

10. Telegram from Dagerman to Svanström, 20 July 1948 (NA). As stated on p. 76, Dagerman was also planning a novel entitled *Ökenminnen* [Desert Memories] while in France.

11. See p. 59 above.

Chapter Six

1. The term is discussed in greater detail on p. 109 ff.

2. The information is taken from telegrams in Norstedts archives (7 February 1949, 8 February 1949) and statements made by Annemarie Dagerman in conversation with me.

3. Quoted by Lagercrantz on p. 192 of his biography.

4. The details are in interviews given by Dagerman at the airport on his return; e.g., *Svenska Dagbladet*, *Dagens Nyheter*, *Morgon-Tidningen*, all 11 July 1949. Dagerman describes the journey and his inspiration for *Wedding Worries* in the article "Bröllopsbesvär och andra," *Morgon-Tidningen*, 19 November 1950 (reprinted in *Vårt Behov av tröst*, pp. 28—34).

5. Details of the contracts are recorded in Svanström's memorandum 12 January 1949, and his reservations about the voyage in a memorandum dated 20 April 1949 (NA).

6. Information provided by Annemarie Dagerman.

7. Memoranda by Ragnar Svanström, 25 April 1949, 10 May 1949, 20 January 1951 (NA).

8. Page 33 in *Vårt behov av tröst* (see note 4).

9. Such tramps frequently figured in contemporary literature, the best-known instance being Bolle in Harry Martinson's novel *Vägen till Klockrike* (1948; Eng. tr. *The Road* [London: Jonathan Cape, 1955]). Some of the comments made by Dagerman's tramps can be seen as an attack on Martinson's *luffarromantik* ("tramp romanticism").

10. See note 4.

11. Annemarie Dagerman confirms that her husband was aware of an anonymous seventeenth-century poem with almost the same title as the novel, "Bröllopsbesvärs ihugkommelse" [Memories of Wedding Worries]. The reference gives extra justification for the old-fashioned language of the chapter headings, but apart from a confused atmosphere featuring rustic merry-making, drunkenness, and scurrility there seems to be no close connection between the novel and the poem.

12. Here and in connection with all subsequent quotations from and reference to *Bröllopsbesvär*, the figure in parentheses refers to the page number of the 1949 edition published by Norstedts.

13. "Var är den vän som överallt jag söker?" was written by Johan Olof Wallin in 1818, and is no. 564 in the Swedish Hymn Book.

14. Kerstin Anér, "Kärlek utan fula ord," *Damernas värld* 3 (1950).

15. Stig Dagerman, "Vårt behov av tröst är omättligt," *Husmodern* 13 (1952) (reprinted in *Vårt behov av tröst*, pp. 285–91).

16. Stig Dagerman "Bröllopsbesvär och andra" (see note 4).

17. Es An (= Elis Andersson), "Bondbröllop med besvär," *Göteborgs-Posten*, 24 December 1949.

18. The Swedish wording is "Man tager vad man haver," which uses obsolete verb forms and sounds distinctly old-fashioned, hence the biblical language of the English rendering. It should be pointed out, however, that the phrase is used colloquially in modern Swedish in the expression "'Man tager vad man haver,' säger Kajsa Warg" ("You take whatever you've got," says Kajsa Warg). Kajsa Warg was the author of a famous cookbook, published in 1755. The modern usage is similar to the English reference to Mrs. Beeton in the phrase: "First catch your rabbit. . . ." Apart from a typically amusing juxtaposition of ancient and modern, sublime and ridiculous, it is difficult to see any deeper relevance in the reference to Kajsa Warg, whereas the use of what sounds like biblical language has obvious significance.

19. The German-Jewish poet Heinrich Heine (1797–1856) first published his poem "Die Lorelei" as no. 2 of the cycle "Heimkehr," which formed part of his book *Reisebilder* (1826). The third and fourth verses run:

"Die schönste Jungfrau sitzet, / Dort oben wunderbar, / Ihr gold'nes Geschmeide blitzet, / Sie kämmt ihr goldenes Haar. // Sie kämmt es mit goldenem Kamme, / Und singt ein Lied dabei; / Das hat eine wundersame, / Gewaltige Melodei" (The most beautiful of maidens sits up there, looking wonderful: her golden trinkets are glistening as she combs her golden hair. She combs it with a golden comb, and as she does so she sings a song which has a strange but powerful melody). The siren sits on a cliff by the Rhine at St. Goar and lures boats onto the treacherous rocks below by beguiling the sailors with her beauty and her song.

Chapter Seven

1. A list of foreign performances of *The Man Condemned to Death* is appended to the 1978 edition of *Den dödsdömde* published by Federativs, Stockholm. The translation published by the American Scandinavian Foundation, New York and Princeton, 1951, calls the play *The Condemned*; a radio version broadcast in England in 1950 (translated by Alan Blair) called it *The Shadow of Death*. I prefer the literal translation used throughout in this book.

2. Ebbe Linde, "Skuggan av Mart," *Dagens Nyheter*, 11 September 1948.

3. Ivar Harrie, "Tragedi pa Lilla Dramaten," *Expressen*, 11 September 1948.

4. Bengt Nirje, "Intervju med aktuell dramaturg," *Expressen*, 19 April 1947.

5. Holger Ahlenius, *Bonniers Litterära Magasin* 2 (1943):145.

6. Viveka Heyman, " 'Den dödsdömde' en märkling pjäs," *Arbetaren*, 19 April 1947.

7. Annemarie Dagerman remembers that her husband was particularly depressed on his return from the London first night, due to the poor production of his play there.

8. Dagerman's program note is reprinted in *Vårt behov av tröst*, pp. 238−40. The theme of a man reprieved when on the point of being executed, but who goes on to commit crimes and is eventually put to death anyway, may well have influenced Pär Lagerkvist's novel *Barabbas* (1950; Eng. tr. New York: Random House, 1951; London and Toronto, 1952): Dagerman even has a character named "The Almost Crucified." Cf. J. Mjöberg, *Livsproblemet hos Lagerkvist* (Stockholm: Bonniers, 1951), p. 190.

9. This theme is at the heart of "En spelmans mössa" [A Fiddler's Cap], a "scene for radio" broadcast in 1955 but written some six years earlier.

10. E.g., Elis Andersson, *Tjugofem säsonger* (Gothenburg: E. Höglund,

1957), p. 360. The Gothenburg production was in January 1950.

11. Stig Dagerman, "Vägen till Paris," *Expressen*, 29 March 1948.

12. The program note for the first performance states that it was finished "over Christmas." In his Dagerman bibliography, pp. 222 – 23, Lagercrantz reveals that the circumstances of the play have a factual basis and that the characters are modeled on real people.

13. The title *Sorgeår* [Year of Mourning] was first mentioned in a memorandum by Ragnar Svanström dated 10 January 1949 (NA). An exchange of letters between Dagerman and Svanström, 10 March 1949 and 15 March 1949 (NA), refers to the change of title—the theater authorities presumably thought *Year of Mourning* sounded too gloomy—and also to the postponement of the first performance since rehearsals were behind schedule.

14. Dagerman's comments are quoted in an unsigned interview in *Göteborgs Handels – och Sjöfartstidning*, 8 October 1952.

15. Among Dagerman's papers was a handwritten sheet headed "General plan for the next few years' production." It seems to have been written before *Bränt barn*, i.e., in the first half of 1948, and contains plans for the 1950s—including a whole series of six or seven peasant plays. (I am grateful to Hans Sandberg for supplying me with this page.) The quoted comments are from the article referred to in note 14.

Chapter Eight

1. A complete list of Dagerman's daily verses can be found on pages 115 – 29 of Sandberg's bibliography. The title "Dagermans dagsedlar" contains a number of plays on words which cannot be rendered into English. Dagerman frequently signed articles in *Arbetaren* with the abbreviation "dag," which occurs in both words; *dagsedel* means literally a "daily scrap of paper," which is perhaps one way of describing Dagerman's contribution to the feature page, while the Swedish idiom *utdela en dagsedel* means "to give someone a box on the ear." "Dagermans dagsedlar" was the title used in *Arbetaren* from 22 September 1952. Prior to that a number of titles were used, notably "Qrolls nidvisor" [Qroll's Lampoons] from 3 June 1944 to 30 October 1947.

2. "Höst" [Fall] appeared on 26 October 1954.

3. Both these poems, as well as "Fall," are reprinted in *Dagsedlar*. The English translations appeared first in Laurie Thompson, "Stig Dagerman marching on," *Swedish Books* 3 (1979).

4. Both poems were first published in *40-tal* 4 (1945) and are reprinted in *Vårt behov av tröst*, p. 185 – 87. "The Rat in the Hole" figured prominently

in a series of letters to the editor in the national evening newspaper *Aftontid-ningen* in June 1945, in which correspondents argued the case for and against modernism in poetry—albeit on a rather superficial level.

5. First published in *Prisma* 1 (1950), the cycle is reprinted in *Vårt behov av tröst*, pp. 195–99.

6. Page 6.

Chapter Nine

1. The more important projects are discussed in this chapter. Others include:

> *Mannen på gatan* [The Man in the Street]—play. (Charles, "Människan contra blocken nästa pjäs av Dagerman," *Norbottens-Kuriren*, 30 November 1949.)
>
> *Främmande makt* [Foreign Power]—novel based on experiences in France. (Memorandum by Svanström 9 June 1952 [NA]). By late summer Dagerman was telling journalists that it was to have a Stockholm background. (Anon. "Anita Björk och Dagerman har flugit till Hollywood," *Lunds Dagblad*, 25 July 1952.)
>
> *Tigerhjärtat* [Tiger Heart]—novel. (Letter from Dagerman to Svanström 3 June 1953 [NA].)
>
> *Snöflingan* [The Snowflake]—novel. (Memorandum by Svanström, 11 August 1953 [NA].)
>
> *Världens största rus* [The Biggest Booze-Up in the World]—novel. (R. Svanström, pp. 16–19; cf. also Lagercrantz's biography, p. 189 ff.)

2. Details of the circumstances are given in Sandberg's dissertation, p. 246.

3. Ramström's comments appeared in *Dagstidningen-Arbetaren*, 8 November 1954, and his detailed account of the Branting article in *Verdandisten* 9 (1957).

4. Dagerman first refers to the novel in a letter to Svanström dated 30 June 1950; Svanström's enthusiastic reaction and Dagerman's account of the plot come in several subsequent letters preserved in Norstedts archives.

5. Telegram from Dagerman to Svanström, 12 September 1950, with a more detailed letter 13 September 1950 (NA).

6. Stig Dagerman, "En hund begraven," *Prisma* 5–6 (1950): 11–17; reprinted in *Vårt behov av tröst*, pp. 68–85.

7. The estimate of Dagerman's debt is based on numerous memoranda and letters in Norstedts archives, and is mentioned since some observers have

been inclined to suggest that Dagerman's financial problems were exaggerated. Annemarie Dagerman has commented to me that her former husband's unsophisticated, lower-class background made him particularly sensitive to and uncomfortable about debts which he saw no hope of repaying. See also Ake Ohlmarks, *Drömfabriken. Äventyr i filmens värld*, (Gothenburg: Zinderman, 1970), pp. 71−81.

8. The planned book is first mentioned—though not by name— in a memorandum by Ragnar Svanström 29 December 1950 (NA), and references to it recur in correspondence between Dagerman and Norstedts throughout the spring and summer of 1951. Ohlmarks's comments on Dagerman (see note 7) refer mainly to *Full Orchestra*.

9. Letter from Dagerman to Svanström, 12 September 1951 (NA).

10. The poem by Erik Blomberg (1894−1965) is entitled "Gravskrift" [Epitaph]: "Here lies / a Swedish worker. / Died in peace-time. / Weaponless, defenseless. / Executed / by anonymous bullets. / His crime was hunger. / Forget him never."

11. See note 15 to Chapter 6.

12. For more information about Almqvist, see the volume in Twayne's World Authors Series entitled *C. J. L. Almqvist* (TWAS 401; by Bertil Romberg, 1977).

13. In conversation with me.

14. Stig Dagerman, *Tusen r hos Gud* (Stockholm, 1954; reprinted in *Vrt behov av tröst*, pp. 157−81). An English version, translated by Naomi Walford, is included in the volume *The Games of Night* (London, 1959), pp. 189−215, under the title "A Thousand Years with the Lord." There is an indirect reference to Almqvist in the prologue in that God assumes the human form of Claes Jensen: this name is thought to have been an alias used by Almqvist during his exile.

15. Information supplied by Anita Björk.

16. Memoranda by Svanström, 23 July 1954, 9 August 1954 (NA).

Chapter Ten

1. The latter aspect is stressed by Gunnar Brandell in his *Svensk litteratur 1900−1950* (Stockholm: Aldus, 2d ed., 1967), and *Svensk litteratur 1870−1970*, 2, 1975 (an extended version of the earlier work). Of the standard works Erik Hjalmar Linder's *Fem decennier av nittonhundratalet*, (Stockholm: Natur och Kultur, vols. 1 and 2, 1965−66), gives what is probably the fullest and most positive account of Dagerman's achievements, including him under the subheading "The Young Dead."

2. Kai Henmark (1932—1980) registered for a postgraduate thesis on Dagerman but seems never to have completed it. He published a number of perceptive articles in the late 1950s but almost all of them appeared in popular journals or newspapers. The most notable "academic" study of Dagerman was Agneta Pleijel's discussion of imagery, "Djuret och skräcken," *Samlaren* 1965, pp. 96—114.

3 Ola Loslkk, "Billedsprk og symbolikk i Dagermans roman 'De dömdas ö," *Edda* 5 (1970):289—310.

4. Egil Törnqvist, "Berättartekniken i Stig Dagermans roman Bränt barn," *Svensk Litteraturtidskrift* 4 (1969):25—37. The comparison with Umballa refers to a poem by Heidenstam, "Moguls kungaring" [The Royal Ring of the Mogul], published in 1888; Umballa, a Turk, found the lost ring without effort and was described as a favorite of the gods who was able to achieve remarkable things with consummate ease.

5. Georges Périlleux, "L'oeuvre de Stig Dagerman dans ses rapports avec les théories philosophiques de Kierkegaard, Sartre et Camus," Ph.D. diss., University of Liège, 1975.

6. A list of reprintings and new editions to 1973 is to be found in Sandberg's bibliography.

7. Details of foreign translations of Dagerman's works are also given in Sandberg's bibliography.

8. See for instance Le Clézio's article "Hej, Stig Dagerman," *Bonniers Litterära Magasin* 2 (1969):87, and "J.M.G. Le Clézio et la 'parole éblouissante' de Stig Dagerman," *La Quinzaine*, 1—15 February 1977, pp. 9—10.

9. In conversation with me, January 1975.

Selected Bibliography

PRIMARY SOURCES

(Unless otherwise stated, all are published by P. A. Norstedt & Söner in Stockholm.)

Ormen. Stockholm: Steinsviks, 1945.
De dömdas ö. 1946.
Tysk höst. 1947.
Nattens lekar. 1947.
Dramer om döda. 1948. Contains *Den dödsdömde* and *Skuggan av Mart.*
Bränt barn. 1948.
Judasdramer. 1949. Contains *Streber* and *Ingen går fri.*
Bröllopsbesvär. 1949.
Den yttersta dagen. Stockholm: Radiotjänst, 1952.
Tusen år hos Gud. 1954.
Dagsedler. Stockholm: Dagstidningen Arbetaren, 1954. Edited by L. Bergström and Ö. Wallqvist.
Vårt behov av tröst. 1955. Edited by O. Lagercrantz.

1. Bibliography
   Sandberg, H. *Stig Dagerman—författare och journalist.* Stockholm: Federativs, 1975.

2. English Translations
   A Burnt Child. Translated by Alan Blair. London: Chatto & Windus, 1950; New York: Morrow, 1950.
   The Condemned. Translated by Henry Alexander and Llewellyn Jones. In: *Scandinavian Plays of the Twentieth Century.* Third Series. Princeton: Princeton University Press, 1951.
   The Games of Night. Translated by Naomi Walford. Stockholm: Norstedts, 1959; London: The Bodley Head, 1959; Philadelphia: Lippincott, 1961. Contains a selection from *Nattens lekar* and *Vårt behov av tröst.*

SECONDARY SOURCES

1. Books and Articles

Bergmann, S. A. "Blinded by Darkness. A Study of the Novels and Plays of Stig Dagerman." *Delta* (Cambridge, England) 11 (1957): 16–31. A sound, brief survey—until now the only one in English.

Björck, S. "Den dödsdömde." *Dagens Nyheter*, 26 September 1958. Review of Lagercrantz's biography, but contains some sound judgments on Dagerman generally.

Gran, U. "Stig Dagermans 'Bröllopsbesvär.'" *Perspektiv* 1962, pp. 158–61. Useful introduction to the novel.

Hallingberg, G. "Stig Dagermans filmnovell Att döda ett barn." In: *Novellanalyser*. Edited by Vivi Edström and Per-Arne Henricson. Stockholm: Prisma, 1970, pp. 159–67. The only published analysis of what is probably Dagerman's most widely read short story.

Henmark, K. "Gud och Stig Dagerman." *Vår lösen* 1956, pp. 221–30. Examines religious motifs in Dagerman's works.

———. "Dagerman och anarchismen." *Ord och Bild* 1957, pp. 362–66. Brief comments on Anarcho-Syndicalist traits in the early novels.

———. "I begynnelsen var skräcken." *Kristet forum* 1957, pp. 227–28. *Ångst* and its symbols in Dagerman's works.

———. "Stig Dagerman och ångesten," "Stig Dagerman och religionen," "Stig Dagerman och tystnaden," "Döden och den dömda," "Den fyrtiotalistiska prosans flygande fästningar." In: *En fågel av eld. Essäer om dikt och engagemang*. Stockholm: Rabén och Sjögren, 1962. The essays contain perceptive comments on various aspects of Dagerman's writings and suggest fruitful lines of thought.

Lagercrantz, O. *Stig Dagerman*. Stockholm: Norstedts, 1958. Excellent and revealing biography, demonstrating that many of Dagerman's problems were psychological. Has a few gaps, and does not attempt to analyze any works except *De dömdas ö* and *Tusen år hos Gud*.

Le Clézio, J. M. G. "Hej, Stig Dagerman." *Bonniers Litterära Magasin* 2 (1969):87–92. An enthusiastic reaction from a French novelist on reading *Ormen*.

Leiser, E. "Den dödsdömde.—Anteckningar om Stig Dagerman." *Tiden* 1955, pp. 43–48. One of the best brief accounts of Dagerman's works, although not everyone will agree with the judgments.

Lindgren, E. "Ovanlig debut." *Bonniers Litterära Magasin* 1946, pp. 64–66. Admiring review of *Ormen* by the *doyen* of the 1940s in Sweden.

———. "Skräckens lag och fruktans evangelium." *Bonniers Litterära Magasin* 1946, pp. 779–80. Reprinted in *40-talsförfattare*. Edited by L-O. Franzén. Stockholm: Bonniers, 1965, pp. 169–71. One of the reviews of *De dömdas ö* Dagerman prized most highly.

Losløkk, O. "Billedspråk or symbolikk i Dagermans roman 'De dömdas ö'." *Edda* 5 (1970):289–310. Valuable and illuminating analysis of imagery and symbolism in *De dömdas ö*.

Pleijel, A. "Djuret och skräcken. En studie i Stig Dagermans författarskap." *Samlaren* 1965, pp. 96–114. Analysis of animal symbolism, mainly in *De dömdas ö*.

Romberg, B. *Att läsa epik.* Lund: Gleerups, 1972. Contains a detailed analysis of the story "De röda vagnarna" on pp. 159–75.

Sandberg, H. "De dömdas ö—en politisk idéroman." *Samlaren* 1972, pp. 62–90. Argues persuasively for a political interpretation of *De dömdas ö*.

———. *Den politiske Stig Dagerman.* Stockholm: Federativs, 1979. Invaluable adaptation of Sandberg's dissertation, containing analyses of *Ormen* and *De dömdas ö* (the latter very similar to the previous item), and on Dagerman and anarcho-syndicalism in Sweden of the 1940s.

Sastamoinen, A., ed. *Stig Dagerman och syndikalismen.* Stockholm: Federativs, 1974. Contains several articles about Dagerman and his anarcho-syndicalism.

Spector, R. D. "The Troubled World of Stig Dagerman's Art." *Nordstjernan-Svea* (Brooklyn, N.Y.), 10 February 1977, and "Dagerman's Outsiders." *Nordstjernan-Svea*, 16 June 1977. Both articles deal with Stig Dagerman's short stories in *The Games of Night*.

Svanström, R. *Stig Dagerman. Några minnesbilder.* Stockholm: Norstedts, 1954. Contains three short articles with interesting biographical details.

Thompson, L. *Stig Dagerman: Nattens lekar.* Hull: University of Hull, 1975; 2d ed. 1979. Studies in Swedish Literature, No. 5. Analyzes themes and technique in the stories and adds notes and vocabulary explanations for English-speaking students of Swedish.

———. "Prose in the 1940's." In: *Essays On Swedish Literature. From 1880 to the Present Day.* Edited by I. Scobbie. Aberdeen: University of Aberdeen, 1979, pp. 219–36. Discusses the background of the

1940s and devotes several pages to *Ormen*.

————. *"Stig Dagerman Marching On." Swedish Books* 3 (1979):19—22. Contains translations into English of five "daily verses."

Törnqvist, E. "Berättartekniken i Stig Dagermans roman Bränt barn." *Svensk Litteraturtidskrift* 4 (1969):25—37. Good introduction to the novel without claiming to be comprehensive.

————. "Stig Dagerman: Den dödsdömde (1948)." In: *Svenska dramastrukturer*. Stockholm: Prisma, 1973, pp. 108—27. Contains fruitful comparisons between the play and the original story.

Unpublished

Périlleux, G. "L'oeuvre de Stig Dagerman dans ses rapports avec les théories philosophiques de Kierkegaard, Sartre et Camus." Vols. 1 and 2. Thesis awarded a "Docteur en Philosophie et Lettres" degree at the University of Liége, 1975. Discusses Dagerman's links with Existentialist philosophy.

Sandberg, H. "Det frihetliga alternativet. Anarkismen-syndikalismen och de svenska 40-talisterna, främst Stig Dagerman." Thesis awarded a "fil. lic." degree at the University of Uppsala, 1969. Excellent on biographical details and Dagerman's politics; contains analyses of *Ormen*, *De dömdas ö*, and several less important works, all from a political point of view. More comprehensive than the book cited above, based on the dissertation.

Index